Y0-ABG-408

Morality and the Mail in

Nineteenth-Century America

Morality and the Mail in Nineteenth-Century America

Wayne E. Fuller

UNIVERSITY OF ILLINOIS PRESS
URBANA AND CHICAGO

Manufactured in the United States of America
C 5 4 3 2 1

∞ This book is printed on acid-free paper.

Library of Congress Cataloging-in-Publication Data
Fuller, Wayne Edison, 1919–
Morality and the mail in nineteenth-century America / Wayne E. Fuller.
p. cm.
Includes bibliographical references and index.
ISBN 0-252-02812-0 (cloth : alk. paper)
1. Postal service—United States—History—19th century.
2. Sunday legislation—United States—History—19th century.
I. Title.
HE6371.F846 2003
383'.4973'09034—dc21 2002011213

To the memory of my father and mother,
who would have understood

CONTENTS

PREFACE

> *Therefore choose life, that thou and thy seed may live, that thou mayest love the Lord thy God and that thou mayest obey his voice and that thou mayest cleave to him. . . . that thou mayest dwell in the land which the Lord swore to your fathers, to Abraham, to Isaac, and to Jacob to give them.*
>
> —*Deuteronomy* 30:19–20

In March 1630, the *Arabella,* a ship of thirty tons, lay off the Isle of Wight waiting for favorable winds that would bear it to the New World. Unknown to the world at large, its cargo contained a historic band of religious dissenters, the first of many, who would leave England that spring and summer for the shores of America. They were Puritans, adherents of John Calvin's stern theology, who, having failed to purify the Church of England of all its Catholic forms, proposed to found a *new* England in the wilderness where they could worship God in the simplicity that they believed would be pleasing to him.

On board the *Arabella* that spring was John Winthrop, leader of the enterprise and first governor of the Massachusetts Bay Colony. Educated at Cambridge and proprietor of a large estate at Groton, Winthrop had given up much that was earthly to follow his conscience and his God to the new land. And somewhere on that voyage, as the *Arabella* rolled and rocked with the waves, he delivered a famous sermon that explained in memorable prose the purpose of the Puritan sojourn into the wilderness with instructions on how life must be lived in the new plantation:

> For wee must consider that wee shall be as a Citty upon a Hill, the eies of all people are uppon us; so that if wee shall deal falsely with our God in this worke wee have undertaken, and so cause him to withdraw his present help from us, wee shall be made a story and a by-word through the world, wee shall open the mouthes of enemies to speak evill of the wayes of god, and all proffessours for God's sake; wee shall shame the faces of many of god's worthy servants, and cause theire prayers to be turned to Curses upon us till wee be consumed out of the good land whether we are going. . . . Therefore lett us choose life that wee and are seeds may live, by obeying his voyce and cleaving to him, for he is our life and our prosperity.[1]

Winthrop's sermon, like the Declaration of Independence that was to follow long years afterward, was a blueprint for a new nation. It was to be a model for the world, a city set upon a hill that future colonists could see and say, "Lord, make it like that of New England."

This model plantation was to be achieved by obeying God's will, which was made known to them though the Holy Scriptures. These they pondered daily, followed rigorously, and upon their understanding of them ordered their society. Theoretically, church and state were separate in the new colony, but the Puritans could not conceive of a government that would not uphold the biblical laws of the Christian state they had come to build. Consequently, they severely punished, and even banished, those who blasphemed, dissented from the true religion, disturbed the worship service, and profaned the Lord's day.

Punishment for such crimes lingered long in the land as Puritans worked with almost superhuman effort to build a godly kingdom on earth. When at times they faltered, their ministers called upon them to repent, railing at them in jeremiads that reminded them that they had broken their covenant with the Lord and prophesying doom for the community that turned its face from God.

From these beginnings, whether by happenstance or God's will, as they supposed, the United States was born British, Christian, and Protestant, and all profoundly shaped its history. Long after the pristine Puritanism of the early years had faded and many had forgotten that God had covenanted with them to support them as long as they obeyed him, a moral majority of evangelical Protestants remembered and, informed by biblical morality and their Puritan past, struggled in the rapidly changing world of the nineteenth century to sustain the Christian nation of their forebears against the threat posed to it by a communication revolution spawned by a rapidly developing and innovative postal system.

The U.S. postal service of those years was the radio, telephone, television, fax, and Internet of the time and the principal purveyor of the nation's culture. Favored by postal innovations and cheap postage and laws designed by Congress to diffuse knowledge among the masses, publishers of every sort filled the mail with more than two billion pieces of their work, weighing more than 450 million pounds by 1900 and bringing the good and the bad of American civilization into the nation's homes.

No postal system in the world distributed so many publications, and none so widely. From its earliest days, as post roads carved trails into the wilderness to humble post offices, the mail followed the nation's moving population by means of post riders, stagecoaches, and steamboats. And when at last trains moved the mail, railroad post offices, the marvels of the age, were developed.

Skillful railway postal clerks could sort mail on the run and speed it from coast to coast in 118 hours and forty-five minutes at the end of the century.

To keep abreast of the ever-expanding amount of mail and provide more services to the American people, postal innovations followed one another in rapid order as the nation grew and cities filled the land. The use of stamps and envelopes, free delivery, special delivery, money orders, registered letters, a parcel service, and fast trains made the American postal service the most usable in the world.

No arm of the national government was more intimately tied to the daily lives of American people than the post office, and because Congress controlled it none was as closely connected to American politics or subject to more pressures from various interest groups. Politicians, publishers of all kinds of publications, ordinary businessmen, rogues, free-lovers, free-thinkers, and everyday patrons all sought to use it to serve their own purposes.

Among these interest groups were evangelical Protestants, some of whose ancestors had founded the country and many whose Scotch-Irish forebears of Calvinistic persuasion had strengthened it. From 1810, when Congress first aroused their apprehensions by opening post offices on the Sabbath, and throughout the century evangelicals found much that was troubling in the consequences of the post office's growth and improvements, just as their descendants more than a century later would discover baffling social problems emanating from their own infinitely more complicated communication revolution. But a great cultural chasm divides the two societies. So far has modern American secular society retreated from its religious roots that nineteenth-century evangelists' strenuous objections to opening the nation's post offices on the Sabbath, to Sunday newspapers, and to the mailing of birth control information, lottery tickets, dime novels, and pornography are not just quaint but incomprehensible to all but a handful of contemporary Americans. For nineteenth-century evangelicals, immersed in Christian values as they were, such material in the U.S. mail and post offices that were open on the Sabbath threatened to paganize the Christian nation.

Morality and the Mail in Nineteenth-Century America is a history of the postal improvements that sparked the communication revolution and of the ways in which the evangelical Protestants, in a different age, challenged what they perceived to be the evil effects of a revolution that threatened to paganize the Christian nation that they were determined to save. Without indulging abstract motivational theories, this study takes the evangelicals' word in recounting what they were trying to achieve in their long struggle with the post office. It also attempts to capture their sense of outrage at the post office's violation of the Sabbath and the indecent publications that came through the mail. In tracing the course of their crusade through the century, I hope to shed light on the postal innovations of the time, on religion in politics, the church-state controversy, cultural changes in American society, politics and publishing, the expansion of the postal power, censorship, the supremacy of national over state law, and the waning dominance of the Protestant evangelical religion in an increasingly secular society.

A word of clarification. The evangelicals referred to in this study are those Protestants who belonged to the Presbyterian, Methodist, Baptist, and Congregational churches particularly and to diverse other Protestants sects as well. In spite of the variety of evangelical organizations and differences among them, they all believed, generally speaking, in the Bible as the authoritative Word of God, in the divinity of Jesus Christ, the Trinity, and in most of those orthodox Christian doctrines embodied in the Apostles Creed. Until the twentieth century they were not regarded as right-wing fundamentalists as many of them are today, although their beliefs were much the same. But in the nineteenth century, as Robert T. Handy wrote in his pathbreaking book *A Christian America: Protestant Hopes and Historical Realities,* evangelicals "made up the dominant religious subculture of nineteenth century America."[2]

Not all Protestants were evangelical, of course, but because they formed the dominant religion of the century I found it convenient to use the term *evangelicals* to more accurately define those with whom I am concerned without noting the differences among them. Although all evangelicals were Sabbatarians in the sense that they believed in the strict observance of the Sabbath, not all of them, for various reasons, were willing to support legislation that would close post offices on the Sabbath or stop the transportation of mail on that day. Neither were all of them engaged in other Christian postal reforms of the period, in part because of politics (or reluctance to become involved in it) and sectionalism. Nevertheless those reforms were led by, and in general supported by, the evangelical Protestants who presided over the religious landscape during the century.

• • •

I am much indebted to Richard B. John, professor of history at the University of Illinois, Chicago and a postal history authority, whose many critical suggestions were immensely valuable. Alorha South, guardian of the postal records at the National Archives, was of inestimable help in making available the materials needed for this study. Over the years, my graduate seminar students at the University of Texas at El Paso worked on various aspects of postal history, and I thank them for their contributions to this book. I also wish to thank the personnel at the Library of Congress, who graciously and patiently answered my many requests, and those at the interlibrary loan desk at the University of Texas at El Paso, whose aid has been invaluable. I am especially grateful for the skill and care with which Mary Giles edited the final manuscript. I also acknowledge the extraordinary assistance of my daughter, Jamie, a writer and freelance editor, who read the original manuscript carefully, erased many superfluous words, discovered dangling modifiers, and made a number of sentences say what was intended, and that of my wife, Billie, who, with remarkable patience, photocopied much of the material in the National Archives and encouraged me in darker days.

Notes

1. Daniel Borstin, ed., *An American Primer* (Chicago, 1966), 22–23.
2. Robert T. Handy, *A Christian America: Protestant Hopes and Historic Realities* (New York, 1971), vii.

Morality and the Mail in

Nineteenth-Century America

1 Mail on the Sabbath

Remember the Sabbath day, to keep it holy.
—Exodus 20:8

On the first day of every week in the early winter months of 1810 an almost eerie stillness lay upon towns and villages along the great post roads from Maine to Georgia and from the nation's capital to Tennessee. Shops were closed, government buildings silent, and places of amusement empty. Only that labor considered necessary was performed, for this was the American Sabbath and almost no one except worshipers on their way to church was abroad in the land.

In Boston, where horses could not be watered in public on Sundays or ridden through the Commons, and elsewhere throughout New England the Sabbath was still kept from midnight on Saturdays to the following sunset. But it was not just the heirs of Puritanism who kept the Lord's Day holy in the young republic. Keeping the Sabbath was a practice that Americans from Maine to Georgia had inherited from their Protestant forebears. Observed as a day set aside for rest and worship, it was also enforced with varying degrees of rigidity by state and local laws.[1]

So strictly was the day kept free of activity that even drivers of mail stages, traveling "of necessity" on Sundays along the great post roads, were forbidden to blow their horns and trumpets when they entered villages and towns lest they disturb worship services. And where they had to exchange mail at post offices along the way, they did so with as little commotion as possible. When they had gone, post offices closed. At only a few was mail delivered on Sundays, and those not involved in the exchange of mail rarely opened their doors on the Lord's Day.[2]

But in 1810 the peace of those quiet Sabbaths was threatened when Congress abruptly, almost furtively, decreed that the nation's post offices must remain open on Sundays. This needless addition to the postal laws embroiled the post office in the nation's first dispute over church and state and inspired a controversy that was to last throughout most of the nineteenth century. It was initiated and kept alive by sectional and political animosities and jealousies.[3]

During the Jeffersonian era, the nation's postal system had expanded so rapidly to stay abreast of the country's growth that it became nearly unmanageable. Between 1800 and 1810 post roads increased in miles from 20,817 to 36,406, and each year they marked the moving edge of American settlement. In that same period the number of post offices went from 903 to 2,300, and postal revenues grew from $280,804 to $551,684 as the economy boomed along the eastern seaboard.[4]

Expansion of the postal service placed a heavy burden on the young post office department. Creating hundreds of new post offices, appointing postmasters, and letting contracts to carry the mail over new post roads that Congress continually created in response to constituents' demands overwhelmed the department's employees. Moreover, the condition of the roads, and the wilderness they traversed, delayed the mail, made it vulnerable to theft, and rendered the postal system so untrustworthy that Thomas Jefferson, among others, was fearful of disclosing privileged information in his letters. These and a myriad of other problems were exacerbated by Congress's delay in enacting a new postal law needed to administer the expanding service.[5]

By 1810 it had been eleven years since Congress passed a postal act regulating the post office, and the law that seemed adequate in 1799 failed almost completely to provide for the changed conditions of 1810. But Congress, preoccupied with threats to the nation's neutrality stirred up by English and French attacks on American shipping, allowed the first decade of the new century to elapse before enacting a new postal law designed to remedy the flaws of the old.[6]

The new law added to the staff in the post office department, tightened the postal monopoly, provided stiff penalties for robbing or obstructing the mail, set new postage rates, and made a startling innovation: It opened the nation's post offices on Sundays. Section nine of the act stipulated that every postmaster, or his assistant, be on duty "every day on which a mail . . . shall arrive by land or water, as well as on other days" and "at all reasonable hours" each day of the week deliver "on demand any letter, paper, or packet" to any authorized person.[7] Not only that, but the postmaster was also to receive as well as deliver letters for mailing every day of the week.

Section nine was only one of forty-two sections of the new postal act and seemingly so trivial that it required no debate. Strangely, considering the far-reaching consequences of doing so, Congress opened the nation's post offices on Sundays without any overt demand from the public, special interests, or even the government, whose need for swift communication was obvious. That did not mean, of course, that there was none. Fingerprints on the bill suggested it was partly designed to equalize the arrival of commercial news among towns and cities along the East Coast for the benefit of businesspeople and to enlarge newspaper circulations for politicians, publishers, and the reading public. But there was more. Members of Congress from the sparsely settled South and West believed that opening post offices on Sundays would increase the number of post roads as well as mail and transportation facilities in their areas.[8]

When all these interests were added up, however, they scarcely seemed important enough for the government to have deliberately violated the traditional Sabbath that was so much a part of the American way of life. A great mystery surrounds the passage of section nine. Why, for instance, did Congress open all post offices? Most were small and received no mail at all on Sundays, yet Congress determined that they, too, should remain open. Even harder to explain was why, if Sunday mail delivery was so urgent, there were no petitions from businesspeople and newspaper publishers demanding it? Moreover, why were there no great arguments in the press and in Congress to support it?

So little was said about this innovation that it was impossible to know for certain who demanded that post offices be open on Sundays. One of President Madison's correspondents, a loyal follower, surmised shortly after section nine was passed that those who pushed for the law were "the less moral, & consequently the less respectable part of Society." Certainly, he wrote, they were not the majority of Americans. He was much perturbed because the Philadelphia postmaster, a Christian of excellent reputation who objected to working on the Sabbath, threatened to resign if the law was enforced. "I am sorry, that Congress should have passed such a law," he wrote. "It is hard to expect virtue in a people, when those who are selected for the guardianship of virtue shew so great a disregard for it."[9] Indeed, the need for such a Sunday service, even for business purposes, seemed less than overwhelming to many observers. "For many years," some disturbed Philadelphians wrote, "the city of Philadelphia has carried on a prosperous and extensive commerce, without violating what they deem it their duty to state to be, both the law of God and of man."[10]

That comment suggested, as did others, that Sabbath mail service had been created to appease business interests. Even if their demand for such a convenience had been urgent, however, no law was necessary to force the postmaster general to keep post offices open on Sundays. He had always ordered the transportation of mail on Sundays and opened post offices on that day so it could be exchanged. In some instances he had even permitted, although he did not require, postmasters to deliver mail on the Sabbath. Indeed, just two years before the enactment of section nine, Hugh Wylie, a Presbyterian elder and postmaster at Washington, Pennsylvania, had been ordered to open his post office on Sundays to sort the mail. When he also opened it to the public on that day the postmaster general supported him.[11]

Wylie's violation of the Fourth Commandment eventually led the Presbyterian General Assembly to expel him from the church, and it is possible that this situation inspired Congress to open all post offices on the Sabbath. It may have been that Congress wished to relieve postmasters of the responsibility of deciding whether to open their facilities on demand. No mention was made of that in Congress, however, and it is not clear that Congress even knew of Wylie's problem. If it did, it deliberately subjected all postmasters to possible expulsion from their churches by ordering them to open on the Sabbath.[12]

In any event, the origin of section nine appears to be more complicated than Wylie's problem. Years after its passage, a former member of Congress who had been in office at the time of its enactment explained that Congress had acted without fully understanding the impact the bill would have on the Sabbath. But that is most unlikely. Early in 1810 amendments to the Postal Bill of 1810, which would have opened post offices on Sundays, had twice been proposed in the Senate, but thanks to the opposition of senators from Sabbath-keeping New England were twice rejected. It was a repudiation of which even the most obtuse member of Congress must have been aware. Moreover, the secrecy with which members enacted section nine, as well as the flexibility they gave the postmaster general to fix the hours that post offices could be opened on Sundays to avoid interrupting church services, were surely indications that they knew they were encroaching upon a sacred tradition that would offend many Americans.[13]

No debate had accompanied the Senate amendments to open post offices on the Sabbath, even though senators at one time thought it important enough to require a roll-call vote. Nor was there debate in the House on that most controversial proposal. Instead, section nine was quietly squeezed into the law sometime between April 5 and April 26, 1810, without so much as a roll-call vote and after the bill had been juggled between the House and Senate numerous times.[14] If they understood that they were deliberately violating the Fourth Commandment, and if there was apparently neither pressing demand—or even necessity—for a law allowing post offices to be open on Sundays, why did members of Congress insist on undermining the Sabbath?

Perhaps, after all, the new Sunday service was only a victory of Mammon over God. Yet the passage of a measure so repugnant to so many Americans suggested that Congress had other reasons unrelated to business interests for its determination to establish a Sunday mail service. In the end, the law owed more to the quarrel over post roads and to sectional jealousies, cultural differences between the North and South, and enduring animosities between Federalists and Republicans, the nation's two political parties, than to various business interests.

Emerging in the 1790s over differences arising from Alexander Hamilton's financial policies and willingness to stretch the Constitution and Thomas Jefferson's strict constructionism, Hamilton's Federalist and Jefferson's Republican parties had become bastions of hatred toward one another during the first decade of the nineteenth century. The strife intensified over an array of issues and jealousies, not the least of which was the nation's postal policy.

Because of a great demand for mail, both in settled areas and the new territories, Congress was forced each year or so to consider a bill to create new post roads. In the race for post roads, however, the nation's postal policy, which required the post office to be self-sustaining, favored New England, the stronghold of federalism. There, where people were more likely to use the mail, post roads ran through densely settled areas that generated enough mail to make the roads self-sustaining. But in the South, the seat of Jefferson's Republican Party, where new lands were constantly being opened and population was sparse, it was difficult to establish post roads that would pay for themselves.

Consequently, Federalists, fearing the inability of the post office to cover the cost of an ever-increasing number of nonpaying post roads, tried to restrict their establishment in the South and West. Southern Republicans, however, minimized the importance of the postal policy as it applied to their section and justified their position with the argument that New England had many more post roads than the South. In their view, it was distinctly unfair, as a member of Congress from North Carolina contended in 1807. "Many large counties in the Southern States had no post roads," he said, "while scarcely a town in the Northern States was without one."[15]

Haggling between Federalists and the Republican majority over post roads on which mail stagecoach lines could be established to improve the nation's transportation system continued throughout the Jeffersonian years. Only the expectation that stagecoach operators would be likely to contract to carry mail to small post offices open on Sundays could explain Republican demand that such facilities be opened on the Sabbath. The controversy between Federalists and Republicans over post roads aggravated southerners' jealousy of the North and added to their mistrust of the postmaster general, Gideon Granger, who was another source of friction between the two parties. Granger was an outsider in the Jeffersonian political family. He was one of the very few Connecticut Yankees to support Jefferson in the election of 1800, and the president had rewarded him by appointing him postmaster general, considered a minor position at the time. Retained in office by Madison for a time, by 1810 Granger had served as postmaster general for nine years and accumulated no small amount of ill-will among Republicans.[16]

In all that time he had also gained an unexpected amount of political power because he could appoint postmasters and make contracts with the owners of stagecoach lines. The unstable representative from Virginia, John Randolph, who was jealous of Granger's growing political power and alleged appointment of Federalist postmasters as well as his seeming favoritism toward New England, ruthlessly attacked Granger in Congress in 1806. The postmaster general had, Randolph charged, attempted to bribe members of Congress by awarding lucrative mail contracts to their constituents in exchange for votes to approve settlement of a corrupt New England company's land claims. It was through the use of this power, Randolph argued, that Granger was able to send "a jackal, fed . . . not upon the offal of a [mail] contract, but with the fairest pieces" to prowl at night "through the streets of this vast and desolate city, seeking who he may tamper with" to buy votes for the company. For this and other alleged perceived misdeeds, Republicans demanded a congressional investigation of Granger. Jefferson supported him in this controversy, but it is likely that Republican animosity toward the postmaster general, their jealousy of his political power, and their understanding that he opposed opening post offices on the Lord's Day were all part of the decision to do just that.[17]

Adding to the bitterness that fueled the rancorous environment in which section nine was passed were important religious differences between the two political parties. During the Republic's first twelve years a national law to keep post offices open on the Sabbath would have been unthinkable. Leaders of the Federalist Party then in control of the government, although scarcely orthodox Christians, valued religion and morality as the "pillars of human happiness." Especially was this true of Washington, who believed that "of all the dispositions and habits which lead to political prosperity, religion and morality are indispensable supports."[18]

This was so common an opinion in 1789 throughout the nation—and particularly in New England, stronghold of the Federalist Party—that few Americans thought it strange Washington should have taken the oath of office with his hand on the Bible, added "so help me God" to the prescribed presidential oath, and attended a church service at St. Paul's chapel immediately following his inauguration. Nor did it seem odd in succeeding years, even after the Constitution had been amended to read that Congress must "make no law respecting the establishment of religion," that Congress should employ chaplains to pray at its meetings or that both Presidents Washington and Adams should have asked for days of fasting and Thanksgiving.[19]

But times had changed by 1810. One year into the new century, Thomas

Jefferson, leader of the Republican Party, became president after a torrid election in which Federalists and members of the New England clergy vilified his religious views, which exalted reason over revelation and exuded contempt for the orthodox religion of New Englanders.

Jefferson believed in one God, the creator who had endowed humanity with natural rights, and the moral teachings of Jesus; like Washington, he may even have believed "that no nation has ever yet existed or been governed without religion." But he rejected the divinity of Jesus and all traditional Christian doctrines other than a belief in immortality. His was a religion which, if it lacked emotion enough to inspire great reforms, was reasonable, and Jefferson believed it would become the accepted religion. Perhaps not all of this was understood before the election of 1800, but it was enough for the New England clergy, knowing that Jefferson had once written that it did him "no injury for his neighbor to say there are twenty gods or no god" and that he was a friend of those who were overthrowing Christianity in France, to brand him an infidel. No doubt they also knew of his nearly fanatical hatred for institutional religion, especially that of Presbyterians, Congregationalists, and Episcopalians.[20] Nor did this seemingly benign man ever outgrow his intolerance of these Christian denominations. Because they were mostly Federalists, Jefferson had come to associate them with a plot to overthrow the government and establish a monarchy. Even his famous statement, inscribed on his memorial in Washington, which proclaimed his enmity to "every form of tyranny over the mind of man," and which he swore "upon the altar of God," was directed at Congregationalists and Episcopalians.[21]

Jefferson's hostility to revealed religion, and the New England clergy in particular, inevitably led him to consider the proper relationship between church and state. Unlike Presidents Washington and Adams, he asked neither for days of prayer nor Thanksgiving during his presidency. Nor was a worship service connected with his inauguration. "I . . . have undertaken," he said in his second inaugural, "on no occasion to prescribe the religious exercises suitable to it [the national government]; but have left them as the Constitution found them, under the direction and discipline of the Church or State authorities acknowledged by the several religious societies."[22]

But not quite. Writing to the Baptists in Danbury, Connecticut, in 1802, he went beyond what the Constitution had said about the freedom of religion. The Constitution, he declared, provided a "wall of separation" between church and state. It was an opinion destined to become a reference point in future discussions of the issue.[23]

Without doubt, Jefferson's religious views contributed to abiding bitterness between the two parties. Indeed, it was people's animosity toward a privileged class, especially toward an educated, haughty clergy of Calvinist theology stirring in the young nation since the 1790s, that brought Jefferson to power. Because there was no debate in Congress over the opening of post offices on the Sabbath and so little written about it elsewhere, there is, of course, no way of knowing the degree to which Jefferson's religious views, and those of his followers in Congress, influenced the enactment of section nine. Nevertheless, it is certain that Jefferson set such a tone of religious indifference that his followers who dominated Congress during the early 1800s had no qualms about opening post offices on the Sabbath and trampling on the religious sensibilities of New Englanders.[24]

Whatever their reasons may have been, by opening post offices on Sundays the Republicans provoked the young republic's first confrontation between church and state with a needless law that had perhaps even bent the First Amendment forbidding Congress to pass any law restricting the "free exercise" of religion. It was one thing to affirm separation of church and state and quite another for the government to restrict by law, however obliquely, a postmaster's ability to worship on the Sabbath. At the very least, Republicans had surrendered the government's position of neutrality in religious affairs. Moreover, they had prevented states from enforcing their own Sabbath laws insofar as the post office was concerned, for Congress alone could regulate the post office.

The new law, enacted in April 1810, went into effect later that same year after Postmaster General Granger had composed regulations to govern Sunday mail service. With the latitude Congress had given him, he did his best to ameliorate the effect of the new law on the Sabbath. His regulations provided that post offices at which mail arrived on Sundays were to be kept open for one hour after the arrival of mail and its sorting so letters and papers could be delivered. Where that interfered with church services, the post office was to close and reopen for one hour after the usual ending of the services. Moreover, if mail arrived at a post office too late for a delivery on Saturday, the postmaster was to deliver it on Sunday "at such early hour as not to intrench upon the hours devoted to public religious exercise." Apparently, then, small offices at which mail did not arrive on Sundays, or even Saturdays, could remain closed unless people demanded that they open.[25]

These regulations did nothing, however, to stifle the anguished outcry of evangelistic Christians against their government's violation of the Sabbath. By the time Congress met in December of that year for its next session, their protests against Sabbath mail service had already arrived at the capital. Shortly thereafter they began the first of their antebellum moral reforms with a campaign to end mail delivery on Sundays.[26]

The timing of the crusade was propitious, for when the Sunday mail controversy began in 1810 evangelical Christianity was just recovering from the blows it had sustained during the Revolutionary Era. By the 1750s the first great Christian revival in the American colonies had spent itself, and the Revolution itself, the age of reason, and the lure of Deism had so demoralized orthodox Christianity that many of churches had closed. Others had barely survived, in spite of the great contributions Presbyterian and Congregational ministers had made to the war effort. In 1800 perhaps fewer than 10 percent of the nation's population belonged to a church.[27]

Even then a shift no larger than a man's hand was underway in the nation's religious mood. In the 1790s, both in his classes at Yale University and in his book *The Nature and Danger of Infidel Philosophy* (1798), Timothy Dwight, heir to the Puritan tradition and president of Yale, had begun the change with slashing attacks upon the religion of reason. He was not alone. After the War of 1812, although temporarily disquieted by the Jeffersonians, others followed his lead until the nation was alive with an orthodox religious reawakening that tore thousands from complacent lives and made them reformers.[28]

The evangelical Protestant ministers who led the movement against the opening of the nation's post offices on Sundays during this Second Great Awakening were largely, but by no means exclusively, from New England. They were predominately Congregationalists and Presbyterians—Calvinistic in theology—and with their roots in Puritan America they formed the vanguard of that great host of evangelical Christians who dominated American religion in the nineteenth century. They were among the nation's most fervid nationalists and patriots and had great expectations of their new nation. "Columbia, Columbia," wrote Timothy Dwight, "to glory arise,"

> the queen of the world and child of the skies!
> Thy genius commands thee; with rapture behold,
> While ages on ages thy splendors unfold.
> Thy reign is the last, and the noblest of time,
> Most fruitful thy soil. Most inviting thy clime;
> Let the crimes of the east ne'er incrimson thy name,
> Be freedom, and science, and virtue, thy fame.[29]

Through the years they had largely forgotten whatever reservations they may have had about the Constitution, which contained only an oblique reference to the Deity, and even welcomed the states' disestablishment of particular churches as an opportunity for church growth. They now revered the nation, which God, they believed, had set aside for the purpose of working out his plans on earth. Accepting the government's authority over the nation's civil affairs, they sought to form a moral majority to uphold Christian morality, which alone, in their view, could preserve a Christian nation, ensure democracy, and save the nation from paganism.[30]

Like their Puritan ancestors, they saw Americans as a people chosen by God to create a model nation, a city set upon a hill, a beacon of righteousness in a corrupt world. Here in this new land, set apart from the degradation of the old, they believed God had predestined them to build a new and different kind of nation, which they meant to do by obeying the word of God insofar as that was humanly possible.[31]

Although they gloried in the nation's freedom, democracy, and republicanism and even deemphasized their doctrine of predestination to win souls to Christ, evangelicals never forgot Calvin's premise that humanity was basically sinful, whether born so or made so after birth, and in need of repentance. Unlike Jefferson, whose confidence in democracy was strengthened by his belief in humanity's innate moral sense, evangelicals, wary of human goodness, stressed the necessity of forgiveness, which only Christ could give.[32]

This understanding of human nature made them acutely aware of the hazards sewn into the fabric of their new government. A nation ruled by a monarch or a despot, they agreed, could disregard the Sabbath, restrain its citizens, and control their ignorance by physical force. But that was not possible in the American republic, where no despot ruled and people were free. In America, where people were left to their own devices, only the Christian religion could avert paganism and maintain freedom. In the end, Christianity's survival depended upon the nation's observance of the Sabbath.

Yet near the nation's beginning the very government whose birth and foundations rested on the Christian religion and whose leaders sought God's favor in prayer and in days of Thanksgiving, and whose nation was to be a model for the world, had enacted a law profaning the Sabbath that would, if left untouched, destroy the Christian religion. To evangelicals, section nine was a monstrous act that they felt compelled to oppose with all their being.

Of course, evangelical ministers were not without their own special interests. Even in the early 1800s the influence of the Protestant clergy was not what it once had been. Congregations begrudged them their salaries and ignored their sermons. Moreover, and symbolically, the pulpits of newly constructed churches were often lower than they traditionally had been. No great foresight was needed to see that the continual profanation of the Sabbath would deplete church membership, reduce ministers' already lowered status in their communities, and, in the competition between themselves and politicians, diminish their voice in national affairs. In addition, Protestant ministers could scarcely have been unaware of the possibility that striking out against profanation of the Sabbath and other evils of their day would allow them once again to exert a powerful influence on the life of the nation.[33]

The opposition against opening post offices on Sundays sprang from their hearts, however, and neither egos nor lust for power dominated it. Fervent believers in the sovereignty of God, ministers were steeped in the lessons of the Old and New Testaments and took seriously the word of the Lord. Their fierce struggle to terminate the Sunday mail left no doubt that they firmly believed that the government's violation of the Fourth Commandment would force earnest Christians to resign postmasterships; fill the land with rowdy, profane crowds at post offices on the Sabbath; weaken religion; and, worst of all, as one of their adherents told Congress, expose the "country to the judgments of Heaven."[34]

Indeed, the evil effects of section nine were already evident as the War of 1812 with England raged on into 1814. For some evangelicals, the war was a judgment upon the people for the government's deliberate violation of the Sabbath. For others, the disorderly, boisterous crowds that gathered to await the opening of post offices were the disastrous fruits of the new law. As it turned out, it was not the businessmen for whom the law was presumably enacted who went for their letters on Sundays. Rather, it was as often non-church-goers who collected to hear the news, share gossip, and enjoy each other's company. The disturbance they sometimes caused when the mail stage rolled into a village on a Sunday was implied in the remarks of one senator who had a solution to the problem. "If no distribution of letters and newspapers were made on Sunday," he wrote, "the arrival of a mail stage . . . would excite no unusual attention, and, consequently could occasion no material interruption in religious worship."[35]

That was obvious, of course, but by 1814 evangelicals had become concerned not only about opening post offices and delivering mail on the Sabbath but also about the arrival of the mail stage on that day. The law had said nothing about mail stages, which had always traveled on Sundays. But year by year, supported by government mail contracts, stages traveled ever more miles on the Sabbath, which encouraged businessmen and pleasure-seekers to take passage in them instead of spending the day in worship, study, or quiet contemplation. By the end of the War of 1812, transporting the mail and passengers on Sundays had become an abomination that evangelicals condemned as passionately as they had the opening of the post offices on that day.

But how to repeal section nine and end the transportation of mail on Sundays? At the beginning of the war, in 1812, the House Committee on Post Offices and Post Roads, dominated by Republicans, had easily sloughed off the evangelicals' earliest petitions asking for the law's repeal by appealing to the nation's grave emergency. It could make no changes, its report concluded, "at this peculiar crisis of the United States." But between September 1814 and January 1815, with the war still raging, evangelicals captured Congress's attention more forcefully by bombarding its members with some eighty-five petitions against transporting and opening mail on Sundays. Even more would stream into Congress over the next two years.[36]

These pleas for the repeal of the law of 1810 were not, as might be supposed, from New England alone but from states as widely separated as Virginia and Ohio and as far removed from New England as Tennessee and North and South Carolina. Some were from ordinary citizens like those in Beaver County, Pennsylvania, and others were from organized groups such as the Convention of Congregational Ministers of Massachusetts.[37]

A petition from Congregational ministers, like so many of those that filled congressional mail, was inspired by Lyman Beecher, heir of Connecticut Puritanism, a graduate of Yale University, where he had been Timothy Dwight's student, and Presbyterian-Congregational minister. He was the father of sons and daughters who would become illustrious, but none was more dedicated to preserving the Christian character of the country than he. In 1814 he was the minister of the Congregational church in Litchfield, Connecticut, which was then an intellectual center of New England. There, in the 1780s, Tapping Reeve had begun the nation's first independent law school, to which young men from around the country flocked to learn the law through lectures and the use of a moot court that Reeve had developed. John C. Calhoun, Aaron Burr, and numerous other prominent men who became senators, members of Congress, and Supreme Court justices in the young republic attended Reeve's one-room school of law. There, too, in the 1790s and early 1800s crossing stage lines to New England cities brought a busy and restless humanity that Beecher saw had become increasingly forgetful of the Lord. "Our vices," he said in 1812 in a sermon on the reformation of morals, "are digging the grave of our liberties, and preparing to entomb our glory." What he saw, among other things, were parents who failed to discipline their children, neglected their religious educations, and omitted family prayers. He saw the "enormous consumption of ardent spirit," heard profanity in the streets, and witnessed the outrageous growth of "travel, and worldly labor, and amusement on the Sabbath."[38]

Determined to restore the influence of the church and improve the nation's morals, Beecher found in Congress's establishment of a Sabbath mail service the very cause around which to begin his campaign to exert the church's moral authority. His report, which was approved, to the Connecticut Congregational Ministers Association in June of 1814 recommended petitioning Congress to end Sunday mail delivery, and it circulated far beyond Connecticut. The report marked the beginning of a prolonged battle. Years later, after his memory had dimmed, Beecher was to claim that it was "the origin of the famous petitions against Sunday mails."[39]

Members of Congress had never seen so many petitions on a single subject as were now before them, all demanding an end to transporting and opening mail on Sundays. Frustrated and embarrassed, doubtless fearful of the loss of stage lines that closing the post offices on the Sabbath would bring, they wanted no debate on this problem they had unnecessarily caused. Over the next two years Congress twisted first this way and then that to defeat the repeal of section nine as quietly as possible.

Between 1814 and 1817 the proposal to repeal the law forcing postmasters to open their facilities on Sundays was presented to Congress seven times, twice in the Senate and five times in the House. Each time it was pushed aside, nearly always without debate and without a vote. At first the House Committee on Post Offices and Post Roads attempted to avoid the question by shunting the petitions to the postmaster general and asking the House to dismiss the committee from acting upon them. Reminded by one irate colleague that this was a violation of their own rules, the members first rejected and then reluctantly accepted by a narrow vote a resolution ordering the committee to consider the petitions and report its findings to the House.[40]

After considering the matter but four days, the committee reported, as did a select committee in the Senate a few days later, that because of the war it was "*inexpedient* to make any alteration in the present regulations respecting the transportation and opening the mails on the Sabbath." An attempt failed in the House to change the word *inexpedient* to *expedient.* So determined, indeed, was the Republican majority to maintain Sunday mail service that it even refused to accept amendments that would have added the words *during the present war* to the committee's report after the word *Sabbath* and restricted delivery of newspapers, but not letters, on Sundays.[41]

Neither would the House or Senate accept any other compromise on Sunday mail service. Two committees during this period, one in the Senate and one in the House, brought in minority reports asserting, in effect, that the law keeping post offices open on Sundays was unnecessary (which, in fact, appeared to be true). Twice, once in the Senate and once again in the House, Congress was offered an opportunity to change the law to permit transportation of mail but forbid its delivery on Sundays. But Congress would have neither. In both houses these proposals were summarily rejected without debate or recorded vote.[42]

Committee reports did make clear, however, why it was inexpedient to stop transporting mail on Sundays. The mail, the reports noted, had always traveled on that day, and there was no question that not allowing it to do so would cause great delays. In 1815, according to the postmaster general, mail would be delayed two days from Washington to St. Louis, three days to New Orleans, from New Orleans to Boston as much as five days, and the system of transportation would be disordered "on more than seven hundred routes."[43]

But delay was less important to Congress than what might happen to stagecoach lines if mail was prohibited from traveling on Sundays. Having nourished stagecoach lines for years with mail subsidies that supplemented the passenger trade, members of Congress argued that owners of lines prevented from operating their stages on the Sabbath would lose passenger trade to those that would. They might, in the end, be forced either to surrender their government contracts or, at the very least, charge the government more for carrying the mail. Moreover, the loss in postage to the department would be considerable. In any case, stopping the transportation of mail on Sundays would not keep people from traveling on that day.[44]

If these arguments were sufficient to render transportation of mail on Sundays a "work of necessity," none so logical were offered for keeping post offices open on that day. Indeed, some of the reasons that had apparently instigated the passage of section nine in 1810 were no longer relevant in 1816. Members of Congress then had no reason to fear Gideon Granger's power, for Madison had replaced him with Return J. Meigs two years before. Moreover, in 1816 a member of Congress from Connecticut reminded colleagues that the war could no longer be used as an excuse to keep post offices open on Sundays. "'Happily for the country,'" he said, "'this heavy judgment [the war] has been removed, and we are now at peace with all the world. A more favorable time may probably never occur to retrieve our national character, and wipe out this foul reproach from our system.'"[45]

With Granger gone and the war's close robbing Republicans of their favorite argument for Sabbath mail, it appeared the time had come to close post offices on the Sabbath, even if transportation of mail could not be stopped. Still, there remained the great obstruction of politics, which, had it been only one reason for the enactment of section nine in 1810, was the major barrier to its repeal in 1816.

In that year, when the Sabbath mail controversy was bedeviling Congress, Jefferson's Republican Party, now the Democratic-Republican Party, was the country's only viable political party as the nation moved into the "era of good feeling." The old Federalist Party of Washington, John Adams, and Alexander Hamilton that had founded the new government was dying of self-inflicted wounds. Its members had thought of their nation as a virtuous republic ruled over by the "better people"—the educated, right-thinking, and commercial classes. Unfortunately for them, membership in such classes was limited. It was a foolish mistake to suppose that voters in a democracy would always elect those who considered themselves more virtuous, better educated, and better able to govern than the masses.

In addition, Federalists had opposed the war. The resolutions of the Hartford convention they had called in 1814 to consider dismembering the Union reached Washington early the next year, about the time that news of Jackson's victory at New Orleans and the Peace of Ghent ending the War of 1812 arrived. As fate would have it, it was also at this time that reformers' petitions to stop Sabbath mail were being discussed. Indeed, it was an unlucky happenstance for the reformers that debate over the issue took place in a makeshift building that reminded everyone that the British had burned the capital during a war that New Englanders had opposed.[46]

Yet in spite of their domination of Congress and the presidency, members of the Republican Party lived in fear that Federalists would find some issue that would revive their party and restore them to power. Their fear that this would happen loomed ever larger as the nation approached the election of 1816. Just as they would see in the Missouri question four years later a Federalist attempt to rebuild the party on the issue of the nonextension of slavery, so they apparently saw in the Sabbath mail controversy an issue that might reinvigorate that party.[47]

This Democratic-Republican phobia had surfaced in 1815 at the very outset of the fight over the transportation and delivery of mail on Sundays, when leadership of the House Committee on Post Offices and Post Roads Committee boldly declared petitions against Sabbath mail service invalid, presumably preventing their consideration. In the short debate that followed this strategy, Tennessee's John Rhea, chair of the committee, and other Republicans argued that the petitions were tainted because they had been circulated across the Union by those attempting to "blend the affairs of church and state." In addition, Democratic-Republicans suspected that "some political party considerations" might have entered into the motives which produced them.[48]

As undemocratic as the maneuver was, seventy members of Congress voted with the leadership to invalidate the petitions. That, however, was going too far, even for many Republicans, and a majority of eighty-one agreed to submit the petitions to a committee's consideration. But it proved a hollow victory for the evangelicals. In the end, the House accepted the committee's report that it was inexpedient to stop Sabbath mail service.[49]

Democratic-Republicans used a new argument that stretched the First Amendment for the sake of sustaining the party's political and economic interests: Evangelicals' petitions were somehow a violation of the prohibition against the "establishment of religious clause" of the Constitution. What was really of concern, however, were the "political considerations" that Democratic-Republicans suspected to be behind evangelical efforts to force post offices to close on the Sabbath. Never before had a committee of Congress tried to declare any people's petitions invalid, and the willingness of Democratic-Republican leaders to use that bold strategy indicated how fearful they were that Sunday mail, deplored by so many Americans both North and South, might become an issue around which the Federalist Party might be reborn.

The politics involved in this issue became even clearer in 1816, the year of the presidential election, when Cong. Benjamin Tallmadge presented an amendment that would have ended transportation and delivery of mail on the Sabbath to a postal bill then under discussion. Tallmadge, a Federalist from Litchfield, Connecticut, the same intellectual center in which his friend Lyman Beecher preached God's word, made a fervent plea for the amendment. But the members paid little heed to the arguments of the old Revolutionary War colonel. The most they would do—no small concession considering their avoidance of it in the past—was to honor his specific request that a roll-call vote be taken on his amendment. When it was taken, however, only thirty-five members voted with him; one hundred were opposed.[50]

The vote on Tallmadge's measure was a clear reflection of the party and sectional factions into which the nation had drifted and the determination of Democratic-Republicans to abort a potentially troublesome political issue. Eighty-two Republicans and eighteen Federalists opposed the amendment. Only eight Republicans voted for it, although twenty-six Federalists did so. Twenty-three of the twenty-six were from the New England states, where the Sabbath had been so rigorously observed and where Calvinism retained much of its strength. Only eight of all members of Congress from New England deserted their section to vote against Tallmadge's amendment. Two of these were from Rhode Island, which had always been estranged from the rest of New England, and three were Democratic-Republicans.[51]

A solid South was already forming, however, against the bill. Sixty-eight of the eighty-one members of Congress who voted to continue Sunday mail service were from slaveholding states, even though many petitions against its continuance had come from those states. Only three members from the South voted for the Tallmadge amendment.[52]

Obviously, transportation and delivery of mail on Sundays were sectional as well as political issues that pitted the South, and to some extent the Middle States, against New England, and reflected the division of the country into the sectional political factions Washington had feared. Remnants of the Federalist Party found refuge in New England, while the dominant Democratic-Republican Party increasingly supported southern interests.[53]

Democratic-Republicans might have feared injecting religion into politics and blurring Jefferson's "wall of separation," but that is more than doubtful. Rather, it was an appealing argument to avoid debate over the Sabbath mail issue that might have proven politically useful to Federalists in the election of 1816. Had they not feared the political ramifications of the issue, they might easily have agreed to repeal section nine, which had always been unnecessary, even for expansion of mail service. As it was, they could not close post offices on Sundays and still transport mail on that day without risking a debate on both and losing control of an issue likely to be advantageous to the Federalists.

However it might have been, it was significant that the Republicans themselves had deliberately raised the specter of the fusion of church and state in Congress for the first time in the nation's history—and for political purposes. It would not be the last time Jefferson's party would use the argument as a weapon to frighten Americans and sustain its position in Congress. The issue was destined to become more emotional and divisive in the 1820s, when evangelicals once more mustered their forces to rid the nation of Sunday mail.

Notes

1. See Edward Channing, *A History of the United States: A Period of Transition, 1815–1848* (New York, 1927), 5:230–32, for laws in various states. See also Harold Kirker and James Kirker, *Bulfinch's Boston, 1787–1817* (New York, 1964), 90–91.

2. *American State Papers, Post Office Department, 1789–1833* (Washington, 1834), no. 26, 45 (herefter *ASP: P.O.D.*).

3. *The Debates and Proceedings in the United States, with an Appendix, etc. . .* (Washington, 1853), 11th Cong., 2d sess., 2578, appendix (April 30, 1810) (hereafter *Annals of Congress*).

4. *ASP: P.O.D.*, no. 95, 253.

5. Jefferson worried about spies in the post office and the opening of his letters. See Jefferson to E. Randolph, June 27, 1797, and Jefferson to Madison, April 5, 1798, in *The Works of Thomas Jefferson*, ed. Paul Leicester Ford (New York, 1904), 4:156, 4:230.

6. For the law, see *Annals of Congress*, 11th Cong., 2d sess., 2567–82 (May 1, 1818), appendix.

7. Ibid., 2570.

8. *ASP: P.O.D.*, no. 25, 44–45. For the interests of towns and cities in the mails, see *Annals of Congress*, 11th Cong., 2d sess., 637–38 (Apr. 3, 1810). For Congress's interest in stagecoach lines, see *ASP: P.O.D.*, no. 9, 21–22, and no. 12, 29. By 1805 a line of mail stages was in operation from Maine to Georgia (*ASP: P.O.D.*, no. 15, 34).

9. Samuel Carswell to Madison, June 16, 1810 in *The Papers of James Madison: Presidential Series*, ed. J. C. A. Stagg et al. (Charlottesville, 1992), 1:318–19. Madison apparently never answered this letter. Nor does it appear that Madison, although a Presbyterian, was opposed to opening the post office on the Sabbath. He was from the South, where

mail routes were sparse, and it was his party that drove through legislation (which he signed and never looked back upon) opening the offices on that day.

10. *ASP: P.O.D.,* no. 26, 45.

11. See also Oliver W. Holmes, "Sunday Travel and Sunday Mails: A Question which Troubled Our Forefathers," *New York History* 26 (Oct. 1939): 413–24. For a thorough investigation of the postmaster at Washington and the origins of section nine, see Richard R. John, *Spreading the News: The American Postal System from Franklin to Morse* (Cambridge, 1995), 170–71, and Richard R. John, "Taking Sabbatarianism Seriously: The Postal System, the Sabbath, and the Transformation of American Culture," *Journal of the Early Republic* 10 (Winter 1990): 522.

12. See John (*Spreading the News,* 170–71) for this argument, which omits other possible reasons for Congress's action.

13. For the Senate amendments, see *Annals of Congress,* 11th Cong., 2d sess., 637, 643 (April 3, 5, 1810). For the idea that Congress passed this without due consideration, see "Petition of Truman Hastings and Others," doc. 12, 25th Cong., 2d sess., 15 (Dec. 12, 1838).

14. *Annals of Congress,* 11th Cong., 2d sess., 1987–89 (April 26, 1810).

15. For the quotation, see *Annals of Congress,* 9th Cong., 2d sess., 623 (Feb. 25, 1807); for the position of the two parties on postal policy, see *Annals of Congress,* 10th Cong., 1st sess., 2082–83 (Apr. 12, 1808).

16. "Gideon Granger," *Dictionary of American Biography* (New York, 1931), 4:443–44 (hereafter *DAB*). For the success of Republican efforts to gain new post roads in spite of opposition, see *Annals of Congress,* 7th Cong. 1st sess., 1370–22 (May 3, 1802); *Annals of Congress,* 8th Cong., 1st sess., 1283–86 (Mar. 26, 1864); *Annals of Congress,* 8th Cong., 2d sess., 1666 (Feb. 14, 1805); and *Annals of Congress,* 9th Cong., 1st sess., 1295–96 (Apr. 21, 1806), all in the appendices.

17. *APO: P.O.D.,* no. 26, 45. For Randolph's attack upon Granger, see *Annals of Congress,* 8th Cong., 2d sess., 1031–33 and 1105–6 (Jan. 29, 31, 1805). For the Republican accusation that Granger had appointed Federalist to be postmasters, see Caleb Atwater to Madison, Dec. 20, 1809, in *Papers of James Madison,* ed. Stagg et al., 2:138–39. For the investigation of Granger, see *Annals of Congress,* 9th Cong., 1st sess., 831–34 (Mar. 21, 1806), and *ASP: P.O.D.,* no. 20, 40. Granger's explanation of his part in the affair is in *Annals of Congress,* 8th Cong., 2d sess., 1110–13 (Feb. 1, 1805). The vote taken to accept the report of the Committee on Claims was 63 to 58, with almost all southern members of Congress opposed to the acceptance. *Annals of Congress,* 8th Cong., 2d sess., 1173 (Feb. 2, 1805). Congress adjourned before the investigation of Granger could begin.

18. See Washington's farewell address in *Annals of Congress,* 4th Cong. 2d sess., 2876 (Sept. 17, 1796), appendix.

19. *Annals of Congress,* 1st Cong., 1st sess., 25, 29 (April 30, 1789); see also Anson Phelps Stokes, *Church and State in the United States: Development and Contemporary Problems* (New York, 1950), 1:486.

20. For the quotation, see "Notes on Virginia," in *Writing of Thomas Jefferson,* ed. Andrew Lipscomb (Washington, 1904), 221. Jefferson's brief statement of his religion is found in Jefferson to Benjamin Rush, April 21, 1803, in *Works of Thomas Jefferson,* ed. Ford, 8:223–28. William D. Gould, "The Religious Opinion of Thomas Jefferson," *Mississippi Valley Historical Review* 22 (1933): 191–208, counters the attacks upon Jefferson's religion. See also Daniel Boorstin, *The Lost World of Thomas Jefferson* (Boston, 1960), 151–

66; Adrienne Koch, *The Philosophy of Thomas Jefferson* (Chicago, 1964), ch. 4; and Fawn M. Brodie, *Thomas Jefferson: An Intimate History* (New York, 1974), 25, 54–55, for interpretative accounts of Jefferson's religion. A sympathetic treatment of Jefferson's religious views is found in Dumas Malone, *Jefferson the President: First Term, 1801–1805* (Boston, 1970), ch. 11. See also Edwin S. Gaustad, *Sworn on the Altar of God* (Grand Rapids, 1996), 90–91, 142–46, for an account of the religious question in the election of 1800 and Jefferson's views on immortality and confidence in a universal rational religion. On Jefferson's alleged belief in the necessity of religion in government, see Nicholas Von Hoffman, "In the Stacks: God Was Present at the Founding," *Civilization* 5 (Apr.–May 1998): 39.

21. Jefferson to Rush, Sept. 23, 1800, in *Works of Thomas Jefferson,* ed. Ford, 7:460; see also Gaustad, *Sworn on the Altar of God,* 184–87. In his first inaugural address, Jefferson attempted to heal the wounds that resulted from the election of 1800, but in his second inaugural, in a scarcely veiled description of the aborigines who believed reason was a false god, he struck back orthodoxy. Cf. *Annals of Congress,* 6th Cong., 2d sess., 764 (Mar. 4, 1801); and *Annals of Congress,* 8th Cong., 2d sess., 79 (Mar. 1805).

22. *Annals of Congress,* 8th Cong., 2d sess., 78 (May 4, 1805); see also Gaustad, *Sworn on the Altar of God,* 98–100.

23. Stokes, *Church and State,* 1:335. This was assuredly not what the Founders had in mind when they wrote the Constitution. The keen observation of Joseph Story, associate justice of the Supreme Court and student of the Constitution, was that "the attempt to level all religions, and make it a matter of State policy to hold all in utter indifference, would have created universal disapprobation, if not universal indignation" and surely close to the mark. Joseph Story, *Familiar Exposition of the Constitution of the United States . . .* (New York, 1858), 261, 726.

24. For an excellent account of the revolt against the New England clergy in the 1790s and religious upheaval, see Nathan O. Hatch, *The Democratization of American Christianity* (New Haven, 1989), 17–22, 170–89. On the evangelical fear of Jeffersonian apathy toward religion, see Robert H. Abzug, *Cosmos Crumbling: American Reform and the Religious Imagination* (New York, 1994), 113.

25. *ASP: P.O.D.,* no. 26, 45, and no. 29, 46 (quotation). By 1877, postal regulations actually specified that post offices at which the mail did not arrive on Saturday or Sunday need not open on Sunday. *United States Official Postal Guide* (Boston, 1877), 9.

26. For the early petitions, see *Annals of Congress,* 11th Cong., 3d sess., 487 (Jan. 4, 1811), and *ASP: P.O.D.,* no. 26, 44–45. The petition of the Presbyterian General Assembly, which was early in the fight against section nine, held that Congress had an obligation to honor the Sabbath. John, *Spreading the News,* 177.

27. Robert T. Handy, *A Christian America: Protestant Hopes and Historical Realities* (New York, 1971), 27. See also a perceptive article by Sidney Mead, "America Protestantism during the Revolutionary Epoch," in *Religion in American: Interpretive Essay* ed. John M. Mulder and John F. Wilson (Englewood Cliffs, 1978), 162–80; Russell Nye, *The Cultural Life of the New Nation* (New York, 1960); and Winthrop S. Hudson, *American Protestantism* (Chicago, 1961), 49–51. For a different explanation of the religious situation, see Hatch, *The Democratization of American Christianity,* 63–66.

28. For a searching account of the Second Great Awakening, see Abzug, *Cosmos Crumbling,* ch. 2. See also Martin E. Marty, *Righteous Empire: The Protestant Experience in America* (New York, 1970), 89–99: Charles Kellar, *The Second Great Awakening in Connecticut*

(New Haven, 1942); Alice F. Tyler, *Freedom's Ferment: Phases of American Social History to 1860* (Minneapolis, 1944); and John B. Boles, *The Great Revival* (Lexington, 1972). Boles sees the origin of the awakening in the "feeling of crisis," but George Thomas, in *Revivalism and Cultural Change: Christianity as Nation-building in Nineteenth-Century United States* (Chicago, 1987), attributes the origins of the awakening to "free will" and market forces. Hatch, *The Democratization of American Christianity,* 17–18.

29. Walter Blair et al., *The Literature of the United States: An Anthology and History* (New York, 1946), 1:451. Two streams of evangelistic political thought emerged during the nineteenth century. "At one extreme," notes Richard J. Carwardine, "stood the Calvinist Puritan vision of politics as a means of introducing God's kingdom. . . . In contrast 'pietist' evangelicals viewed politics from a New Testament Pentecostal perspective which magnified the role of the Holy Spirit . . . and . . . led . . . to an essentially negative view of government." Richard J. Cawardine, *Evangelicals and Politics in Antebellum America* (New Haven, 1993), 14. It is the first of these groups that took the lead in pushing for postal reform, although they were in many cases joined by the others.

30. Elwyn A. Smith, *Religious Liberty in the United States* (Philadelphia, 1972), ch. 5, examines evangelical thought of the period. See also Henry May, *Protestant Churches and Industrial America* (New York, 1949), 3–4. For the promotion of a Christian civilization, see Handy, *A Christian America,* ch. 2. On Timothy Dwight and New England's special place in the Second Great Awakening, see Abzug, *Cosmos Crumbling,* 32–38. On a nation set apart for a divine purpose to establish a Christian nation, see James Davison Hunter, *American Evangelism: Conservative Religion and the Quandary of Modernism* (New Brunswick, 1983), 24. As used throughout this text, "moral majority" refers to those evangelical Protestants who sought to persuade Congress to pass legislation to rid the U.S. postal system of those services that threatened to destroy what they perceived to be a Christian nation.

31. On the evangelical debt to the Puritans, see Handy, *A Christian America,* 12–13. From a different perspective, Jefferson, too, in his first inaugural address saw a bright future for his pristine country, which was "separated by nature and a wide ocean from the exterminating havoc of one quarter of the globe." *Annals of Congress,* 6th Cong., 1st sess., 764 (Mar. 4, 1801).

32. Although it was true that Calvinist minsters, such as Lyman Beecher, avoided as much as possible the question of inherited sin and followed somewhat the "New Haven" theology of Nathaniel Taylor during the Second Great Awakening, they never ignored sin or the need for repentance and forgiveness. See Barbara Cross's astute introduction to Lyman Beecher, *The Autobiography of Lyman Beecher,* ed. Barbara M. Cross (Cambridge, 1961), 1:xi–xxxvi (hereafter Beecher, *Autobiography*); see also Abzug, *Cosmos Crumbling,* 38. For Jefferson's views of human nature, see Koch, *The Philosophy of Thomas Jefferson,* ch. 3.

33. Beecher, *Autobiography,* 1:xxxi–ii. For the accusation of the clergy's self-serving, see "Memorial of Citizens of Windom Co., Vt.," H. Doc. no. 115, 21st Cong., 2d sess., 2, 3 (Feb. 24, 1831). Concern for the waywardness of unrestrained citizens was made all the greater by untrained ministers and their following's attacks on the Calvinist clergy.

34. *Annals of Congress,* 14th Cong., 1st sess., 1123 (Mar. 2, 1816).

35. *ASP: P.O.D.,* no. 75, 213.

36. The quotation is from Beecher, *Autobiography.* See also *Annals of Congress,* 13th Cong., 3d sess., 1063 (Jan. 10, 1815); see also *ASP: P.O.D.,* no. 30, 45, and no. 31, 47, as

well as "Sabbath Mails," *Annals of Congress,* 13th Cong., 3d sess., xxiii (index), *Annals of Congress,* 14th Cong., 1st sess., xxxv (index), and *Annals of Congress,* 14th Cong., 2d sess., lxiii (index).

37. *Annals of Congress,* 14th Cong., 1st sess., 26 (Dec. 19, 1815); *Annals of Congress,* 14th Cong., 2d sess., 679 (Jan. 16, 1816). The Presbyterian General Assembly inspired many petitions. John, *Spreading the News,* 173.

38. Beecher, *Autobiography,* 2:191 (first quotation), 192 (second and third quotations). For Litchfield, Connecticut, see Marian C. McKenna, "The Law School of Tapping Reeve," in *My Country* 20 (Autumn 1986): 7–16. On Beecher, see also Abzug, *Cosmos Crumbling,* 36–56, and Howe, *Political Culture,* 150–67.

39. Beecher, *Autobiography,* 1:197. See also John, "Taking Sabbatarianism Seriously," 524–25, for the contribution of the Presbyterian General Assembly to the movement, and Caller, *Second Great Awakening,* 144–48.

40. *Annals of Congress,* 13th Cong., 3d sess., 586 (Nov. 16, 1814); *Annals of Congress,* 13th Cong., 3d sess., 1063–65 (Jan. 10, 1815); *Annals of Congress,* 13th Cong., 3d sess., 1074–75 (Jan. 16, 1815).

41. *Annals of Congress,* 13th Cong., 3d sess., 1084, 1146–47 (Jan. 20, Feb. 10, 1815); for Senate action, see *Annals of Congress,* 13th Cong., 3d sess., 185 (June 27, 1815); see also *ASP: P.O.D.,* nos. 29, 46, and no. 30, 47 on the Senate's Select Committee.

42. *Annals of Congress,* 14th Cong., 1st sess., 28 (Dec. 22, 1815); *Annals of Congress,* 14th Cong., 1st sess., 302 (Apr. 9, 1816); *Annals of Congress,* 14th Cong., 2d sess., 419, 1045–47 (Jan. 6, Mar. 1, 1817).

43. *ASP: P.O.D.,* no. 29, 46

44. *Annals of Congress,* 14th Cong., 2d sess., 1047 (Mar. 1, 1817); see also *ASP: P.O.D.,* no. 75, 213–14.

45. *Annals of Congress,* 14th Cong., 1st sess., 1124 (Mar. 2, 1816). A brief account of Granger's removal is in White, *The Jeffersonians,* 301.

46. On the Federalists, see Shaw Livermore, Jr., *The Twilight of Federalism: The Disintegration of the Federalist Party, 1815–1830* (Princeton, 1962), 3–14. For Congress's temporary building, see *Annals of Congress,* 14th Cong., 1st sess., 379–80 (Dec. 7, 1815).

47. On the Missouri question, see Glover Moore, *The Missouri Controversy, 1918–1821* (Lexington, 1953), 106. See also Livermore, *Twilight of Federalism,* 20–22, for Democratic-Republican fears in 1816 and chapter 5 for a modification of Moore's interpretation of the Federalists and the Missouri Compromise.

48. *Annals of Congress,* 13th Cong., 3d sess., 1074–75 (Jan. 16, 1815).

49. Ibid., 1075.

50. *Annals of Congress,* 14th Cong., 1st sess., 1123 (Mar. 2, 1816). On Tallmadge, see Beecher, *Autobiography,* 1:136, 1:148–49.

51. *Annals of Congress,* 14th Cong., 1st sess., 1123 (Mar. 2, 1816).

52. Ibid.

53. For Washington's warning, see *Annals of Congress,* 4th Cong., 2d sess., 2872–73 (Sept. 17, 1796), appendix.

2 Sabbath Mail and the Separation of Church and State

That your memorialist conscientiously believe that the people of the United States in their national capacity and character, constitute a Christian nation.
—Petition to Congress, December 10, 1829

In the twelve years following the defeat of the evangelicals' crusade against Sabbath mail, the post office, freed from whatever restraints that closing facilities and terminating transportation of the mail on the Sabbath might have had on its growth, expanded rapidly. By 1828 mail was being carried 10,142,000 miles annually, and the Post Office Department had spread its net, spiderlike, over 114,536 miles of post roads to the farthest corners of the nation. Not only was mail going farther over these roads, but it was also going faster. That year the postmaster general boasted that mail was being carried at a speed of one hundred miles a day over many mail routes.[1]

More miles of post roads meant more post offices, too—7,651 in 1828 to be precise. Places that would become household names in years to come—Gettysburg, Chancellorsville, and Fredericksburg—already had post offices; even the small post office at Harpers Ferry did $454.81 worth of business that year. Moreover, an estimated 26,956 employees now worked for the post office. Stagecoaches were everywhere, carrying mail and passengers more than six million miles annually. In 1827 the red coaches belonging to James Reeside, a flamboyant, Scottish-born mail contractor, were already a familiar sight along post roads, carrying the mail 391,194 miles annually over 573 miles of road. On ninety miles of these roads, mail was carried twice a day and at least six days a week.[2]

Accompanied as it was by a blatant disregard of the Lord's Day, such expansion greatly aggravated evangelicals' religious sensibilities, already bruised by the previous protest. Expansion meant, of course, that more Americans than ever were traveling on Sundays and more postal employees were being forced to work on that day. Worse still, the army of postal workers confirmed in more and more American minds that the nation cared nothing for the laws of God and even insisted they be broken. More proof was provided by the new law Congress passed in 1825 that regulated the post office. Given the opportunity to wipe out section nine, Congress had only transferred it to section eleven of the new law.[3]

It was inevitable, then, that the swift extension of the post office, made without thought to the Sabbath, would lead evangelicals to renew their crusade to stop mail on that day, which they did in 1828. This time, however, their attack was brief, cut short by their opponents' charge that evangelicals wished to create a Christian party, blend politics and religion, destroy the separation of church and state doctrine, and put the nation in religious bondage. As was the case in 1816, however, it was a specious argument and would help determine the nation's attitude toward the involvement of religion in politics from then to now. Used by the remnants of the Jeffersonian party, as it had been in 1816, to sway the masses against the termination of Sabbath mail, it was designed less from fear of the union of church and state than to promote Sabbath mail routes and help stagecoach owners secure government contracts to carry mail and passengers on that day, provide transportation in areas where the postal service and transportation were meager, and destroy the last vestiges of the old New England political leadership in national affairs.[4]

The evangelicals' second great effort to stop mail on the Sabbath began in 1826 with a call from an alarmed Presbyterian General Assembly to boycott the growing number of Sabbath-breaking transportation companies. Among those who responded was Josiah Bissell, Jr., of Rochester, New York. Bissell, a Presbyterian elder, had founded the General Union for Promoting the Observance of the Christian Sabbath two years after the organization of the American Society for the Promotion of Temperance with the help of the wealthy and influential Tappan brothers, Lewis and Arthur. Subsequently, Bissell established the Pioneer Line transportation company, whose white stagecoaches with green trim lumbered along the road between Albany and Buffalo every day except Sunday. Built to prove that a coach line refusing to travel on the Sabbath could succeed, the Pioneer Line, which had no mail contract, did not last long. Nevertheless, it and the organization of the General Union for Promoting the Observance of the Christian Sabbath did reawaken the dormant crusade against Sunday mail.[5]

As it happened, 1828 was also the year of the presidential race that brought the return of two political parties to the national arena and positioned the incumbent president, John Quincy Adams, a National Republican, against Andrew Jackson, a Republican. The campaign was bitter and unlike any that had preceded it. It was waged largely through the post office, whose expansion and improvements, little noticed in the overall scheme of things, had so enlarged the reading public during the 1820s that the post office had become a major catalyst in changing the course of American politics and ushering in the "era of the common man." Partisans of both parties filled the mail with more pamphlets, political newspapers, broadsides, and circulars than could have been imagined just four years before.[6]

Not to be outdone by the politicians, the General Union also used the mail to appeal "to the consciences and hearts of men," as its constitution provided. It mailed out across the country some thirty thousand copies of Lyman Beecher's stirring attack on transporting and delivering mail on Sundays. These circulated side by side with hundreds of copies of the "coffin handbill," which accused Jackson of murdering six soldiers, and newspapers stamping John Q. Adams as unfit for the presidency because he had traveled and made a campaign speech on a Sunday.[7]

Passing through the mail that year, too, was a Philadelphia newspaper edited by the Rev. Ezra Ely, a Presbyterian minister who called for a "Christian party in politics." Actually, Ely had issued his call in a Fourth of July sermon the year before, and his newspaper had continued to urge Christians to support good men for office. It was not clear whether he was proposing an actual political party or merely urging Christians to vote for supporters of Christian causes. In that most political of times, however, it was everywhere assumed that he meant an actual political party.[8]

Whatever Ely's purpose, when the furor of the campaign had abated at the end of 1828 Andrew Jackson, symbol of the common man and heir to the Jeffersonian party, had won the election. When Congress met in December of that year it had before it some 467 petitions from twenty-one states demanding an end to the transportation and delivery of mail on Sundays. Those from New York were said to have been signed by seven thousand people and one from Boston by two thousand, suggesting that a moral majority was indeed forming against the government's violation of the Sabbath.[9]

The Sabbatarians' appeals contained compelling arguments that reasonable men, in the absence of political and religious prejudices, might have accepted. Essentially, they questioned the authority of the government to violate God's commandments, declared the law opening the nation's post offices unconstitutional, and elaborated on the awesome consequences awaiting the nation's continued profanation of the Sabbath.[10]

Believing, as surely most Americans did at the time, that the United States was a Christian nation, founded by Christians and inhabited by citizens who were nearly all Christian and whose very Constitution was "done in convention . . . in the year of *our Lord one thousand seven hundred and Eighty seven,"* they reasoned that the government must therefore also be Christian. If that was so, the government was bound by the laws of God and not at liberty to require unnecessary work that included, they believed, delivering and transporting mail on the Sabbath. "Indeed, it will hardly be contended now, by any one," wrote a group of North Carolina Sabbatarians, "that there is an *absolute necessity* for this labor; the question seems to rest altogether on the *expediency* of the measure. And shall mere human expediency make void the law of God?" This, for evangelicals, was unthinkable.[11]

It was not, however, just God's law that Congress had violated by its legislation. It was the Constitution itself. The evangelicals' position, in fact, was not without substance. Almost as clearly as the Constitution recognized slavery, it also recognized the Sabbath; one section provided that a bill would become law if the president had not signed it within ten days after it was presented to him, "Sundays excepted." Obviously, the Founders meant Sunday to be a day of rest, a supposition borne out by the fact that Congress did not meet on that day, nor were any government offices open except post offices.[12] This particularity was not lost on evangelicals. They were quick to point out that no other government employees—no judges, no members of Congress, and no lesser federal employees—were forced to work on Sundays. Only postmasters and postal workers had been singled out for that purpose, which was unfair discrimination in their view and unconstitutional as well.

Beyond that, Sabbatarians charged, the law requiring postmasters to work on the Sabbath violated the First Amendment, which prevented Congress from passing or enforcing any law restricting freedom of religion. Did not that law, they asked, restrict the religious freedom of those conscientious Christian postmasters who were forced either to surrender their positions in order to comply with the Fourth Commandment or violate their consciences by laboring on Sunday?[13]

Finally, the Sabbatarians argued, opening post offices on Sundays violated the Tenth Amendment, which guaranteed the states all powers "not delegated to the United States." Nearly all states, they contended, had laws that precluded activities such as mail delivery on Sundays. "Yet," ran the reformers' complaint, "they are in effect repealed; for they are completely set aside by that part of the Post Office law . . . which renders impractical the effectual execution of any of the State laws by which a due observance of the Lord's day is enjoined."[14]

It was a question of the rights of states and would plague the nation for more than half a century. "Can Congress," Sabbatarians asked, "by one or two sentences in regulating her Post Office Department, virtually repeal and annul all these State laws? If they come into collision, which is to yield?" Evangelicals had no answer. They would scarcely have thought to bring the matter to the Supreme Court, which to that time had only once declared a law of Congress unconstitutional, and they had no idea, of course, that their questions would one day be settled on the battlefield. Their only contention was that Congress, in opening post offices on Sundays, had gone too far. "We know Congress cannot," wrote a gathering of Kentucky citizens in 1828, "and ought not, to enforce the duties of the Sabbath. We ask them not to do this; but we ask them to keep their hands from pulling down, destroying, and disregarding a day, the duties of which are established by another and infinitely superior power."[15]

Briefly put, Sabbatarians contended that Congress had not kept religion where the Constitution had left it but had taken sides against it. Reflecting on the legislation some years later, one newspaper editorialized that the law was "*against* religion. It does not leave Christianity in the same circumstance as before it was passed." Not only had Congress ranged the government against religion, but it had also done so for no reason other than expediency. Not without reason, then, the national law creating a Sunday mail service for which there was no apparent need appeared to evangelical Christians to be a deliberate effort by Congress to distance the nation from Christianity.[16]

As fervent as were their arguments against the injustice and unconstitutionality of the law opening post offices, the great weight of evangelicals' appeals was reserved for the consequences awaiting a nation that profaned the Sabbath by its ordinances. Members of Congress might look with equanimity upon the profanation of the Sabbath, and others might see no harm looming in the distance to the nation from travel and pleasurable excursions on the Sabbath. Not so the evangelicals. Awed by God's power and with their beliefs anchored in the Bible, they were as certain that the deliberate violation of the commandments would bring ruin to the soul of the nation as they were sure of God's sovereignty. "Let our nation but trample on the Sabbath," wrote a Sabbatarian in 1829, "and neglect its sacred duties, and we shall soon be heathens, or come to a condition like the French nation when they abolished the Sabbath."[17]

In their minds, section nine of the 1810 Postal Act was a national sin that made it impossible "for the friends of good order to . . . protect this holy day from profanation while the Government allows the mails to be carried on Sundays, and requires postmasters to deliver letters, papers and packets 'on every day in the week.'" It was one thing for individuals to ignore the Sabbath, but it was quite another for Congress, representative of the government and all the people, to require them do so. Every postmaster forced to open his post office on Sundays and every mail carrier—from stagecoach driver and helper to those on horseback and in sulkies—lumbering along post roads on that day, greeting people, or stopping to share a bit of news was, in effect, a symbol of a pagan nation whose laws contravened those of God.[18] Moreover, they were deplorable examples for others. "Many thousands," an assembly of Boston citizens wrote to Congress in 1830, "are, as a consequence of this practice, led into habits of business; and many other thousands still are gradually enticed into habits of dissipation and idleness in those very hours which would otherwise have been consecrated to instruction and devotion." If that should continue, they warned, "the restraints of religion will be removed from the community at large . . . or be consigned to a comparatively small number of retired and obscure individuals."[19]

A loss of the "restraints of religion" was the evangelicals' overriding concern. They were persuaded not only by their faith but also by the overthrow of religion in France scarcely four decades earlier that so monstrous an evil would result from this loss that people's freedoms would be swallowed in a quagmire of vice and crime and the government itself overturned. "No maxim in politics is better established," a Philadelphia memorial contended, "than that virtue and good morals are the only basis on which free government can permanently rest; and no truth is more clear or important than that which was inculcated in the farewell address of the Father of his country—that morality cannot be preserved without religion; and to this it may, with truth as unquestionable, be added, that, without a Sabbath, a day of sacred rest, religion cannot be maintained in an extensive community."[20]

For Sabbatarians, Sunday was not just a day of worship. It was also a day of rest, spiritual renewal, and study, which they greatly valued. Its observance, to quote the Bostonians, was "conducive to good morals, intelligence, and happiness." Its desecration, "if it should become universal . . . would be followed by general ignorance, licentiousness, and vice; and, in such a state of things, it would be impossible to sustain our republican institutions, or those religious privileges which are more valuable than life itself."[21]

Finally, and not forgotten by evangelicals in their summary of evils issuing from the violation of the Sabbath, was the realization that the law opening post offices on Sundays had exposed the nation to God's "fearful judgments," the consequences of which no one could know.[22]

As the petitions against transportation and delivery of mail poured into Congress in 1828 they were speedily sent to the Post Office Committees of both houses. In the House, the committee agreed with the petitioners that the law opening post offices on Sundays, if not transportation of mail on that day, was unnecessary and recommended that it be repealed. The Senate Post Office Committee, however, controlled by the Democratic Party, formerly the Democratic-Republican Party that had been responsible for the controversy, took the opposite stand. This committee was headed by Richard M. Johnson, a Democrat of Kentucky, and its report was a sharply worded attack upon the Sabbatarian movement and designed to put it to rest forever.[23]

Actually, there were two Johnson reports. One was presented early in 1829 to the Senate, where Johnson, having been defeated for reelection, was serving his last term. The other was communicated in 1830 to the House, to which he had been elected in 1829 and where he had immediately been made chair of the Post Office Committee. The arguments of both were much the same, but the latter, made after the first had failed to stop the flow of petitions, was more caustic and confrontational and overcame whatever sentiment that lingered in Congress for repeal of the law opening post offices.[24]

Historians have praised Johnson's reports as significant guideposts in the nation's tortuous path between church and state, and indeed they were. They were also cleverly disingenuous, and one cannot miss, even at this distance, the animus toward Calvinistic evangelicals, so reminiscent of Jefferson's consuming hatred of Presbyterians and Congregationalists, that pervaded both documents. Because the Sunday mail controversy was a moral issue, emotional responses to it were to be expected. Johnson's attack, however, seemed born of something more than the moral issue involved.[25]

Richard Mentor Johnson served in Congress from 1807 to 1837. Usually he boarded when in Washington at the home of Obadiah B. Brown, the chief clerk in the Post Office Department in 1829 and a political appointee who had long lived in Washington. Presumably it was Brown, a shrewd and calculating Baptist minister with a sharp pen, who composed Johnson's reports. But it must be supposed that Johnson fully agreed with the reports, the emotionally charged language of which was reminiscent of that he had used to castigate Federalists in Congress through the years.[26]

However it may have been, Johnson was an early opponent of the Calvinistic evangelicals' effort to abolish Sunday mail service. As a fervent Jeffersonian anticlerical, he had probably supported the law of 1810 opening the nation's post offices. If not, he had at least become an obdurate foe of the Sabbatarian movement by 1815. That year, although not a member of the Post Office Committee and presumably without direct interest in the bill, he was one of only three members of the House to argue that evangelicals' petitions were invalid because they united church and state and involved "political party considerations."[27]

Why this early opposition to the termination of mail on the Sabbath? It could not have been that Johnson did not understand the religious revival taking place at the time or that he disapproved of it. Nor could it be that, notwithstanding his argument in 1815, he was overly concerned about the connection between church and state or did not appreciate the power of Christianity to improve civilization. In 1820, when Congress was debating the proposal to prevent the extension of slavery into Missouri, Johnson had argued against the proposition on the ground that allowing slavery to spread to the new state would be the best way to ameliorate its effects and even end them. "The more you suffer them [the slaves] to disperse," he had said, "the more rapidly you will accelerate this desirable state of things [emancipation]. The energies of the Christian world are now combined in the diffusion of evangelical light, and the principles which it inculcates are every day relaxing the bonds of slavery. . . . Encourage Sunday schools," he continued, "multiply Bible societies; increase missionary exertions; animate to deeds of benevolence, abolition societies, and perfect the system of colonization. Then trust the kind providence of God for the result, and you will perform the duties of Christians and patriots, in the service of God and his creatures."[28]

No, it was not so much his fear of the intrusion of religion into politics that motivated Johnson's opposition to the Sabbatarians as it was the Presbyterians and Congregationalists, and behind them the Federalists, who were its leading lights. Like so many Democrats of the time, Johnson was a sincere Jeffersonian idealogue who had often crossed swords with Federalists, whom he regarded as traitors for their opposition to the measures leading to the War of 1812 and to the war itself.[29]

As it had for so many in his party, this harsh view had only hardened with Federalists' efforts to prevent slavery in Missouri in 1820, which Johnson saw as a maneuver on their part to regain political control and "gratify a lust for power." Indicative of his disdain for New England was his attitude toward President John Q. Adams, whose roots lay in Puritan Massachusetts. Meeting Johnson shortly after Adams's election, the editor of the *National Intelligencer* recalled suggesting to him that the administration might pursue a policy in the public interest. "I don't care," Johnson was quoted as saying, "for by the eternal, if they act as pure as the angels that stand at the right hand of the throne of God, we'll put them down."[30]

So profound did Johnson's loathing of the Federalists appear that it is difficult to know whether it was inspired by their principles or by who they were—for they were everything Johnson was not. Not only were most of them New Englanders, but they were also likely to be educated, commercial, wealthy, and given to aristocratic pretensions. They were, as some of Johnson's supporters attested, "men of talents and influence." In short, they were the so-called better people. More than that, they were likely to be Congregationalists and Presbyterians, the elect of God, who did indeed give the impression of exclusiveness, superiority, and self-righteousness. These were the people who presumably would form Ely's "Christian party" and possibly take over the government.[31]

Like many who supported his position, including John Leland, the great

Baptist leader who greatly influenced him, Johnson was outside this pale. A sometime member of the Baptist Church, born into an obscure pioneer family, largely self-educated, a slaveholder who sired two daughters by his female slave, with whom he lived openly, and a westerner, he and New Englanders had little in common except their dislike of each other. No doubt that dislike had much to do with the venom in his reports rejecting petitioners' efforts to terminate Sunday mail.[32]

From the outset, Johnson's reports, approved by the committee majority, seemed deliberately intended to offend evangelicals who supported termination of Sabbath mail. The first report began with the gratuitous implication that there was no difference between the Christian Sabbath and the pagan day of rest, and both made it appear that evangelicals were really asking Congress to mandate the first, instead of the seventh, day of the week as the day of rest for the nation. This, the reports contended, Congress had no constitutional right to do. "The committee look in vain," Johnson wrote, "to that instrument [the Constitution] for a delegation of power authorizing this body to inquire and determine what part of time, or whether any, has been set apart by the Almighty for religious exercises."[33]

As if that sneering tone and the distortion of their position were not enough to exasperate the reformers, Johnson taunted them with the suggestion that they seek help from the states. "Let the petitioners turn to *them,* and see if they can induce the passage of laws to respect the observance of the Sabbath; for if it be sinful for the mail to carry letters on Sundays, it must be equally sinful for individuals to write, carry, receive, or read them."[34] Of course none knew better than Johnson that the states already had Sabbath laws and were, insofar as the postal system was concerned, powerless to act. Only Congress could close, or open, post offices on Sundays.

Johnson's most effective argument was directed at Ezra Ely's unfortunate call for a Christian party and the evangelicals' imagined efforts to thrust a religious party into politics. It was fortunate, he thought, that the question of a religious party had arisen so early in the nation's history "while the spirit of the Revolution yet exists" and, presumably, while he was there to oppose such a party. In any case, it allowed him to position himself and his committee as defenders of religious liberty. "The extensive religious combinations to effect a political object are," he wrote, "always dangerous. This first effort of the kind calls for the establishment of a principle, which . . . would lay the foundation for dangerous innovations upon the spirit of the constitution, and upon the religious rights of the citizens."[35]

Once the nation yielded to this kind of religious pressure, Johnson continued, there would be no end to the horrible consequences that would follow this religious despotism. He had no difficulty finding examples of the terrible fate of nations in which church and state were connected. In fact, the entire world, with one exception, offered an illustration. "With the exception of the United States, the whole human race . . . is in religious bondage; and in reviewing the scenes of persecution which history everywhere presents, unless the committee could believe that the cries of the burning victim, and the flames by which he is consumed, bear to Heaven a grateful incense, the conclusion is inevitable that the line cannot be too strongly drawn between church and state."[36]

Not only was the evangelicals' attempt to develop a Christian party dangerous in Johnson's view, but it was also treasonous. He regretted that a question involving the "dearest privileges of the constitution" should have been brought before Congress by those who "enjoy its choicest blessings" and compared them to traitors: "*We* should all recollect that Catiline, a professed patriot, was a traitor to Rome; Arnold, a professed Whig, was a traitor to America; and Judas, a professed disciple, was a traitor to his Divine Master."[37]

Preposterous as this was, it was not the end of the Johnson's tirade. Searching for every base motive the evangelicals may have had, he intimated that their purposes were economically motivated, for they had been unable to profit from government mail contracts or from becoming postmasters because of their religious scruples. "If this be their motive," Johnson wrote, "then it is worldly gain which stimulates to action, and not virtue or religion. Do they complain that men less conscientious in relation to the Sabbath obtain advantages over them by receiving their letters and attending to their contents? Still their motive is worldly and selfish."[38] If, however, their motive had been to lead Congress to "sanction their *religious opinions* and *observances,* then their efforts ought to be resisted as in their tendency fatal both to religious and political freedom."[39]

Except to say that it was imperative that postmasters should keep their offices open at least some time every day of the week, Johnson's emotional reports never addressed the issue of whether the law forcing them to do so was necessary or even constitutional. Nor did the reports give any hint as to why the law had been enacted in the first place. Instead, they justified the need to transport mail on the Sabbath and noted that the postmaster general had always had authority to do this. "Congress," wrote Johnson, "have never legislated upon the subject. It rests as it ever has done, in the legal discretion of the postmaster general, under the repeated refusals of Congress to discontinue the Sabbath mails. His knowledge and judgment in all the concerns of that Department will not be questioned."[40] That, of course, was true, but the statement made it appear that Congress had nothing to do with the origin of the controversy. It cleverly skirted the evangelicals' principal argument that there had been no necessity for Congress to pass a law forcing postmasters to keep their offices open at some time each day of the week.

A minority report that accompanied Johnson's to the House attempted to correct its obvious distortions. The petitioners, it said, had not asked Congress to "meddle with theological controversies," nor to blend religious and civil affairs, nor to interfere with the religious "feelings of any portion of the inhabitants of the Union." Furthermore, they had not asked Congress to enact a law making the Sabbath the first day of the week or approached the government "for personal emolument," as had been implied, nor were they traitors. Instead they had come "as patriots and Christians, to express their high sense of the . . . necessity of the Sabbath for the perpetuity of our republican institutions."[41] Moreover, if transporting mail on Sundays was a work of necessity, the same could not be said for keeping post offices open on that day where no mail arrived.[42]

Others outside Congress also saw the guile in Johnson's reports. One observer, writing to the editor of the *Niles Weekly Register* in 1829, complained that "Col Johnson and his Committee pretend to see in the prayer of the memorialist what is not in it, nor would be allowed by those presenting it to have been in it, in any form, either expressed or implied." Early in 1830 a minister revealed his anguish at the duplicitous first report. "Oh, if ever the spirit of a good man falters," he wrote, "and his heart dies within him, it is when he finds his motives misrepresented and his efforts counteracted by a brother's influence."[43]

But these rebuttals to the deliberate perversions of the evangelicals' petitions were as chaff in the wind. The Senate had ordered three thousand copies of Johnson's first report to be printed for its use, and the House required ten thousand copies of his second, together with the minority opinion. These, circulating through the mail in 1829 and early 1830, roused the country against efforts to stop mail on the Sabbath and broke the ranks of the evangelical moral majority, many of whom observed the Sabbath but in that age of the common man were anticlerical.

Having nurtured the frightening specter of a religious party blending church and state, Johnson had done his work well, establishing a fear that burned itself into the American psyche from that day to this. Memorials supporting the reports were presented to Congress from nearly every section of the nation, including New England. State legislatures, excited by the controversy, drew up remonstrances against stopping transportation of mail on Sundays and the repeal of the law opening post offices on that day.[44]

As might have been expected, all these remonstrances reflected the arguments in Johnson's report and were couched in much the same emotional language. In that era, people saw in the evangelicals' campaign all the dangers to their liberties and to the Republic that Johnson had seen and more. It seemed obvious that the campaign was an effort to unite church and state, the first step of a religious party to interfere in civil affairs, and an attempt to fill all public offices with men who would accept the "faith and doctrine of a powerful party" and be zealous enough to control people's consciences.[45]

Participants in one meeting held in Tammany Hall late in January 1830 and organized by Preserved Fish, a prominent New York merchant and archfoe of evangelicals, saw in their campaign a massive conspiracy "to influence and control public opinion, to make all our literary and benevolent institutions subservient to sectarian purposes."[46] They also saw a frightening connection, which augured ill for the Republic's future, between the reformers' effort and the New York legislature's compliance with a religious sect's request to adjourn for a day of fasting.

Some remonstrances were even more vituperative than Johnson's report. One attacked "a certain party styling themselves the 'Christian party in politics,' which under moral and religious pretenses, are officiously and unremittingly intermeddling with the religious opinions of others, and endeavoring to effect by law . . . a systematic course of measures, which, we believe, are tending to favor the dominancy of particular creeds . . . infusing a spirit of religious intolerance into the political institutions of the country which, unless opposed, will result in a union of church and state."[47]

The authors of this memorial had gathered with other citizens of Windham County, Vermont, early in 1831, and, like the Johnson report, they accused the reformers of mercenary motives and of concealing their objective by "many artful pretexts." Nor were they deluded by "any professions of the petitioners' benevolent motives." Instead they saw in those professions "the common artifice of ecclesiastical ambition—of that ambition which deceives only to destroy; which rears in its van the emblems of meekness, charity, and philanthropy, and carries in its train the engines of persecution, torture, and massacre; which commences with soothing flattery, and ends in a furious and brutalizing tyranny; which sweeps from its path every vestige of civil and religious liberty, and perishes at last, as perish it must, gorged with human blood, the victim of its own detestable depravity."[48]

Throughout their arguments, however, it was clear that these evangelicals of the different denominations in the West and South hated and feared what Jefferson had hated and feared: the power and exclusivity of Congregationalists and Presbyterians and their leaders. "When we consider the number, talents, and influences," they wrote, "of this body of men; their zeal and activity; the intimate union that exists among them . . . ; the support they derive from numerous religious corporations and societies, rapidly increasing in numbers and in wealth; the almost unlimited control which they exercise over our colleges and other literary institutions, with no power but the laws, which they are ambitious to control . . . we see reason to dread even their unassisted efforts to deprive us of our liberties."[49]

In the end, such fearful and angry remonstrances so intimidated Congress that it refused to even consider resolutions or memorials against Sunday mail. Shortly after Johnson gave his second report in March of 1830, New Jersey's senator, Theodore Freilinghuysen, sometimes called the "Christian statesman" and arguably the most respected man in the Senate, offered a resolution requesting the Post Office Committee to submit a bill ending Sunday mail service. But this was laid on the table, and the committees were discharged from further consideration of the subject without so much as a recorded vote in either the Senate or the House.[50]

Then, late in 1830, when still one more memorial against Sunday mail was presented to the House of Representatives, Johnson objected to its being sent to the Post Office Committee. "The committee had acted on the subject," he said, "and would not do so again unless compelled to do so by an express order of the House." Apparently confident that none would dare confront him, he challenged any of the memorial's "advocates on this floor" to say "what could be said in favor of Congress interfering with religious considerations."[51]

Johnson had correctly judged the apprehensions of the legislators. The member of Congress from Pennsylvania, who had introduced the memorial, denied he was an advocate of the petitioners' position, and no one else rose to defend the discontinuance of mail on Sundays. The memorial was sent to the Committee of the Whole on the State of the Union and buried there. Three days later Johnson boasted that the postmaster general was now free to change the number of times that mail was carried over postal routes from three times a week to six and "even to seven times, thank God, when it was necessary."[52]

Johnson's boast inadvertently revealed that more than hatred of New England politicians and clergy or fear of the union of church and state had inspired his and the Democratic opposition to the evangelicals' crusade. What motivated it was a desire to help stagecoach owners develop Sunday stagecoach lines. Indeed, the Sunday mail controversy had from the first been as much about stagecoach lines as governmental exigencies. In the months that followed Johnson's speech it was obvious that one of his purposes had been to help his good friend James Reeside as well as other owners of large lines obtain contracts to carry mail on Sundays.

Johnson may have known Reeside as early as the War of 1812, in which he served as a soldier and Reeside as a wagoner. Probably, however, their friendship dated from the 1820s, when Johnson served on the Senate Post Office Committee and Reeside was already securing large mail contracts. Certainly they had become close friends by 1828, and it is likely that Reeside advised Johnson to oppose the Sabbatarians' effort to abolish Sunday mail. If so, Reeside had more reason for doing so than merely speeding or protecting mail, which had been the usual arguments for carrying mail in coaches.[53]

Contracts to carry mail seven days a week were much sought after by owners of large stagecoach lines like Reesides's. Under such contracts they profited not only from the additional money the post office department gave them for carrying mail an extra day but also from many people who, much to the dismay of evangelicals, found it more pleasurable and convenient to travel on Sundays.

Still, little notice might have been given to this close relationship between the chair of the House Committee on Post Offices and Post Roads and Reeside, the nation's largest mail contractor, had the Post Office Department not pursued the rapid development of the mail service as soon as William T. Barry, another of Johnson's friends from Kentucky, became President Jackson's postmaster general in 1829. Even as Johnson was exulting in the postmaster general's freedom to transport mail seven days a week Barry had already set just such an expansion in motion.[54]

With the help of Johnson's other friend, Obadiah B. Brown, chief clerk of the Post Office Department in charge of awarding mail contracts, Postmaster General Barry was busily engaged by 1830 in upgrading the conveyance of mail from horseback and sulky to stagecoach over hundreds of post roads. To do so, the department lifted contracts from original contractors and awarded them to those who ran the great stagecoach lines. When that was accomplished, the frequency of carrying mail increased to three, six, or seven days a week, and the new contractor was given additional money for improved service.

The manner in which these improvements were made was illustrated by routes 1215 and 1230, the first running from Bedford to Blair Gap and the second from Bedford to Cumberland in Pennsylvania. Because mail over these routes was extremely light, they were advertised in 1831 as weekly horse routes at $275 per year. James Clark was awarded the contract, but in less than a year the routes were upgraded to triweekly, four-horse, post coach routes, taken from Clark, and given to James Reeside, who contracted for them for $4,500 a year. Shortly thereafter, in 1833, one was made a daily route, and Reeside was given an additional $2,911.72 for the improvement.[55]

Throughout President Jackson's first administration this procedure was repeated hundreds of times until the number of miles that mail was carried annually in two-horse stages or four-horse post coaches had increased from some six million in 1829 to 17,693,839 in 1833, and the frequency of mail had been improved over thousands of routes. How many were converted to Sunday mail catering to the passenger trade is uncertain, but they were numerous. In 1834 Reeside alone transported mail over ninety miles of post roads three times a day, more than 526 miles twice daily and more than 881 miles daily. Altogether, his coaches carried the mail more than 1,743,910 miles annually, and he received $119,810 per year.[56]

These changes were expensive of course, and each year under Barry's management the post office ran a deficit. By 1834 the department's debt was so enormous that Barry, when Congress refused to appropriate money to cover it, was forced to borrow from private banks to pay contractors their due. That was unprecedented. Postal policy had always dictated that the post office must pay its own way, neither making money for the treasury nor taking appropriations from it but using surplus funds to expand the service.[57]

How had it happened, then, that Postmaster General Barry had gone so far astray from the original policy? One reason was Johnson, who in his role as chair of the House Post Office Committee had been able, even in the face of postal deficits, to push a new post roads bill through Congress in 1832. Dismissing the apprehensions of his colleagues, who feared the postmaster general had no money to establish new post roads, Johnson said he was under no "imperious obligation to ascertain whether the funds of the department would or would not enable that officer to execute the will of Congress." Furthermore, he remarked that he was not averse to having the government appropriate money for them if need be, even in the face of postal deficits.[58]

Given the close connection between the postmaster general and Johnson, it was not surprising that Johnson's disregard of the postal policy and determination to expand the postal system should have given Barry so little pause in running up the deficit by putting into operation the new post roads for which Johnson's bill had called. Some members of Congress believed that more than postal deficits was to blame for the new post roads bill, however, and even before it had been passed they spoke of appointing committees to investigate the Post Office Department. The Senate, controlled by Whigs, did appoint such a committee in 1830, but Johnson took offense at a similar proposal in the House and temporarily blocked the effort.[59]

In 1833, however, Johnson was no longer the chair or even a member of the Post Office Committee, and committees in both the Senate and the House mounted massive investigations of the Post Office Department. At first Postmaster Barry refused to surrender the documents for which the Senate Committee called and on the peculiar grounds that the Senate was the jury in an impeachment trial and had no right to investigate him until he was impeached. Both the Washington *Daily National Intelligencer* and the New York *Evening Star* professed to be alarmed at this state of affairs. "Would the King of England dare to assume such power?" asked the *Evening Star*. Nevertheless, two years later, and after three thorough investigations, the committees produced reports that provided a sordid picture. Corruption and greed in the management of the post office were pervasive enough to have produced postal deficits even had no new post roads at all been established. Although the reports of the Whigs were more critical of postal officials than those of Democrats, the situation was so serious that even they could not dismiss all the charges leveled at Postmaster General Barry and his chief clerk Obadiah Brown. "They [the House Committee] have, in their conclusions, at least, done justice to the subject," the *Intellingencer* explained, "in terms too explicit to be either misunderstood or misinterpreted."[60]

Rifling through mail contracts, sorting out the department's financial records, and taking testimony from numerous witnesses, the committees followed a trail of broken postal laws, favoritism in awarding contracts, suspicious loans made to postal officials by mail contractors, and the waste of thousands of dollars in improving weekly or triweekly routes to dailies, more to help stagecoach lines make connections for passengers than for the good of the service. Contrary to President Jackson's antimonopoly preachments, the committees found that stagecoach owners, abetted by the Post Office Department, were using their mail contracts to monopolize passenger trade. Nor could they ignore the evidence of collusion among Barry, Brown, and the great mail contractors in awarding contracts.[61]

Obadiah Brown, who had presumably written so loftily in the Johnson reports accusing the evangelicals of mercenary motives, was the principal target of the committees' attack. Among his many misdeeds were borrowing unsecured loans from Reeside and another mail contractor to whom he had given lavish mail contracts, investing money in a stagecoach line to whose owner he awarded mail contracts, and opening bids for routes before all bids were gathered, presumably to make certain the proper bidder received the contract. When questioned about why certain peculiar mail contracts had been made with large stagecoach lines, either his memory failed him or he did not know. Moreover, he had covertly received extra compensation for superintending the post office building.[62]

Even Postmaster General Barry was not beyond suspicion, for he had also borrowed from Reeside, who was the big winner in the great mail contract sweepstakes. Barry, however, had at least attempted to be discreet in receiving borrowed money from contractors. In this instance, according to the Democratic minority report, his friend Johnson borrowed "from a friend of his, who was a contractor . . . without . . . knowledge of Major Barry" and gave the money to Barry to pay off a debt. Because that was done, the minority continued, "without the agency or knowledge of the postmaster general, it cannot furnish suspicion of any wrong on his part."[63]

No scandal of similar proportions had yet been discovered in the young republic. To be sure, it was not entirely Postmaster General Barry's fault. Members of Congress insisted on having new post roads for constituents, and Barry was to some degree a victim of their demands. Moreover, Barry did believe, as had his predecessor, that increased postal services would produce revenues enough to pay for them. Besides all that, this was the age of "boundlessness" as free enterprise flowered and influence-peddling was in its infancy.

Still, the almost brazen audacity of the four close friends—Johnson, Barry, Brown, and Reeside—involved in the systematic bleeding of the post office was amazing, and the Senate majority's report did not overlook it. "The very large amount of the extra allowances made to Reeside and some other individuals," noted the report, "gave, in the judgment of your committee, strong ground for the opinion, that a portion of those allowances were used for secret purposes, or that they were shared by individuals having authority or influence in granting them."[64]

It may never be known whether a part of Johnson's wealth of his later years came directly or indirectly from Reeside and other mail contractors for his help in defeating the Sabbatarians' effort to stop Sunday mail and ramming through the Post Roads Act of 1832. His name was only tangentially mentioned in the reports, and he was never accused of taking money from Reeside. Nor did his behavior prevent him from becoming vice president under Martin Van Buren in 1836. Still, his friendship with those who profited from lucrative mail contracts cast suspicion upon him and was doubtless the reason he was no longer on the Post Office Committee after December 1832.[65]

As for Johnson's friends, Brown was moved from his position in charge of awarding contracts and in 1833 made treasurer of the post office, where he remained until early 1835 when he resigned under pressure. That same year Barry also resigned to become minister to Spain. Both men declared their innocence in appeals to the people and hoped to be vindicated of wrong-doing. They never were. Barry died in Spain shortly after arriving there, and Brown faded from the scene, fortunate enough not to have been indicted for his violations of postal laws.[66]

Before he left office Barry had already begun to curtail much of the postal service he had put in place, going so far, indeed, as to reduce even James Reeside's compensation by some $13,000 by 1834. More stringent measures were taken against some of the large contractors by Barry's successor Amos Kendall, another Kentuckian and the once powerful but enigmatic member of President Jackson's "kitchen cabinet." Faced with the post office's financial burdens that Barry had left, Kendall forthrightly suspended payments to contractors he determined had been overcompensated. Among them was James Reeside, who spent the rest of his life and much of his money suing the government for what it supposedly owed him. He died in 1842, a poor man.[67]

In his efforts to clean up the post office, Kendall had the help of a new postal law, enacted in 1836 and designed to prevent the problems the committees had uncovered. It included special rules for making contracts with mail contractors, defined more precisely the postmaster general's duties, and forbade postal employees to be financially involved in postal affairs. It also completely changed the way the Post Office Department did business. From that time forward, postal revenues were to be turned into the treasury, postal budgets containing estimated needs for each year were to be submitted to Congress, and each year Congress was to appropriate money from the general fund to operate the postal system.[68]

Evangelicals may have regarded the fall of the Kentucky clique as the Lord's retribution for their violations of the Sabbath, but other than the forced curtailment of some daily mail routes they could not have drawn much comfort from it. Nothing except the department's financial straits had caused the postmaster general to curb mail transportation on Sundays, and the law requiring post offices to remain open on that day, which had been at the root of evangelicals' concerns, was untouched.

Furthermore, their General Union for Promoting the Observance of the Christian Sabbath had been unable to withstand Johnson's onslaught. Dispirited and unable to find a permanent secretary for the organization, torn between those who wished to close businesses on the Sabbath as well as post offices and those who did not, members had abandoned the General Union by 1832. By then their interests, including those of the Tappan brothers, who had been the union's prominent supporters and quintessential evangelical reformers, had turned elsewhere. Abandoning the idea of freeing slaves by helping them emigrate to Africa, the Tappans were already becoming intrigued at the prospect of seeking immediate freedom for slaves, and the next year they helped form the American Anti-Slavery Society.[69]

Led by Lewis Tappan, the more aggressive of the two brothers, the New York committee of the new society prepared to educate the American public by distributing antislavery material nationwide through the mail, much as had been done in the Sabbatarian campaign. Consequently, in July 1835 bags loaded with papers such as *Human Rights* and Arthur Tappan's *Emancipator* were mailed to community leaders everywhere. Some of the material made its way through the mail to Charleston, South Carolina, where the postmaster retained it and requested Postmaster General Kendall to tell him whether to pass it southward. While he waited for Kendall's answer, however, the Charleston post office was raided, and the material was seized and burned.[70]

Meanwhile, Postmaster General Kendall advised the Charleston postmaster that he had no legal authority to instruct him on what to do but that circumstances did justify retaining the offending papers. In presenting the matter to the president in his annual report, Kendall later argued that states were united only for certain purposes, that they retained sovereignty in matters pertaining to protecting their institutions, and that neither the national government nor another state or person had a right to disseminate literature within a state whose laws forbade the dissemination of such literature.[71]

That position, which was virtually substantiated by Congress's benign neglect in the ensuing years, meant, in effect, that although the national government could not use its postal power to violate a state's law designed to protect slavery, such power could be used to override a state's law protecting the Sabbath. If Sabbatarians who remained devoted to their cause saw the irony of this double standard, they did not mention it in the petitions they sent Congress in 1838, scarcely two years later, urging that body once more to repeal the law opening post offices on Sundays.[72]

By then Martin Van Buren had become president and Richard Johnson vice president. With their adversary removed from Congress, the time seemed favorable for bringing the issue of closing post offices on Sundays before Congress once more. Besides, for some Sabbatarians the need to do so was more urgent than ever. In the seven years since the collapse of the General Union for Promoting the Observance of the Christian Sabbath a budding transportation revolution promised fulfillment of evangelicals' dire predictions about what would happen if the government did not stop Sunday mail.

By 1838 the Erie Canal, connecting New York City with Lake Erie and the West, had been in operation for nearly thirteen years, and others were being built westward from eastern cities. That same year, stagecoach lines carried mail more than twenty million miles annually to 12,553 post offices. And, as it turned out, 1838 was also the year that Congress declared all railroad lines to be post roads. Just ten years after the groundbreaking ceremony that launched the building of the Baltimore and Ohio Railroad, railroads and steamboats were already carrying mail nearly 2,500,000 miles annually.[73]

The nation seemed filled with Americans traveling on Sundays. "We are a Sabbath breaking people," declared Harmon Kingsbury, a Cleveland resident and one-time missionary. On any Sunday, he wrote, Americans were to be seen "in every stage and post office; in every steam and canal boat; in every rail car and omnibus; in every place of public resort, and in most houses kept for the entertainment of the travelers." All classes violated the Sabbath, including even those who were in high places and circulating "through every artery of this great nation, filling with pain and sorrow the heart of those who sincerely love their country, and that kingdom which Jesus Christ came into the world to establish."[74]

The situation along the canals and waterways and in the Great Lakes region was especially alarming to evangelicals. There the desecration of the Sabbath was almost universal. The Erie Canal was singled out for particular reproach when a group of businessmen whose products were transported along it memorialized the canal's managers concerning the harm done to employees forced to work seven days a week. The practice, they said, deprived the men of a day of rest, fostering their ignorance and immorality.[75]

It was not surprising, therefore, that evangelicals from Buffalo to Cleveland, led by Kingsbury, should have asked Congress in 1838 to once more confront the problem of Sunday mail. The petitioners, however, said little about transporting mail on Sundays and asked only that the part of the postal law opening post offices on the Sabbath be repealed to remove the sanction unnecessarily given "to an immorality, shielding it from the operation of the Legislatures of the States, and hindering the efforts of the benevolent."[76]

To the Sabbatarians in the late 1830s that seemed little to ask. Repeal of that law, they pointed out, would not necessarily close any post office, for the postmaster general had authority to instruct postmasters to keep facilities open if need be. But repeal would mean that Congress could no longer require anyone to work on Sundays, and "no man could then say . . . that the 'supreme law of the land *requires* labor to be done on Sunday . . . and therefore I am justified in breaking the fourth commandment.'"[77]

The petitions were passionate pleas, as they had always been, that drew upon history to prove that the nation was not pagan but Christian. They cited example after example to illustrate how Christian religion had been woven into the fabric of government and traced once more the story of evangelicals' efforts to change the postal law since its inception.[78]

One petition ran to forty-one pages and revealed throughout how absolutely convinced Sabbatarians were that the fate of the Republic rested upon observing the Sabbath. Urging Congress to remember that the nation was destined to be "occupied by hundreds of millions of souls," and admonishing it to "lay carefully the foundations upon which depend the perpetuity of our institutions," petitioners explained once more, as forcefully as they could, how important keeping the Sabbath was to the permanence of the Republic. "Now, when it is said," ran their argument,

> the strict religious observance of the Sabbath is essential to intelligence, peace, morality, and republican institutions, we have in view this great, enterprising, and prosperous nation, whose only law is the will of the *people,* not of a despot; also the truths, that *ignorance,* clothed in her mantle of intemperance, immorality, and sloth, cannot guide this mighty ship over the trackless, restless sea upon which she is launched, that an immoral community cannot be an intelligent and peaceful community; and that the appropriate exercises of the Sabbath, such as devout reading, and the faithful preaching of the gospel, are the greatest incitements to a peaceful, industrious, temperate, moral, and sober life.[79]

A nation of peaceful, industrious, temperate, moral, and sober Christian people who were devoted to reading and the faithful preaching of the gospel was the evangelicals' grand vision of the future of the country about which they cared so much. As much spiritual as material, it could be achieved, in their view, only by strict observance of the Sabbath. Given their orientation, they were unable to understand "how any lover of his country" could "lend his influence to desecrate that day or withhold that influence to prevent its further desecration."[80]

In these petitions, as in many of those sent to Congress earlier, were dire prophecies, reminiscent of Puritan jeremiads, of the fate awaiting the nation that violated God's laws. One called attention to the Prophet Isaiah's warning that the nation that disobeyed God would perish and applied his warning to the contemporary situation. "And let it not be supposed," it read, "that God will long suffer his day to be thus trampled upon by a people, favored like ancient Israel, though they have been. He will not with impunity, suffer this or any other nation to blot out one of his commands of the decalogue, especially the one on which, more than any other, rests the foundation of his religion."[81]

For those whose minds were so thoroughly attuned to the Bible and who remembered how often God had punished his people for their sins, such prophecies of doom were no idle threats but firmly held convictions. But the Democratic Congress, determined to uphold the policy it had begun, ordered the Sabbatarian petitions to be printed and returned to the Post Office Committees, from which they never emerged.[82]

Except for a brief effort in the 1840s, it was the evangelicals' final legislative attempt before the Civil War to force Congress to destroy that disrespect for God's law embedded in the legislation opening post offices on the Sabbath. But throughout that decade and the next, and in the midst of political realignments and controversies, determined evangelicals kept this violation of the Decalogue before the American people until, in the aftermath of that war, a postal revolution and a changed society forced Congress to consider it once more.

Notes

1. *American State Papers, Post Office Department, 1789–1833* (Washington, 1834), no. 72, 183 (hereafter *ASP: P.O.D.*).

2. Ibid.; *ASP: P.O.D.* no. 73, 195, 200–201; *Report of the Postmaster General, 1828,* 180 (this and subsequent citations to postmasters general reports can be found in the *Congressional Information Service Serial Set Index* [Washington, 1997]); "Affairs of the Post Office Department," *Register of Debates,* 23d Cong., 1st sess., 234 (June 9, 1834), appendix (hereafter *Register*). On Reeside, see Philip Jordan, *The National Road* (1948, repr. Gloucester, 1966), 180–83.

3. *Register,* 18th Cong., 2d sess., 91 (Mar. 3, 1825), appendix.

4. Between 1817 and 1828 only two efforts were made in Congress to revive the Sunday mail issue. One attempt was made in 1822 by Cong. Robert Wright of Maryland, but it was rejected. *Journal of the House of Representatives,* 17th Cong., 1st sess., 312–13 (Mar. 4, 5, 1822).

5. Richard F. Palmer, *The "Old Mail Line": Stagecoach Days in Upstate New York* (Lakemount, 1977), ch. 12. The most detailed account of the organization and work of the General Union for the Promotion of the Observance of the Sabbath is found in Richard R. John, "Taking Sabbatarianism Seriously: The Postal System, the Sabbath, and the Transformation of American Political Culture," *Journal of the Early Republic* 10 (Winter 1990): 535–39. See also Lewis Tappan, *The Life of Arthur Tappan* (1870, repr. Westport, 1970), 96–98; and Bertram Wyatt-Brown, *Lewis Tappan and the Evangelical War against Slavery* (Cleveland, 1969), 52–55. The Tappan brothers were quintessential evangelical reformers involved in nearly every evangelical cause of the period, from the American Bible Society to the American Anti-Slavery Society.

6. Glydon G. Van Deuson, *The Jacksonian Era, 1828–1848* (New York, 1959), 26–29. On the importance of the spread of newspapers, see Robert V. Remini, *The Election of Andrew Jackson* (Philadelphia, 1963), 76–80. Jackson's party was soon to be the Democratic Party, of course.

7. Tappan, *The Life of Arthur Tappan,* 98; see also John R. Bodo, *The Protestant Clergy and Public Issue, 1812–1848* (Princeton, 1954), 39–41. The coffin bill appears in Remini, *Election of Andrew Jackson,* 154–56, 419–28. As many as one hundred thousand copies of Beecher's paper may have been circulated (John, "Taking Sabbatarianism Seriously," 539). John Q. Adams, who might have been expected to oppose Sabbath mail because of his New England background, apparently did not. He raised no objection to the law of 1825, which repeated opening post offices on the Sabbath and became law as he was taking office. Throughout his four years of state of the union messages he praised the operation of the post office. In 1844, however, he did support the Sabbath in a speech to a Sabbatarian convention. Reverence for the Sabbath, he maintained, was necessary to keep the nation's liberties safe. *Niles Weekly Register,* Dec. 21, 1844, 246.

8. Bertram Wyatt-Brown, "Prelude to Abolitionism: Sabbatarian Politics and the Rise of the Second Party System," *Journal of American History* 58 (Sept. 1971): 323–24; see also

Arthur Schlesinger, Jr., *The Age of Jackson* (New York, 1950), 137. Ely had actually favored Jackson for president. Richard J. Cawardine, *Evangelicals and Politics in Antebellum America* (New Haven, 1993), 13–14.

9. "Petition of Hastings and Others," S. Doc. no. 12, 25th Cong., 3d sess., 15 (Dec. 12, 1838); *Niles Weekly Register*, Jan. 10, 1829; see also *Journal of the House of Representatives*, 20th Cong., 2d sess., 231–34 (Feb. 3, 1829).

10. The Sabbatarian arguments were much alike and probably drawn from a circular prepared by Lyman Beecher. See *ASP: P.O.D.*, no. 87, 232–38, for the arguments in full; see also Tappan, *The Life of Arthur Tappan*, 98. The government's violations of the Sabbath were a good example of the Protestant quarrel with the American republic, which Mark Y. Hanley might have used in his fine book on the Protestant resistance to the American culture: *Beyond a Christian Commonwealth: The Protestant Quarrel with the American Republic, 1830–1860* (Chapel Hill, 1994).

11. *ASP: P.O.D.*, no. 87, 232, emphasis added.

12. U.S. Constitution, art. 1, sec. 7. For evangelicals' constitutional arguments, see *ASP: P.O.D.*, no. 87, 234, and "Petition of Truman Hastings," S. Doc. 12, 25th Cong., 3d sess, 1–30 (Dec. 12. 1838), 23–24.

13. *ASP: P.O.D.*, no. 87, 232, 234.

14. Ibid., 234.

15. Ibid., 235 (quotations).

16. Ibid., 232; for the quotation, see "Petition of Truman Hastings," 24.

17. *Niles Weekly Register*, Feb. 22, 1829.

18. On the law as a national sin, see *ASP: P.O.D.*, no. 87, 232, 236 (quotations).

19. Ibid., 237; see also 233.

20. Ibid., 234–35.

21. Ibid., 237. On the importance of the Sabbath to evangelicals, see Robert T. Handy, *A Christian America: Protestant Hopes and Historical Realities* (New York, 1971), 48–51, and Robert H. Abzug, *Cosmos Crumbling: American Reform and the Religious Imagination* (New York, 1994), 111–14. "The Puritan Sabbath was probably the most distinctive symbol of evangelical civilization in the English speaking world," observed George Marsden, "and remained a major reform issue where religious and social interests coincided" (*Fundamentalism and American Culture: The Shaping of Twentieth-Century Evangelicalism* [New York, 1980], 13).

22. Marsden, *Fundamentalism and American Culture*, 233. For a detailed analysis of Calvinistic evangelicals' opposition to opening mail on the Sabbath, see Richard John, *Spreading the News: The American Postal System from Franklin to Morse* (Cambridge, 1995), 190–93.

23. *House Journal*, 20th Cong., 2d sess., 236–37; *ASP: P.O.D.*, no. 74, 212–13.

24. *ASP: P.O.D.*, no. 74, 211–12; *ASP: P.O.D.*, no. 87, 229–31.

25. For favorable views of Johnson's reports, see Schlesinger, *Age of Jackson*, 140–43; and Joseph L. Blau, ed., *Cornerstones of Religious Freedom in America* (New York, 1964), 109–12.

26. For the pertinent facts of Johnson's political career, see *Biographical Dictionary of the United States Congress, 1774–1989* (Washington, 1989), 1270. For a friendly account of Johnson's position on the Sunday mail controversy, see Leland Winfield Meyer, *The Life and Times of Colonel Richard M. Johnson of Kentucky* (New York, 1932), 257–63.

27. *The Debates and Proceedings in the United States; with an Appendix, etc...*, 13th Cong.,

3d sess., 1075 (Jan. 16, 1815) (hereafter *Annals of Congress*). Although it is not certain, he may have had a direct interest in opposing the closing of post offices, as will be seen.

28. *Annals of Congress,* 16th Cong. 1st sess., 353–54 (Feb. 1, 1820).

29. *Annals of Congress,* 10th Cong., 1st sess., 1152 (Dec. 11, 1807); Meyer, *Life and Times of Colonel Richard M. Johnson,* 327–28.

30. *Annals of Congress,* 16th Cong., 1st sess., 355. When his statement on Adams was made public, Johnson tried to cast it in a favorable light but in essence admitted the truth of it. *Niles Weekly Register,* April 28, 1827; see also Meyer, *Life and Times of Colonel Richard M. Johnson,* 220–21.

31. *ASP: P.O.D.,* no. 87, 238.

32. Meyer, *Life and Times of Colonel Richard M. Johnson,* 290–91, 301–2. On John Leland, his anticlericalism, and his influence, see Nathan O. Hatch, *The Democratization of American Christianity* (New Haven, 1989), 95–101.

33. *ASP: P.O.D.,* no. 87, 229.

34. Ibid., 230.

35. Ibid., 229; *ASP: P.O.D.,* no. 74, 211.

36. *ASP: P.O.D.,* no. 87, 230.

37. Ibid. For those who "enjoy its choicest blessings," read Congregationalists and Presbyterians, men of wealth whom Johnson could not forbear to castigate.

38. Ibid.

39. Ibid., emphasis in the original.

40. *ASP: P.O.D.,* no. 74, 211; *ASP: P.O.D.,* no. 87, 229–30.

41. *ASP: P.O.D.,* no. 87, 231.

42. Ibid.; *ASP: P.O.D.,* no. 74, 213; see also *Register,* 21st Cong., 1st sess., 1–3 (May 8, 1830).

43. *Niles Weekly Register,* Feb. 22, 1829; *Home Missionary and Pastor's Journal,* Jan. 1, 1830, 139.

44. *ASP: P.O.D.,* no. 87, 238–41. For the printing of the first report, see *Journal of the Senate,* 20th Cong., 2d sess., 79 (Jan. 19, 1829); see also *Journal of the House of Representatives,* 21st Cong., 1st sess., 369–70 (Mar. 5, 1830). The vote to publish Johnson's second report was ninety-three for and sixty-seven against. The majority of New England votes were cast against publication, Middle Atlantic states were almost evenly divided on the issue, and slaveholding states voted by a large majority to publish. Much of the opposition to terminating mail on Sundays came from anticlerical evangelists, those who hated what Jefferson feared and hated. On evangelical opposition, see John, *Spreading the News,* 199–200.

45. Ibid., 238–39.

46. "Preamble and Resolutions Adopted at a Meeting of the Citizens of New York," S. Doc. no. 64, 20th Cong., 2d sess., 1–2 (Feb. 9, 1829). On Preserved Fish, see *Dictionary of American Biography* (New York, 1931), 3:401–2 (hereafter *DAB*); for other participants in the meeting, see John, *Spreading the News,* 194.

47. "Memorial of Citizens of Windham County, Vermont," H. Doc. no. 115, 21st Cong., 2d sess., 1 (Feb. 24, 1831).

48. Ibid., 3, 5.

49. *ASP: P.O.D.,* 87, 238. Unlike Jefferson, however, they were generally orthodox evangelicals but anticlerical. There was much anticlerical sentiment among Protestants, inspired in part by John Leland, the Baptist minister, and Jefferson supporters who had

influenced Johnson. On John Leland and organized Christianity, see Hatch, *The Democratization of American Christianity,* 93–100.

50. *Register,* 20th Cong., 2d sess., 43 (Jan. 17, 1829); *Register,* 21st Cong., 1st sess., 427 (May 8, 1830). It was said of Freilinghuysen that no man of his time belonged to more Christian and charitable institutions than he. *DAB,* 4:16–17.

51. *Register,* 21st Cong., 2d sess., 358 (Dec. 14, 1830).

52. *Register,* 21st Cong., 2d sess., 374 (Dec. 17, 1830).

53. For the connection between Reeside and Johnson, see Meyer, *Life and Times of Colonel Richard M. Johnson,* 258, 310–11. As early as 1831, one senator suggested the problem involved in the connection between Johnson and large mail contractors. *Register,* 21st Cong., 2d sess., 5–6 (Dec. 15, 1830).

54. For a friendly account of Barry's life, see *DAB,* 1:656–58; see also Leonard D. White, *The Jacksonians: A Study in Administrative History, 1829–1861* (New York, 1954), 251–53.

55. "Reports of the Majority and Minority of the Committee of the Senate on Post Office and Post Roads," S. Doc. no. 86, 23d Cong., 2d sess., 39–47 (Jan. 27, 1835) (hereafter "Reports"). The Democratic majority report, "Examination of the Post Office," H. Rept. no. 103, 23d Cong., 2d sess., 32–33 (Feb. 15, 1835), substantially confirms the Whig-dominated Senate report and indicates that Postmaster General Barry felt free to establish Sunday mail as a result of Johnson's successful reports. His predecessor, Postmaster General John McLean, who had also pursued a vigorous expansion of the service, had adopted "the practice . . . on each route where a daily mail is not established, so to regulate the conveyance, where practicable, as to make the Sabbath a day of rest" (*ASP: P.O.D.,* no. 75, 214). The report, in the testimony of Harper and Dundas ("Reports," 357ff), contains testimony showing how Brown urged daily mail upon contractors.

56. *Report of the Postmaster General, 1833,* 286. For the extent of Reeside's empire, see "Affairs of the Post Office Department." Comparison of the numbers of daily mail on selected routes in the Northern Division in 1827 with the numbers in 1834 suggests how greatly Sunday mail was extended. H. Rept. no. 103, 23d Cong., 1st sess., 866–74 (Feb. 18, 1835).

57. Much controversy existed over the amount of the deficit, but it was probably more than $3 million for the four years of Barry's administration. "Affairs of the Post Office Department," 217. The effort of the Democratic majority's report of the House to explain the deficit is in "Examination of the Post Office" (3–9); see also White, *The Jacksonians,* ch. 13, for the complete story.

58. *Register,* 21st Cong., 2d sess., 366–67 (Dec. 17, 1830).

59. *Register,* 21st Cong., 2d sess., 7 (Dec. 15, 1830); *Register,* 22d Cong., 1st sess., 2809–10 (May 7, 1832).

60. The Senate's Democratic minority of 1834 found no evidence that any contractor was specially favored ("Affairs of the Post Office Department," 235). Its report of 1835, however, made no such claims ("Reports," 61, 107–8). See also the *Daily National Intelligencer,* Oct. 25, 1834, 2, for quotations from both the *Intelligencer* and New York *Evening Star.* On the post office scandal, see John, *Spreading the News,* 241–52.

61. White, *The Jacksonians,* ch. 13, contains an excellent summary of the committees' findings.

62. "Reports," 86, 81–89. For Brown's complete testimony before the committee, see S. Doc. no. 96 in the report; see also "Examination of the Post Office," 29–30, 62–72, 87.

63. "Examination of the Post Office," 57–60; "Affairs of the Post Office Department," 234.

64. "Reports," 81. The Senate minority exculpated Barry by citing the pressure upon him (ibid., 15).

65. *House Journal,* 22d Cong., 2d sess., 22 (Dec. 6, 1832). For suspicions raised against him, see *Register,* 21st Cong., 2d sess., 5 (Dec. 15, 1830).

66. *Niles Weekly Rigister,* Feb. 7, 1835, 395, Feb. 21, 1835, 436. Barry's appeal and rebuttal to the charges are in the *Niles Weekly Register* of April 25, 1835 (139–44).

67. On Barry's curtailment of Reeside's service, see S. Doc. no. 138, 23d Cong., 1st sess., 248–52 (Mar. 3, 1834); on his death, see Jordan, *The National Road,* 183–84. Claims were eventually settled, but before the controversy was over a judgment was made against Kendall, and he was jailed within the confines of the District of Columbia for more than a year. S. Doc. no. 178, 27th Cong., 3d sess. (Feb. 16, 1843); H. Rept. no. 147, 27th Cong., 3d sess. (Feb, 8, 1843). Shortly before Reeside's death, however, a jury in the circuit court of appeals in Philadelphia awarded him $180,496 (*Niles Weekly Register* Dec. 11, 1841, 8). On Kendall, see *DAB,* 5:325–27.

68. *United States Statutes at Large* (Boston, 1856), 5:80–90; see also White, *The Jacksonians,* 274–83.

69. On the formation of the American Anti-Slavery Society, see Wyatt-Brown, *Lewis Tappan,* 102–11; Louis Filler, *Crusade against Slavery* (New York, 1960), 65–67; and Gilbert Barnes, *The Anti-Slavery Impulse, 1830–1840* (New York, 1957), 54–56. The Sabbath crusade had been hurt by the division between those who wanted to boycott Sabbath-breaking businesses and those who did not (Abzug, *Cosmos Crumbling,* 114–16). For the despair of the evangelicals following the Johnson reports and the abuse heaped upon the Sabbatarians, see Paul Boyer, *Urban Masses and Moral Order in America, 1820–1920* (Cambridge, 1978), 8.

70. *Report of the Postmaster General, 1835,* 396–98; Clement Eaton, "Censorship of the Southern Mails," *American Historical Review* 48 (Jan. 1843): 266–80.

71. *Report of the Postmaster General, 1835,* 396–98.

72. President Jackson asked Congress to use the postal power to forbid the mailing of such incendiary literature, but John C. Calhoun, fearful lest this seeming violation of the Constitution set a precedent for overturning slavery, proposed a law making it illegal for any postmaster to deliver any material touching on slavery to any person or post office in any state where by law such material is prohibited. Although the bill was defeated after a lengthy debate, the practice it provided for was generally followed. See S. Doc. no. 118, 24th Cong., 1st sess., 1–12 (Feb. 4, 1836), and for the failure of the bill, see *Register,* 24th Cong., 1st sess., 1737 (Jan. 9, 1836).

73. *Report of the Postmaster General, 1838,* 664.

74. "Petition of Harmon Kingsbury. . . ," H. Doc. no. 36, 25th Cong., 2d sess., 7 (Dec. 18, 1837).

75. "Petition of Truman Hastings," 16. For an interesting scholarly view of canal workers' conditions, see Peter Way, "Evil Humors and Ardent Spirits: The Rough Culture of Canal Construction Laborers," *Journal of America History* 79 (March 1993): 1397–428.

76. Petition of Truman Hastings," 1. Hastings's petition included Kingsbury's and an appendix containing material from other pertinent sources.

77. Ibid., 11.

78. Ibid., 4–8.

79. Ibid., 8.

80. Ibid., 8; see also Handy, *A Christian America,* 48.

81. "Petition of Harmon Kingsbury," 10.

82. *Journal of the House of Representatives,* 25th Cong. 2d sess., 92–93 (1837); *Senate Journal,* 25th Cong., 3d sess., 42, 293 (1838).

3 Changing the Sabbath to a Day of Rest

As the government of the United States of America is not in any sense founded on the Christian Religion . . . it is declared by the parties that no pretext arising from religious opinion shall ever produce an interruption of the harmony existing between the two countries.

—*Treaty between the United States and the bay and subjects of Tripoli of Barbary,* United States Statutes at Large, *8:155*

We deny that this is Christian nation. . . . Almighty God is not the "source of all authority and power" in our government.

—*Horace Greeley, March 7, 1865*

On March 4, 1841, twelve years of Jacksonian democracy came to an end when the Whigs installed their man, William Henry Harrison, in the White House. The old general, hero of the War of 1812, had been elected in a campaign that appeared to be more about log cabins and hard cider than serious issues. But beyond the bonfires and illuminations that lit the night skies, some sober soul-searching was taking place among evangelicals as they sought the party most likely to take seriously their concern for keeping the Fourth Commandment.

Not unreasonably, many of them had shunned the party of Richard Johnson to support Harrison for president and so helped push the young Whig Party toward the North and Protestant reform as the Democratic Party, conversely, edged toward the South. During the campaign, Harmon Kingsbury, instigator of the petitions to repeal the law opening post offices on Sundays in 1837, informed Harrison that the candidate was to be the Lord's "'instrument for the removal of this great national sin [Sunday mail] from our beloved Country.'"[1]

It is unlikely that Harrison, who died a month after taking office, would have measured up to the evangelicals' trust had he lived. Yet over the course of the next few years Whig postmasters general did, in fact, drastically reduce the number of miles that mail was carried on Sundays. By June of 1842, they had saved nearly $40,000 by curtailing Sunday service on what had been daily routes; at the end of the Whig administration in 1845, mail stagecoach travel had been reduced by more than a million miles annually, largely by eliminating Sunday travel.[2]

To be sure, the Whigs had inherited this reduction policy from the Democratic postmasters general, who had been forced by three successive years of postal deficits to reduce Sunday service over many stagecoach routes. But unlike the Democrats, Whigs were willing to openly suggest a connection between religion and the ending of the seven-day service on mail routes. Accepting the need to reduce mail service because of postal deficits, Whig Postmaster General Francis Granger, son of Gideon Granger, noted in 1841 that "the religious sense of the community, will certainly approve the feeling, that selects the Sabbath as the day on which that service should not be performed."[3]

That evangelicals expected the Whigs to be sympathetic to their cause was suggested by the smattering of their petitions begging for termination of Sunday mail—a smattering of those which had filtered into Congress during the early 1840s. Whatever might have been their opposition to Sunday mail, however, Whigs made no effort to change the law that opened post offices on Sundays. Nor did they respond to more such petitions when their party controlled the White House after 1849. Apparently, after twenty years they were still too cowed by Richard Johnson's devastating reports inveighing against closing post offices and terminating mail transportation on the Sabbath to propose closing post offices on that day.[4]

Nevertheless, evangelicals kept the issue of Sunday mail alive by using changes in the postal laws and expansion of postal routes to spread their concern for the violations of the Sabbath far and wide via a torrent of publications that traveled on Sundays with the rest of the mail. Forced by the competition of private carriers who during the 1840s began to violate the government's monopoly by carrying letters and packages outside the mail over newly established railroads for less than the government charged, Congress enacted a series of laws. One of them reduced postage on religious newspapers to one-fourth that of regular newspapers. It was a nod to the pervasiveness of the religious sentiment of the age but far short, of course, of closing post offices on Sundays.

"I concur," said James Duncan of Massachusetts as he sponsored the new postage rate for religious newspapers, "with the sentiment of that enlightened French statesman, Guizot [a nineteenth-century historian as well], that the reason why the American people have been enabled to establish and maintain a well-regulated system of Republican liberty, and the French people have failed in all their attempts to do so, is, that in this country there has been a pervading religious sentiment, of which the French people have been devoid." Like the Sabbatarians before him, he believed that the post office might be used to help maintain "the same principles and the same influences which have established and perpetuated our free institutions."[5]

The law was prompted by vigorous benevolent societies—the American Bible, Tract, and Home Missionary Societies and the Sunday School Union—founded years before in the postmillennial enthusiasms of the Second Great Awakening. Pledged to spread the Christian message, they had from the beginning published and disseminated enormous quantities of material. But many of their publications, because of the high postage rates on printed matter, had been distributed by colporteurs. After 1851, however, the societies were quick to take advantage of the postage rates favoring religious papers.[6]

There were no more prolific writers in the nation during the 1850s than those who wrote on religion and no press more voluminous or widespread than the religious press. Most denominations had weeklies, monthlies, and quarterlies and mailed them, together with the papers of various benevolent societies, over the nation's principal arteries of communication, which in 1860 stretched across 240,594 miles of post roads to nearly 28,500 post offices. Among these was an antislavery paper, the *National Era,* founded by Lewis Tappan, whose editor began running a serial entitled *Uncle Tom's Cabin* the year after the cheap postage act passed.[7]

Unlike the *National Era,* however, not all religious pamphlets were deliberately antislavery papers, although as carriers of the Christian message they could not always avoid voicing antislavery sentiments. Nearly all of them, however, decried the desecration of the Sabbath, with the result that observance of the Lord's Day—and, in fact, the Christian message itself—was never far from the minds of people and their politicians. Indeed, the great outpouring of religious publications that swelled the mail from one end of the country to the other following the reduction in postage did much to nurture a Protestant age of faith. It also produced, near the end of the decade, a sharp resurgence of revivalism during which the Republican Party, tinged with the religious causes of the era, emerged from the bosom of the old Whig Party.[8]

In the political turmoil of the 1850s the Whig Party had been torn apart by antislavery and anti-immigrant dissidents. Unable to find any unifying principal around which they might rally within the party, many of its members left to join either the anti-immigrant American Party or the antislavery Republican Party. In the end, the Republican Party absorbed most dissidents of both persuasions, which included temperance and Sabbath Day advocates as well as Christian reformers of various other causes. It was to be as close to a purely Protestant party as the nation was to have.[9]

True, the Republican Party never promised to close post offices on Sundays, but the Sabbatarian impulse within its ranks was reflected in New York in 1860. That year the Republican-dominated state legislature enacted legislation to enforce its old Sabbath law. The law was intended to curb the free and easy Sabbaths of German immigrants and the always troublesome ideological antisabbatarians. Democrats for the most part, they complained bitterly against the law, calling Republicans "blue-light Puritans" and reminding listeners that they were of the ilk that had once tried to stop the mail on Sundays. "'Presbyterian-Puritanism,'" observed the New York *Sunday Mercury*, "'bestrides the Republican party'" like the "'Old Man of the Sea bestrode Sinbad the Sailor.'"[10]

There was much truth in the charge. Even President Lincoln, preoccupied as he was with the war, felt the force of Sabbatarianism within the party, and in 1862 he ordered the nation's troops to observe the Sabbath. "The discipline and character of the national forces," his order read, "should not suffer, nor the cause they defend be imperilled, by the profanation of the day or name of the Most High." Perhaps it was significant that Lincoln's order came only after the bloody battle of Antietam seemed to have made clear that the Union's cause might indeed "be imperilled."[11]

That terrible battle, like so many that were to follow, was, in the eyes of both the evangelicals and the president, the price that had to be paid for a war caused by the nation's sins. It was as if the war could account for the calamities that Sabbatarians had so long predicted for Congress's disobedience of God's law by opening post offices on Sundays. It affirmed their belief that God was not mocked and that a nation, like individuals, must pay for its sins. The hand of God rested, too, upon the war's outcome. Religious Americans could not help but notice that Gen. Robert E. Lee's surrender coincided with the day set aside to commemorate Jesus' triumphal entry into Jerusalem and that Lincoln, like Jesus, who was said to have died for the sins of humanity on Good Friday, was also slain on that day "in order that the whole nation might not perish."[12]

For some time following Lee's surrender and President Lincoln's assassination, such religious reflections were on many minds, and as the country entered the postwar period evangelicals could still believe that the United States was a Christian nation. But if they thought that the somber events of that Holy Week and the terrible cost of a war fought over the nation's sins might lead Americans to a renewed awe of God's power and greater respect for the Sabbath, they were mistaken. Instead, in the modern America that emerged in the aftermath of the Civil War the vision of a Christian nation dimmed before evangelicals' eyes, even as they fought vigorously to maintain it.[13]

One major source of this great change was the rapid expansion of the nation's railroad network. Between 1865 and 1900 busy Americans constructed more than two hundred thousand miles of track. Built hurriedly over vast tracts of empty land, they spanned the continent, running through thousands of villages, towns, and cities and binding the nation with time zones and bands of steel. The rails brought raw material to manufacturing centers, scattered finished products to distant markets, created a national industrial economy, dominated financial markets, helped homogenize the American population, produced a business-dominated urban society, and became the symbol of a mechanized America.[14]

As the moon draws the tides, so railroads, factories, and new businesses drew Americans from the land and immigrants into the jaws of cities. In 1860, only 141 of the nation's cities had populations of eight thousand or more; by 1900, 545 had that many—and even more. During the 1880s alone, 161 cities of eight thousand or more were added to the total; nearly 30 percent of the population in 1890 lived in such places. Chicago, New York City, and Philadelphia all had more than a million inhabitants by the turn of the century.[15]

The new and mechanized world of big business and huge cities posed staggering problems for Protestants dedicated to maintaining a Christian nation. From the Puritan past to the Civil War, their religion, like themselves, had been nurtured in a predominately homogeneous, rural, and uncrowded society in which individualism and the direct relationship with God that characterized it were especially compatible. But the cities of the new America—vibrant with humanity's rampant rage for wealth, nearly bereft of Protestant churches among the poor, rife with saloons and bawdy houses, inundated with immigrants so different from the founders of the nation whose Protestant religion had shaped it, and so crowded that "people who live in the country," according to one observer, "can have no idea of the way in which people are packed together in our great cities"— eclipsed hopes of saving society from paganism. Indeed, a series of articles, "Home Heathen of Our Great Cities" in the *Christian Union,* began early in 1885 and suggested that the battle may already have been lost.[16]

The Eleventh Ward of New York City illustrated the source of evangelicals' anxieties. In 1880 it contained 68,779 people, 39,025 native- and 29,754 foreign-born. In 1885 it also possessed 346 saloons (one for every two hundred persons) and only nineteen churches and mission chapels (one for every 3,700 persons). New York was not alone. In 1879 Chicago had some three thousand saloons, nearly all of which were open on Sundays before church and long after it. "It has become difficult to attend church in portions of the city," the *Christian Union* reported, "without passing from five to one hundred open saloons boisterous with vile speech. On those days they are the special haunts where young bootblacks gather dimes and new skills in crime."[17]

Evangelicals were not alone in their forebodings about cities. James Bryce, the Englishman who surveyed the nation in the 1880s and commented on the widespread religiosity of the American people, wondered what would happen to society if cities were to rob people of their faith:

> Sometimes, standing in the midst of a great American city, and watching the throngs of eager figures streaming hither and thither, marking the sharp contrasts of poverty and wealth . . . knowing that before long a hundred millions of men will be living between ocean and ocean under this one government—a government which their own hands have made and which they feel to be their own hands—one is startled by the thought of what might befall this huge yet delicate fabric of laws and commerce and social institutions were the foundation it has rested on to crumble away.

Should they cease to believe in a power above them, would "custom and sympathy . . . replace supernatural sanctions, and hold in check the violence of the masses and the self-indulgent impulses of the individual?" Bryce's answer to his own question revealed doubt. "History," he concluded, "if she cannot give a complete answer to this question, tells us that hitherto civilized society has rested on religion, and that free government has prospered best among religious peoples."[18]

The evangelicals, of course, were of a like mind. Many times they had said that free government rested upon religion and that maintaining religion was dependent upon keeping the Sabbath. But that had become a greater problem than it had been before the war. In a new urban environment in which people were now referred to as "the masses" instead of individuals, keeping the Sabbath Day holy was impossible except in small towns and the countryside. The desecration of the Lord's Day was seen on every hand. "The Puritan Sabbath has gone," the *Christian Union* announced in 1879, "not threatened; not going; but gone."[19]

And so it was. Far from that Puritan Christian Sabbath Harriet Beecher Stowe remembered as "the golden day," when "all its associations, and all its thoughts, words, and deeds, were . . . entirely distinct from the ordinary material of life," Sundays in cities were filled with noise and activity. Freight trains thundered through on that day as on the other days of the week; elevated trains and horse cars, filled to overflowing with passengers, rattled over and through the streets; milkmen's carts broke the early-morning Sabbath silence; and joyous, boisterous crowds of assorted backgrounds and creeds joined excursions destined for the countryside, beaches, and amusement parks to spend the Sabbath in pleasure and, not infrequently, in drunkenness and debauchery.[20]

To the apprehensions of evangelicals, immigrants were transforming the American Sabbath into a European Sunday holiday filled with hours spent in beer gardens, saloons, and parks. "If we were simply Anglo-Saxons," Lyman

Abott told his Protestant readers in the pages of the *Christian Union,* "and if we had only ourselves to take care of, our problem would be a very simple one; for the Anglo-Saxon race, as we all know, is very intelligent, virtuous, and self-restrained. But in this nation God has been pouring, by his providence, all classes and condition of men, until in our nation to-day there is a greater variety of race, of tongues, and of character, than is to be found anywhere else on the face of the globe."[21]

But it was not just European immigrants who violated the Sabbath. Consider a Sabbath Day on Martha's Vineyard in 1879. Founded years before by religious people for a religious purpose, camp meetings were still being held on its grounds. "Its cottages," according to the *Christian Union,* "are still mainly owned by men in whose veins flows Puritan blood." But on Sundays, excursion boats emptied their human cargoes upon the shore at Oak Bluff, where they enjoyed the parade of a brass band, drank soda water and lager beer, and wandered through the streets. "The crowd," ran the story, "was orderly, good-natured, happy . . . ; but unmistakably a crowd of pleasure-seekers, not of worshipers either of God or nature, and as unmistakably a crowd not of Germans, or Irish, or French, but full blooded New Englanders; of sons and daughters of the Puritans."[22]

All who had eyes to see and ears to hear had to agree that the old Puritan Sabbath was dead. There were even those Protestants who rejoiced that the day had lost its grim Puritan face. But as the profanation of the day grew worse even they were disturbed enough to support a revival of the Sabbatarian movement that emerged in the middle of the Gilded Age. Beginning in the late 1870s, and almost abruptly, as if they had just awakened to the new encroachments upon the Sabbath, ministers once more began denouncing violators and violations of the Lord's Day. Nearly dormant Sabbath organizations were suddenly revived, new ones created, and old Sabbath laws, long since forgotten or ignored, were strengthened or revised to meet the new conditions.[23]

The Sabbath crusade of the 1880s has been dwarfed in historical memory by the temperance movement to which it was related, but it was no small affair. Enforcement of New York's recently revised penal code by a quickly formed Sunday Closing Committee nearly emptied the streets of New York City when the law first went into effect in December 1882. In that city, too, and in Philadelphia, where the Philadelphia Sabbath Association had been intact for forty-three years by 1889, Sabbatarians had been able to prevent the Sunday openings of museums and theaters against ever-mounting pressures.[24]

From these cities westward to Cincinnati, Chicago, and elsewhere, where saloons were open on Sundays and Sunday excursions were common, citizens banded together to enforce old Sabbath laws and reclaim the day for the Lord.

In this effort they were supported by the Law and Order Society, a national organization formed by middle-class urban vigilantes who were outraged by disregard of Sabbath laws. At the time of its fourth annual meeting in Cincinnati in 1886, some thirteen Law and Order Society state organizations had been formed and between six and seven hundred local leagues. Acting everywhere to support blatant violation of the Sabbath laws, society members, according to the *Christian Union,* had virtually closed saloons to minors in Chicago.[25]

Yet year by year evangelicals' efforts to preserve the old Sabbath against forces of an urbanized, multicultured society lost ground. In Milwaukee during the 1870s, violations of the Sunday law were so numerous that an editor of a Christian paper asked whether the law had been changed. In Chicago, where a return to strict enforcement of Sabbath laws seemed impossible in 1879, ministers bargained with saloon-keepers to close their establishments during hours of worship. That same year, a Norwich minister's attempt to shut down the Sunday excursion business of a steamship company whose boats were, in his opinion, nothing more than "floating brothels," led to such an outcry of bigotry and fanaticism against him that the prosecutor lost courage and failed to uphold Connecticut's Sabbath law, which supported the minister's attempt.[26]

Moreover, enforcement of Sabbath laws frequently had unwelcome consequences for evangelicals. New York's revised penal code of 1882, which provided stricter enforcement of the Sabbath law, precipitated a clamor from liquor dealers and other businessmen. As a result, the following year brought new legislation that still permitted, even after Gov. Grover Cleveland's modifications made it more palatable to evangelicals, some Sunday openings and inspired a continuing effort to lift restrictions against the liquor trade.

By the mid-1880s if not before, it was clear to the most earnest evangelicals that the struggle to preserve the Sabbath with state laws, even with the help of Law and Order societies, was being lost. It was not just that state laws were virtually impossible to enforce, and neither was it that strict enforcement of those laws too frequently led to their weakening as saloon-keepers and others pressured state legislatures to change them. Rather the battle was being lost because such laws could not prevent the national government from violating the Sabbath.[27]

Discouraged by the faltering struggle to enforce Sabbath laws, latter-day Sabbatarians saw that they could never rely on state laws alone as long as the expanding postal service remained as the greatest offender of the Sabbath. "Ever more important," the *Christian Statesman* reported in 1888, "is the vast post-office system of the country, which has become the most conspicuous and influential Sabbath-breaking institution in the nation. Its hundred of thousands of employees are wholly dependent on the government for the opportunity to observe the Sabbath and enjoy the benefits which it affords. The postal service, through its connection with the railway system and through the facilities which it affords . . . stimulates Sabbath-breaking agencies to a pernicious activity."[28]

That was undeniably true, and it was ironic that the very mechanism through which the culture of a supposedly Christian nation was purveyed should be the means of sending an irreligious message to the American people. Moreover, that message was being spread farther and faster than ever before by a postal system that was as unlike that of the 1820s as the stagecoach was unlike the steam locomotive. Between 1828 and 1887 the number of post offices increased from 7,651 to well over 55,000, and the miles the mail was carried grew annually from 3,608,540 to more than 257,000,000. In 1828 the post office had not quite 27,000 employees; in 1887 that number neared 150,000, an estimated 100,000 of whom had to work on Sundays.[29]

Massive as these figures were, they scarcely began to tell the story of the communications revolution wrought by railroads and imaginative postal innovations in the aftermath of the Civil War. By 1880 envelopes had long since replaced letters folded and sealed with wafers, three-cent stamps prepaid the mailing of a letter sent anywhere in the nation, registration of letters was possible, as was the use of money orders, and mail had been divided into four classes and was being delivered free to homes in cities.

But the principal arm of this communications revolution was a remarkable new railway mail service that took advantage of the expanding railroad network. Congress had made the railroads into post routes in 1838, and their use by the post office had expanded rapidly. Before the Civil War, railway mail was worked by a route agent who sorted and distributed for post offices along his route but sent "through mail" directed beyond that route to various distributing offices. There it was delayed until it could be re-sorted and prepared for the next step on its journey. The system was clumsy at best, and as volume grew heavier year by year mail began to pile up at distributing offices, virtually forcing postal authorities to find a better way to handle it.[30]

A better way was found during the Civil War and perfected in the 1870s. By then the Post Office Department had developed railway post offices, which, for efficiency, had no equal anywhere in the world. They were housed in specially made railroad cars equipped like regular post offices. In addition to the usual letterboxes and racks for mail bags, they had ingeniously devised catcher arms, which, to the amazement of onlookers, could capture mail bags from stationary cranes as the train sped by. That mail, and all through mail so retrieved as well as picked up at major junctions, was sorted aboard the moving train by highly trained railway mail clerks. They, having memorized train schedules, postal divisions, and post offices in order of their appearances, would work furiously to separate it into appropriate pouches according to its destination.

"With wonderful memory and almost unerring judgment, formed in the twinkling of an eye," according to one admiring member of Congress, railway mail clerks sorted and pouched mail destined for post offices along the way and flung it to waiting mail messengers as the train hurried on. The clerks sorted mail routed to distant places into other pouches and transferred it to connecting trains, which then took it to one of eleven postal districts scattered about the country in 1889. "If a letter is mailed in Portland, Maine destined for Portland Oregon," a member of Congress told colleagues in 1886, "the deft fingers of these skillful agents guide the inanimate missive from train to train and from road to road, so that the most experienced and well-posted traveler, starting at the same time, destined to the same point, cannot get ahead of it." In this fashion railway postal clerks handled an almost incredible 13,792,607,160 pieces of mail in 1900, excluding registered mail, and achieved the Post Office Department's dream of mail traveling as fast as travelers.[31]

Postal officials rightly regarded railroad post offices as one of the wonders of the age. Indeed, they were marvels of efficiency. In the 1870s they had already eliminated the cumbersome distributing post offices and made possible mail trains that sped about the country at nearly forty miles an hour. Moreover, they made it possible for the efficient distribution of 1,347,145,180 pounds of mail at century's end, most of which had been generated by American businesses.[32]

For evangelicals, however, there was a costly religious price to be paid for this great service, as there was for many of the new postal services that were such a vital part of the communications revolution. Supported by mail contracts as the stagecoaches had been, railway mail trains ran night and day each day of the week and required the services of a regiment of Sunday postal workers. Besides railway mail clerks, who sorted mail, mail messengers, wagon masters, and local agents were needed on the ground to oversee its transfer from depots to various post offices. Beyond these employees who were forced to work on Sundays, unnecessarily the Sabbatarians concluded, an estimated five hundred thousand railroad and newspaper employees also had to labor on that day to operate the mail trains and market the Sunday newspapers.[33]

Railway mail clerks, however, were the Sabbatarians' special concern, perhaps as much because so many of them were skilled, white, middle-class, and Protestant, much like themselves, as because they were forced to work long hours and on Sundays. There had been a time, according to one Sabbatarian, when railway clerks out of New York worked "seven days a week, eighteen hours a day" on alternate weeks. This kind of brutal duty had been reduced over the years, but the hours of labor still required in 1888 left the "Post Office of the United States the dishonor of being the 'champion man-killer.'"[34]

Actually, a railway mail clerk's route in 1886 varied from approximately 106 to 133 miles per day, although there were many exceptions. The average was 120 miles, which meant that, traveling at a speed of thirty miles an hour and excluding the time he spent preparing mail before leaving, he worked the mail en route only about four hours before the end of a run. There the clerk usually laid over until the next day, when he returned over the same route. Commonly he either traveled or laid over on the Sabbath, which in either case kept him from church on Sundays. "While you are sitting in your cushioned pew listening to the charming theology of this day and age," a member of Congress told colleagues in 1886, "the [railway] postal clerk is handling 3,424 pieces of mail matter, so that before you return to church for the evening service you can spend a couple of hours in the pleasant recreation of opening and assorting from thirty to fifty letters from your constituents."[35]

Sabbatarians also found much in the conditions under which railway mail clerks labored to support their lamentations against working on the Sabbath. Aside from the grueling, pressure-ridden, everyday task of distributing nearly 3,500 pieces of mail in an unconditioned and swaying postal car that sometimes made them ill, there were other dangers in their work that might have been alleviated had they and railway employees—engineers especially—been able to rest on the Sabbath.[36]

Often lost in the story of the railroads in the nineteenth century is an appalling number of train accidents, to which the statistics of injuries, and even death, of railway postal clerks bore witness. Between 1875 and 1900 railway mail clerks suffered 6,889 casualties and 127 deaths from train wrecks. In 1897 alone, fourteen were killed, five of them in one accident when their train, Number 6 on the Wabash Railroad, traveling at high speed near Missouri City, Missouri, came upon an unstable trestle that gave way, plunging the train into roiling waters below. Such was the cost in human lives of the nation's new communications system. Worse still, when such accidents occurred there was no help for the bereaved, neither were there benefits or insurance, until 1902, when Congress, after nearly two decades of pleading by postmasters general, finally provided for $1,000 grants to victims' families.[37]

The number of postal employees engaged in the railway mail service in 1889 was 5,640, virtually all of whom were forced to work on the Sabbath at one time or another. But that number was infinitesimal compared to the host of postal clerks, postmasters, and mail carriers who were required to work—all unnecessarily, Sabbatarians claimed—on Sundays.[38]

From 1810, when Congress first opened post offices on Sundays, to 1887, postal laws were completely revised and updated only three times. On each occasion, however, the section keeping post offices open on Sundays was retained. This provision, together with new postal services, huge mails boiling up from the business world, and perpetually running trains that brought the mail to post offices day in and out, compelled most urban postmasters to force clerks and carriers to work on the Lord's Day. Postmasters in New York City, Philadelphia, and Chicago kept as many as half their regular week-day employees working on the Sabbath in the 1880s. "Practically," the New York City postmaster said in 1884, "the general delivery window of this office is never closed" because people would drift in throughout the day and into the night to get their mail.[39]

It was rare that either the large city post offices or the hundreds of smaller ones had as many clerks as were needed to keep up with the expanding mail. Deep in the often unsanitary bowels of every large post office, unseen by a public that knew nothing of their work, clerks sorted tons of mailable matter—newspapers, letters, circulars, books, and packages—and endlessly prepared it for destinations far and near. Upstairs, other clerks met the public, issued money orders, registered letters, sold stamps, answered inquiries, and delivered mail at general delivery windows. In addition, hundreds of carriers showed up every Sunday morning to sort mail for the next day's delivery or help with other chores. In 1889 the postmaster general counted 47,466 postal clerks and 8,830 mail carriers at free-delivery offices, most of whom were employed at least part of every Sabbath or at least on every other Sabbath.[40] Deplorable as Sabbatarians found that to be, it was by no means all that worried them. Their fears multiplied with each mile that the railroads expanded to bring mail to more and more country post offices on Saturdays and Sundays.

Unlike their urban counterparts, rural Americans had been unable to take advantage of various new postal services. Their mail service throughout many of the post–Civil War years was scarcely different than it had been before the war. In 1889 mail was brought over star routes (those marked in schedules by an asterisk) by contractors who carried it by buggy, horseback, or stagecoach from rail centers to more than fifty-six thousand small fourth-class post offices scattered throughout the land. To these facilities, farmers and villagers went for their mail, once, twice, or perhaps three times a week. "I represent a rural district," explained a member of Congress from Alabama in 1876, "and many of my people do not get a mail but once a week. Many have to go twenty-five miles to get a letter. I myself have but three mails a week from the railroad to the town in which I live."[41]

Because no mail arrived at most rural post offices after closing on Saturdays or before six o'clock on Sunday afternoons, postal regulations did not require that postmasters open their post offices on the Sabbath, and usually they did not. This left the Sabbath in the countryside nearly as undisturbed as it had always been. But mail contracts forced railroads, pushing incessantly toward the setting sun, to move the mail on Saturdays and Sundays to more and more post offices in previously isolated villages and small towns. When that happened, those post offices were forced to remain open on Sundays in order that the incoming mail might be sorted and delivered to those who asked for it. But it was not just the small post offices on railroad lines that were so affected. Many offices on star routes in the West also had to remain open on Sundays when mail stages, which connected with the new railroad centers, were upgraded to daily service and mail arrived on Sundays.[42]

Ordinarily, a postmaster's chores could be done in a short time, but it troubled Sabbatarians that postmasters had authority to keep their post offices open on Sundays for as long as they wished. The result was that not a few remained open during the church hour and beyond to enrich the postmasters. Postal regulations forbade them to sell money orders or register letters on the Sabbath, but they could, and did, sell stamps on that day, which, when canceled in their offices, increased their compensation.[43]

The expansion of Sunday service into rural America was especially frightening to Sabbatarians, who saw the communications revolution spreading the desecration of the Sabbath into rural towns and villages—the very heart of Protestantism. In some ways the problem was even worse in small towns and villages than in cities. Except for those who received mail at general delivery windows, most urban patrons waited until Monday for their mail, when it was delivered to their homes. But in small towns and villages, where no free delivery existed, people flocked to get their mail when post offices were open on Sundays. "Over wide sections of the country," one minister wrote, "the arrival of the Sabbath morning mail from the city is the signal for the resort of multitudes to the post-office. Christian men and women on their way to and from the sanctuary, swell the throng. The afternoon of the day is surrendered to secular things."[44]

The intrusion of Sunday mail into the quiet of a rural Sabbath was a harbinger of worse things to come for Sabbatarians. Always fearful of the unwelcome possibilities of new postal services, they envisioned a not-too-distant time when free delivery, already established in towns and cities, would become a major threat to keeping the Sabbath holy, not only in cities and large towns but also in small rural villages and hamlets.

By 1889 the free delivery of mail to urban homes had been in operation for more than two decades. Established in 1863 when the South was otherwise engaged and unable to oppose it, city free delivery measured the trek to the cities, just as post roads had marked the pioneers' advance into the wilderness. After authorizing the postmaster general to establish service in large cities of his choice, Congress removed his discretionary power two years later and ordered him to establish free delivery only in cities with a population of fifty thousand or more. Under this imperative, free delivery was first reduced to forty-five cities and then extended to fifty-two by 1873. Between 1874 and 1887, however, when Congress first authorized free delivery in towns of thirty thousand and then reduced this to twenty thousand, 137 more towns were given the new service, bringing the total to 189.[45]

Movement to urban America was not restricted to the largest cities, however. Americans were on the move from farms to villages and from villages to towns. Congress, under constant pressure, authorized the postmaster general in 1887 to establish free delivery in towns that had populations of ten thousand. Almost overnight another 169 towns were added to the list, and by 1900 the nation had 795 free-delivery towns and cities.[46]

Sabbatarian fears that this astounding growth of free-delivery towns might lead to Sunday mail delivery were not entirely groundless. Extensions of the service had been so constantly demanded by townspeople and villagers that there was no certainty that members of Congress, whose respect for the Sabbath had never been obvious insofar as mail was concerned, might not at some time attempt to curry favor with constituents by ordering Sunday delivery. True, Postmaster General Marshall Jewell's apparent effort to establish a Sunday delivery service in New York City in the 1870s ended in failure, but there was no assurance that the effort might not be made again.[47]

This prospect became imminent when Postmaster General William F. Vilas, President Cleveland's postmaster general, expanded a fledgling special delivery service in 1885. This postal innovation provided for immediate, everyday delivery of letters, when stamped with a special delivery stamp, at post offices in towns of four thousand or more. At first the service was rendered by youthful messengers who were paid a nominal fee, but it seemed clear to evangelicals that this would soon change. "When this practice becomes common in one place," predicted a disturbed Sabbatarian, "it will soon become common in all, and when *special* delivery by [regular] carriers becomes common, *general* delivery by carriers on Sunday will follow almost as a matter of course."[48]

One Philadelphia minister was worried enough over the direction this new service might take to protest to Postmaster General Vilas. "'What I have done, I have done'" that official responded, prompting the frustrated minister to complain to President Cleveland. But the president's intervention was less helpful than the Sabbatarians had hoped. Vilas assured Cleveland that he sympathized with the need to worship and meditate on Sundays but maintained that the government was obligated to deliver special delivery letters on that day.[49]

To complicate matters, the very next year, 1886, Congress permitted the postmaster general to extend special delivery service to all mailable matter and to all post offices, subject only to the postmaster general's discretion. The sole reflection of the Sabbatarians' efforts and President Cleveland's intervention showed up in postal regulations stipulating that postmasters "were not required to make delivery of special-delivery matter on Sunday, nor to keep their office open in any manner different on that day from that provided by regulation."[50]

Rebuffed by the postmaster general, fearful of the possibility of further encroachments by the postal service on the Sabbath, and with no place else to turn in their quest to preserve the Sabbath, evangelicals launched a vigorous effort in 1886 to secure a national law closing post offices on Sundays and forbidding transportation of mail on that day. Such a law, they believed, would go far toward restoring a sacred Sabbath and have glorious results. Not only would it terminate Sunday mail deliveries at post offices, but it also would reduce the number of Sunday mail trains subsidized by mail contracts and so limit the number of passengers traveling on the Lord's Day.[51]

Beyond that, the Sabbatarians, optimistic in their yearning for a return to the old ways, persuaded themselves that the passage of a national Sabbath law was achievable. The post office was, after all, the people's post office, and Congress could be compelled to stop Sunday mail if enough Christian people demanded it. No other government institution offered evangelicals such an opportunity for making a statement for Christianity or preserving a Christian nation. Nor did any present a better opportunity to restore the waning power of the clergy and their followers to influence government policy.

To be sure, Sabbatarians knew this effort had failed before, but they also believed they were better prepared for the battle than were their forebears in the 1820s. In the first place, unlike the older Sabbatarians who had pushed for a strictly Christian Sabbath, their descendants in the 1880s agitated only for a day of rest instead of a day of worship. Sunday was now to become a day free of labor for the health and welfare of hard-pressed workers as well as, or even instead of, a day of worship.

It was not a new idea in 1887. Nearly a decade before the moderate *Christian Union* had argued that justification for national Sabbath laws, in a nation committed to separation of church and state, had to stem from the need to provide a day of rest for laborers rather than from the requirements of religion. It was not, of course, a viewpoint popular with all Sabbatarians. One member of the clergy complained that it was tantamount to saying, "'We the people,' regardless of God's law, 'do ordain and establish' a day of rest purely as a 'civil Sabbath, a 'police regulation,' as any pagan Government would do." But realists among the Sabbatarians knew the nation had already become too secularized to turn back and that a day of rest was their only hope of securing a national Sabbatarian law and, perhaps, a less obviously profane Sabbath.[52]

A more inclusive Sabbath was not the only difference between the Sabbatarians' campaign of the Jacksonian era and those of the 1880s. In the Gilded Age, not surprisingly, when Americans were organizing themselves into various groups, Sabbatarians were much better organized than their forebears had ever been. They had the support of three powerful organizations unheard of before the war: the National Reform Association, the Woman's Christian Temperance Union (WCTU), and the American Sabbath Union.

Of the three, the oldest and most ambitious was the National Reform Association. Following a preliminary meeting in Xenia, Ohio, on February 3, 1863, the group's founders, representing eleven Christian denominations, met again in May of the next year in Allegheny, Pennsylvania, to form an organization whose purpose was nothing less than to preserve the nation's Christian character and prevent "the heathenizing of America." Perceiving in those dark days of the Civil War that the war was God's judgment upon the nation for the sin of slavery, for the Founders' original sin of omitting God from the Constitution, and for a growing secular rejection of Christianity, they formulated a program designed to thwart the ambitions of freethinkers, who were as determined to sever the connections between religion and the state as association members were to preserve them.[53]

From its beginning, the Republic had included freethinkers, although their major organization, composed of many local associations formed over the years, was not established until the National Liberal League was begun on July 4, 1876, in Philadelphia. By that time, freethinkers' agenda had been promulgated and even partially implemented. Adhering strictly to Jefferson's "wall of separation" between church and state, freethinkers proposed abolishing the chaplaincy corps, repealing all state Sabbath laws, forbidding the reading of the Bible in schools, eliminating the tax-exempt status of churches, eradicating the use of oaths, preventing the proclamation of days of prayer and Thanksgiving, and abrogating all laws enforcing Christian morality.[54]

By the beginning of the Civil War, secularists had failed to persuade Congress to abolish the nation's chaplains, but by taking advantage of the omission of the word *God* in the Constitution and Jefferson's wall of separation doctrine they had been able to persuade the Supreme Court of California to declare that state's Sabbath law unconstitutional in 1858. Still to come in the next decade was the Ohio Supreme Court's decision that made it unconstitutional to read the Bible in that state's public schools.[55]

Frightened by the possibility of secularists actually achieving through the courts what they had failed to accomplish by legislation, the National Reform Association attempted to correct loopholes in the Constitution by amending that document's preamble to include acknowledgment "of almighty God as the source of all authority in civil government; of the Lord Jesus Christ as the ruler of nations," thereby certifying that the United States was a Christian nation. Only in this way, association members believed, could they deprive opponents of religion of the argument that the Constitution did not recognize the existence of God. Nor were they content to merely write the word *God* into the Constitution, as some urged, without mention of Jesus Christ. "A pagan nation may be content simply to acknowledge God," said one of the association's founders, "but no Christian nation can consistently refuse to acknowledge Christ."[56]

Whether Lincoln knew of the determination of the Christians who first met in May 1863 to write the name of God into the Constitution when he spoke of "this nation *under God*" at Gettysburg six months later is unknown. In any case, the sentiment was widespread, and for these deeply religious people the stakes were very high. "We must wrest this argument [of an un-Christian nation] from the unbeliever," warned one minister, "or he will wrest from us every argument which defends our Christian institutions. We can no longer leave so precious, so vital a body of laws and usages as those which defend the Sabbath, Christian marriage, the sacred name of God, and the oath, exposed to argument drawn from a Constitution which contains no utterance in their favor. We must throw around them the shield of constitutional provision . . . or they perish out of our life as a nation."[57]

The National Reform Association had strong leadership that included a number of prominent men of faith—ministers, academicians, and members of Congress alike, many if not all of whom could trace their ancestry to the Puritans. Perhaps the most notable was William Strong, an ardent Presbyterian, an associate justice of the Supreme Court in the 1870s, and an early president of the association. But influential leadership was not enough to overcome the reservations of other prominent men such as Horace Greeley. "We deny," he wrote in the New York *Tribune* at the first stirrings of the movement in 1865, "that this is a Christian nation. . . . Almighty God is not the 'source of all authority and power' in our government."[58]

Like so much they attempted, the association's effort to amend the Constitution had failed by the 1880s, as had its drive to secure a national law against divorce (evangelicals believed that the rapidly rising divorce rate threatened to destroy the institution of the family). Undaunted by their early defeats, however, the National Reform Association remained committed to these reforms. It also backed another constitutional amendment that would direct each state to establish public schools that would educate children "on the principles of the Christian religion" as well as on the traditional aspects of learning. Furthermore, association members continued to protect the use of oaths and urge proscription of blasphemy even as they, along with thousands of Sabbatarians, joined with the Woman's Christian Temperance Union to put an end to Sunday mail.[59]

The Woman's Christian Temperance Union was founded in 1874 in Cleveland, Ohio, after groups of earnest Christian women in New York and elsewhere began singing hymns in front of saloons and praying for their closure. Its motto, "For God and Home and Native Land," proclaimed its patriotic roots, as did its membership composed of many women who also traced their lineages to the Puritans. Indeed, the organization's 1877 convention was attended by the descendants of "Governor Bradford, John Alden, General Warren, and a score of equally historic names." In purpose and in the Puritan heritage of its membership of earnest evangelical women, the WCTU was much like the National Reform Association and closely allied with it. Founded to rid the nation of John Barleycorn and under the dynamic leadership of Francis Willard, former president of the Evanston, Illinois, Women's University, it became actively involved in diverse Christian crusades, not the least of which was the campaign to reclaim the Sabbath.[60]

For this purpose, the WCTU established the Department for the Observance of the Sabbath in 1884 and made the spirited Josephine Bateham of Painsville, Ohio, its superintendent. By December 1887 she had energized local WCTU groups throughout the country, which inspired thousands of sermons for a day of rest and raised petitions with some 1,500,000 names to demand that Congress eliminate the "needless Government work and interstate commerce on the Christian Sabbath."[61]

The American Sabbath Union, the third leading organization to support the Sabbatarians' crusade, was by far the largest. It was, however, a late-comer, formed in 1888 when the struggle for a day of rest was far spent. Its prime mover was Wilbur F. Crafts, an energetic and ambitious man who at one time or another was a Methodist, Congregational, and Presbyterian minister. Born in 1850 in Fryburg, Maine, of Puritan forebears and educated at Wesleyan University in Connecticut, he was the prolific author of a number of books, among them *The Sabbath for Man,* a statistically drenched argument for keeping the Sabbath Day holy. In May of 1888 Crafts successfully persuaded the Methodist quadrennial conference to invite other Protestant denominations to unite in support of a national Sabbath law, and from that time on he became the principal spokesman for the Sabbatarians. In time, all of the major

Protestant denominations and many of the smaller ones, allegedly representing ten million people, joined the American Sabbath Union.[62]

Crafts reached out not only to Protestant denominations for support for a Sabbath day-of-rest law but also to organized labor and even to the hierarchy of the Catholic Church. In December 1888, Cardinal James Gibbons of Baltimore wrote to Crafts that the observance of the Sabbath could not "fail to draw upon the nation the blessings and protection of an overruling Providence" and added his name, and by inference that of the Catholic Church's, to those millions seeking a Sabbath law. Moreover, taking advantage of the movement's more inclusive direction that aimed for a day of rest as well as a day of worship, Crafts was able to win support for a Sunday law from the Knights of Labor and the Brotherhood of Locomotive Engineers, many of whose local assemblies added their petitions to the great numbers piling up in the Senate chambers.[63]

The new inclusive strategy had come at an opportune time for winning the support of the Knights of Labor. Only two years before, in 1886, Samuel Gompers had founded a rival organization, the American Federation of Labor, whose goal was the eight-hour day. That demand had led to the great strike against the McCormick Harvester plant in Chicago in 1886 and to the subsequent violent Haymarket Square riot. The Knights of Labor, whose members reflected middle-class aspirations, was only remotely tied to these events, but it was nonetheless tainted by them, which precipitated a decline in membership. What better way then to recoup its fortunes than to support a law that would at least decrease the number of hours that many members were required to work each week?[64]

Yet a more inclusive Sabbath and the support of spirited organizations were still not enough to ensure passage of a national law terminating mail on Sundays. Sabbatarians needed a sympathetic ear in Congress, and they found it in the person of Sen. Henry Blair of New Hampshire. One of the boldest and most contentious and reform-minded senators of the late nineteenth century, Blair, for all his efforts at social reform, remains largely ignored by historians. Born in New Hampshire in 1834 and left fatherless at the age of two, Blair had no easy life. He was raised on a neighbor's farm until he was seventeen, attended schools as farm work permitted, studied law in the office of a lawyer, was admitted to the bar, served in the Civil War, and was wounded at Port Hudson. Climbing the political ladder of local politics after the war, he eventually won election to the House of Representatives in 1875 and to the Senate in 1879. In the 1880s he became chair of the Senate Committee on Labor and Education. From that position he launched an invaluable investigation into the relations between capital and labor and wrote a law providing for national aid to education and a joint resolution to amend the Constitution to require that states provide public schools in which students would be taught the common branches of learning and principles of the Christian religion.[65]

A New Englander who had firm religious convictions, Blair was perhaps the only U.S. senator in the 1880s to give Sabbatarians a hearing. No doubt it was for that reason that the Sabbath law petitions were directed to his committee rather than to the Post Office Committee as might have been expected. In any event, by the end of 1887 a crumpled mass of petitions, "aggregating many thousands," according to Blair, "from all parts of the country, and from the best influences in the country," had descended upon his committee. They came in such numbers as to give Senator Blair an excuse to rouse national interest in the Sabbatarians' campaign by holding hearings on the subject in April of 1888.[66] In May, Blair introduced a sweeping bill in the Senate that would stop Sabbath mail, eliminate most interstate railroad traffic on the Sabbath, and abolish military parades on that day. Certain exceptions to these strictures were permitted for emergencies, but it was a wide-ranging bill that provided a Sabbath law for the Territories similar to those that states possessed.[67]

Blair's bill, so long sought by evangelicals and the first of its kind, inspired a frenetic flurry of activity among Sabbatarians, who mobilized their troops to force Congress to enact it. "Let us overwhelm Congress with petitions and letters and we shall get our desires" the *Christian Statesman* urged readers (who needed no urging). Hundreds of secretaries of the National Reform Association—whose affiliated associations had grown from forty-seven, with fifteen thousand members, in 1864 to more than 1,200, with 175,000 members, in 1889—fanned out across the East and the Midwest. They spoke for the Sabbath law on college campuses, at religious meetings, and wherever else they could secure an invitation. At churches large and small they gave numerous sermons related to the evils of alcohol and the consequences of profaning the Sabbath.[68]

The work of the Department for the Observance of the Sabbath of the WCTU was even more encompassing. In November, Francis E. Willard declared that support for the bill would be made the organization's "special of specialties" for the next three months. "Think what it would mean," she said in anticipation of its passage, "to have a railroad quiet on the Sabbath. No trains, no excursions, no Sunday papers, for they would soon die if there were no mails, one and half million men released from toil, and the correct example of the national government to influence every legislature and court in the country."[69]

No one thought more about that than Josephine Bateham. Tireless and hopeful, she was the "Deborah of the movement" and like the biblical Deborah led her troops into the face of the enemy. Rarely resting, she had organized

Sabbath departments in forty-one states and territories, with more than seven hundred superintendents to oversee them, by the end of 1888. The work was hard and often discouraging. "Postoffices open [on Sundays]," the Dakota superintendent wrote about her area in 1888. "Christians and ministers use Sunday trains and are indifferent, people careless about God's law and civil law." Still, Bateham's forces persevered, and by October 1888 the department had been responsible for more than two thousand sermons relating to the Sabbath, organizing several hundred prayer and public meetings, teaching the Fourth Commandment in hundreds of Sabbath schools, and distributing nearly eight hundred thousand pages of leaflets on the subject.[70]

As if the possibility of securing a Sabbath law were not enough to rouse their excitement, the evangelicals' enthusiasm was compounded by the presidential campaign of that year. "The air is all astir," Bateham observed in the fall of 1888, "with moral questions as well as political." And so it seemed. Neither the party of Democratic incumbent Grover Cleveland nor that of Republican candidate Benjamin Harrison supported the Sabbath law. But the Prohibition Party, luring many evangelicals from the Republican Party by its stand against alcoholic beverages, did support, if somewhat timidly, preservation of "the Sabbath as a civil institution."[71]

When the exciting campaign ended many Sabbatarians whose hopes of a third-party victory had been unrealistically raised assuaged disappointment over Gen. Clinton B. Fisk's poor showing as the prohibitionist candidate with the knowledge that Harrison at least, a Republican and devout Presbyterian elder, would be the next president. Still, they had little time to ruminate about the election. Senator Blair, whose Committee on Labor and Education had been swamped by new petitions requesting passage of his day of rest bill, called the committee together for a second hearing on December 13, 1888, this time to consider the bill, which had languished during the first session of the Fiftieth Congress.[72]

The new hearing was an extended version of the previous one. From ten in the morning until after four in the afternoon, Blair and three other senators listened to the testimony of twenty-three witnesses, nearly half of whom were Protestant ministers. Only three of the group—those representing the Seventh Day Baptists, Seventh Day Adventists, and the Secular League of the United States—spoke against the measure. Many of their arguments went back to the 1820s and centered on the biblical origin of the Sabbath Day, correct interpretation of the Decalogue, the Constitution, and separation of church. What was new was the testimony revealing how the communications revolution—expansion of railroads and growth of the post office—had transformed American life and the American Sabbath.[73]

Again and again, supporters of the Sabbath law described how far Sunday mail service had reached into the nation's small towns and villages to profane the Sabbath and alter old patterns of life, how each new postal service had added to the labor of those forced to work on Sundays, and how the greed of publishers and railroad owners were perpetuating the profanation of the Lord's Day. More than that, they made a creditable case for the fact that all this was unnecessary. They pointed out that urbanites in free-delivery cities, whose mail was not delivered on Sundays, did not suffer. Nor was Sunday mail necessary to send emergency messages when the telegraph was available for just such exigencies. Finally, the testimony of Gen. A. S. Diven, long-time director of the Erie Railroad, showed by detailed illustrations that it was not necessary to run trains on Sundays, even those carrying perishables or the mail. "With regard to mail trains," he said, "I see no necessity for the distribution or movement of mails on Sunday. The mail is not resorted to now in cases of emergency. . . . Almost all the great business of the country for which the mails are used is suspended on Sunday."[74]

Proof of Diven's testimony was to some extent demonstrated during the year when railroad managers began to reduce their Sunday trains. It had not been easy to persuade railroad executives to do this when, like William Vanderbilt, they agreed only to "stop Sunday trains when other railroads do." But the advocates were persistent. To one manager who professed ignorance of the divine law governing the Sabbath, a minister quoted from Isaiah, whose counsel was to "turn away thy foot from the Sabbath, from doing thy pleasure on my holy day." In this case, that apparently had less impact than the possible loss of dividends. Still, the New York Central and Hudson River, the Pennsylvania, and a number of other railroads, under mounting pressure, had reduced the number of their trains that traveled on Sundays by 1889.[75]

Following the hearing, Sabbatarians looked forward to the beginning of the second session of the Fiftieth Congress in January 1889. At that point, they believed, their Sabbath law would be acted upon, and they had some reason to be hopeful that it would at least pass in the Senate. On January 16, Senator Blair had presented to the Senate the "petition of fourteen million," as it was called, asking for the passage of the law. It was the fruitful harvest of many laborers and seemingly too impressive to ignore.[76]

True, critics noted that the millions represented mostly the numbers of members of organizations rather than actual names of people, but Josephine Bateham, who had worked among the people, refused to accept that attack. Admitting that she was unsure how many actual individuals had personally signed petitions, she contended nonetheless that it was no small number. "I do know," she said, "that, pasted on red cloth and arranged as drapery in the

Foundry [Methodist] Church of this city [Washington, D.C.] . . . the petition is over half a mile in length, much of it in double columns; and yet this wonderful petition, doubtless by many millions the largest ever presented to this or any Government, is not yet full grown."[77]

However many names were there, the evangelicals rolled thousands of them up in red cloth; tied them with red, white, and blue streamers; and placed them on each senator's desk. All that energy and zeal for the cause could do, they had done. Success or failure waited upon the Senate's decision, to which they looked forward hopefully in the spring of 1889. In their heart of hearts, however, many knew that the political influence of the millions of evangelicals who had lent their names to promoting a day of rest was unequal to the naysaying power of the publishers who distributed their Sunday newspaper through Sunday mail.

Notes

1. As quoted in Richard J. Cawardine, *Evangelicals and Politics* (New Haven, 1993), 100. For a perceptive analysis of the relationship between the evangelicals and the Whig party, see Daniel Walker Howe, *The Political Culture of the American Whigs* (Chicago, 1979), ch. 7.

2. *Report of the Postmaster General, 1842,* 736 (this and subsequent citations to postmasters general reports can be found in the *Congressional Information Service Serial Set Index* [Washington, 1997]). Actually, more than $58,000 had been saved before some Sunday service was restored. For the reduction in the use of mail stagecoaches, cf. *Report of the Postmaster General, 1841,* 481, and *Report of the Postmaster General, 1845,* 850. For the Sabbatarian influence on postal policy, see also Richard R. John, "Taking the Sabbath Seriously: The Postal System, the Sabbath, and the Transformation of American Political Culture," *Journal of the Early Republic* 10 (Winter 1990): 562–63.

3. *Report of the Postmaster General, 1840,* 478. For some Sunday mail routes curtailed by December 1840, see H. Doc. no. 27, 26th Cong., 2d sess., 1–15 (Dec. 23, 1840); for the quotation, see "Documents from the Post Office Department," S. Doc. no. 1, 27th Cong., 1st sess., 68 (May 29, 1841). Granger noted that in many areas the changes had been welcomed but that he had suffered many complaints and demands for restoration of the old service. For the plight of the post office before Kendall's resignation in 1840, see H. Rept. no. 524, 26th Cong., 1st sess., 26 (May 26, 1840). Congress's belated recognition that stagecoaches had been put "on many routes where travel does not warrant keeping up the stages" led to legislation in 1845 directing the postmaster general to contract with the lowest bidder to carry the mail without specifying the kind of conveyance contractors must use other than that necessary to provide "celerity, certainty, and security" for the mail. Consequently, the postmaster general contracted to have mail carried by horseback or sulky on more and more routes over which mail was rarely carried on Sundays, which relieved congressional pressure on the postmaster general to use stagecoaches on many seven-day mail routes. The law was permissive until 1859, when Postmaster General Joseph Holt stopped the practice of requiring stage-

coaches on any route. *Congressional Globe,* 28th Cong., 1st sess., 520 (Apr. 16, 1844); see also *United States Statutes at Large* (Boston, 1856), 5:738, and *Report of the Postmaster General, 1859,* 1402.

4. *House Journal,* 27th Cong., 2d sess., 1632–33 (Dec. 6, 1841–Aug. 31, 1842), index. For petitions to Congress following the Whigs' return to office in 1849, see *Journal of the Senate,* 32th Cong., 1st sess., 894 (Dec. 1, 1851–Aug. 31, 1852), index.

5. *Congressional Globe,* 31st Cong., 2d sess., 245 (Jan. 15, 1851). For the postal law favoring religious newspapers, see *United States Statutes at Large* (Boston, 1856), 10:38–40, 641–42. Debate over the bill is found in *Congressional Globe,* 31st Cong., 2d sess., 25, 55 (Dec. 10, 13, 1850). Southerners were much opposed to favoring the religious press, arguing once more that it was a violation of the separation of church and state.

6. See also David Paul Nord, "Systematic Benevolence: Religious Publishing and the Marketplace in Early-Nineteenth-Century America," in *Communication and Change in American Religious History,* ed. Leonard I. Sweet (Grand Rapids, 1993), 238–69.

7. *Report of the Postmaster General, 1860,* 417–18. On the religious press, see Nathan Hatch, *The Democratization of Christianity* (New Haven, 1989), 141–46; Carwardine, *Evangelicals and Politics,* 38–39; David Paul Nord, "Evangelical Origins of Mass Media," *Journalism Monographs* 85 (May 1984): 1–30. On the *National Era,* see Bertram Wyatt-Brown, *Lewis Tappan and the Evangelical War against Slavery* (Cleveland, 1969), 279, and Philip Van Doren Stern, *The Annotated Uncle Tom's Cabin* (New York, 1946), 19–20.

8. The abolitionists, for example, castigated directors of the American Tract Society because of their refusal to attack slavery. Louis Filler, *Crusade against Slavery, 1830–1860* (New York, 1960), 261–63; New York *Daily Tribune,* Jan. 21, 1858, 3; *The Independent,* Jan. 31, 1856, 36. For the revival of 1858, see Timothy L. Smith, *Revivalism and Social Reform* (New York, 1957), 63–79. For tracts decrying the desecration of the Sabbath, see Frederick L. Browner, "The Observance of the Sabbath in the United States, 1800–1865," Ph.D. diss, Harvard University, 1937, 229–30. For the connection between the mass media and "the triumph of Christianity in the antebellum period," see Mark Noll, "The Evangelical Enlightenment and Theological Education," in *Communication and Change in American Religious History,* ed. Leonard I. Sweet (Grand Rapids, 1993), 270–300.

9. For the political chaos from which the Republican Party emerged, see David M. Potter, *The Impending Crisis, 1848–1862* (New York, 1976), 225–65; and for the Protestant evangelical role in the development of the new party, see Cawardine, *Evangelicals and Politics,* ch. 8.

10. As quoted in the New York *Tribune,* June 12, 1860, 4.

11. For the origins of Lincoln's Sabbath Day order to the troops, see Carl Sandburg, *Abraham Lincoln: The War Years* (New York, 1936), 3:374–75; for a different view of the origin of the order, see Bronner, *The Observation of the Sabbath,* 332–34. The fact that the Battle of Bull Run was fought on a Sunday concerned those who held the day sacred, and Gen. Irwin McDowell was berated for his failure to properly observe the day (*The Independent,* Nov. 20, 1862; see also the New York *Tribune,* Nov. 17, 1862).

12. Lincoln's most moving statement on sin as a cause of the war was in his Second Inaugural Address. James D. Richardson, comp., *A Compilation of the Messages and Papers of the Presidents, 1789–1897* (Washington, 1897), 6:276–77. A summary of sermons on Lincoln's death appears in Sandburg, *Abraham Lincoln,* 3:357–66, and in Merrill D. Peterson, *Lincoln in American Memory* (New York, 1994), 7–8. For the quotation, see the

sermons following Lincoln's death in David Chesebrough, *No Sorrow Like Our Sorrow: Northern Protestant Ministers and the Assassination of Lincoln* (Kent, Ohio, 1994), 88.

13. For evangelical euphoria following the war, see Henry F. May, *Protestant Churches and Industrial America* (New York, 1949), 125–35, and Smith, *Revivalism and Social Reform*, 232–37.

14. Edward C. Kirkland, *Industry Comes of Age: Business, Labor, and Public Policy* (New York, 1961), 46. On railroads as a symbol of mechanized America, see Alan Trachtenburg, *The Incorporation of America: Culture and Society in the Gilded Age* (New York, 1982), 57–59; see also Daniel Boorstin, *The Americans: The Democratic Experience* (New York, 1973), 120–21.

15. Kirkland, *Industry Comes of Age*, 237; *Twelfth Census of the United States, Population* (Washington, 1900), pt. 1:lxxxiii. See also Josiah Strong, *Our Country* (Cambridge, 1963), 172–73, on the growth of cities and their attraction for immigrants.

16. *Christian Union*, Feb., 19, 1879, 170, Feb. 26, 1885, 4; see also Robert T. Handy, *A Christian America: Protestant Hopes and Historical Realities* (New York, 1971), 73–79.

17. *Christian Union*, Feb. 19, 1885, 7 (a map of the Eleventh Ward); for the situation in Chicago, see *Christian Union*, May 21, 1879, 462.

18. James Bryce, *The American Commonwealth* (New York, 1897), 2:726–27.

19. *Christian Union*, Aug., 27, 1879, 166 (quotation), Sept. 10, 1879, 202. The Protestant literature of the period was filled with references to "the masses," sometimes, perhaps unconsciously, conveying the sense of "the others" as opposed to themselves (*Christian Union*, April 2, 1885, 7).

20. On Stowe, see *Christian Statesman*, July 21, 1881, 4.

21. *Christian Union*, Aug. 31, 1882, 181.

22. *Christian Union*, Sept. 10, 1879, 220.

23. See Handy, *A Christian America*, 84–88, for the importance of the Sabbath to American Protestants. Editors of *Christian Union* (Aug. 9, 1879, 384, May 21, 1885, 4) wanted no return of the Puritan Sabbath and envisioned a different kind of Sabbath, neither European or Puritan.

24. New York *Times*, Dec. 2, 1882, 2, Dec. 4, 1882, 1; *Christian Union*, Jan. 1, 1879, 26, Dec. 7, 1882, 487, July 5, 1883. On the Philadelphia Sabbath Association, see "Sunday Rest Bill," S. Misc. Doc. no. 43, 50th Cong., 2d sess., 141 (Jan. 17, 1889) (hereafter "Day of Rest").

25. On the Law and Order Society, see *Christian Union*, Feb. 11, 1886, 4; see also *Christian Union*, Nov. 15, 1883, for Law and Order activities in Cold Springs, New York. For law enforcement in Cincinnati in 1889, see *Christian Statesman*, Sept. 5, 1889, 9.

26. *Christian Statesman*, Aug. 14, 1873, 1; *Christian Union*, May 21, 1879, 462, Aug., 27, 1879, 166.

27. See *Christian Union*, May 3, 1883, 346, and March 19, 1885, 3, for the weakening of New York's Sabbath law. The problems that evangelicals faced in various larger cities are detailed in articles on "Heathen Cities" in *Christian Union* (e.g., April 2, 1885, 7).

28. *Christian Statesman*, Dec. 20, 1888, 3.

29. *Report of the Postmaster General, 1828*, 179; *Report of the Postmaster General, 1887*, 9, 405. *Report of the Postmaster General, 1887* does not give the number of postal employees for that year. The figure used is drawn from the *Report of the Postmaster General, 1889*, 12. For the estimated number of postal employees forced to work on Sundays, see "Day of Rest," 17.

30. For a description of the early railway mail service, see *Niles Weekly Register,* May 18, 1838, 178; *Report of the Postmaster General, 1868,* 12–14; and *Congressional Record,* 44th Cong., 1st sess., 2927 (May 3, 1876).

31. "History of the Railway Mail Service," Senate Ex. Doc. no. 40, 48th Cong., 2d sess., 45–46 (Jan. 21, 1885); "Report of the Special Commission on Railway Mail Transportation," S. Misc. Doc. no. 14, 45th Cong., 2d sess., 27 (Dec. 14, 1877); *Report of the Postmaster General, 1900,* 582. The tenth and eleventh postal divisions were added to the original nine in 1889. *Report of the Postmaster General, 1889,* 478–79; quotation in *Congressional Record,* 49th Cong. 1st sess., 2764–65 (Mar. 25, 1886) (quotations); see also Carl H. Scheele, *A Short History of the Mail Service* (Washington, 1970), 94–97.

32. *Report of the Postmaster General, 1900,* 243. For a brief overview of the railroad mail, see Superintendent of Railway Mail Service to Hannibal Hamlin, *Congressional Record,* 44th Cong., 1st sess., 5170–72 (Aug. 4, 1876).

33. For those employed in the railway mail service, see "Day of Rest," 17; see also "Postal Regulations," H. Misc. Doc. no. 63, 50th Cong., 1st sess., 304, 367–78 (Oct. 20, 1888) (hereafter "Postal Regulations"). The duties of mail messengers and local agents are on page 77.

34. "Day of Rest," 4, 5.

35. *Congressional Record,* 49th Cong., 1st sess., 2764 (Mar. 25, 1886).

36. Ibid.

37. For the total casualty statistics, see *Report of the Postmaster General, 1900,* 584; for the accident rate of 1897, see *Report of the Postmaster General, 1897,* 491. The law for the compensation to a deceased postal worker's family is found in *United States Statutes at Large* (Washington, 1963), 32:2:115. The first postmaster general to recommend compensation for the family of a postal clerk killed in the line of duty was William F. Vilas in 1885 (*Report of the Postmaster General, 1885,* 57–58).

38. *Report of the Postmaster General, 1889,* 11.

39. "Day of Rest," 5 (quotation); *United States Statutes at Large* (Boston, 1846), 4:102; *United States Statutes at Large* (Boston, 1856), 5:80; *United States Statutues at Large,* rev. (Washington, 1885), 18:750.

40. *Report of the Postmaster General, 1889,* 11–12. For an excellent description of the work of postal clerks, see Marshall Cushing, *The Story of Our Post Office: The Greatest Government Department in All Its Phases* (Boston, 1893), 181–86.

41. *Congressional Record,* 44th Cong., 1st sess., 3053 (May 12, 1876); see also *Report of the Postmaster General, 1889,* 230, for money-order post offices.

42. "Postal Regulations," 210. On Sundays, Bryce remarked, the "American part of the rural population, especially in the South, refrains from amusement as well as from work" (*American Commonwealth,* 2:715). Beginning in the late 1870s during the administration of Rutherford B. Hayes, many star routes were unjustifiably upgraded to daily and speedier service. That led to the great star route scandal of the 1880s, reminiscent of the postal scandal in the Jackson admininstration. Those involved in the scandal, contractors and postal officials, were brought to trial but escaped conviction. A summary of the story may be found in "Frauds in the Star Route Mail Service—Investigation of Expenditures in the Department of Justice," H. Rept. no. 2165, 45th Cong., 1st sess. (July 3, 1884).

43. For the Sabbatarians' complaint against the authority given postmasters, see "Day of Rest," 4–6. See also "Postal Regulations," 210.

44. "Day of Rest," 34.

45. *Report of the Postmaster General, 1900,* 108; see also "Extension of the Free Delivery Service," H. Rept. no. 2215, 49th Cong., 1st sess, 1–5 (May 5, 1886).

46. *Congressional Record,* 49th Cong., 1st sess., 71–78ff (July 19, 1886); *Congressional Record,* 49th Cong., 2d sess., 71–73 (Dec. 9, 1886); see also *Report of the Postmaster General, 1900,* 109.

47. One minister alluded to Marshall's attempt to establish a Sunday free-delivery service in New York City, but if the effort was made it apparently drew little attention. "Day of Rest," 8.

48. Ibid., 8, emphasis in the original; *Report of the Postmaster General, 1885,* 32–37.

49. "Day of Rest," 8. For Vilas's explanation, see *Report of the Postmaster General, 1885,* 34–35.

50. *United States Statutes at Large* (Washington, 1887), 24:220–21. The debate over extension of special delivery service appears in *Congressional Record,* 49th Cong., 1st sess., 3620–21 (April 19, 1886); see also "Postal Regulations," 280.

51. *Union Signal,* Nov., 22, 1888.

52. "Day of Rest," 3–4; *Christian Union,* April 9, 1879, 384, and Sept. 17, 1879, 222; *Christian Statesman,* Oct. 15, 1874, 1, and April 25, 1889, 4 (quotation). For the opposition to a civil Sabbath, see *Christian Statesman,* Sept. 26, 1889, 3

53. David McAllister, *The National Reform Movement: Its History and Principles, a Manual of Christian Civil Government* (Philadelphia, 1890), 24–27; see also *Christian Statesman,* April 25, 1889, 4.

54. McAllister, *The National Reform Movement,* 163–66; see also Hal D. Sears, *The Sex Radicals: Free Love in High Victorian America* (Lawrence, 1977), 34–36.

55. McAllister, *The National Reform Movement,* 159–60. On Congress's refusal to act to eliminate the Chaplaincy Corps, see "Chaplains in Congress and in the Army and Navy," H. Rept. no. 124, 33d Cong., 1st sess., 1–10 (Mar. 27, 1854); see also "Report of the Committee on Judiciary on Chaplains," S. Report no. 376, 32d Cong., 2d sess., 1–4 (Jan. 19, 1853); and, for the Ohio decion, *Report of the United States Commissioner of Education for 1874* (Washington, 1873), 328.

56. McAllister, *The National Reform Movement,* 9; *Christian Statesman,* April 25, 1889, 4.

57. McAllister, *The National Reform Movement,* 136. The words *under God* appear to have been Lincoln's sudden inspiration; they were not in the text from which he read his address. Gary Wills, *Lincoln at Gettysburg The Words That Remade America* (New York, 1992), 192, 194.

58. New York *Tribune,* Mar. 7, 1865; Gary Scott Smith, *The Seeds of Secularization: Calvinism, Culture, and Pluralism in America, 1870–1915* (Grand Rapids, 1995), 59. On Justice Strong, see *Dictionary of American Biography* (New York, 1936), 9:153–55 (hereafter *DAB*). The House Judiciary Committee, to whom the proposed amendment was sent, studied the debates held in the constitutional convention and concluded that the Founders had discussed the question of referring to God in the Constitution and decided against including anything that "might be construed as a reference to any creed or doctrine." "Acknowledgment of God and the Christian Religion in the Constitution," H. Rept. no. 143, 43d Cong., 1st sess., 1 (Feb. 18, 1874).

59. McAllister, *The National Reform Movement,* 9–10; "Day of Rest," 127.

60. For the origins of the WCTU, see Allan Nevins, *The Emergence of Modern America* (New York, 1928), 338–39. For the Puritan heritage and close relationship with the Na-

tional Reform Association, see *Union Signal,* Nov. 11, 1886, 2, May 17, 1888, 4, 24–26, and May 27, 1886, 12 (quotation). On Francis E. Willard, see *The Outlook,* Mar. 5, 1898, 575–77.

61. "Day of Rest," 21–22, 131; *Christian Statesman,* Oct. 25, 1888, 2; *Union Signal,* May 27, 1886, 12, and Nov. 11, 1886, 23.

62. *Christian Statesman,* Dec. 20, 1888; see also "Day of Rest," 18. It might have been supposed that Dwight L. Moody, one of the leading evangelists of the day, would have been a leader of this organization. Certainly, he fervently believed in observing the Lord's Day and counted violation of that day as one of humanity's major sins. But Moody was not given to politics or legislative endeavors. His emphasis was upon saving souls, not on crusades to save the Christian nation through legislative endeavors. George M. Marsden provides an excellent analysis of Moody's place in late-nineteenth-century evangelism in *Fundamentalism and American Culture: The Shaping of Twentieth-Century Evangelism* (New York, 1980), 32–39.

63. "Day of Rest," 18–21 (quotation on 131). An account of the work of Wilbur C. Crafts among labor organizations appears in *Christian Statesman* (Nov. 22, 1888, 1).

64. For the Knights of Labor connection with the eight-hour movement and Haymarket Square riot, see Paul Avrich, *The Haymarket Square Tragedy* (Princeton, 1984), 183, 219–20, 309–10. See also "Letter from the Postmaster General," H. Exec. Doc. no. 71, 49th Cong., 1st sess., 1–2 (Feb. 12, 1886); "Hours of Letter Carrier per Day," H. Rept. no. 265, 50th Cong., 1st sess., 1 (Feb. 7, 1888); and *United States Statutes at Large* (Washington, 1889), 25:157. A Sunday day of worship as well as rest may have appealed to many laborers who were still tied emotionally to the Protestant faith. Herbert G. Gutman, "Protestantism and the American Labor Movement: The Christian Spirit in the Gilded Age," *American Historical Review* 72 (Oct. 1966): 74–101.

65. *DAB* (Washington, 1932), 1:334–35; see also Barbara Stokes, "A Puritan in Washington: The Legislative Career of Henry Blair," master's thesis, University of Texas at El Paso, 1965. For his educational amendment to the Constitution, see *Congressional Record,* 50th Cong., 2d sess., 433 (Dec. 1, 1888). Blair introduced the school amendment on May 25, 1888, as Joint Resolution 86; see *Senate Journal,* 50th Cong., 1st sess., 877 (May 25, 1888).

66. "Notes of a Hearing before the Committee on Education and Labor, United States Senate, Friday, April 6, 1888, on the Petitions Praying for the Passage of Legislation Prohibiting the Running of Mail Trains, Interstate Commerce Trains . . . and Other Violations of the Sabbath," S. Misc. Doc. no. 108, 50th Cong., 1st sess., 1 (April 15, 1888).

67. "Day of Rest," 1–2; *Congressional Record,* 50th Cong., 1st sess., 4455 (May 21, 1888).

68. The figures appear in *Christian Statesman,* May 16, 1889, 8; an example of the work of the secretaries is in *Christian Statesman,* Feb. 28, 1889, 8.

69. *Union Signal,* Nov. 12. 1888, 12 (quotation), Nov. 22, 1888.

70. *Christian Statesman,* October 25, 1888, 2.

71. Kirk Porter, *National Party Platforms, 1840–1956* (Urbana, 1956), 76–82. The *Christian Statesman* (Oct. 25, 1888, 2) contains an account of Josephine Bateham's critical attitude toward older parties.

72. "Sunday Rest Bill," 1; see also *Christian Statesman,* Dec. 20, 1888, 5–6. For Sabbatarian comments about the outcome of the election, see *Christian Statesman,* Dec. 6, 1888, 6–7.

73. For the substance of the Sabbatarian argument, see the statement of Wilbur Crafts ("Day of Rest," 2–21); for a rebuttal, see the testimony of John B. Wolff ("Sunday Rest Bill," 56–62, 105–14).

74. "Sunday Rest Bill," 29, passim; see also Charles Worcester Clark, "Day of Rest," *Atlantic* 64 (Sept. 1889): 373.

75. For the quotation from Isaiah, see "Sunday Rest Bill," 147; on the reduction of Sunday railroad traffic, see *Christian Union,* Jan. 3, 1888, 4; *Christian Statesman,* Feb. 28, 1889, 1 (first quotation); and New York *Times,* Apr. 24, 1889, 2, Apr. 25, 1889, 8, and Apr. 29, 1889, 12.

76. *Congressional Record,* 50th Cong., 2d sess. 831–32 (Jan. 16, 1889). Of Protestant churches submitting petitions in favor of the Sabbath law, the largest number by far were Presbyterians, followed by Methodists, Congregationalists, and Baptists. The membership of these churches was overwhelmingly old-stock English, Scotch, and Scotch-Irish. The regions most supportive of the bill were the Midwest in addition to Pennsylvania, New York, and Massachusetts. As it had been in 1828 and 1830, the South was the least supportive of the bill. John Henry Dixon, "Henry William Blair, the American Sabbath, and the Sunday Rest Bill," M.A. thesis, University of Texas at El Paso, 1989, 42–45.

77. For criticism of the petition, see *Christian Union,* Feb. 14, 1889, 212; for Crafts's assessment of the petitions and Josephine Bateham's statement, see "Day of Rest," 18, 22.

4 Sunday Newspapers and the Day of Rest

Never in the world was such a scepter of power placed within hands of an individual as is wielded by the editor of one of our leading papers.
—Christian Statesman, *August 28, 1889*

In the fall of 1888, as the crusade for a day of rest rushed toward its conclusion, a Protestant minister singled out one of the greatest evils radiating from Sunday mail. It was, he declared, "the Sunday newspaper in whose behalf the hills of all our larger thoroughfares echo with the shriek and groan of flying locomotives; our towns and villages are inundated with the typographical deluge, and even the comers to the House of God, many of them baptized before entering upon worship, with the shock of news and gossip and fiction—not to say of scandal and crime."[1]

For so many of those trying to preserve remnants of the Puritan Sabbath in the late nineteenth century Sunday newspapers, sold far and wide and read by thousands on a day set aside for spiritual reflection, were the ultimate desecration of the Lord's Day. For evangelicals, the putative evil spawned by these newspapers was compounded by the realization that they were made possible only by the government's generous subsidization of the post office in collaboration with publishers, and railroads. "The 'Sunday newspapers,'" the Rev. T. S. Stevenson, secretary of the National Reform Association, wrote in 1885, "the United States mail service, and the railroads, constitute a triple unholy alliance against the right observance of the day of rest by the American people."[2]

Sunday newspapers were not new in the 1880s, of course. At least one had appeared briefly as early as 1796, and, before the Civil War, larger cities were familiar with independent Sunday sheets that contained miscellaneous information and some news. But the first daily newspaper of importance to have a sustained Sunday edition was James Gordon Bennett's *Sunday Herald.* Bennett had built circulation in the 1830s with stories of seduction, crime, murder, and suicide, for which he was roundly condemned by other publishers and moral reformers in the "moral war" of 1840. Impervious to these attacks, scornful of Sabbath-keepers, and anxious to turn a profit, Bennett, after two failed attempts, began publishing a Sunday edition continuously in 1841 in spite of the outcry against him.[3]

After that other large urban dailies, spurred by the demand for news during the Civil War and competition for readers and profits, gradually added Sunday editions. In cities, however, a lingering respect for the Sabbath prevented many publishers of daily newspapers from joining in profaning the Lord's Day with Sunday editions. Fewer than fifty daily newspapers had Sunday editions in 1870, and those editions were little different in content from the dailies. Yet twenty years later Sunday editions of more than 250 urban daily newspapers reached virtually every town, village, and hamlet in America, overwhelming the influence of omnipresent weekly rural and Christian newspapers, profaning the Sabbath, and, from an evangelical perspective, threatening to shatter American society itself.[4]

The phenomenon was not merely the inevitable result of the rise of urbanization. Of course cities provided publishers with wealth, readership, and the advantages brought by improvements in printing and the telegraph and the development of national news services. But it was Congress's generous postage laws, written in part for the dissemination of public information and in part from fear of the great urban press, that subsidized them and made them so prosperous and numerous. Moreover, expansion of the railroads, extension of the postal service, and postal innovations gave newspapers national prominence that in turn invigorated and eventually defeated the evangelical crusade to stop mail on the Sabbath and secure a day of rest.[5]

Prompted by the political power of newspapers and the argument—repeated again and again through the years—that the success of democracy rested upon a diffusion of knowledge, Congress had from the beginning rigged the postal system to support the nation's press. The first postal law of 1792 suggested the direction that legislation would take. That law set the postage rate of a letter going no farther than thirty miles at 6 cents. On newspapers, which Congress admitted into the mail for the first time, the rate was 1 cent for each newspaper traveling a hundred miles—1.5 cents for a greater distance. Newspapers sent more than a hundred miles (but all of those within the state of publication) were mailed at the 1 cent rate. The law also generously permitted editors to exchange newspapers through the mail at no cost whatever. Government documents mailed free to editors under their legislator's frank provided another source of free information.[6]

Favored by such laws, the American press expanded wonderfully. Needing little more than the free exchanges, franked government documents, cheap postage, and the rapid expansion of the postal service to succeed, scores of ambitious men and institutions went into the publishing business. For more than half a century and under the government's benign laws, diffused information—political, religious, and business—traveled through the mail in an abundance unmatched in any other country. By 1850 more than 2,500 newspapers, to say nothing of a vast number of tracts and pamphlets, were being published.[7]

It was only natural, in that fledgling rural republic whose states were still wary of one another, that Congress's early postal laws should protect the state and local press from outside competition by charging newspapers mailed across state lines a half-cent more than those sent within the state of publication. Publishers tried repeatedly, and in the name of diffusion of information, to end that discrimination and even to abolish postage on publications altogether, but without success. Already perceiving in 1832 "a prevailing curiosity in the interior to see and read the papers . . . published in the large cities," the Senate Post Office Committee concluded that the abolition of postage on newspapers would entice rural people to purchase urban newspapers and so supplant smaller ones. That, in turn, would result in the "monopoly of influence of the large cities and foster a political atmosphere uncongenial to a spirit of independence." Protecting that independent spirit was a matter of grave concern in a time when it appeared to many of his opponents that President Andrew Jackson was acting the part of a king. "A concentration of political power," noted the committee, "in the hands of a few individuals is, of all things, most to be dreaded in a republic. It is, of itself, an aristocracy more potent and dangerous than any other; and nothing will tend so effectually to prevent it as the sustaining of the newspaper establishment in the different towns and villages throughout the country."[8]

Despite such warnings, the urban press at mid-century was already threatening to "invade the simple, pure, conservative atmosphere of the country" with what a member of Congress from North Carolina called "the poisoned sentiments of the cities concentrated in their papers," thereby forcing Congress to consider the complex postal problems that a rapidly spreading urban press posed.[9]

Because doing so was prudent as well as politically necessary, Congress first had to find a way to protect rural newspapers from being swallowed by the urban press. Then, with so many publications entering the mail and publishers demanding reductions in postage, a new method was needed to replace the old and unwieldy system of determining postage according to the distance a newspaper was being sent.

Finally, with reduced rates in the offing, Congress hoped to force publishers to prepay postage. That was no simple matter. Although it would soon force private individuals to prepay postage on their letters, Congress, hesitant always to aggravate the press, was exceedingly reluctant to change a system that had always required postmasters to collect from subscribers at the post office of delivery.

At the end of the Civil War, however, some of these problems had been solved. Congress had appeased rural publishers by permitting their publications to be mailed free throughout the county of publication, substituted the weight of a newspaper and the frequency of its publication for the distance sent, greatly reduced the postage on urban newspapers, and brought order from chaos in determining postal rates by separating mail into the first, second, and third classes, giving each its own postage rate. But the law that newspaper publishers must prepay postage on second-class publications, either at the post offices of mailing or those of delivery, was unsuccessful. Given a choice, most publishers chose to have the postage on their newspapers paid at offices of delivery, which meant involving thirty thousand postmasters. Like all collection agents, postmasters were given a commission for their efforts, but these were sometimes small enough not to bother with. If postmasters did, they did not always report such collections to the post office, which had no ready means of determining whether the payments had been made.[10]

That system of collection, so beneficial to the press, was a disaster for postal revenues. Statistics based on the census of 1870 and a month-long winter 1873–74 survey of mail in seven principal cities revealed that only $835,727 was collected of the $2,794,271 postage due on second-class matter under the law of 1863. Other figures showed that it cost the government $26,000,000 in 1873 to transport second-class matter that paid only $1,100,000 in postage.[11]

For postal officials, that constituted an outrageous subsidy for the press, even for the noble purpose of diffusing information. That same year the postmaster general asked Congress to end the old law's ambiguity and force publishers to prepay postage. His plan required them to take their publications to post offices of mailing. The material would be weighed in bulk and charged by the pound at a rate some 40 percent below the previous rate. This unparalled reduction, the postmaster general believed, was necessary to secure the approval of the press, without which Congress was unlikely to act. Publishers would then purchase stamps that would be affixed not on each newspaper but on an entire bundle.[12]

The postmaster general had made this proposal four years earlier, but Congress, apparently fearing the wrath of urban publishers at having to pay postage on their newspapers, had been reluctant to act upon it. By 1874, however, so massive and so costly had the transportation of printed matter become that Congress was forced to reconsider the postmaster general's proposal. The thorniest problem became the amount to charge for mailing a pound of newspapers.

Publishers had already solved that puzzle, however. Realizing some time earlier that forced prepayment was imminent, some thirty-five of the leading publishers in New York, Boston, and Cincinnati, led by the Harper brothers, petitioned Congress to suggest that "in the interest of the people, the rate of postage should be as low as would be compatible with the efficient working of the Department." This, they determined, was 1 cent a pound on newspapers and 2 cents on periodicals.[13]

When a bill proposed in the House by Joseph Cannon of Illinois, a member of the Post Office Committee serving the first of what would be many terms, came before Congress in the summer of 1874, it called for a cent and half a pound for newspapers published weekly or more often and 3 cents for those, mostly periodicals, less frequently published. Several days later, however, Cannon's bill was vastly revised in the Senate. Leading the debate, John Sherman from Ohio induced setting the postage rate at 4 cents a pound for all publications, regardless of frequency of publications.[14]

Urban publishers reacted to Sherman's proposal as if mortally wounded. The Senate, and Senator Sherman especially, they charged, had acted out of spite against publishers' attacks on franking privileges—a seemingly outrageous entitlement—which Congress had been forced to temporarily suspend in 1873. "The Senate," the Chicago *Tribune* reported, "has always evinced a horror of the newspapers, and a strong desire to punish them."[15]

Early attempts failed to reconcile the differences between the House and Senate bills, but at the end of the session, when Congress hurried through a mass of legislation, a compromise was reached. The postage per pound on newspapers published weekly or more frequently was set at 2 cents not 4 cents, and periodical literature became 3 cents a pound. The exception was that newspapers published and mailed in a free-delivery city would be charged an additional cent if delivered by carriers. For 2 cents a pound, daily newspapers could be mailed everywhere—not only to subscribers but also to newsdealers (of which there were many). For the same rate, dealers could return unsold publications.[16]

Set to begin January 1, 1875, this little-noticed but highly successful postal innovation was a significant part of the communications revolution of the time and no mean achievement. After some twenty or more years of trial and error, the old system, charging postage on each individual newspaper for the distance it traveled, was gone, although frequency of publication and weight remained factors in setting postage rates. Gone, too, was the clumsy, inefficient method of collecting postage on printed matter. In 1875 the postmaster general's office announced after a year of trial that postage, which in the previous year had been collected at thirty-five thousand post offices, was now collected at just 3,400. There, publications were weighed in bulk, and stamps purchased at greatly reduced cost were affixed to bundles of newspapers. In view of the commercialization of urban newspapers and the nation, it was fitting that the $35 stamp on so many bundles featured the Goddess Commerce clothed in full garments and holding a miniature ship in her right hand and a caduceus, the rod of the crafty Mercury, in her left.[17]

Still, as generous as this huge reduction in postage on printed matter was, it was not enough to appease eastern publishers. Those who published periodicals were especially aggrieved because newspapers were charged only 2 cents a pound while they had to pay 3 cents. Determined to equalize matters, a group again led by the Harpers and composed of members of boards of trade from various cities, publishers of some of the largest publications in New York, Boston, Cincinnati, and Chicago, and a spokesperson for the American News Company met in the fall of 1878 in the New York City post office with the chair of the House Post Office Committee, North Carolina's Alfred Waddell, to discuss a bill that would reduce the postage on periodical literature to 2 cents a pound.[18]

Born in 1834 in Hillsboro, North Carolina, a graduate of the University of North Carolina, and a southern lawyer, Waddell might have been expected to be unsympathetic to urban publishers, given the previous record of southerners on postal affairs. But he had once been publisher of the Wilmington *Herald* and was a supporter of the industry, eager to fashion the kind of a bill that publishers wanted. This meeting was followed by other conferences among businessmen, publishers, and members of the House Post Office Committee. Among the latter was Hernando Desota Money from Mississippi, former chair of the Post Office Committee and also a former newspaper editor. Money was especially sympathetic to publishers of periodicals, which were, he believed, great educators and much more deserving of cheap postage than newspapers "with their load of gossip and scandal."[19]

In this cozy atmosphere of togetherness publishers and members of Congress prepared a bill that would reduce postage on periodicals to 2 cents a pound; force publishers to register their publications with postmasters, who would determine eligibility for the second-class mail privilege; add a fourth class of mail; and broaden the definition of second-class mail. Publishers were even permitted to add supplements to their newspapers, and, with overweening magnanimity, the law permitted them to distribute sample copies for advertising purposes—all at the low postage rate. When the wrangling over these proposals stopped late in the summer of 1879 and the bill had passed through a metamorphosis peculiar to Congress, only the provision for registration was eliminated because some in Congress thought it would lead to censorship. Others believed it would create a privileged status for urban periodicals.[20]

Once again, however, the law was not the extent of Congress's generosity to the publishing industry. Taking advantage of a movement in the early 1880s to reduce letter postage from 3 to 2 cents, Congress began toying with the idea of abolishing postage on second-class matter altogether, as it had done for weeklies circulating in counties of publication. President Arthur's postmaster T. O. Howe favored that, but the idea was too generous for even a Congress anxious to please the press. Instead, convinced by publishers' friends in Congress that the postage rate on publications was an unfair tax to be paid as a price of doing business—and amid paeans of praise for the press, that "greatest of educators"—Congress quietly reduced postage on second-class matter to 1 cent a pound in 1885. It was exactly the rate for which publishers had asked twelve years before and the acme of Congress's support for the press.[21]

Inevitably, cheap postage laws, expanding postal service, fast mail trains, and competition encouraged the proliferation of Sunday newspapers. Even the New York *Tribune,* long a holdout, began publishing on Sundays in 1879 after its publisher, Whitelaw Reid, discovered that his efforts to set "a noble example for observance of the Sabbath" had only resulted in readers subscribing to another newspaper. Although late in the field, the *Tribune* lost no time in meeting its competition. By 1883, in the absence of a mail train to the summer resorts of Saratoga and Newport, managers of the newspaper were employing a special train to take their Sunday papers there. They would beat the competition and satisfy the American public's nearly insatiable appetite for Sunday newspapers.[22]

Other than its day of publication, the *Tribune,* like most other Sunday newspapers of the 1880s and 1890s, no more resembled that of 1870 than rural weeklies resembled urban dailies. Over the years it had grown to twenty-five pages or more. Thanks to the postal law of 1879 publishers were permitted, without extra cost, to divide those pages into supplements, which, taken together, contained something of interest for virtually every family member. Endlessly fascinating and titillating and novel as electricity, Sunday newspapers of the 1880s had become habit-forming, and thousands of American families looked forward to them. "The family appetite for the newspaper," wrote a journalist in 1886, "is at no time so keen or so universal as on Sunday morning, when all the household has time to bestow upon it its perusal and when the plans for the coming week both for business and pleasure are determined by the contents of the paper."[23]

Ministers of the old faith and their followers, those who longingly hoped to preserve what they believed was the Christian nation of their ancestors, watched the growth of Sunday newspapers as if it were a cancerous tumor rapidly destroying the tissues that held society together. The Sunday newspaper was one more cross to bear for those already beset by decreasing church attendance and the undermining of faith by science, biblical criticism, and spokespersons for variations of a new theology. Sunday newspapers cluttered the minds of worshipers, who read of everyday concerns before church, and replaced Christian publications as the preferred reading material on Sabbath afternoons. They not only profaned the Sabbath but also competed with Protestant ministers for souls.[24]

Ironically, the Christian press had been partly responsible for the laws that made Sunday newspapers ubiquitous. Like other publishers, they, too, needed the postal system to spread the Christian message. Representatives of such publications as the New York *Evangelist* and the *Christian Union,* in addition to the American Tract Society, had helped fashion laws that established the pound postage system and equalized rates between newspapers and periodicals. The religious press had flourished under those laws. For years the *Christian Herald and Signs of Our Times,* among many others, was replete with new sermons, brief news dispatches from which moral lessons could be drawn, and biographies of outstanding Christians—all designed "to make known the way of salvation and to keep alive the expectation of our Lord's return to earth." They were mailed at midweek as second-class material at the New York City post office to hundreds of the faithful for $1.50 a year and to newsdealers everywhere. But the *Christian Herald* was no match for the Sunday newspaper. Neither was the *Christian Union,* which had a "Sunday Afternoon" column filled with Bible lessons for adults, younger people, and children. *"Harper's Weekly* and *The Christian Union* lie together on the parlor table," the *Christian Union* reported in 1879, "and the Puritan glances at [Thomas] Nast's caricature before he takes up the *Union*'s religious editorial"—if, indeed, he took it up at all.[25]

Sunday newspapers were doing more than superseding religious weeklies. Steadily, almost stealthily, and through an expanding postal service they brought an alien urban culture into American homes, displacing the older rural folkways in which evangelicals' Christianity was rooted and confronting them each week with clashing moral values. To say, as a journalist did in 1886, that Sunday newspapers jarred "upon the convictions of those who still adhere to the ways of their fathers" failed to capture the depth of concern. As children of the Puritan way, evangelicals were acquainted with sin and its manifestations as revealed in even rural weeklies, but they were scarcely prepared for the messages of urban culture they found in Sunday newspapers. Columns devoted to drama and the adulation of actors and actresses, in addition to sports pages, women's pages, hundreds of columns of advertisements (including those of dresses "fashioned in infidel France"), and revelations of the ways of the rich and the conditions of the poor all reflected overpowering materialism. Such information was new and shocking, no doubt even titillating, to evangelicals who regarded the theater as the devil's workshop and looked askance on the emphasis on women's fashions, Sunday baseball, and the Sunday sports page.[26]

Worse still, the great urban Sunday newspapers were, like dailies, filled with sensational stories of city life. The columns of gossip, the gory details of murder, the intimate particulars of seduction and divorce, the casual accounts of suicides, and the lurid depictions of gambling halls, saloons, and dens of vice were as stabs to the hearts of evangelicals hoping to preserve a Christian nation. "The agency of the reputable press, in spreading intelligence and enlightening and guiding public sentiment, is thankfully recognized by the wisest men," commented the *Christian Union* in 1885, "but the agency of the satanic press, in spreading the germs of vice and crime and in misleading and debauching public opinion and public morality, fills the mind of thoughtful observers with horror and alarm."[27]

Nothing disturbed evangelical values more than Sunday newspapers' stories of seduction, adultery, and divorce. Members of the National Reform Association were especially dismayed by such reports. Pledged to secure "the Purity and Permanence of the family," they had worked for years for a national divorce law that might make divorces more difficult to obtain, thus reducing their numbers and protecting traditional family structure. Now they saw their efforts being undercut by the sensational stories of stolen love and family breakups glamorized in Sunday newspapers.[28]

As with stories of crime, it was not enough for reporters to fill Sunday newspapers with the facts of each seduction. They must instead embellish every story with sordid details. "Every divorce case before the courts," the *Christian Union* noted in 1885, "every case of domestic infidelity, every case of common scandal, is rehearsed with the utmost fullness. Every salacious incident is deftly woven in to make the story as delectable as possible to the class of readers for whom it is prepared."[29] What concerned the *Christian Union,* and in fact the majority of evangelicals, was the effect that would have on the nation's young people. "There is little profit," continued the *Christian Union,* "in keeping our young people out of vile houses and away from disreputable characters if we bring such newspapers into our homes and suffer them to spread before our children these pictures." There were few cities, it surmised, in which directories of houses of ill-repute could not be obtained from newspaper columns. In addition, more than half of the daily newspapers in the country were "wholly unfit, by reason of their circumstantial reports of vice and crime, to be admitted to any family."

In the early 1870s, when Sunday editions were taking shape, publishers had been careful to include religious columns in them. But, indicative of the waning Christian fervor, these had been reduced in the 1880s to little more than tokens. A survey of New York Sunday newspapers for December 9, 1888, revealed that the New York *Tribune* had eighty-one columns on gossip and political, social, sensational, and criminal issues and only three-fourths of a column on religion. The material in the others was roughly the same. The *Times* and the *World* devoted the least space to religion, and the *Sun* gave the most, a column and a half. "O for a breath of the old Puritanism!" one minister proclaimed. "I believe his Sabbath was a little too grim. But what men it made! Men of the martyr spirit. Men of heroic mould. . . . You could trust them, lean on them, depend on them."[30]

Nor did the worldly contents of Sunday newspapers improve with age as some supporters prophesied they would. One optimistic journalist, writing for *Forum Magazine* in 1886, speculated that the day would come when Sunday newspapers would "be regarded as the adjunct, the complement, the extension of the Christian Church into society at large." Seven years later, however, another journalist in the same periodical found that the contents of Sunday newspapers had grown more secular. Comparing the Sunday editions of the New York *Tribune, World, Times,* and *Sun* between April 17, 1881, and April 16, 1893, he discovered four and a half columns of gossip in 1881 but 116 and one-quarter in 1893 in addition to seven and a half columns of scandal. On the first page of the *Sun* on that Sunday morning in April 1893 were accounts of an English nobleman's alleged indecent assault, a woman whose lover had made her drunk, a barkeeper's wife's attack in the streets upon her husband's mistress, and one story the like of which the journalist believed had never been printed in a respectable newspaper.[31]

These lurid stories of urban life revealed violations of all ten commandments and were offensive enough to evangelicals trying to conserve biblical morality in the daily press. Their appearance in the Sunday morning newspaper, which was already profaning the Lord's Day with its publication, seemed almost blasphemous. Small wonder then that evangelicals, so strongly committed to the old ways, struck out at Sunday newspapers from the pulpit and podium as well as in the press. Accusing Sunday newspapers of monstrous evils, they urged their congregations not to read or purchase them. In Cleveland in 1886, a ministers' alliance urged Christians to refuse to advertise in newspapers that continued with Sunday editions. Moreover, at its convention in 1889 the National Reform Association produced a resolution appealing to publishers of Sunday newspapers "as patriots and lovers of humanity to cease their publications" on the Lord's Day.[32]

Such appeals were like asking rivers to flow backward. Sunday newspapers, subsidized and spread across the country by the government's mail service, were immensely profitable and popular, and their publishers seemed untroubled by the possible evil effects that their stories of divorce, or accounts of murder, rape, and other crimes, might have upon the nation's youth or family structure. The New York *Times* mocked the Cleveland ministers' efforts and remarked that they were either insincere or more impractical and "out of touch with the facts of the case than clergymen usually are when they take excursions into the field of secular agitation." The *Times* recognized that people in small communities could still lose caste if they acted on Sundays as they did on other days. "But," it added. "this sentiment does not extend to Sunday papers," and it warned that the "admirers of the Puritan Sabbath should not push its observance too far."[33]

Defenders of Sunday newspapers, including a Chicago minister who scorned his counterparts for having small minds and fearing competition, argued that evangelicals did not understand that newspapers were supposed to print news and could not always print exalted themes lest they lose their audiences. The public, he said, demanded exciting stories. The Chicago *Daily News,* not altogether unfamiliar with sensationalism itself, understood that. "'The Sunday paper,'" it reported in 1884, "'itself has created the only demand there is for it. It is made the vehicle for gossip, choice pieces of scandal, stories, and the like which fill its columns, and it is purchased and read because of these features. A Sunday paper in Chicago containing matter that was proper and suitable for Sunday reading would not find a hundred purchasers in the city.'"[34]

The only New York city newspaper bold enough to test the proposition that readers demanded sensation was Elliott Shepard's *Mail and Express,* which took a lofty moral tone and printed news without the lurid details that characterized other newspapers' reporting. The New York *Times* scoffed at the attempt of this "esteemed" and "good-text editor" to "evangelize the secular press by force of example." Yet in spite of the jeers of rival editors the *Mail and Express*'s circulation was at least enough to keep it alive, suggesting a steady market for those who shunned lurid journalism. Even so, it was not clear that those who read the *Mail and Express* read no other newspaper. Shepard was president of the American Sabbath Union, and the *Mail and Express* did not, of course, appear on Sundays, but it is likely that many, if not most, who read it also read a Sunday newspaper.[35]

Those readers, however, would scarcely have made some of the claims that their defenders did. As the evangelical attack on Sunday newspapers became more strident in 1888, for example, a secularist lawyer in Chicago declared that the newspapers' "moral teachings have superseded that of the pulpit." Far from influencing the young to stray into evil paths, newspaper stories taught the dreadful consequences of crime and ill-advised marriage. "It sways people," the orator continued, "not indeed with torture and persecution and burnings but through the spirit of rationalism," and it, not the churches, should be exempt from taxation.[36]

Publishers, of course, believed they had not only a right but also a duty to publish news in any way they saw fit. Nor would they brook any effort to "improve" their newspapers as some defenders delicately hoped they would. They had, after all, the constitutional right of freedom of the press. At an 1888 Milwaukee conference on the freedom of the press Charles A. Dana, once an important figure in the Lincoln administration and editor of the New York *Sun,* told a cheering, laughing crowd of newspapermen that "whatever Divine Providence permitted to occur he was not too proud to report," which obviously relieved him of the responsibility of what was reported in his newspaper.[37]

Thus, unrestrained and made ever more profitable by the insatiable American appetite for the salacious, Sunday newspapers expanded their markets as the postal service expanded, hastening the day when, according to A. T. Stevenson, secretary of the National Reform Association, the Christian religion itself would be overthrown. "As public sentiment learns to tolerate and to demand this supply of secular reading on the Sabbath," he wrote in 1885, "all the instruments of diffusing it will be enlarged and extended. The number of post offices permitted to remain closed on the Sabbath will steadily diminish. The number of persons who will consent to receive, or will demand, their mail on the Sabbath, will continually increase. The demand of the delivery of letters from house to house in cities on the Sabbath will be renewed and granted. Stores and counting-rooms will gradually be thrown open that the letters thus delivered may be received and answered. Open for this purpose, other business will be transacted. . . . Merchants who would prefer to respect the Sabbath will grow restive under the seeming advantages gained by conscienceless competitors."[38]

But there was an even greater price to be paid for the Sunday newspaper. "Christian principle," the secretary continued, "weakened by small concessions and undermined by treacherous currents on every side, will gradually cease its resistance . . . ; and the Sabbath of the Lord . . . whose due observance is the chief pillar of national virtue and welfare, will to all appearances be lost in a rising tide of lust for pleasure and lust for gain. With the loss of the Sabbath religion will perish. . . . Infidelity and irreligion will sweep over the land; churches will be neglected . . . ; the children of those who throng our sanctuaries to-day will become infidels and worldlings; our schools and colleges perverted to secular education, will be seminaries of atheism; and only as she is scourged back to God and to duty by terrible judgments, can it be hoped that the nation will recover the advantage which to-day she is so wantonly casting away."[39]

Many shared Stevenson's apocalyptic vision, including those who had labored so hard for a national "day of rest." Virtually all believed that a rejection of God's laws spelled doom for the nation. For the most dedicated at least, it was not such a far step from the publication and distribution of Sunday newspapers to the nation's downfall. In the spring of 1889, then, their only hope of saving the nation appeared to rest upon enactment of the national day of rest bill pending in Congress. That alone, they believed, could end the government's profanation of the Sabbath, provide a day of rest for workers, silence Sunday mail trains, and, above all, stop the spread, if not the publication, of Sunday newspapers.

Meanwhile, the Senate had been slow to take up Sen. Henry Blair of New Hampshire's "day of rest" bill. It was the short session of Congress, and the Senate had busied itself with appropriation and private pension bills. It was still engaged in these and sundry matters on Saturday, March 2, 1889, when the session technically came to an end. Their business unfinished, however, senators met the next day to act upon the remaining agenda, including the Blair bill, which had not been recommended by Blair's Committee on Labor and Education and, indeed, was apparently supported by Blair alone.[40]

The scene in the Senate on the evening the Blair bill was finally brought forward was chaotic and even disgraceful. It was a Sunday, not the day evangelicals would have wished for the Senate to consider their bill. A large crowd had packed the gallery and watched amusedly as the Senate hurried through its business. Once, when a senator presented two petitions, one for and one against the passage of the day of rest bill into law, a ripple of laughter wafted among the spectators. At several points the proceedings were interrupted by Harrison Riddleberger of Virginia, who was inebriated and disruptive and at last had to be whisked from the chamber by the sergeant-at-arms and an assistant. Then, finding a moment when there was nothing before the Senate, Oregon's Joseph Dolph moved that the Committee of Education and Labor be discharged from further consideration of the Blair bill. Dryly, George Hoar of Massachusetts observed that it clearly was "not proper to work upon that subject on Sunday" and objected to Dolph's motion on the ground that Senate rules required such motions to lie over one day. The Senate president pro tempore agreed and announced that "the motion would go over," presumably to the next day.[41] But there was no next day, as all knew there would not be. The Senate would not meet again that session, and the day of rest bill in which so many had invested so much was ignominiously abandoned with no voice raised in its defense.

The Senate's contemptuous rejection of the Blair bill was a devastating blow to the evangelicals' Sabbatarian crusade for a day of rest, and they never really recovered. Wilbur Crafts, ever the optimist and perhaps believing that the incoming Republican administration would be more sympathetic to the cause, told some of the disheartened that the Sabbath bill would have good chance of passing in the next Congress. But that was not to be. Senator Blair did reintroduce it, and a similar bill was submitted to the House of Representatives. Yet in spite of another huge outpouring of supporting petitions no action was taken on either bill.[42]

Sadly, their failure was followed by a demoralizing rift in the American Sabbath Union at the organization's convention in December 1890. Unable to work with the president, Elliott Shepard, Wilbur Crafts resigned his secretary's post in April of that year and went to the convention determined to defeat Shepard's reelection. Claiming that Shepard was forcing him out of the Union he had created, Crafts scattered fliers among the delegates. Shepard, he charged, dominated the organization by undemocratic means, and the *Mail and Express* monopolized the Union's literature.[43]

Congress's rejection of the Sabbath bill may have been the real cause of the dissension, or perhaps it was the clash of two ego-driven men who could not abide one another. The New York *Times* blamed Shepard. It headlined its story "Disgraceful Political Methods Introduced into a Religions Convention" and accused Shepard of using his money to buy the presidency. However it occurred, Shepard was reelected president, but the organization's effectiveness was diminished.[44]

Even had there been no split in the American Sabbath Union it would have made no difference in the outcome. It seemed clear that the nation, although a moral majority of evangelicals supported the Sabbath bill, had moved too far from its Puritan roots to accept a law depriving people of Sunday mail and newspapers. Arrayed against the bill were not only Seventh Day Adventists and secularists but also railroad managers, saloonkeepers, steamboat companies, and liberty leagues. The leagues were composed in part of people of foreign birth, and they wanted saloons exempted from any Sabbath law. The strongest foes of all were the editors of Sunday newspapers. "Never in the world," a minister remarked after the bill's failure, "was such a scepter of power placed within hands of an individual as is wielded by the editor of one of our leading papers." Josephine Bateham, superintendent of the WCTU Sabbath Department, had foreseen such opposition long before the bill's defeat. "As nearly all of the large dailies publish a Sunday edition," she had remarked, "greatly to the damage of public morals, and derive therefrom their greatest income, they are expected to throw their whole influence against any law which would prevent their publishing or circulating such edition."[45]

Neither churchgoers nor ministers, those who had actually been opposed to the bill and those who were indifferent, were blameless in the eyes of people who had fought the battle. "The guilt of the Government and of the people in either requiring or tolerating this wholesale Sabbath-breaking institution, the Post Office Department," wrote a disappointed Sabbatarian, "is as great as the Sunday mail is unnecessary. And if the church is the light of the world, what shall we say of those church members who patronize the post office on the Sabbath, and who help the government in its work of demoralizing the masses and grinding down its vast array of employees to restless toil? Will not God avenge the wrong?"[46]

The foes of a Sunday day of rest reflected the ever-increasing secularization and urbanization of American society, and no number of petitions could change that fact. Even the incoming Harrison administration, which was sympathetic to the Sabbatarians, could not alter such realities. Nevertheless, Harrison, to the delight of evangelicals, had appointed John Wanamaker, founder of the great Wanamaker department store in Philadelphia, as postmaster general. This imaginative man, perhaps the nation's most aggressive postmaster general, was a devout Presbyterian and a Sunday school teacher whose contributions to the Harrison campaign (allegedly corruptly used) evangelicals were willing to overlook in their joy over his sympathy for their cause. Indeed, he was sympathetic. He was the first postmaster general to mention Sunday mail in his report to the president. "The Government," he remarked in 1889, "should, as far as possible, make no requirements which will prohibit its employes [*sic*] from the enjoyment of a day of rest." He promised to "make use of all proper means tending toward the minimizing of post-office work upon Sunday."[47]

To make good on his promise, he sent a letter to the postmasters of the nation's hundred largest post offices and asked that they record the amount of work done in their offices on Sundays compared to other days. Summed up, the postmasters' reports disclosed that the sale of stamps on Sundays, as well as the number of people who called for mail on that day, was small. But, they agreed, as long as railroads brought mail on Sundays it would either have to be handled or allowed to accumulate until Mondays, when sorting and distribution would cause derangement of business.[48]

The report was less than helpful to the evangelicals, but Wanamaker promised further study of the problem. In the meantime, in June 1889, he closed Post Office Department offices in Washington on Sundays, where so many had worked for so long on that day to catch up on back work. He tried, too, to reduce the hours all postal employees worked. In the end, however, he found it impossible to stop transportation of mail on Sundays. "It is wholly impractical," he wrote in his final report to the president in 1892, "with the mails in transit from the beginning of the year to the end of it, by day and night, on lands and sea, starting every hour from points thousands of miles apart, to stop, at 12 o'clock midnight on Saturday night, all work for twenty-four hours, then start again."[49]

Wanamaker did suggest, however, that it would be possible for local communities, if they voted to do so, to close their post offices on Sundays and require railroads to hold their mail for that day. Perhaps that option would have been a workable solution to the problem in the antebellum period, but in the 1890s the patrons of small-town and village post offices were apparently more interested in receiving their Sunday newspapers than in closing post offices.

That became clear early in the next century when Congress once more considered a proposal to close post offices on Sundays. Although supported by a new Sabbatarian organization called the Lord's Day Alliance and remnants of the day of rest battle, the proposal was initiated by urban members of Congress anxious to secure a day of rest for city postal clerks whose hours of labor, unlike those of city mail carriers, were largely unregulated. Indeed, in 1911 the postmaster general was not even enforcing a law of that year intended to award them compensatory time off when they were forced to work on Sundays. Frustrated by the department's evasion of the law and pressured by clerks to do something, the next year legislators from cities proposed closing all post offices on Sundays as the surest way to secure a day of rest for postal clerks.[50]

Ironically, their proposal was opposed by those who represented the rural districts that had once been strongholds of Sabbatarianism. To close post offices on Sundays, said one member of Congress, would raise "a howl of discontent going up all over the land," primarily because in the country it would mean the loss of the Sunday newspaper. Unlike in cities, where newspapers had their own delivery systems, Sunday newspapers were still being mailed to post offices in small towns and hamlets, and subscribers would pick them up on Sunday mornings. "We all know," an Illinois legislator explained, "that the news on Sunday is as eagerly sought on that day as it is on any other day. It is sought by the layman in the cross-roads district the same as it is by the politicians or the professional aristocrat, and to close the mails all day on Sunday . . . in my opinion, is very unwise."[51]

In the end, Congress compromised, as it did so often on postal conflicts between rural and urban interests. It stipulated that only urban post offices of first and second class would be closed on Sundays for mail delivery. Third- and fourth-class post offices, usually located in rural areas, would remain open to ensure that country people could receive the newspapers that for so long had disturbed the Sabbath.[52]

The settlement, which became effective August 24, 1912, pleased those in small-town America who were accustomed to stroll down Main Street on quiet Sunday mornings to retrieve newspapers from post office boxes. But it was a grievous blow to urban newspaper publishers, who saw in it a threat to Sunday deliveries to larger, third-class post offices. Unaccustomed to postal laws inimical to their interests, they vented their wrath against what they called this "backwoods legislation," this "Puritanic labor law" that had been surreptitiously "snooped in to the appropriation bill in the closing days of Congress."[53]

Publishers neither knew nor cared that Congress had used precisely the same maneuver in 1810 to open post offices on Sundays. What mattered to them was continuation of the old postal service through which they could send Sunday newspapers, and that they received. By loosely interpreting the law, an accommodating postmaster general permitted newspapers and the mail of special groups to be delivered from even first- and second-class post offices on Sundays as always.[54]

The Independent, that enduring Christian weekly, had favored the new law because it provided a needed day of rest for hard-pressed postal workers. At the same time, it recognized that the law was not made to protect the Christian Sabbath, for the United States was not a Christian nation. "Politically ours is not a Christian nation," ran the editorial, "nor a Jewish, nor a Mohammedon country although by the preponderance of religious faith we are Christian." It was a fact often repeated by infidels and liberal Christians alike throughout the nineteenth century and as often rejected by evangelicals who yearned to force their government to reflect the nation's Christian roots by not only terminating Sunday mail but also by eradicating the prurient publications that the swiftly spreading postal network was pouring into American homes.[55]

Notes

1. *Christian Statesman* (Philadelphia), Sept. 6, 1888, 6.
2. "Sunday Rest Bill," S. Misc. Doc. no. 43, 50th Cong., 2d sess., 34 (Jan. 17, 1889) (hereafter "Day of Rest").
3. On the development of Bennett's New York *Herald,* see James L. Crouthemel, *Bennett's New York* Herald *and the Rise of the Popular Press* (Syracuse, 1989), ch. 2; on the

"moral war," see Oliver Carson, *The Man Who Made News: James Gordon Bennett* (New York, 1942), 184–90; on Sunday newspapers to 1870, see Aldred McClung Lee, *The Daily Newspaper in America: The Evolution of a Social Instrument* (New York, 1937,) 376–80, 391–400, and Frank Luther Mott, *American Journalism: A History,* 3d ed. (New York, 1962), 318, 397, 480–82.

4. Mott, *American Journalism,* 480–81; Lee, *The Daily Newspaper,* 393–94.

5. On the development of the urban press, see Mott, *American Journalism,* ch. 30.

6. *United States Statutes at Large* (Boston, 1845), 1:238. Postal workers carried newspapers outside the mail before 1792. Postage rates from 1789 to 1876 may be found in "A Compilation of the Laws of the United States, Showing the Changes in the 'Domestic Rates of Postage etc.,'" S. Misc. Doc. no. 88, 44th Cong., 1st sess., 3 (Apr. 3, 1876) (hereafter "A Compilation of the Laws").

7. *A Compendium of the Ninth Census* (Washington, 1872), 510.

8. *American State Papers: Post Office Department, 1789–1833* (Washington, 1834), no. 120, 347–48.

9. *Congressional Globe,* 31st Cong., 2d sess., 74 (Dec. 18, 1850).

10. *United States Statutes at Large* (Boston, 1850), 9:587–91; *United States Statutes at Large* (Boston, 1855), 10:30–40; *United States Statutes at Large* (Boston, 1863), 12:701–9; see also *Congressional Record,* 41st Cong., 1st sess., 5207 (June 19, 1874).

11. *Congressional Record,* 41st Cong., 1st sess., 4659–60 (June 6, 1874). These figures are estimates at best and vary from report to report. See "Transmission of the Mails and Revenues Derived Therefrom," S. Misc. Doc. no. 98, 43d Cong., 1st sess., 1–2 (Apr. 16, 1874); see also New York *Times,* Apr. 17, 1874. 1.

12. *Report of the Postmaster General, 1873,* xxi–xxii (this and subsequent citations to postmasters general reports can be found in the *Congressional Information Service Serial Set Index* [Washington, 1997]).

13. "A Uniform Rate of Postage on Newspapers, etc.," H. Misc. Doc. no 287, 43d Cong., 1st sess., 1 (June 4, 1874) (hereafter "Uniform Rates of Postage on Newspapers").

14. *Congressional Record,* 43d Cong., 1st sess., 4659 (June 6, 1874); *Congressional Record,* 43d Cong., 1st sess., 5027 (June 16, 1874).

15. For the publishers' petition, see "Uniform Rates of Postage on Newspapers"; Chicago *Tribune,* June 20, 1874, 6 (quotation). Two years later, when the postal deficit had reached $6 million, Sherman again flailed at the newspapers. "Is there such a fear of the newspaper, that we fear to do what is right?" he asked. *Congressional Record,* 44th Cong., 1st sess., 3712 (June 9, 1876).

16. "A Compilation of the Laws," 25–26. The struggle over the reconciliation of the postage rate between the House and Senate may be found in *Congressional Record,* 44th Cong., 1st sess., 3720–21 (June 9, 1876).

17. *Report of the Postmaster General, 1875,* 19–20. Such was the accumulation of New York newspapers in New York City by 1873 that postal officials, with the urging of publishers, established a fast train from New York to Chicago in 1875 to carry nothing but mail. Although the New York *Times* assured readers that the experiment "was not gotten up in the interests of newspapers," the 633 canvas bags filled with newspapers aboard the train, the train's departure at four in the morning to ensure morning editions a place onboard, and the New York publishers who accompanied the train belied the headlines. In spite of the great opposition of the rest of the country to the appropriation for the fast train, which eventually ran only along the eastern seaboard, it con-

tinued through the century, a witness to the power of the eastern press. *Report of the Postmaster General, 1874,* 207–8; see also "History of the Railway Mails," S. Exec. Doc. no. 40, 48th Cong., 2d sess., 100 (Feb. 6, 1885).

18. *Report of the Postmaster General, 1878,* 51–53; see also *Harper's Weekly,* Feb. 15, 1879.

19. *Congressional Record,* 45th Cong., 3d sess., 2135 (Feb. 28, 1879); on Waddell, see *Dictionary of American Biography* (Washington, 1932), 10:301 (hereafter *DAB*); on Money, see *DAB* (Washington, 1934), 7:85–86.

20. *Congressional Record,* 45th Cong., 3d sess., 2136–37 (Feb. 28, 1879); *United States Statutes at Large* (Washington, 1879), 20:359; see also New York *Times,* Jan. 5, 1878, 8. In the place of actual registration, local postmasters were to determine a publication's eligibility for second-class privilege, which was not much different than registration. Determination of eligibility was later determined in Washington after pertinent documents were received from local postmasters.

21. *Congressional Record,* 47th Cong., 2d sess., 332–32 (Dec. 15, 1882), *Congressional Record,* 47th Cong., 2d sess., 383 (Dec. 16, 1882); *Congressional Record,* 48th Cong., 2d sess., 1438 (Feb. 7, 1885); see also *United States Statutes at Large* (Washington, 1885), 23:387.

22. For the quotation, see James Melvin Lee, *History of American Journalism* (New York, 1917), 380; see also "Day of Rest," 34, and *Christian Union,* Dec. 10, 1879, 486.

23. James Parton, "Newspapers Gone to Seed," *The Forum* 1 (Mar. 1886): 18.

24. Chicago *Tribune,* Dec. 10, 1888, 2; J. H. Ward, "The Future of Sunday Journalism," *The Forum* 1 (June 1886): 389. On the effect of science on the religious, see James Turner, *Without God, without Creed* (Baltimore, 1985), 116–26.

25. For Christian publishers' support of the pound postage laws, see "Uniform Rates of Postage on Newspapers," 1; *Report of the Postmaster General, 1878,* 51; and New York *Times,* Oct. 10, 1878. See also *Christian Statesman,* July 11, 1889, 6; *Christian Union,* Sept. 10, 1879, 202; and *Christian Herald and Signs of Our Times,* May 27, 1880, 344.

26. For a minister's comment on dresses fashioned in France, see Chicago *Tribune,* Sept. 23, 1888, 3; on materialism, see Josiah Strong, *Our Country* (Cambridge, 1963), 160–70; for the opinion of a Presbyterian minister in 1889 concerning the theater, see *The Nation,* Mar. 14, 1889, 218. See also Joseph Leeds, *The Case of a Friend of the Commonwealth versus the Sunday Newspaper: With Special Relation to the Pubic Ledger* (Philadelphia, 1902) for a comment upon the contents of the Sunday edition of the Philadelphia *Public Ledger* when it began issuing a Sunday edition in 1902. Of particular interest for insights into the urban newspaper and urban culture, see Gunther Barth, *City People: The Rise of Modern City Culture in Nineteenth-Century America* (New York 1980), ch. 3. For the quotation, see Ward, "Future of Sunday Journalism," 389.

27. *Christian Union,* Jan. 8, 1885, 3.

28. David McAllister, *The National Reform Movement: Its History and Principles, a Manual of Christian Civil Government* (Philadelphia, 1890), 31.

29. *Christian Union,* Jan. 8, 1885, 3.

30. *Christian Statesman,* Mar. 27, 1889, 8.

31. Ward, "Future of Sunday Journalism," 358; Gilmer Speed, "Do Newspapers Give the News?" *The Forum* 14 (Aug. 1893): 707–9.

32. New York *Times,* Apr. 25, 1886, 8; *Christian Statesman,* May, 2, 1889, 3.

33. New York *Times,* Apr. 25, 1886, 8.

34. C. R. Miller, "A Word to Critics of Newspapers," *The Forum* 15 (Aug. 1893): 716; Chicago *Daily News,* as quoted in Wilbur F. Crafts, *The Sabbath for Man: A Study of the Origin, Obligation, History, Advantages, and Present State of Sabbath Observance with Special Reference to the Rights of Workingmen* (New York, 1892), 325.

35. New York *Times,* Apr. 30, 1888, 5, Dec. 26, 1888, 4, May 18, 1889, 4; Mott, *American Journalism,* 374, 449.

36. Chicago *Tribune,* Dec. 24, 1888, 8.

37. Chicago *Tribune,* July 25, 1888, 5 (quotation), Dec. 14, 1888.

38. "Day of Rest," 35.

39. Ibid.

40. None of the committee members who sat in on hearings for the bill appeared to favor it. Some, like Senator Payne of Ohio, were closely allied with big business and perhaps all felt the pressure of newspapers. Only James Wilson of Iowa, a well-known advocate of prohibition and Christian causes, might have been sympathetic, but he, too, supported the railroads.

41. *Congressional Record,* 50th Cong., 2d sess., 831, 2639–40 (Jan. 16, 1889); *Congressional Record,* 50th Cong., 2d sess., 2640 (Mar. 2, 1889). The correct date would be March 3, but the *Congressional Record* gives March 2 (see also *Christian Statesman,* Mar. 14, 1889, 2, and New York *Times,* Mar. 9, 1889, 1).

42. *Christian Statesman,* Mar. 7, 1889, 7; *Congressional Record,* 51st Cong., 1st sess. (1894–95), index (under "Blair").

43. New York *Times,* Dec. 9, 1890, 1.

44. Ibid.

45. *Christian Statesman,* Aug. 29, 1889 4. For Josephine Bateham's comment, see "Day of Rest," 23–24.

46. *Christian Statesman,* July 11, 1889, 6.

47. *Christian Statesman,* Jan. 3, 1889, 1, and Jan. 31, 1889, 1; *Report of the Postmaster General, 1889,* 23.

48. *Report of the Postmaster General, 1889,* 23.

49. *Report of the Postmaster General, 1892,* 60.

50. For the postal clerk law of 1911, see *United States Statutes at Large* (Washington, 1911), 36, 1339. A summary of the compensatory time problem and the amendment to the post office appropriation bill for 1913 providing for closing post offices on Sundays are in *Congressional Record,* 62d Cong., 2d sess., 4658 68 (Apr. 12, 1912); *Congressional Record,* 62d Cong., 2d sess., 4888 (Apr. 16, 1912). On the role of the Lord's Day Alliance, see "Sunday Postal Law," *The Independent,* Sept. 5, 1912, 573.

51. *Congressional Record,* 62d Cong., 2d sess., 4888–89 (Apr. 16, 1912).

52. *United States Statutes at Large* (Washington, 1913), 37, pt. 1, 543.

53. "Sunday Mail," *Literary Digest,* Sept. 7, 1912, 356.

54. *Report of the Postmaster General, 1912,* 13–14; New York *Times,* Sept. 1, 1912, 10. Although most third- and fourth-class post offices were to remain open on Sundays, the old regulations survived that provided they need not do so if mail did not arrive after closing on Saturdays or before 6 P.M. on Sundays.

55. *The Independent,* Sept. 5, 1912, 575.

5 The Post Office, Protestants, and Pornography in the Gilded Age

Put to death, therefore, what is earthly in you: fornication, impurity, passion, evil desire, and covetousness, which is idolatry.

—Colossians 3:5

Deborah Leeds, superintendent of the Department for the Suppression of Impure Literature of the Women's Christian Temperance Union, struck a discouraging note in her report of 1888. She had undertaken the task of ridding the country and the mails of impure literature for the Woman's Christian Temperance Union, and she was finding it difficult to find helpers. Few, she said, wanted to become involved in this work because of the "exceeding repulsiveness of some of its aspects" so that "our lips be dumb when we ought to speak and we become unfaithful."[1]

Her work did have repulsive aspects, it was true, especially for women of the Gilded Age. For many men, too, the work was too odious to discuss. Still, notwithstanding her complaint there were those, even some like herself, in that post–Civil War period who felt compelled to speak out against it. Indeed, the purification of literature that passed through the mail, like the struggles against Sunday mail and Sunday newspapers, was another of those Herculean tasks born of the improved postal service that evangelical Protestants shouldered in their quest to preserve a Christian nation. In this encounter, however, unlike their crusade to establish a day of rest, an effort that faltered on the constitutional principle of separation of church and state, the Constitution's freedom of the press clause was not allowed to stand in the way of achieving their principal goals.

In the burgeoning mails that the revolution in communications had brought, evangelicals confronted a completely new kind of publication, more satanic and loathsome to them than newspapers with all their sordid stories had ever been. Composed of books, papers, pamphlets, poems, and pictures deliberately designed to be obscene, the new publications, to the horror of evangelicals, had surfaced during the Civil War and were spreading their poison by mail throughout the nation even as the country fought for its life in the 1860s.[2]

Until the expansion of the postal service in the 1850s and 1860s, evangelicals were little troubled by the mailing of obscene publications; their issue was the fight against Sunday mail. True, such material was not unheard of and may have surfaced in the early 1840s. The few states that had laws prohibiting obscene publications pointed to its presence. So did laws that Congress enacted in 1842 and again in 1857 forbidding importation of "indecent and obscene prints, paintings, lithographs, and transparencies" as well as daguerreotypes and certain wooden and metal figures. Not until the Civil War, however, did the postal system become a major conduit for obscenity, much of it so unspeakably depraved by evangelical standards as to strike at the very foundation of Christianity.[3]

Because of the spreading railroad network and the postal reforms of the 1850s and early 1860s, mail was moving more efficiently than ever, and reduced postage rates on printed matter yielded a great rushing river of publications. Briefly put, cheap postage and an expanding, efficient postal service made the trade in obscene literature both profitable and possible. Still, another factor was also responsible for a great outpouring of licentious literature in the 1860s. A market was needed for this kind of material, and it was found among the boys in blue during the Civil War.[4]

The appearance of this literature among the troops made the Union Army something of a battleground between Christian and obscene publications in a contest for the minds of soldiers. "The temptations of the camp are proverbial," wrote a chaplain with the Union troops in New Orleans in 1863. Men succumbed to them, he believed, because they lacked a "fit and healthy stimulus for [their] *minds,"* and he urged people to send the troops good reading material, either by mail or by express.[5]

Evangelicals needed no urging. They were already in the field with an organization called the United States Christian Commission, holding church services, consoling the wounded on battlefields and in hospitals, and delivering thousands of pages of Christian tracts, bibles, and books. By March of 1864 the commission had already delivered a million testaments and as many hymnbooks to soldiers, and it was distributing more than four hundred thousand standard religious publications each month. "The usual baneful influences of war upon the morals of the soldiers, have, by these means," according to *The Independent,* "been greatly mitigated, and the prevalence of profanity, gambling, and debauchery, in many regiments, greatly abated."[6]

Undoubtedly the commission's prayer meetings and church services, as well as the distribution of familiar religious literature, brought comfort to lonely, homesick, and often frightened farm boys far from the religious influences of their homes. But even the optimistic *Independent* could "not say that all, or even a majority have become religious men" through those efforts. In fact, some evidence suggested that if the Christian Commission, for all its mighty work, was not losing, then neither was it winning. The battle continued for the minds of young men being sullied in a swamp of obscene publications circulating among them. Even the famous Ironsides Regiment, the 176th New York, raised by men connected with the New York branch of the Christian Commission and composed of selected Christians, was not, according to one observer, "fully equal to the high standard originally adopted for it."[7]

Details are scant concerning the quantity of obscene publications distributed among soldiers during the war. The numbers were enough, however, to alarm Lincoln's first postmaster general, Montgomery Blair. Alerted to the degrading books and papers circulating to soldiers, Blair, who was deeply religious, had them removed from the mail along with a number of disloyal newspapers.[8] Questioned in 1863 by members of Congress about his authority to do this, Blair cited precedents of censorship that other postmasters general had set over a span of twenty-five years and explained to the House Judiciary Committee that he had used his authority to withdraw both obscene matter and newspapers friendly to the South from the mail. The one was withdrawn for criminal immorality, the other for treason, both being a threat to the safety of the country.[9]

The Judiciary Committee recognized the dangers involved in censorship but agreed that the postmaster general had the right, even the duty, in the absence of congressional legislation on the matter to ban treasonous and obscene publications. Every citizen, the committee argued, had the duty to prevent crimes from being committed. "How, then," it asked, "could the Postmaster General, who, having charge of the mail service of the country, knowingly permit a newspaper, letter, or other message to be carried in the mails, advising and conspiring the destruction of life or property, or knowingly permit the passage of obscene and unlawful publications destructive of public morals?" Certainly, the committee continued, it was his duty to ban these publications from the mail lest the "postal system, established and sustained for the benefit of the people, might be turned into the means of the destruction of life, property, and morals."[10]

Yet obscene publications continued to reach the troops, either because William Dennison, who replaced Blair as postmaster general in 1864, was reluctant to withdraw such material from the mail without the specific approval of Congress or because it was impossible to remove it all. As the war ended obscene publications were still being mailed, prompting Congress, at the request of Postmaster General Dennison, to consider a law permitting postmasters to remove such material from the mail and punish those responsible for them. "It is said," remarked Vermont's Jacob Collamer as he introduced the measure in the Senate early in 1865, "that our mails are made the vehicle for the conveyance of great numbers and quantities of obscene books and pictures, which are sent to the Army, and sent here and there and everywhere, and that it is getting to be a very great evil."[11]

Collamer, who had once been postmaster general himself, approached the Senate and the subject cautiously. He knew how bitterly senators had resented southern postmasters' removal of antislavery papers from the mail and acknowledged at the outset that senators might wish to strike out the section of his proposed legislation allowing postmasters everywhere to disallow obscene publications. This, after some debate, the senators did, but such was their abhorrence of the new kind of literature that no senator rose to object to banning it, whether on constitutional grounds or any other.

Even the problem of determining whether a publication was or was not obscene without opening its wrapper was not allowed to stand in the way of the bill's passage. "I think the prohibition against publications of this character ought to stand," said Ohio's Senator John Sherman. "We are well aware that many of these publications are sent all over the country from the city of New York with the names of the parties sending them on the backs, so that postmasters without opening the mail matter may know that it is offensive matter, indecent and improper to be carried."[12] As a result, Abraham Lincoln, on the eve of his second inaugural, signed the first law prohibiting every "obscene book, pamphlet, picture, print, or other publication of a vulgar or indecent character" from the mail. Violation was a misdemeanor punishable by a $500 fine or imprisonment of not more than one year or both.[13]

Because Congress had provided no specific means of enforcing the law, obscene material continued to be mailed. The trade in indecent literature flourished, especially in New York City where it was centered. There, in the aftermath of the war, its publishers found a new market for their wares among thousands of young men who had taken themselves and their dreams of making a fortune to that bustling city. Far from the restraints of their homes in the country, working at lowly jobs in scores of businesses, living in cheerless boardinghouses, shunning the churches they could not afford to attend, and idling away their Sundays and evening hours, they were susceptible to the overwhelming vices of the city.[14]

In 1866 the enticements for dissipation strewn in their path were prodigious indeed. A survey made that year revealed that more than 181,000 men between the ages of fifteen and forty lived in New York City. Contributing to their downfalls were saloons that housed 653 billiard tables, 7,786 licensed porter houses and bar rooms wherein six hundred barrels of spirits were consumed daily, 223 concert saloons, and thirteen theaters. The saloons employed 1,191 semiclad waitresses, many of them prostitutes, who attracted 29,900 visitors every day. Some visitors, according to the New York *Tribune,* were "men who were not yet totally ruined." Not a few were from "the best, most cultivated, and highest circle of society." In addition, 730 houses of prostitution and "gambling hells" were located within a nest of streets and lured young men into depravity.[15]

Worse still was the incredibly open street sale of obscene books and papers, publications of the kind that would eventually be mailed. "As illustrating the audacity with which this temptation is flaunted in the face of young men, it might be stated that in one place, on a principal thoroughfare, there are openly exposed for sale two vile weekly papers which can be purchased for ten cents a copy, and more than fifty kinds of licentious books, each one illustrated by one or two cuts, at prices ranging from thirty-five to fifty cents, while on each copy there is a catalogue of more than one hundred of the same character. If the purchaser manifests a deep interest in the books for sale, the proprietor will show him a catalogue of large numbers much more vulgar and atrocious, illustrated with the most obscene cuts, from which selections can be made."[16]

The survey was sponsored by the directors of the city's Young Men's Christian Association, founded in 1852, who were, for the most part, men of wealth and position. Like the Sabbatarians, they had migrated to New York City and were imbued with the biblical Puritan values of their youths and a patriotic zeal to preserve a Christian nation. Appalled at the possibilities of young men being lost to drink and dissipation and led to brothels by sordid books and papers, they influenced the New York state legislature in 1868 to prohibit publication and sale of such material. Unwilling to stop with that, four years later the association created the Society for the Suppression of Vice.

Some peddlers of pornography in New York City were arrested under the New York law, although state laws, like state Sabbath laws, were of limited effectiveness. They could no more prevent publishers of obscenity from infecting the nation's morals by mailing their products throughout the country than states could stop the Sunday mail. Congress alone could say what might and might not be mailed, and evangelicals were forced to turn once more to Congress, as they had for a day of rest, for stronger laws to prevent obscene literature from going through the mail, and, it was hoped, help preserve the nation's Christian character. This time, however, they were not to be denied as they had been in previous efforts. Such was the loathing of salacious literature among middle-class Americans in the Gilded Age that the evangelical community, even the part that had refused to support a day of rest law, united to embrace laws against obscenity.[17]

The federal law of 1865 prohibiting mailing obscene literature, enacted when Congress discovered that the nation's soldiers were being inundated with immoral literature, had rarely been enforced. Still, it remained on the books, and when Congress undertook to revise and consolidate all laws relating to the post office in 1872 it was necessary to amend the prohibition law, or to include it in the revision as it was, or to erase it. Unwilling to discuss so nefarious a business as mailing obscene publications, yet aware that it thrived by means of the postal service, Congress with little debate included the law of 1865 in the revision and made one addition. Fearful that some people might use postcards, which it had just authorized, to defame their enemies and send them scurrilous messages visible to all mail-handlers, Congress specified that every postcard or envelope upon which a scurrilous writing or demeaning epithet appeared would, like other obscene writing, be unmailable.[18] Passed in midyear, the act and the previous law became immediately useful to the New York City's YMCA's Society for the Suppression of Vice. The society's agent Anthony Comstock, with the help of the police, was already rounding up purveyors of smut under the state law, and he was more than willing to enforce federal laws.

Anthony Comstock was just twenty-eight when he was appointed an agent of the committee. Born in 1844, he had been shaped by the rigors of life on a Connecticut farm, a devout Christian mother who reared him on stories of biblical heroes, and a lingering Puritan environment in that "Land of Steady Habits," which was one of the earliest participants in the Second Great Awakening. Of powerful, stocky build and five feet ten inches tall at age twenty, he was filled with the patriotic zeal common to his upbringing, and he enlisted in the army, serving in a quiet sector in Florida. Ridiculed for his religious convictions but undaunted, he became a delegate of the Christian Commission and spent much time arranging for chaplains to preach to the soldiers and conducting prayer services himself, although he was ridiculed for his religious convictions. Mustered out in 1865, in 1866 Comstock, like so many other young men from Connecticut, migrated to New York City, where he worked as a clerk in a dry goods store.[19]

In the city, Comstock found all the vices the YMCA survey had reported. Unlike other young men, however, and because of his Christian convictions, he was repelled rather than attracted by the iniquity he saw about him, especially the open trade in obscene literature. Indeed, he appeared to be among the first to understand that new and burgeoning business. "'Early in 1872,'" he wrote, "'the appalling fact was revealed to me that there was an organized business, systematically carried on, where 169 [obscene] books were openly advertised in circulars.'" Comstock rigorously and unapologetically began enforcing the laws against trafficking in obscenity and used the police to make arrests of the offenders he found.[20]

At first he worked on his own, a single, lonely figure securing the arrest of publishers and sellers alike who were growing rich by the trade. But to overcome such a growing business he needed help, and in 1872 he sought the support of the secretary of the New York YMCA. The secretary laid Comstock's letter on his desk, where by chance Morris K. Jesup, then president of the organization, read it, called on Comstock at the store where he worked, and invited him to his Madison Avenue home to discuss the matter.[21]

A wealthy merchant, banker, philanthropist, and devout Christian, Jesup, like Comstock, was originally from Connecticut, that birthplace of Christian reformers. Descended from a long line of Puritan ancestors, he was to become over the course of years vice president of the Evangelical Alliance and president of the American Sunday School Union and the New York Mission and Tract Society. He had also been an organizer of the United States Christian Commission and was, in all probability, familiar with the obscene literature scattered among the troops. He was immediately drawn to Comstock's work and character, and their meeting led to Comstock's appointment as special agent of the YMCA's Society for the Suppression of Vice in 1872. It was also the beginning of a long friendship that lasted until Jesup's death in 1908. He never wavered in his support of Comstock.[22]

Beginning in the spring of 1872 and working under the authority of the YMCA throughout that year, supported by Jesup, who funded much of his work, and by the newly revised postal law, Comstock had by late August caused the arrest forty men who were, as the New York *Times* put it, "sending their vile goods through the mails." One man arrested was Patrick Bannon, who was mailing circulars and cards advertising his obscene publications in a "covert but perfectly comprehensible way" to students, those most susceptible to temptation. He was sentenced to prison for one year or until his fine of $500 was paid.[23]

Comstock's arrests continued through the fall, and by December publishers were beginning to move their businesses to adjoining states. Still, Comstock had already discovered that the law of 1872 was not strong enough to rid the nation of the obscene literature in which New York City was mired. He also knew that publishers were using the mail to disseminate their wares among the young. The law of 1872 did not adequately define obscenity, did not proscribe obscene advertisements among the unmailable items, and did not provide a clear means of enforcement. Discouraged by the weakness of the law but determined to smash the purveyors of unsavory literature, Comstock, at Jesup's expense, went to Washington late in December 1872 and again in early 1873 to impress upon Congress the necessity of enacting a new law, which he had prepared.[24]

It may seem surprising that Comstock, only recently an obscure clerk in a dry goods store, virtually unknown outside of New York City, and with no idea that he would one day slash his way through American life to become famous (or infamous as many thought) should have had the temerity to approach Congress or to believe that he could persuade that body to pass a law which he had a major part in writing. But he was young, still handsome although beginning to bald, and firm enough in his Christian morality to confront Congress single-handedly if need be. In fact, he did not do so alone. He had the invaluable help of a network of like-minded and influential Protestant Puritans, representative of the nation's evangelical moral majority, who remembered their own moral upbringings. In addition to Jesup, he had the support of the members of the YMCA's Society for the Suppression of Vice as well as powerful members of the YMCA's board of directors. Among the latter group was the president of the board, William Earl Dodge, Jr., who had been raised in a religious home. His father, a product of Connecticut's Puritan religiosity, had helped found New York City's YMCA and contributed generously to worthy Christian causes. William Dodge, Jr., continued his father's religious interests and became president of the Evangelical Alliance and vice president of the Sunday School Union.[25]

Beyond that, Comstock had the support of no less a person than William Strong, associate justice of the Supreme Court, who helped him draft the law he presented to Congress. Strong's Christian credentials were unquestioned. Also born in Connecticut and son of a Congregational minister, he was a devout life-long Presbyterian. He had been president of the American Sunday School Union and the American Tract Society and vice president of the American Bible Society. He had also been president of the National Reform Association, which was just then, in February 1873, meeting in New York, where it sought to add a sixteenth amendment to the Constitution to include reference to God and Jesus Christ in the preamble of that document.[26]

Armed with a draft of his bill and an exhibit of obscene books, pamphlets, catalogs, and letters he had seized from their peddlers and publishers, Comstock traveled to Washington in February 1873 because he was determined to secure a law that would banish obscene publications. There, through Strong and A. H. Byington, another friend from Connecticut and editor of the Norwalk *Gazette,* Comstock met a number of important senators. One, William Buckingham, was the former governor of Connecticut and had among his Puritan ancestors the original founders of New Haven and a founder of Yale University. William Windom of Minnesota also promised to support the bill.

Windom, in fact, had already written a bill similar to Comstock's, which he presented to the Senate in February. It was Windom who introduced Comstock to Vice-President Henry Wilson, in whose office Comstock displayed his exhibit and explained the magnitude of the obscenity trade.[27]

In assembling the exhibit Comstock had much from which to choose. In a little more than a year as agent of the YMCA's Society for the Suppression of Vice he had seized more than twelve tons of books and pamphlets, sheets of letter-press, and stereotyping plates for printing presses, much of which he had stored in the American Tract Society Building, an incongruity that could only be explained by the evangelicals' support for Comstock's work. His collection also included more than two hundred thousand obscene items of various kinds, including photographs, rings, watch and knife charms, songs lyrics, catalogs, and playing cards. Only a small part of this could have been in his exhibit, of course, but a representative sample, including at least some of the fifteen thousand letters written by boarding school students of both sexes ordering obscene materials from dealers, made a potent argument for the necessity of a more stringent law against mailing obscene literature.[28]

The men who viewed Comstock's exhibit were not unsophisticated. They were men of the world who understood corruption and human frailty. Even as they spoke with Comstock, they wrestled with the issue of corrupt members of Congress who had, in effect, taken bribes from the construction company that built the Union Pacific Railroad. But Comstock's exhibit revealed corruption of a different kind, the kind that struck at the family, always considered the cornerstone of American Christian civilization. As one member of Congress noted, it "threatened to destroy the future of this Republic by making merchandise of the morals of our youth," and even "the purity and beauty of womanhood has been no protection."[29]

In that era of Protestant dominance the canons governing sexual morality were founded upon biblical authority that condemned all sexual excess, from fornication to adultery and everything in between, violations of which produced a kind of spiritual corruption more difficult than bribery for legislators to touch. They were stunned at the pervasiveness of the obscene publications Comstock's exhibit revealed. "It may well be doubted, Mr. Speaker," remarked New York's Cong. Clinton Merriam, referring to Comstock's collection, "if war, pestilence, or famine could leave deeper or more deadly scars upon a nation than the general diffusion of this pestilential literature."[30] Although he had no idea of the extent of the trade, Merriam was no stranger to the problem. In the previous session of Congress he had sponsored a bill forbidding the sale and manufacture of obscene publications in Washington,

D.C., and the Territories, and it was he to whom Comstock turned to introduce his bill in the House of Representatives in January 1873.[31]

In spite of many assurances of help, however, the bill moved through Congress at an agonizingly slow pace. Comstock stayed in Washington, visiting first one and then another legislator and fretting over the delays, which he knew would give the bill's enemies time to defeat it. "'It is very slow work and trying to patience,'" he wrote in his diary. As always, however, he turned to God for strength and comfort. "'I know there is *One above all* others. I can but pray to Him for his blessing.'"[32]

The problem, at first, was that several bills on the same subject were before Congress, a sure sign that biblical morality lived and that Comstock was not alone in his anxiety about the danger to the American family of the hideous nature of the new publications. The bills had to be reconciled, and once again a New Englander of distinction came to Comstock's aid—Benjamin Vaughn Abbott, one of the outstanding legal minds of the day. Abbott integrated the various bills so that, in the end, Comstock's law was really a composite of several others. Still, the complex nature of the proposed law, the novelty of it, and questions about its meaning caused the bill to be further delayed.[33]

In the Senate, the bill was first reported from the Post Office Committee without amendment, then recommitted, then returned to the Senate with amendments, and then laid over two days to accommodate one senator who wanted to give it "very careful consideration." Even that time was insufficient to satisfy everyone. When it was brought forward again, New York's Roscoe Conkling, fearing that in "the indignation and disgust which everybody feels in reference to the acts which are here aimed at," asked that the bill be printed so all could read it and thus avoid error.[34]

There was more hesitation in the House, where the bill had been introduced as early as January 25, 1873. Enough time had elapsed for at least one legislator, Benjamin Butler from Massachusetts, who had himself proposed a similar law, to peruse the bill at home. Then, when the bill seemed headed for passage, it was discovered that enactment would wipe out pending prosecutions against those Comstock had brought before the courts under the old law. He objected and was even willing to see the bill's defeat rather than have the persons charged go free.[35]

Finally, as Saturday became Sunday, March 3, and with Congress still in session at one in the morning, the bill was brought up once more, hurriedly amended to provide that its passage would not change the status of those being prosecuted under the old law, and passed amid protests against acting in "hot haste." By that time Comstock, believing his bill was lost had left the capital, torn between keeping the Sabbath and remaining to see the bill's fate, "so crushed, so broken down, so tempted to sin against God." He did not know until the following day that at the last moment Speaker James G. Blaine, possibly because of the influence of Jesup and William E. Dodge, permitted the bill to be called up and passed.[36]

The Comstock law reflected the sense of the evangelical moral majority in Protestant America in 1873. Passed at a time when American women were alerting the nation to the curse of prostitution, the law reflected the evangelicals' dread of the damage that spreading what they considered to be filthy literature through the mail might do to young people. Delayed, amended, covertly attacked, ridiculed, and supported principally by Comstock, his small circle of influential friends at the New York YMCA influenced by his exhibit, the legislation was pushed forward by a handful of senators and members of Congress determined to make a stand for decency in American life.[37]

The seriousness with which they regarded the new law became obvious when Senator Windom told Comstock before the bill had actually passed that Postmaster General John Angel James Creswell intended to appoint Comstock as a special agent to enforce the law. Moreover, the Committee on Appropriations was prepared to put money aside for his salary. "Windom seems determined," Comstock wrote in his diary, "that I shall be sustained and says that he means to see that this goes through the House and that I am thus commissioned as Special Agent P.O. Dept."[38]

The YMCA Society for the Suppression of Vice, however, instructed Comstock not to take the money should it be appropriated, and Comstock readily agreed. He had not, after all, worked for the passage of a law to create a government job for himself. Nevertheless, Postmaster General Creswell did appoint him as a special agent of the Post Office Department, a position he held without pay until well into the next century when he was finally given a salary.[39]

The new law went far toward giving Comstock and other postal agents the tools they needed to stamp out vile literature. It contained five sections. The first section prohibited the sale and publication of immoral material in Washington, D.C., and in the Territories. The second could not, of course, prevent publication of such material within the states, but it could and did broaden the definition of objectionable mailed matter so no "lewd or lascivious" or obscene "book, pamphlet, picture, paper, print, or other publication of an indecent character" could be mailed. Of great importance to Comstock was section five, which provided a clear method of enforcement. It spelled out a procedure that judges could use to destroy obscene material when they received any properly substantiated complaint.[40]

Nationwide, the press seemed much less interested in the passage of the

Comstock law as the Forty-second Congress ended than it did about the retroactive pay increase the members had just voted themselves. But not in New York City. There, where the trade in obscenity centered, the city's major newspapers, aside from the *Herald* and a few others that had been accustomed to advertising what was then regarded by evangelicals as obscene material, welcomed the new law. Doubtless reflecting the hope of its readers, the *Journal of Commerce* prophesied that "those wretches who are debasing the youth of our country . . . will soon be in the strong grip of the government." The *Journal* even seemed willing to forgive Congress for its "salary grab" because of its enactment of the Comstock law. "'Something will be forgiven,'" ran the account, "'to a Congress which thus powerfully sustains the cause of morality,'" and it went on to explain how vital the Post Office had been to the success of the trade. "'By far the larger share of their gains [publishers of obscenity] comes through the mails. Cut off from the Post Office . . . they will find their business unprofitable and for the most part quit it.'"[41]

The New York *Times,* too, which had published the full text of the law in February, was pleased with the prospect of obscene literature and advertising being suppressed by the law. It was "disgusting," the *Times* commented, "even for a hardened man of the world to see the circulars and books which are sent by post to the girls and boys in our schools."[42]

Provided with the new law and his appointment as a special agent of the Post Office Department, Comstock, like the biblical Samson, began smiting the peddlers of obscenity "rib and thigh." Using fictitious names and addresses, he ordered the obscene material he saw advertised, and when it was sent through the mail he brought about the arrest of its publishers. He also kept a wary eye on newspapers and twice arrested the Claflin sisters, Victoria and Tennessee, whose most grievous offense had been to describe in their *Woodhull and Claflin's Weekly* the lurid details of the alleged adultery of the illustrious Henry Ward Beecher, pastor of the wealthy Pilgrim Congregational Church.[43]

So vigorous was Comstock's attack on what he viewed as obscenity in the mail, and so unfavorable was the publicity his exploits received, that he soon became an embarrassment to the more squeamish members of the YMCA. Their sensitivity to this nasty business led some of them to believe it was better to do nothing than to stir up trouble. Acting on this supposition, in January 1874 they severed the organization's connection with the Society for the Suppression of Vice and with Comstock, who remained the society's executive secretary throughout his career.[44] Except for such prominent men as Jesup, Samuel Colgate, a soap manufacturer and devout Baptist, and other members of the new society's board of directors who remained solidly behind him and his work, the embattled reformer was left virtually alone to fight the battle against obscene publications whose nettles YMCA members hated but were afraid to touch.[45]

Comstock thought them fearful, but their position was little different from that of many evangelicals of the period. Horrified by the vile literature passing through the mail, so tempting to the young and so contrary to Christian morality, they were reticent to speak of it but desperately anxious to have it destroyed, even at the risk of jeopardizing their freedom of speech. That was confirmed by the gingerly manner in which members of Congress addressed the amendment to the Comstock law in 1876.[46]

By that time the Comstock law had been in operation nearly three years and had left a trail of angry opposition in the wake of the arrests it occasioned. The Chicago *Tribune* called Comstock a "prurient prude" who hurt innocent people and violated their rights with "rummaging of the mails." Perhaps it had in mind the case of John A. Lant, spiritualist and editor of the Toledo *Sun,* whose arrest Comstock had instigated for publishing and mailing theological articles written by the eccentric millionaire George Francis Train. The commissioner before whom Lant was tried considered them "unfit to be read by any decent person" and the jury convicted him, although there was apparently not an obscene or scurrilous word in the articles.[47]

Yet even in the face of the venomous attacks, when the House Post Office Committee learned that the Comstock law had failed to provide punishment for mailing lewd, lascivious, or obscene material it wrote a bill to correct that omission. What the committee wanted, according to Joseph Cannon of Illinois, who introduced the measure in the House, was a bill so "sharply drawn" that it would "cover almost any conceivable kind of obscene literature, for if there is one evil more than another . . . which is sapping and corrupting the morals of the youth of the country, it is this thing of circulating surreptitiously through the mails and otherwise, this class of obscene literature. I think," he went on, "it does more harm every year than all the pulpits are able to do good."[48]

Joseph Cannon was appointed to the Post Office Committee in 1873 during his first term in office, and he would help shape postal legislation for more than two decades. Coarse in manner and speech, he was once known as the "hayseed from Illinois" and later, more affectionately, as "Uncle Joe." Generally sympathetic to publishers, he was no friend of pornography, and his amendment to the Comstock law broadened the category of unmailable publications and made it affirmative. Instead of saying that "no obscene, lewd, or lascivious book, pamphlet, picture, paper, or print, or other publication of an indecent character" could be mailed, his amendment declared that *"every* obscene, lewd, or lascivious book, pamphlet, picture, paper or print, or other publication of an indecent character," including *"writing,"* was unmailable.

The amendment also provided penalties that could not be mistaken should the law be violated.[49]

Although it was mostly a rewrite of the original Comstock bill, its severe, positive nature gave members of Congress pause. Did not the bill go too far they asked? Ohio's James Garfield, a former minister, thought that the case against Train's articles, which seemed more blasphemous than obscene, had set a dangerous precedent. "Where freedom of opinion and of the press lie on the border of obscenity," he said, "is a difficult question to determine." Others thought the penalty of a fine not less than $100 and not more than $500, or imprisonment for no less than one year and no more than ten, was so severe that courts would ignore it. And one legislator feared the power being given to thousands of postmasters to interfere with people's correspondence.[50]

But those were mostly words. Obscenity in the mail was not to be tolerated, aided, or abetted in Protestant America, and whatever his reservations virtually every member of Congress who doubted the bill felt compelled to assure Cannon that he was for it. Still, the bill was recommitted to the Post Office Committee for revisions, and the Chicago *Tribune* promised that legislators would speak against it when it came back for debate. But that never happened. When the committee returned the bill to the House with only a few words changed, the House accepted it without debate and passed it on to the Senate, where it also passed without serious questioning. Nor did President Ulysses S. Grant hesitate to sign it.[51]

The new law assured Comstock that the publishers and peddlers of filth whom he had caused to be arrested could now be punished; it also prepared the way for a fierce struggle over the right to send licentious material via the nation's mail. On the one side of the battle were the evangelicals and Comstock, struggling to preserve Christian morality and a Christian nation; on the other side was the National Liberal League, the omnipresent arch-enemy of Christianity and all its works in the nineteenth century. Composed of freethinkers of nearly every persuasion—"freelovers," atheists, and, free religionists—members of the league considered themselves defenders of free speech and freedom of the press. In the middle, of course, were the courts, which finally had to decide whether publishers of obscene publications could use the mail to distribute their goods.[52]

The struggle began in earnest with Comstock's arrest of Ezra Heywood in Boston in November 1877. Reared in an orthodox Christian home in Connecticut and educated at Yale University to become a minister, Heywood had become an anarchist, freethinker, and, like the Claflin sisters, an advocate of free love. In 1876 he had published and mailed a pamphlet entitled *Cupid's Yokes,* which urged the abolition of marriage.[53]

Although an anarchist and an enemy of monopoly, Heywood was not averse to using a government-owned monopoly to distribute his pamphlet and also his paper *The Word,* which went through the mail at a cheap postage rate. In mailing *Cupid's Yokes,* however, his timing was exceedingly bad. He had published his attack upon the nation's most cherished institution at the very time when many evangelicals, particularly those in the National Reform Association, were asking for a national divorce law to reduce the rising number of divorces. They believed that divorce violated the sanctity of marriage and foreshadowed the instability of families and that the nation's well-being rested upon the institution of the family. When, therefore, in November 1877 Comstock maneuvered through a free-love gathering to arrest Heywood for violating the postal laws and rushed him headlong from the convention to jail just ahead of a mob of freelovers who sought to prevent the arrest, he challenged the freethinkers' right to oppose Christian morality through the mail.[54]

Some seven months later in a Boston courtroom crowded with free-love advocates, Heywood was sentenced to two years at hard labor in the Dedham, Massachusetts, jail for violating the postal laws. The verdict, which followed what Heywood's supporters believed to be an unfair trial, inspired a massive protest. On August 1, 1878, not quite two months after Heywood had been sentenced, an enthusiastic crowd estimated to be as many as six thousand gathered in Boston's Faneuil Hall to denounce the verdict and petition President Hayes to pardon Heywood. Unable to find in *Cupid's Yokes* material fitting the definition of obscenity and knowing Heywood to be in ill-health, the president did pardon him in December 1878, much to the dismay of the evangelical clergy who had supported Hayes's election.[55]

Meanwhile, in the spring of 1878, freethinkers, stirred by Heywood's arrest and that of others for violating postal laws, petitioned Congress to repeal the five sections of the U.S. revised statutes that defined unmailable matter and banned it from the mails. Robert G. Ingersoll of Illinois, son of a Presbyterian minister but, ironically, the nation's most outspoken, flamboyant, and best-known "infidel" of the day, headed the petition presented to the Senate in March.[56]

Benjamin Butler introduced the petition in the House of Representatives in February "without expressing an opinion" on its merits, saying only that it contained fifty thousand signatures and measured 2,100 feet in length. In four lengthy paragraphs the petition argued that the antiobscenity laws had been passed without the knowledge of the petitioners; that the government of the United States was established to protect, not limit, the rights of personal liberty, freedom of conscience, and the press; that antiobscenity laws were in violation of those rights; that they were being used for purposes of moral and religious persecutions; and that protection from obscenity should be left to the states.[57]

The petition, obviously too large to ignore, was referred to the Committee on the Revision of the Laws of the United States. The committee accorded the freethinkers a hearing, at which Comstock testified. "As I entered the Committee room," he remembered, "I found it crowded with long-haired men and short-haired women, there to defend obscene publications . . . by repealing the laws. I heard their hiss and curse as I passed through them. I saw their sneers and their looks of derision and contempt." Several liberals spoke, including one physiologist, but in the end the committee was no more sympathetic to obscenity in the mail than Congress had been. In May 1878 it rejected the freethinkers' petition with the assertion that the laws were not unconstitutional and should not be changed; moreover, "the Post Office was not established to carry . . . obscene writings, indecent pictures, or lewd books."[58]

Furious at the rejection of their lengthy petition, the National Liberal League, composed of nearly two hundred individual leagues, met in their national convention in Syracuse in October 1878. Most delegates were determined to continue the fight to repeal the laws barring obscenity from the mail. But not all freethinkers could agree on such a drastic step, and the convention quickly turned into a name-calling, epithet-hurling, crowd of angry delegates. The New York *Times* saw the battle as a fight between freelovers, who sought the repeal of the laws, and others—like the woman from Nebraska denied her seat as a delegate because she was no freelover—who shrank from the enormity of supporting the right to send obscene publications through the mail to countless American homes. "Who," asked an opponent of repeal, "desires their daughter raped in mind by obscene literature?"[59]

That eventuality, should the laws be repealed, failed to move the majority of delegates. They not only resolved to repeal the laws but also grabbed control of the convention. As a compromise to the disaffected they proposed a year's moratorium on discussions of repeal, but the compromise failed when they elected their own people to head the league. Denouncing the action of the majority, Francis Abbott, the league's president and an avowed opponent of repeal, withdrew from the organization together with a handful of individual leagues. The majority passed resolutions for repeal of the laws.[60]

In the aftermath of the battle, Courtland Palmer, a wealthy New York lawyer and founder of that city's Nineteenth Century Discussion Club, wrote to the *Times* to protest its coverage of the convention. Palmer, the newly elected treasurer of the league, denied that he was a freelover, that he supported obscenity in the mail, that the majority of delegates were freelovers, or that freelovers even attended the convention. Instead, he was struggling, he wrote, along with many of those in the minority, for "freedom of speech, freedom of the press, and [a] free Post Office."[61]

Palmer was not, however, the most vigorous opponent of antiobscenity laws. That place was reserved for Dr. DeRobigne Mortimer Bennett, another freethinker, publisher of a small paper, *The Truth Seeker,* and Comstock's implacable foe. It was he more than perhaps any other who had been instrumental in gathering signatures for the great petition asking for the repeal of the laws. No freelover but clearly a freethinker defiantly opposed to Christianity, he had been arrested by Comstock in late 1877 for mailing an "Open Letter to Jesus Christ." In that letter Bennett had asked if the Almighty had "intercourse with the virgin Mary" and had written much more that Comstock thought "too horrible to write." Much to Comstock's dismay, however, Bennett was not indicted. The "Open Letter" was considered blasphemous but not obscene. Within a year Bennett again deliberately challenged the Comstock law by republishing the already banned *Cupid's Yokes.* Undaunted by his previous defeat, Comstock had him arrested him once more in December 1878, shortly before Hayes pardoned Heywood.[62]

In March of the following year Bennett was tried before a large crowd. If they were eager to hear details of the attack upon marriage they were disappointed. The judge disallowed the testimony of expert witnesses who had found nothing obscene in *Cupid's Yokes* and forbade defending attorneys from reading from classical works to show that those works were more obscene than Bennett's publication. At the trial's conclusion, while the prosecuting attorney pleaded "for the purification of society from the teaching of such works," the judge instructed the jury that it did not have to consider the work as a whole to find the defendant guilty or innocent. It had only to find that certain passages of *Cupid's Yokes* would have a tendency "to deprave or corrupt the morals of those whose minds are open to such influences and into whose hands publications of this sort might fall" to find Bennett guilty. Based on English law, that became the standard definition of obscenity in the nineteenth century.[63]

After a lengthy deliberation, the sequestered jury found Bennett guilty of mailing an obscene pamphlet. His attorneys then appealed the decision on the ground that the whole of *Cupid's Yokes* had not been included in the indictment and the judge had refused to have it read in court. But in that age of evangelical morality, fear of the effects of obscenity delivered through the mail was so pervasive that the three judges who heard *U.S. v. Bennett* brushed aside such objections and sustained the presiding judge's ruling in every instance. In doing so they legitimized the right to deny the mail to certain publications. Four days later Bennett was sentenced to thirteen months at hard labor.[64]

In the meantime, some one hundred of Bennett's supporters, including six women, met in an indignation meeting to condemn the antiobscenity laws as unconstitutional and bemoan the growing strength of Christianity, which they saw as the source of those laws. Before they adjourned they began the circulation of a petition requesting President Hayes to pardon Bennett. The president refused to do so, however, although Bennett's case was similar to Heywood's, because of the pressure exerted by the evangelicals' counter-petition and his reluctance to disturb the Court's decision in *U.S. v. Bennett.*[65]

This was not the end of the freethinkers' efforts to repeal the nation's antiobscenity laws, however. The National Liberal League met in convention once again, this time in Cincinnati, in September 1879. Ingersoll was there, and perhaps as many as two hundred delegates. Among them, in addition to Ingersoll's wife Eva Amelia, who also attended, was a scattering of other women. One allegedly urged the convention to "get rid of these vile, miserable, loathsome dens called homes in our land."[66]

After expressing sympathy for Bennett, delegates again faced the perplexing question that had divided their ranks: How could they demand repeal of antiobscenity laws and still oppose mailing obscene literature, which was obviously objectionable to so many people, at the same time? The problem was finessed with a resolution that opposed mailing obscene literature but called "upon the Christian world to expunge from the so-called 'sacred' Bible every passage that cannot be read without covering the cheek of modesty with the blush of shame." Until that had been done, the resolution continued, liberals demanded "that the laws against the dissemination of obscene literature be impartially enforced." Put another way, obscene literature should be permitted to pass through the mail until certain passages were expunged from the Bible.[67]

That bit of sophistry failed to impress the evangelicals. In 1880 the Rev. Joseph Cook, an influential member of the National Reform Association whose Monday lectures in the Old South Church in Boston drew standing-room-only crowds, called "the Infidel National Liberty League's" resolutions "shrewd and fruitless." They sought, he said, "to use the sacredness of mails as a stiletto through which to stab the youth of the land." He also called for a "vehement uprising of indignant Christian sentiment of the whole land" to support the "righteous laws" and Comstock's work.[68]

The National Liberal League's resolution did indeed seem fruitless, and Cook's clarion call to Christians to support the Comstock law appeared to drive liberals and obscene literature from the field. Only the year before, the *Christian Union* had rejoiced that it was impossible to find a single obscene book where just five years before there had been a hundred different varieties of them. Then, in 1881 the third assistant postmaster general, A. D. Hazen, announced that no obscene book had reached the dead letter office during the previous year.[69]

In fact, however, liberals had not disappeared and neither had obscene publications. In the late 1870s and early 1880s publishers of obscene publications, always quick to discover loopholes in the law where loopholes were discoverable, had found a crafty way to evade the Comstock law as amended in 1876.

The Comstock law had declared all obscene, lewd, or lascivious publications and writings to be unmailable. Addition of the word *writing* raised questions about its meaning, however, when postal patrons began complaining of receiving obscene handwritten letters during the late 1870s. Were the letters in sealed envelopes really "publications" as proscribed by the Comstock law? In 1883 the writer of such a letter in Texas was arrested by a postal inspector but then freed by a judge on the grounds that a sealed letter was not a publication and therefore did not come within the meaning of the Comstock law. The decision was made even though the judge was reminded of a similar case in Illinois in which a judge had sentenced a person to three years in the penitentiary for precisely the same crime.[70]

That same year a more embarrassing problem was created for the Post Office when the famous actress Mary Anderson received a letter containing a fabricated photograph that purportedly showed her with her dress above her knees. The letter also demanded a payment of $9,000 to withhold the photograph from the public. When there was no immediate answer, another letter was sent. Other photographs of her, it threatened, would be produced and scattered throughout the nation and Europe. Her "naked form" would be "familiar to every sporting man and woman in the land" unless she complied with the demands.[71] A postal inspector arrested the writer, who admitted his guilt and implicated others. Because of the confusion over whether the Comstock law could be used to prevent such letters going through the mail, however, the judge dismissed the case before it went to a jury.[72]

Uncertainty about whether the Comstock law banned obscene written material in sealed envelopes provided both creditors and publishers of obscene publications a loophole by which they might mail heretofore unmailable matter with little risk of punishment. By the use of a facsimile stamp that impressed the written, but not printed, notation "Bad Debtors' Association" or some similar inscription on envelopes, creditors brought to public attention an addressee's failure to pay a debt. Similarly, publishers began to copy and mail obscene books by means of a new stylograph that reproduced the books in cursive writing instead of print.[73]

Predictably, these evasions of the law's intent evoked demands for another amendment to the Comstock law that would close its loopholes once and for all. Both the Post Office Department, which was being harassed by patrons who complained of receiving scurrilous and obscene letters, and the evangelicals, whose press kept up a steady volley of attacks against obscenity in the mail, urged a more stringent definition of unmailable matter. In the mid-1880s the *Christian Union* condemned what it called those "secret publications that crawl out of their hiding places only in the darkness, stimulate the passions and feed the imaginations of the young" and attacked those who would apologize for the sin of passion. Compassion for this weakness came at too high a price. "Purity," continued the weekly, "like truthfulness is one of the foundation virtues, and he who weakens these weakens the whole superstructure of moral character built upon them." which "contribute to forces which undermine society."[74]

More specifically and frankly, James Monroe Buckley spelled out the dangers of obscenities in the mail in 1882. Buckley was a renowned Methodist minister, world traveler, and editor of the influential Methodist *Christian Advocate* for thirty-two years. Small, slight of frame, and with a massive, almost completely bald, head, he had great erudition and could present the evangelical Protestant view of obscene publications and their relation to matters sexual in as candid a language as the age would permit.[75]

Tracing the evolution of passion from animals under no restraint sexually to civilized humans who were, or could be, Buckley noted how imagination stimulated passion, whose only legitimate gratification was marriage. "Lust," he wrote, "indulged in thought or deed apart from love is moral impurity; sexual love with lust, apart from wedlock, is the spirit of adultery. . . . Divorce, polygamy, communism, illegitimacy, abortion"—all sins the evangelicals feared for what they might do to the family and the social fabric—"and the overthrow and aberration of the sexual instinct in vices that are 'not so much as to be named' are superficial indications of its [passion's] power."[76]

How dangerous then was obscene literature to the youth of the land, according to Buckley? "The effect of licentious publications upon the imagination of youth is 'evil and only evil and that continually.' . . ; the obscene book, or picture, by premature representation and morbid exaggeration, in which lust is a tyrant smothering love and the rightful sovereign, poisons all the springs of fancy, and turns the fantasies of feeling into stagnant pools, breeding disease. . . . From the corrupting influence of but one such book or picture, it is doubtful if many wholly recover; the hideous and polluting remembrance is a 'damned spot that will not out.'"[77]

Such Christian arguments and the clamor for strengthening the Comstock law in the 1880s, however, renewed the struggle between evangelicals and liberals. In the wake of the new efforts to close the mail to every piece of obscene matter, liberals, who had been quiet but not cowed in the aftermath of Congress's rejection of their great petition, began once more to urge repeal of antiobscenity laws and to warn the nation of the laws' inherent perils.

Contrary to what might have been expected, it was not Ingersoll who developed the liberal argument against the Comstock law in the 1880s. After lending his name to the early petition for the elimination of those laws he appeared to have had second thoughts about their repeal. Instead, the articulate Courtland Palmer and Octavious Brooks Frothingham were among those who challenged antiobscenity laws in the 1880s. Both were freethinkers and well known for their interests in science, philosophy, and art. Palmer, treasurer of the National Liberal League and a socialist whom Andrew Carnegie once accused of living off of a fortune's unearned income, was a man of "education, culture, wealth, and leisure," according to *The Independent,* and the "most active apostle of unbelief in [New York] city." Frothingham was a graduate of Harvard University's School of Divinity and had drifted far from orthodox Christianity to become a Unitarian minister, then leader of the Free-Religionists, and then minister of the Independent Liberal Church in New York City.[78]

Both men opposed the suppression of impure literature in the name of freedom of speech, and both attacked the methods being used to enforce antiobscenity laws. Frothingham indirectly compared Comstock to a general trained to "lurk, deceive, spy; to conceal, disguise, misinterpret motives." Both men also assailed those who supported the Comstock law. One did so because they and the Society for Suppression of Vice were closely connected to the church and violated the separation of church and state, the other because they constituted a "sect" of highly moral men who wished to impose their own "'moral sentiments upon their fellow-creatures, however infirm or debased.'"[79]

Although they fervently opposed the Comstock law, Palmer and Frothingham agreed upon the desirability of preventing obscene publications from reaching young people. The problem was how to do so without the use of antiobscenity laws. Both men offered solutions, but Palmer's was the more specific of the two. His solution—often repeated through the years—was parental responsibility and education. Parents, he suggested, might receive their children's mail and withhold that which was obscene. And although he could not well argue for religious instruction, he did believe that education would solve the problem. "By physiological instructions," he observed, "by healthy occupation, by the cultivation of fine tastes at home and at school, the young will engender ideas utterly antagonistic to indecency."[80]

Because he was a rationalist who believed in a rational universe, Frothingham, too, argued that the education of children would make antiobscenity laws unnecessary. "To raise the level of public opinion by the influence of teaching, knowledge, character," he maintained, "is the desirable consummation. . . . It is the duty of preacher, lecturer, teacher of every description to employ their whole strength in the noble work of diffusing light. But as illumination spreads, vice will flee away."[81]

Still, Frothingham, whose faith in science, education, and progress in that age of science was deep and abiding, was apparently content to let time dissipate the problem even though he denied that he was a "disciple of the 'let alone' philosophy." His optimistic answer to the vexing question was conveyed in a picturesque tableau: "The summer sun draws vapors from the marshes, the clouds collect; the lightening flashes; thunder rolls; rains fall in torrents; the face of nature is covered with darkness; cattle seek the shelter of trees and sheds; the farmer runs to covert. Presently the clouds disperse; the darkness vanishes; the rainbow spans the heavens; diamonds sparkle in the grass; the air is fresh; the kine low in the pasture; the husbandman's heart rejoices that the storm came and went as it did. The lesson is too obvious to be pressed. Usually evils disappear noiselessly, being distanced and outgrown. The silent pressure of public conscience renders resistance unavailing."[82]

It was no accident that Frothingham set his scene of disappearing evils in the countryside instead of the city, where it was less obvious—to evangelicals at least—that resistance to iniquity was not needed. Nor apparently was Congress convinced that evanescent evils were fleeing before an aroused public conscience. Between 1882 and 1886 no less than five bills to lengthen the inventory of unmailable matter had been introduced in Congress only to fail in one house or the other or to die in the post office committees.[83]

In 1886, however, the contest between liberals who struggled for freedom of the mail and evangelicals who sought its purification was reaching a climax. That year, as liberals from Massachusetts and New York and as far as Iowa petitioned Congress to repeal the antiobscenity laws, the Senate passed without debate an amendment to the Comstock law forbidding written obscene matter in the mail. Indicative of just how far senators were then willing to go was the addition of the words *filthy and disgusting* to the list of adjectives describing unmailable publications.[84]

Following the passage of this amendment to the antiobscenity laws, Comstock gleefully reported to the Society for the Suppression of Vice that "in the face of . . . [the Liberals'] opposition a bill to amend the law which they sought to repeal was introduced, passed the Senate, and is now on the calendar of the House of Representatives awaiting action." His exuberance was premature.

The House refused to accept the Senate's bill. The battle between good and evil, as both sides saw it, was prolonged for two years while bills to both repeal and strengthen antiobscenity laws were debated.[85]

In the end, the liberals' bill was ignored. No matter how reasonable their arguments, they and their forces were no match for the moral majority of evangelicals. In their effort to reinforce the antiobscenity laws evangelicals were supported by the National Reform Association; a number of vigorous urban Societies for the Suppression of Vice modeled on that of New York City's; and the Woman's Christian Temperance Union, for whom Comstock had become a "moral hero." Finally, evangelicals had the inestimable support of a national social purity movement, an anti-polygamy quest, and public opinion that had little tolerance for obscenity in the mail in an age when many Americans looked to the Christian past for moral roots.[86]

Strangely, in view of the Democratic Party's stand against sumptuary laws, the man who was to take the lead in amending the Comstock law in the Republican Senate was a Democrat from Missouri, George Graham Vest. A Missouri Confederate during the Civil War, Vest was once described as "that great little fellow . . . with a tremendous intellect" in a "small and emaciated" body." He had entered the Senate in 1879 and in 1888 was serving on the Judiciary Committee when he introduced a bill to once again amend the Comstock law.[87]

Vest's bill, more properly the Judiciary Committee's bill, was shorn of the words *filthy and disgusting.* They had been added in other antiobscenity measures to ban sex-laden health magazines from the mail, but courts had ruled that such magazines, although disgusting, were not obscene because they did not tend "to excite the passions." Even with the adjectives' omission the bill went beyond all previous laws governing unmailable matter. It declared unmailable every obscene writing "whether sealed as first-class matter or not" and provided punishment for anyone who wrote or published obscene mail matter and mailed it under the cloak of first-class mail. The sole proviso was that only those to whom such sealed first-class mail was sent could open it.[88]

At first Vest and the Judiciary Committee had been primarily concerned with the use of transparent envelopes. Barred from blackmailing or shaming debtors by means of scurrilous, defamatory, or injurious epithets on envelopes sent to them, businesses had adopted transparent sealed envelopes through which all the world, as well as the addressee, could see such offending terms as *bad debts.* Having been shown, however, the growing assortment of written, stylographed, and obscene publications that was also passing through first-class mail, the outraged Senator Vest was less concerned with defamatory letters than with obliterating the stench of obscene publications.[89]

Vest's presentation of the committee's bill in the Senate suggested that he had only recently become familiar with the way obscene publications were mailed. Explaining that the present law did not cover obscene written material, he went on to show how publishers had used that omission to mail their publications. "Those scoundrels," he said, "went to work and used the new stylographic process. . . . They took these awful publications, which I shall not name here, and stylographed them from one end to the other, and put them in the mail, and they are being sent forth all over the country to young people."[90]

Like the evangelicals and most others who sought to rid the mail of obscene publications, Vest was alarmed at the dangers that such mail posed for the nation. "It saps the very foundation of society," he said. "It poisons the mind of the young. It outrages the sensibilities of the old." He had little sympathy for colleagues who demurred at the harsh penalties the proposed law would impose. "I have letters in my possession," he said, "letters which are not fit to be read in the Senate . . . for which it would be hard to find any punishment adequate, cases in which these villainous publications have been sent to ladies, to young girls. They are the most villainous things. I would rather see in the hands of one of my children a rattlesnake or a cottonmouth than one of these books."[91] Nevertheless, some senators, while avidly protesting hatred of obscene publications were unwilling to approve the proposed penalties. Fears that the minimum penalties for violating the law—a $100 fine or a year in jail or both—could be too harsh to impose on young boys who might mischievously write an obscene letter led to an amendment eliminating all minimum penalties. With that amendment Vest's bill passed in August 1888.[92]

It was the third and final amendment to the Comstock law in the nineteenth century. Congress had done what it could to drive obscene matter from the mail, and its final willingness to remove the veil of secrecy from first-class mail, albeit under careful guidelines, indicated widespread acceptance of the evangelical moral majority's hatred of obscenity.[93]

Still, evangelicals who had led the fight for a day of rest, attacked Sunday newspapers, and led the battle against obscenity in the mail were not satisfied. In addition to the overtly obscene letters, books, and pamphlets slithering through the postal system they saw an ever-mounting mass of impure literature, barely separated from the obscene and mailed under the second-class privilege to young people, corrupting their morals and imperiling the nation's family structure. This literature, composed largely of paperback books, they also meant to remove from mail.

Notes

1. *Christian Statesman* (Philadelphia), Oct. 18, 1888, 2.

2. L. L. Doggett, *The Life of Robert R. McBurney* (New York, 1917), 79; Alison Parker, *Purifying America: Women, Cultural Reform, and Pro-Censorship Activism, 1873–1933* (Urbana, 1997), 2.

3. *United States Statutes at Large* (Boston, 1856), 5:566–67, 11:168–69 (quotation); see also "Tariff Act of 1842," H. Exec. Doc. no. 126, 34th Cong., 1st sess. (July 16, 1856). As early as 1834, John McDowall, the New York reformer, had collected a body of obscene books as articles. On this and state laws on obscenity before the Civil War, see John d'Emilio and Estelle B. Freedman, *Intimate Matters: A History of Sexuality in America* (New York, 1988), 157–59. Comstock found that the authors and publishers of obscenity had been at work in the 1840s, but their publications were apparently not widespread at the time. Anthony Comstock, *Frauds Exposed; or, How the People Are Deceived and Youth Corrupted* (New York, 1880), 388. On the paucity of obscene material in the Republic's early days, see also Morris L. Ernst and Allen U. Schwartz, *The Search for the Obscene* (New York, 1964), ch. 1.

4. Changes in the laws regulating postal rates to 1875 may be followed in "A Compilation of the Laws of the United States, Showing the 'Changes in the Domestic Rates of Postage . . . , from 1789 to 1875,'" S. Misc. Doc. no. 88, 44th Cong., 1st Sess. (Apr. 3, 1876). Postal innovations relevant to the expanding mails of the 1850s and 1860s are explained in chapters 3 and 4 of this volume. For the argument that each "new information technology has spawned pornography," see Frederick E. Allen, "Behind the Cutting Edge," *American Heritage* 51 (Sept. 2000): 19–20.

5. *The Independent,* Jan. 8, 1863, 4.

6. *The Independent,* Mar. 24, 1864, l; for the statistics on the work of the Christian Commission at the end of the war, see Richard C. Morse, *History of the North American Young Men's Christian Association* (New York, 1918), 63. See also Doggett, *The Life of Robert R. McBurney,* 46–48, for the New York connection to the Christian Commission. Whether this religious and pornographic mail was mailed through the Confederate post office in any great numbers to Confederate troops is doubtful. The Conferate post office was modeled more or less on the Union post office and used forms and documents taken from it but was not well organized before the war ended.

7. *The Independent,* Mar. 24, 1864, 1; Doggett, *The Life of Robert R. McBurney,* 61–62.

8. On Postmaster General Blair's religion, see William Earnest Smith, *The Francis Preston Blair Family in Politics* (New York, 1969), 1:211–12.

9. "Mailable Matter," H. Mis. Doc. no. 16, 37th Cong., 3d sess., 8 (Jan 20, 1863).

10. Ibid., 12.

11. *Congressional Globe,* 37th Cong., 2d sess., 661 (Feb. 8, 1865).

12. Ibid. On Collamer, see *Dictionary of American Biography* (New York, 1930), 2:300–301 (hereafter *DAB*).

13. *United States Statutes at Large* (Boston, 1866), 13:507.

14. For a good description of the condition of young men in New York City in the 1860s, see Doggett, *The Life of Robert R. McBurney,* 23–28.

15. Ibid., 76–77; New York *Tribune,* Jan. 5, 1868, 1.

16. Doggett, *The Life of Robert R. McBurney,* 79–80.

17. Haywood Broun and Margaret Leech, *Anthony Comstock: Roundsman of the Lord*

(New York, 1927), 82–84; Charles G. Trumbull, *Anthony Comstock, Fighter: Some Impressions of a Lifetime of Adventure and Conflict with the Powers of Evil* (New York, 1913), 54.

18. *United States Statutes at Large* (Boston, 1873), 17:304. Debate over the improper use of post cards may be found in *Congressional Globe,* 42d Cong., 2d sess., 2300–2301 (Apr. 9, 1872).

19. The material on Comstock is extensive. The best known, Broun and Leech's *Anthony Comstock,* although written in the patronizingly critical tone of the debunking era of the 1920s, is especially valuable because of the authors' use of the Comstock's diaries, which have not been available to other scholars. Trumbull's *Anthony Comstock, Fighter* is a friendly account written by an author who conferred with Comstock and used the diaries to some extent. One scholarly study by Richard C. Johnson, "Anthony Comstock: Reform, Vice, and the American Way," Ph.D. diss., University of Wisconsin, 1973, is a more objective account. The most malevolent view of Comstock is D. M. Bennett's "Anthony Comstock," in Bennett, *The Champions of the Church: Their Crimes and Persecutions* (New York, 1878). Bennett had been arrested by Comstock and sentenced to jail. In addition, Comstock's own writings provide useful insights into his life; see, for example, *Traps for the Young* (repr. Cambridge, 1967), which has an introduction by Robert Bremner that is critical of Comstock; see also Comstock, *Frauds Exposed.* Nicola Beisel uses class, gender, and ethnicity as tools to interpret Comstock's motivations (*Imperiled Innocents: Anthony Comstock and Family Reproduction in Victorian America* [Princeton, 1997]). For the religious environment of Connecticut, which explains much about Comstock and fellow workers from that state, see Charles Roy Kellar, *The Second Great Awakening in Connecticut* (New Haven, 1942), ch. 1. With his side-whiskers and balding head, Comstock was widely caricatured and ridiculed, particularly in *Life* magazine, as he chased down malefactors of the antiobscenity laws. Such was his faith, however, that he never wavered from what he considered the task the Lord had given him. Descriptions of him appear in Broun and Leech, *Anthony Comstock.* 13–14.

20. Quoted in Doggett, *The Life of Robert R. McBurney,* 107; see also Comstock, *Frauds Exposed,* 389.

21. Trumbull, *Anthony Comstock, Fighter,* 63–65; Doggett, *The Life of Robert R. McBurney,* 107. Of course, he needed the help of the police to make arrests.

22. For Comstock's account of his meeting with Jesup, see Doggett, *The Life of Robert R. McBurney,* 107–8; on Jesup, see the *National Encyclopedia of American Biography* (New York, 1966), 11:93, and New York *Times,* Jan. 23, 1908, 26.

23. New York *Times,* Aug. 28, 1872, 2 (quotation), Nov. 19, 1872, 1.

24. Broun and Leech, *Anthony Comstock,* 129.

25. On William E. Dodge, see Richard Lovitt, *The Merchant Prince of the Nineteenth Century: William E. Dodge* (New York, 1954), esp. 3–15 and 194–203. See the *National Cyclopedia of American Biography* (Ann Arbor, 1967), 13:352, for William Earl Dodge, Jr. On his work for the YMCA, see Doggett, *The Life of Robert R. McBurney,* 74–75. Comstock's law was apparently drafted by Cephas Brainerd, director of the YMCA and a lawyer (John Paul Harper, "'Be Fruitful and Multiply': The Reaction to Family Limitation in Nineteenth-Century America," Ph.D. diss., Columbia University, 1975, 184). A photograph of Comstock at this point in his career appears in Broun and Leech, *Anthony Comstock,* opposite page 78.

26. For Strong, see *DAB* (New York, 1936), 9:153–55, New York *Times,* Aug. 20, 1895, 9, and *The Evangelical,* Aug. 23, 1895, 2. On the National Reform Association conven-

tion, see *The Nation,* Mar. 13, 1873, 174–75, and the New York *Times,* Feb. 27, 1873, 2 and ch. 3. The connection between the men who participated in the antipornography crusade and the benevolent societies and other religious organizations suggests a tightly knit group of Christians, little commented upon, whose influence was widespread in the Gilded Age.

27. Trumbull, *Anthony Comstock, Fighter,* 86; for Windom's bill, see *Congressional Globe,* 42d Cong. 3d sess., 56 (Feb. 11, 1873); for material on the exhibit, see Broun and Leech, *Anthony Comstock,* 131 (Comstock's "Diary" also appears in Broun and Leech, *Anthony Comstock*); see also Trumbull, *Anthony Comstock, Fighter,* 83–85. On Senator Buckingham's background, see *Congressional Record,* 43d Cong., 2d sess., 2000ff. (Mar. 1, 1875); on Windom, see *DAB* (New York, 1936), 10:383–84, and New York *Times,* Jan. 30, 1891, 1.

28. For a catalog of goods Comstock had acquired, see *Congressional Globe,* 42d Cong., 3d sess., 168 (Mar. 1, 1873), appendix. The connection with the American Tract Society is discussed in Johnson, *Anthony Comstock, Reform, Vice,* 55. On one occasion, Comstock was standing in the offices of the American Tract Society when he received a package designed to kill him. It was one of many attempts on his life. Trumbull, *Anthony Comstock, Fighter,* 150.

29. *Congressional Record,* 42d Cong., 3d sess., 168 (Mar. 1, 1873), appendix.

30. Ibid.

31. Ibid.; Broun and Leech, *Anthony Comstock,* 131; Trumbull, *Anthony Comstock, Fighter,* 86.

32. As quoted in Comstock, "Diary," 134.

33. Trumbull, *Anthony Comstock, Fighter,* 87; Broun and Leech, *Anthony Comstock,* 131–32. Benjamin Vaughn Abbott (*DAB* [Washington, 1931], 1:16–17), brother of Lyman Abbott (*DAB* [Washington, 1931], 1:24–25), was publisher of the *Christian Union,* later called *The Outlook.*

34. *Congressional Globe,* 42d Cong., 3d sess., 1307 (Feb. 13, 1873); *Congressional Globe,* 42d Cong., 3d sess., 1359 (Feb. 14, 1873); *Congressional Globe,* 42d Cong., 3d sess., 1371 (Feb. 15, 1873); *Congressional Globe,* 42d Cong., 3d sess., 1437 (Feb. 18, 1873) (first quotation); *Congressional Globe,* 42d Cong., 3d sess., 1525 (Feb. 20) (second quotation); *Congressional Globe,* 42d Cong., 3d sess., 2005 (Mar. 1, 1873).

35. A day-by-day account of the passage of the law, based on Comstock's diaries of the passage of the Comstock law, appears in Broun and Leech, *Anthony Comstock* (128–42). Trumbull's reconstruction of the events, also based on Comstock's diaries and conversations with him, are somewhat different (*Anthony Comstock, Fighter,* 83–89). For the introduction of the bill and its final passage, see *Congressional Globe,* 43d Cong., 3d sess., 856 (Jan. 25, 1873), and *Congressional Globe,* 43d Cong., 3d sess., 2005 (Mar. 1, 1873).

36. Comstock's agony of spirit during this ordeal is recorded in "Diary" (139–42), and in Trumbull, *Anthony Comstock, Fighter* (95–99); see also *Congressional Record,* 43d Cong., 3d sess., 2005 (Mar. 1, 1873). Congress extended its debate, but the *Congressional Record* does not reveal it. For one view of the enactment of the Comstock law, see James C. N. Paul and Murray L. Schwartz, *Federal Censorship: Obscenity in the Mails* (Glencoe, 1961), 22. Ignoring the Christian context in which the law was written, Paul and Schwartz contend that a "group in Congress was enlisted to steamroller the measure into the statute books." True, those who focused on the bill were largely easterners, where the problem was most conspicuous, but those who seemingly refused to believe that there was

widespread support for the Comstock law once pornography became a national problem ignored the fact that there were two additions to the law. Walter Kendrick, *The Secret Museum: Pornography in Modern Culture* (New York, 1987), 143.

37. For the beginnings of women's moral education societies, see David J. Pivar, *Purity Crusade: Sexual Morality and Social Control* (Westport, 1973), 78–83; for Comstock's version of the opposition to the bill, see Comstock, *Frauds Exposed,* 391–92.

38. Comstock, "Diary," 136.

39. Broun and Leech, *Anthony Comstock,* 136–37. In all that time, Comstock was paid by the New York Society for the Suppression of Vice, whose funds were derived in part from the fines of those he arrested.

40. *United States Statutes at Large* (Boston, 1873), 17:598–600. The third section prevented persons from importing the items mentioned in section 2. See also Dorothy Fowler, *Unmailable: Congress and the Post Office* (Athens, 1977), 61–62.

41. As quoted in the New York *Times,* Mar. 8, 1873, 7.

42. New York *Times,* Mar. 12, 1873, 4.

43. Comstock's arrests may be followed in Records of the New York Society for the Suppression of Vice (hereafter RNYSSV), Manuscript Division, Library of Congress. The Claflin episode is covered in detail in Broun and Leech, *Anthony Comstock,* 102–7 and 117–22.

44. For differing versions of this episode, see Broun and Leech, *Anthony Comstock,* 149–50, and Doggett, *The Life of Robert R. McBurney,* 109. One topic of discussion at a July 1873 YMCA convention in Poughkeepsie was obscene literature. Although the secretary of the organization had advised him not to speak on the subject because of his notoriety, Comstock spoke anyway. Lyman Abbott, a Congregational minister and brother of Benjamin Vaughn Abbott, who had helped Comstock write the law, also spoke (New York *Times,* July 11, 5).

45. For those who supported Comstock through the years, see Trumbull, *Anthony Comstock, Fighter,* 237–38, and Broun and Leech, *Anthony Comstock,* 151.

46. Broun and Leech, *Anthony Comstock,* 151.

47. Chicago *Tribune,* Jan. 28, 1876, 4, 5; New York *Times,* Jan. 29, 1875, 2, Dec. 11, 1875, 3; RNYSSV, 55–56. See also Martin Henry Blatt, *Free Love and Anarchism: The Biography of Ezra Heywood* (Urbana, 1989), 110. A defense of Lant and Comstock's cruelty may be found in Bennett, *The Champions of the Church,* 1023–24.

48. *Congressional Record,* 44th Cong., 1st sess., 695 (Jan. 27, 1876).

49. Ibid., emphasis added. On Cannon, see *DAB* (New York, 1931), 2:476–47; for his later career, see Blair Bolles, *Tyrant from Illinois: "Uncle Joe" Cannon's Experiment with Power* (New York, 1951).

50. *Congressional Record,* 44th Cong., 1st sess., 695–96 (Jan. 27, 1876). Cannon's original bill contained the word *any* instead of *every.* See also Fowler, *Unmailable,* 63.

51. *Congressional Record,* 44th Cong., 1st sess., 3656 (June 7, 1876); *Congressional Record,* 44th Cong., 1st sess., 4262 (June 30, 1976); Chicago *Tribune,* Jan. 28, 1876, 5.

52. For the National Liberal League, see Sidney Warren, *American Free Thought, 1860–1914* (New York, 1966), 30–37. See also chapter 3 of this volume on National Reform Association and National Liberal League.

53. Blatt, *Free Love and Anarchism,* 113.

54. For the story of the arrest, see Comstock, *Traps for the Young,* 163–67, and Blatt, *Free Love and Anarchism,* 113–15; for the position of the National Reform Association on di-

vorce, see the New York *Times,* Nov. 2, 1877, 8. On *Cupid's Yokes* and Heywood, see also Hal D. Sears, *The Sex Radicals: Free Love in High Victorian America* (Lawrence, 1977), ch. 10.

55. New York *Times,* June 26, 1878, 5, Dec. 21, 1878. See also Ari Hoogenboom, *Rutherford B. Hayes: Warrior and President* (Lawrence, 1995), 383, and Bennett, *The Champions of the Church,* 1060–61; on the Faneuil Hall meeting, see Blatt, *Free Love and Anarchism,* 129–32. In *Free Speech in Its Forgotten Years* (New York, 1997), David M. Rabban provides a sympathetic account of this aspect of the free speech story (33–44).

56. *Congressional Record,* 45th Cong., 2d sess., 1683 (Mar. 11, 1878). For Ingersoll, see *DAB* (New York, 1932), 5:469–70. In spite of his association with the original petition, Ingersoll could not, finally, support the repeal of antiobscenity laws. Blatt, *Free Love and Anarchism,* 127.

57. *Congressional Record,* 45th Cong., 2d sess., 1340 (Feb. 28, 1878).

58. Comstock, *Frauds Exposed,* 424–30; "Repeal of Certain Sections of the Revised Statutes," H. Rept. no. 888, 45th Cong., 2d sess., 1 (May 31, 1878); C. Thomas Dienes, *Law, Politics, and Birth Control* (Urbana, 1972), 66–71.

59. New York *Times,* Oct. 28, 1878, 5.

60. Ibid.; see also *The Independent,* Jan. 1, 1880, 5. Francis Abbott was apparently no relation to either Benjamin or Lyman Abbott.

61. New York *Times,* Oct. 31, 1878, 2.

62. New York *Times,* Dec. 11, 1878. 8; see also Broun and Leech, *Anthony Comstock,* 176–77; quotation from Anthony Comstock to David B. Parker, June 9, 1879, box 2, Correspondence and Reports Relating to Criminal Investigations, Nov. 1877–Dec. 1903, Records of the Post Office Department, Bureau of Chief Inspector, National Archives (hereafter Case Files).

63. New York *Times,* Mar. 19, 1879, 10, Mar. 20, 1879, 8, Mar. 21, 1879, 3. The judge's instructions followed the English "Hicklin standard" set in *Queen v. Hicklin* (1868) for determining obscenity. Blatt, *Free Love and Anarchism,* 119.

64. New York *Times,* June 1, 1879, 5, June 6, 1879, 8. For *United States v. Bennett,* see Fowler, *Unmailable,* 68. The ruling of the judge in this case in defining obscenity, based upon a ruling in England, set the standard for determining what was obscene and what was not. In 1878 the Supreme Court ruled in *ex parte Orlando* that Congress could determine what could or could not be carried in the mail (ch. 9).

65. New York *Times,* June 4, 1879, 8; Hoogenboom, *Rutherford B. Hayes,* 386–87. The president of the National Liberal League saw pressure from the Protestant clergy as the reason the president refused to pardon Bennett (New York *Times,* Sept. 14, 1879, 1). When it was learned that the petition was circulating, one minister began a counter-petition requesting that no pardon be given (New York *Times,* Aug. 25, 1879, 5). For a petition circulated against Bennett's pardon, see the *Christian Union,* July 30, 1879, 83, which includes a list of prominent members of the clergy, as well as physicians, educators, and businessmen who signed the petition.

66. *The Independent,* Jan. 1, 1880, 6.

67. New York *Times,* Sept. 14, 1879, 1 (quotations); see also *The Independent,* Jan. 1, 1880, 5. On challenges to biblical obscenity, see Theodore Schroeder, *"Obscene" Literature and Constitutional Law: A Forensic Defense of Freedom of the Press* (New York, 1972), 308, 11.

68. *The Independent,* Jan. 1, 1880, 5.

69. *Christian Union,* Feb. 5, 1879, 134; *Report of the Postmaster General, 1881,* 356 (this and subsequent citations to postmasters general reports can be found in the *Congressional Information Service Serial Set Index* [Washington, 1997]).

70. Box 3, file no. 169, Case Files.

71. Box 3, file no. 171, Case Files. On Mary Anderson's career, see the *National Cyclopedia of American Biography* (New York, 1898), 1:243.

72. Box 3, file no. 171, Case Files.

73. "Obscene Mail Matter through the Mails," H. Rept. no. 2676, 49th Cong., 1st sess., 2 (May 29, 1886); New York *Times,* July 13, 1883, 5; *Report of the Postmaster General, 1881,* 336; Fowler, *Unmailable,* 70–71. See also *Congressional Record,* 50th Cong., 1st sess., 6934 (July 24, 1888).

74. *Christian Union,* Sept. 18, 1884, 260.

75. On Buckley, see *DAB* (New York, 1930), 2:231–32.

76. J. M. Buckley, "Suppression of Vice," *North American Review* 135 (Nov. 1882): 495–96, quotation on 96.

77. Buckley, "Suppression of Vice," 496. Perhaps it may seem strange that more than a century later Richard Nixon's commission on pornography found a similar connection between pornography and evil effects. *The Obscenity Report: The Report to the Task Force on Pornography and Obscenity* (New York, 1970), 39–42.

78. On Palmer, see *Appleton's Cyclopaedia of American Biography* (New York, 1888), 3:637, New York *Times,* July 24, 1888, 5, and *The Independent,* Aug. 2, 1888; for Frothingham, see *DAB* (Washington, 1932), 4:44.

79. O. B. Frothingham, "Suppression of Vice," *North American Review* 135 (Nov. 1882): 489–95. Palmer's argument against the obscenity laws is found in the New York *Observer,* as quoted in Comstock *Traps for the Young,* 211–15.

80. Comstock, *Traps for the Young,* 215.

81. Frothingham, "Suppression of Vice," 494–95.

82. Ibid., 494.

83. For examples of these bills, see *Congressional Record,* 49th Cong., 1st sess., 5448 (Jan. 9, 1886), and "Obscene Matter through the Mails."

84. *Congressional Record,* 49th Cong., 1st sess., 440 (Jan. 5, 1886); *Congressional Record,* 49th Cong, 1st sess., 2379 (Mar. 15, 1886). For the passage of the amendment, see *Congressional Record,* 49th Cong., 1st sess., 5448 (Jan. 9, 1886).

85. *The Outlook,* Jan. 27, 1887, 20; *Congressional Record,* 50th Cong., 1st sess., 2210 (Mar. 26, 1888); *Congressional Record,* 50th Cong., 1st sess., 2618 (Apr. 2, 1888).

86. On the establishment of Societies for the Suppression of Vice, see *Union Signal,* Nov. 26, 1885, 2. The *Signal* noted societies in Des Moines, New Orleans, and Buffalo as well as in Indiana, Minnesota, and Illinois. On the role of the WCTU in the fight against impure literature see also chapter 7 of this volume.

87. On Vest, see *DAB* (Washington, 1936), 10:260. It may have been that Republicans had chosen Vest for this task to win Democratic votes for the bill. Serving on the Judiciary Committee was Iowa's senator, James Wilson, a prohibitionist and reformer who had earlier pushed through the Senate a bill to prevent evasions of antiobscenity laws. See *Congressional Record,* 49th Cong., 1st sess., 2645 (Mar. 23, 1886) for his bill.

88. "Obscene Matter through the Mails," 1; *United States Statutes at Large* (Washington, 1889), 25:496–97.

89. *Congressional Record,* 50th Cong., 1st sess., 6734 (July 24, 1888).

90. *Congressional Record,* 50th Cong., 1st. sess., 7661 (Aug. 17, 1888).

91. Ibid.

92. *Congressional Record,* 50th Cong., 1st sess., 7662 (Aug. 17, 1888).

93. There was, however, one more law passed in 1897 that prohibited express companies from transporting obscene material from one state or territory to another state or territory. *United States Statutes at Large* (Washington, 1897), 29:512.

REPORT

Of the Committee of the U. S. House of Representatives,

ON THE PETITIONS AGAINST THE

Transportation of the Sunday Mails.

The report of the Post Office Committee in the House of Representatives (1830) detailed many petitions pleading for the closing of the post offices on Sundays. (Library of Congress)

Cong. Richard M. Johnson of Kentucky. In his right hand are documents inscribed "Sunday Mail Reports," which rejected the voluminous petitions to close post offices and terminate the transportation of mail on Sundays, a proposal considered to violate the principal of separation of church and state. (Library of Congress)

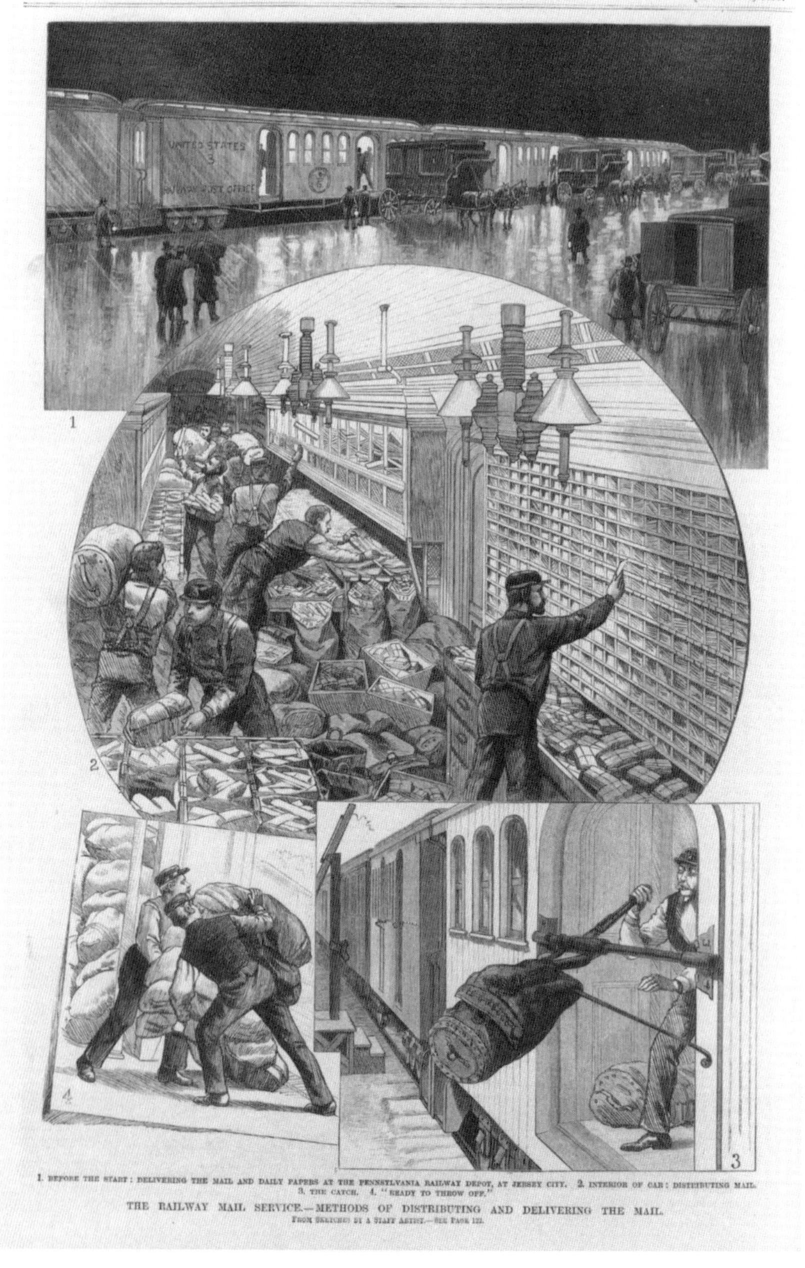

The railway mail service in action, "before the start; delivering the mail and daily papers at the Pennsylvania Railway depot, at Jersey City" (1); "interior of car; distributing the mail" (2); "the catch" (3); and "ready to throw off" (4). (Library of Congress)

Begun as an experiment in 1874, the fast train carrying nothing but the mail and newspapers sped from New York to Chicago in twenty-six hours. In time, various so-called fast trains carried the mail across the country, but the original fast train, supported by a special appropriation, was restricted to the East Coast to accommodate the publishers of eastern newspapers. (Library of Congress)

To the dismay of evangelicals, urban newspapers like the New York *Journal,* which proclaimed New York the "Wickedest City in the World" and reported accounts of sordid city life, were published on Sundays. (Library of Congress)

Flourishing through the use of the improved mail service in the nineteenth century, lotteries brought high hopes, despair, and poverty to thousands and led evangelicals to stygmatize them as sinful and support legislation to banish lottery material from the mail. (Library of Congress)

RECOMMENDED

PRESCRIBED

and Indorsed by

PHYSICIANS!

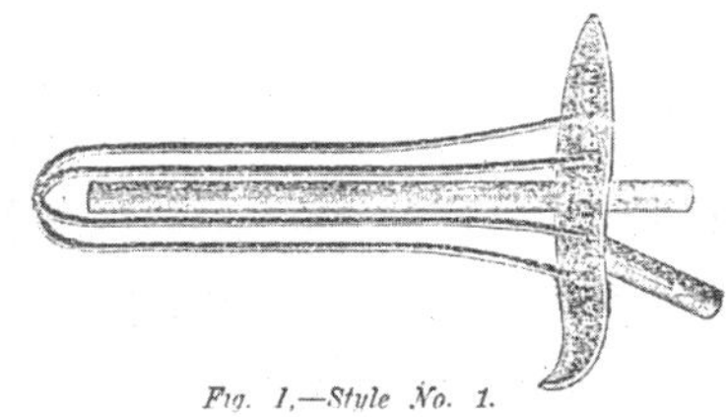

No Testimonials

REQUIRED.

Ask your own

DOCTOR.

Fig. 1.—Style No. 1.

This Instrument was Invented by a practical Physician, making a Specialty of Diseases of Women. It is constructed upon the most scientific principles, fitting closely the parts designed for. Its construction is of the Best Material, and

It Has No Rival.

1. It is the only Syringe which will cleanse the parts thoroughly.
2. It is the only Harmless and Infallible Safe-guard.
3. It is the only one which can be used in bed and do its work.
4. It is the only Practical Syringe for Invalid Ladies.
5. It is a Common Sense Syringe for medical purposes.
6. It Is a perfect Bath Speculum.
7. It cannot get out of order. It is simple and self-cleaning.

IT IS A LITTLE THING, IT IS TRUE, BUT INGENIOUS IN CONCEPTION, AND TO THE POINT FOR ALL PURPOSES, AND WILL DO ALL CLAIMED FOR IT.

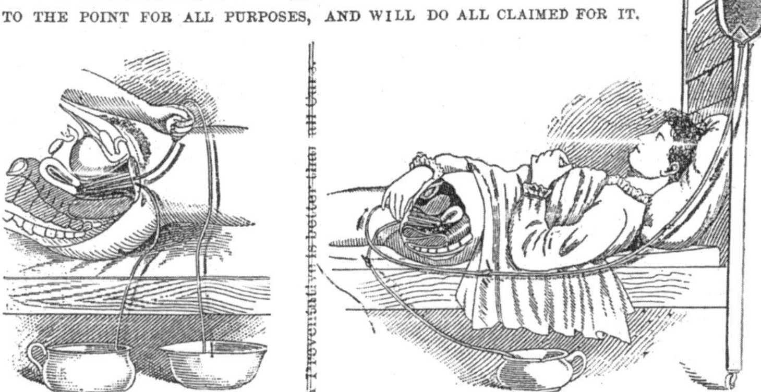

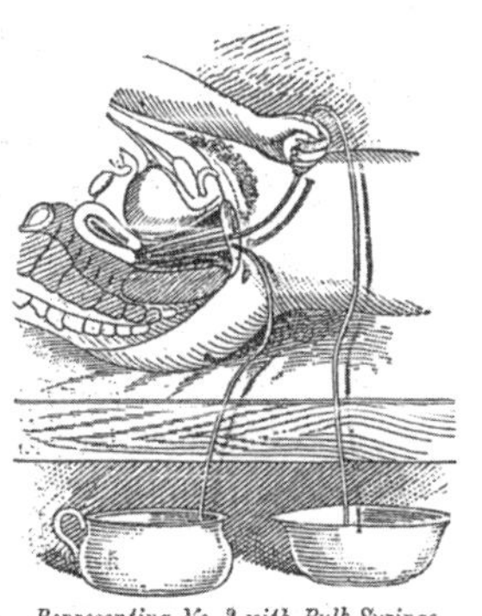

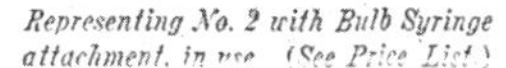

Representing No. 2 with Bulb Syringe attachment, in use. (See Price List.)

Representing No. 3 with Fountain Spring Attachment, in use. (See Price List.)

IT IS A UNIVERSAL FAVORITE WITH MARRIED LADIES. ONE OF THEM SAYS SHE IS USING ONE, NEVER HAS ANY MORE WORRY, AND THAT SHE WOULD NOT TAKE $100 FOR IT, IN CASE SHE COULD NOT GET ANOTHER.

One of the many contraceptive and abortion devices illegally mailed in the late nineteenth century. (Box 104, file no. 150, Correspondence and Reports Relating to Criminal Investigations, Nov. 1877–Dec. 1903, Records of the Post Office Department, Bureau of the Chief Inspector, National Archives)

The Great Secret Revealed

NO MORE NEED OF ABORTION!!

THE GREAT SECRET, HERETOFORE KNOWN ONLY TO THE ELITE OF FRANCE, MADE KNOWN TO THE PUBLIC.

I spent three years in the office of Dr. M. Thiers at Paris, France, studying and practicing medicine, during which time I became possessed of his wonderful secret for the prevention of conception. The prevention is simple, safe, and absolutely certain. There is no medicine or drugs of any kind used. This great secret will be hailed as a boon to the newly married, as well as those contemplating marriage; and especially to ladies in weak and feeble health, whose constitution will not permit of their raising children. There is no need of a woman having a child unless she desires to do so, as any-one possessed of the Doctor's secret can testify.

This wonderful secret, together with four valuable receipts for the promotion of health and beauty, will be sent to any address for $2, and that no mistake may occur, a picture or bed-room scene showing the exact position to be assumed will also be sent.

Address all communications, with your name and address plainly written, enclosing $2, to

DR. J. H. LEROY,
LINCOLN, NEB.

A fraudulent contraceptive advertisement mailed in violation of the Comstock law. Gullible people eager for birth control information received, for a price, this postcard. (Box 5, file no. 191, Correspondence and Reports Relating to Criminal Investigations, Nov. 1877–Dec. 1903, Records of the Post Office Department, Bureau of the Chief Inspector, National Archives)

AL POLICE GAZETTE.

NEW-YORK, SATURDAY, MARCH 13, 1847. FOUR CENTS A NUMBER.

The problem of abortion, drawn to the attention of the American public by widespread advertisements in newspapers circulating through the improved mail service, had barely surfaced when this drawing appeared in the *Police Gazette* on March 13, 1847. (Library of Congress)

6 The Attack upon Impure Literature in the Mail

Blessed are the pure in heart, for they shall see God.
—Matthew 5:8

"If you will not aid him, it only remains for me to die!" This desperate appeal from a "sweet-faced girl" was the opening line in *Old Sleuth, Badger & Co.*, a 5 cent paperback novel published in 1891 by George Munro, publisher of the "Old Sleuth Library" among other publications. Distraught by the imprisonment of her fiancé, whom she believed had been falsely accused of theft, she had come to Old Sleuth, the famous detective, for help. Forty chapters later, following a trail of dastardly intrigue, murder, dissolute men, and a woman made "even more desperate" than the man who had corrupted her, Old Sleuth and his partner Badger have solved the crime, captured the criminals, freed the young woman's fiancé, and had him restored to his former position.[1]

This paperback novel, number 59 in volume 3 of the "Old Sleuth Library," was, it was claimed, issued quarterly. It also had a subscription price of 25 cents and was entered at the New York City post office at the second-class postage rate made absurdly cheap by the pound postage law.[2]

When members of Congress wrote the postage law in 1874, which admitted newspapers and periodicals at the pound postage rate, they little imagined the effect the new law would have on the publishing world. Nor could they have foreseen how creative American publishers would be in transforming almost any publication into a newspaper or periodical in order to mail it at the cheap postage rate. No sooner had the law gone into effect in January 1875 than publications of all kinds—anything and everything that could be made to appear as a newspaper or periodical—entered the second-class mail. To secure low postage rates, businessmen made their house organs into newspapers by wedging snippets of news among blurbs. Wily publishers created an entirely new kind of magazine or "newspaper" composed of little more than advertisements of various businesses and a bit of news. Trade journals of all kinds and "health pamphlets" of dubious merit were all made to conform to second-class mail requirements; so, amazingly, were paper-bound books.

The apparent subversion of the pound postage law was so astounding that the postmaster general, scarcely two years after its adoption and relying on suggestions of the assistant attorney general for the post office, recommended a change in the law that would narrow the definition of which publications were entitled to the pound postage rate. But that was not as simple as it appeared. The publishing business had changed radically in just two years, thoroughly confounding easy definitions of newspapers and periodicals. "Twenty-five years ago," A. H. Bissell, the assistant attorney general for the post office, wrote in 1877 as he wrestled with the problem, "a publication which met all tastes, which was for everybody's use, was all that was demanded by the people, but it cannot be denied that at this day the demand is for division of labor here as elsewhere." Of one thing he was certain: Paperback books were not entitled to the second-class privilege.[3]

That, however, was not the opinion of Charles Devens, the assistant attorney general's superior and President Rutherford B. Hayes's attorney general. If he did little else that was memorable, Devens, a handsome and urbane New Englander who was thrice wounded in the Civil War, left his stamp on the paperback book industry in 1877 for years to come. That year he ruled the volumes in Chicago's Donnelly, Lloyd and Company's "Lakeside Series" to be periodicals and entitled to the second-class mailing privilege.[4]

These opposing views of the matter, given in the same year and from the same office, compounded confusion over what kinds of publications were entitled to the pound postage rate. Ostensibly it was to end that quandary that Congress, two years later and prompted and prodded by eastern publishers, broadened the definition of second-class mail matter at the same time it reduced the postage rate on periodicals to the newspaper rate of 2 cents a pound. Any publication of printed material containing information "of a public character" or "devoted to literature, the sciences, arts, or some special industry" and not bound by "board, cloth, leather, or other substantial binding such as distinguish printed books for preservation from periodical publication" was eligible for a second-class mailing privilege. To obtain it, publishers had only to show that a periodical was issued at least four times a year from a known place of publication and had a legitimate subscription list.[5]

The new law proved it was easier for Congress to broaden the definition of second-class mail matter than to risk the wrath of publishers, whose business was booming, by restricting it. Far from narrowing the pound postage privilege, the new law opened the door to almost every kind of publication. It was an unimaginative publisher indeed who could not include some information of a "public character" in his paper. Congress's respect for publishers' interests, however, was best revealed in the encouragement it gave the paperback book industry. In the face of the Post Office Department's opposition and the assistant attorney general's opinion, its new law conferred the second-class postage rate upon any publication not bound by "board, cloth, leather, or other substantial bindings."

Years later it would be argued that Congress never really meant to admit paperback books into second-class mail by this law, but that argument was hardly sustainable. When the new law was written, the controversy over paperback novels in second-class mail had already surfaced, and Congress could have easily denied them a cheap postage rate had it so desired. Instead, accepting the law that publishers had written, it defined periodicals broadly enough to give them the pound postage privilege. That this was deliberate was acknowledged by Joseph Cannon, the long-time member of the House Post Office Committee from Illinois who helped draw up the bill. Nearly a decade after its passage, Cannon recollected that Congress had intended to give paperback books a cheap postage rate "to encourage the dissemination of sound and desirable reading matter among the masses."[6]

However it was, the new law enticed thousands of new publications into the second-class mail and swelled the weight of that class. In just one year following enactment of the law of 1879, the weight of second-class mail increased from a little more than fifty-six million pounds to more than sixty-one million. Six years later, when its postage was reduced to 1 cent a pound, the second-class mail weighed 109,962,589 pounds; ten years later it weighed 296,640,351 pounds. Between 1895 and 1896 the weight increased by more than thirty million pounds. In scarcely seven years, from 1887 to 1894, the number of publications admitted to the second-class mail totaled 41,717, of which 27,480 were new and 14,237 were reentries. Each year thousands more applied for the privilege.[7]

The immense mound of mail was composed primarily of bona fide newspapers and periodicals, of course. A considerable portion was also made up of paperback books, which rolled off presses in massive numbers throughout the 1880s and 1890s. Published serially from a known place of publication to conform to second-class mail requirements and mailed to newsdealers and subscribers throughout the country, paperbacks owed their existence to the expansion of railroad and postal networks—and most of all to the postal law of 1879. "This business had been created," one New York publisher admitted, "by the low rate of postage on this class of matter."[8]

And a big and flourishing business it was—so large that, according to the postmaster general, one single publisher in Maine was mailing 1,600 tons of paperback books a year. Driven by a seemingly insatiable market, more and more publishers entered the ranks of paperback publishing. By 1897 the industry had thousands of employees, and an estimated $10 million had been invested in plates and copyrights in the nation's largest cities. Publishing paperback books had become, in fact, the nation's largest entertainment industry.[9]

The cheap price of paperback novels contributed immeasurably to their popularity, as did, of course, exciting stories. The development of a new and inexpensive white paper in the 1880s and the invention of new typesetting machines greatly reduced manufacturing costs. Even these were partially defrayed by the sale of assorted advertisements displayed in the books' pages. The result was a novel that publishers could sell for a nickel or a dime and still make a profit.

Still, the success of the industry rested primarily on imaginative marketing and a postal system that not only created a demand for the books but also supplied a market. Many books were mailed in bulk at the pound postage rate to great distributing companies such as the American News Company, which the benign law of 1879 specifically permitted. The news companies mailed them in turn to book and news agents, who sold them from stores and racks. Those unsold after a time could be mailed to other book dealers, who could mail them on to yet others until finally they were mailed back to the distributor, all at the pound postage rate. Curiously, it cost more to return books to a publisher than to large distributors and other newsdealers, a peculiarity probably instigated by the head of the American News Company who helped write the law.[10]

Outside cities the great market for paperback novels was created through sample-copy advertisements, which could be mailed in any number at the cheap postage rate, and through daily and weekly newspapers that went free through the county of publication. Publishers arranged with editors of such papers to sell paperbacks at cheap club rates. The editors in turn offered the books to subscribers for a coupon and a dime or sometimes for a new subscription and a dime or some other kind of prize. They then gave their subscription list to publishers to fulfill the second-class privilege requirement for a bona-fide subscription list, and publishers mailed the books directly to purchasers. It was a system that helped small newspapers to survive and paperback publishers to scatter their publications nationwide.[11]

The publishers called their publications "libraries" or "series," gave each novel in a series a number to conform to the "periodically published" requirement, and each day mailed thousands upon thousands of them. Between 1882 and the spring of 1898, Frank Tousey published 801 issues of his "New York Detective Library"; in approximately the same period 822 issues of Norman

Munro's "Old Cap Collier Library" appeared. Not all issues were new novels, of course. Most were published again and again in different libraries or series. *Her Double Life,* for example, which was number 3 on Robert Bonner's Sons "Choice Series," appeared as number 1 of the "New York Ledger Library." The back of a novel would be torn off and another pasted on to fit the book into a different library.[12]

Among these paperback editions, such as Houghton Mifflin's "Riverside Library" (which was recommended for students by Harvard's president Charles Eliot as well as the presidents of Johns Hopkins and Stanford universities), were reprints of some of the world's best books. Previously affordable only to a few, they were now accessible to the masses, as the expression went, and reached far into the hinterlands over star mail routes. Students in hundreds of schools across the nation used thousands of them.[13]

The paperback revolution also produced less exalted works. Mailed beside the world's best literature was some of its worst. The "blood and thunder" novels were replete with adventure, crime, desperadoes, schemers, and murderers. This collection of dubious literary merit in the second-class mail was accompanied by criminal magazines containing graphic and detailed depictions of crimes. Lured by the second-class mailing privilege, publishers also found a market, especially among young males, for questionable health pamphlets that focused on sexual matters.[14]

No one seemed to know how much it was costing the government to educate the American people by means of second-class mail. The figures were much disputed, especially by publishers, but the postmaster general estimated the loss on the transportation of all second-class mail, without counting the fixed costs of handling and delivering, at nearly $17 million in 1894. Two years later the cost had risen to nearly $25 million.[15]

For evangelicals, however, the dollar loss was far less than the human cost. By the 1880s they considered the nation to be awash in impure literature, indecent pictures, and satanic advertisements. Ever sensitive to the strictures of biblical morality, they seemed never to be out of reach of vicious literature and illustrations. Newsdealers displayed "flash" paperbacks with gaudy covers, unsavory illustrated pamphlets, and "criminal papers" on their racks, even in foyers of public buildings. Small boys hawked lurid papers and novels on railroad cars, in depots, and along city streets. Racy images of actresses advertising theatrical performances filled billboards, and tobacco manufacturers, to lure customers into buying their wares, stashed provocative pictures of females into cigarette packages. Duke's Cigarettes, for example, carried the "fair face" of an attractive and voluptuous actress. Similar advertisements were displayed in cigar-store windows, where young boys could stand and gaze at them for minutes at a time. In barbershops and saloons, too, tables were loaded with trash literature, and obscene paperbacks were passed among saloon patrons. In Chicago, a Woman's Christian Temperance Union (WCTU) worker found that young men lined their hats with "shameless and debauching" pictures. Warning against "'EVIL BOOKS'" and "'EVIL PICTURES'" in 1879, Henry Ward Beecher wrote, "'[T]here is in every town an undercurrent which glides beneath our feet, unsuspected by the pure; out of which, notwithstanding, our sons scoop many a goblet. Books are hidden in trunks, concealed in dark holes; pictures are stored in sly portfolios, or trafficked from hand to hand; and the handiwork of depraved art is seen in other forms which ought to make a harlot blush.'"[16]

Not coincidentally, the paperback revolution developed along with the social purity movement, which swept through the nation in those post–Civil War years when rapidly growing "social evil" exposed the pervasive immorality of an urban society growing just as rapidly. The extent of the problem was astounding. As many as forty thousand "fallen women" were alleged to be involved in prostitution in the 1890s in New York, and ten thousand in Chicago. Brothels, like saloons, blemished the landscapes of all major cities.[17]

As far back as 1870, Alfred C. Roe, a Protestant minister, had used the pages of the *Christian Union* to call attention to the problem of prostitution in New York City and the "satanic press's" relation to it. But the ancient profession had been too horrible to contemplate in 1870. No crusade was mounted against prostitution until evangelicals, especially the Women's Christian Temperance Union, confronted it during the purity crusade of the late 1880s and 1890s. Composed of a host of organizations, the movement's broad goal was nothing less than to purify the nation's sexual morality, to sanitize the environment, as one WCTU speaker explained, by "throwing the protective influences about exposed young people of both sexes in our towns and cities." Among their numbers, which eventually coalesced into the American Purity Alliance, were abolitionists fighting to abolish prostitution as slavery had been abolished; White Cross societies for men and White Shield chapters for women, organized to persuade young people to take an oath saying no to sex without marriage; mothers' clubs to instruct children in purity and pledge that "they would not *do, say,* or *listen,* to anything they could not tell mamma"; and educators of every level whose thousands of purity publications shared the second-class mail with paperback novels.[18]

Into the fray came a number of Protestant ministers, warily at first and then more boldly as they became less afraid to confront the "conspiracy of silence" that surrounded prostitution. The Evangelical Alliance, meeting in Washington, D.C., in 1887 to discuss national perils, devoted time to the study of the social evil. No organization, however, was more outspoken in this fight than the WCTU. Having discovered young women allegedly bound as "white slaves" to serve the sexual appetites of lumberjacks in Michigan and Wisconsin in 1887, the WCTU broke the conspiracy of silence that had heretofore protected prostitution. Demanding a single moral standard for men and women, gravely affronted by man's debauchery of women, and determined to create a pure social environment to protect the American family structure, the organization established the Department for the Suppression of Impure Literature in 1884 and another for social purity the following year.[19]

The publications that evangelicals and WCTU's new department most wished to suppress were criminal magazines, the so-called medical papers that carried advertisements of a "personal nature" and were published allegedly "in the interest of science," and tawdry paperback novels. Mailed side by side with purity pamphlets, paperback novels and criminal magazines negated the Christian message and polluted the environment that crusaders wished to purify. They made brutality, dishonesty, gambling, slang, and disrespect for parents attractive to youthful readers and turned Christian virtues on their heads. By reading the "James boys" novels, complained the southern *Christian Advocate* in 1882, "our boys will hardly know who is the greater hero—the man who whipped the British at New Orleans or the men who rob the trains in Missouri." Even *Peck's Bad Boy and His Pa,* written by George W. Peck and circulated in serial form in the New York *Sun,* was deemed unsuitable, because, as one member of the WCTU complained, the series had a tendency to "make boys disobedient, irreverent, dishonest liars."[20]

Especially repugnant to evangelicals reared in a different world were the novels' urban settings, which featured many of the evils they abhorred. "The whole vile life of the slums of the great cities, reeks and steams in the pages of these books," wrote a WCTU member in 1886, "vile women, vile men, the thief, the pistol, and whole paraphernalia of vice is opened to the impressionable gaze of the youth of both sexes" whose innocence was threatened by such reading.[21]

As bad as cheap paperback books seemed to evangelicals, they were no worse than, or even as bad as, criminal papers, particularly the *National Police Gazette,* which in the 1880s was perhaps first among equals on evangelicals' list of publications to be driven from the mails. Founded as a weekly newspaper in 1845 for the professed purpose of informing Americans of the great horde of felons living secretly among them and to assist police in apprehending them, the *Gazette* was at first welcomed by other newspapers for its possible contributions to law and order—even one Christian paper was complimentary. As it spread across the country in the aftermath of the Civil War and became familiar to Americans everywhere, however, it was obvious the publishers were less interested in eradicating crime than in profiting from it.[22]

Like all publications of the period, the *National Police Gazette* profited enormously from the second-class postage rate and the improved postal service. The subscription price in 1878 was $4 a year, or 10 cents per copy. Club rates of three or more subscriptions reduced the annual price by $1, but postage, of course, was free. Dealers could order the weekly through the American News Company and two other wholesalers, and they were made aware that unsold papers could be returned at the cheap rate. The *Gazette* also assured dealers that circulars and blank orders would be mailed to them free of charge.[23]

The mail carried the *Gazette* to every urban and crossroads post office in the land, bringing its message of violence, crime, and sexual immorality to thousands upon thousands of the nation's youths. The paper employed correspondents in all parts of the country and constantly advertised for more "sketches, portraits of noted criminals, and items of interesting events from all parts of the country and Canada."[24] Just as railroads had nationalized business, so the postal service and the *National Police Gazette* had nationalized crime. Stories of murder and robbery, more especially of rape, adultery, divorce, and suicide, streamed into the paper's offices on Reade Street in New York City from across the nation. There, embellished and enlivened by artists' sketches, they fired the imaginations of callow youths with sensual images of seductions and violence.

The *Gazette* was especially fond of stories of fallen Christian ministers, coverage that carried screaming headlines. The memory of the alleged dalliance of the great Henry Ward Beecher, pastor of the Plymouth Church of Brooklyn, with his friend's wife had scarcely dimmed when the *Gazette* discovered a sinful Episcopalian bishop in Detroit. "BIGGER THAN BEECHER" ran the bold *Gazette's* headline. "An Old and Reverend Episcopalian Bishop charged with Seduction, Lechery, and Debauchery." The *Gazette* had withheld the story for some time, according to the accompanying account, "through a disinclination to hurl the nauseating revelations upon an already scandal-ridden community as long as there was any possibility that it might die and the festering carcass be hidden from view." But when "all such hope proved vain" the paper was not only compelled to publish the story but also to include an engraving of the bishop with his amanuensis on his lap, a bottle of spirits on the table beside them, and his sermons scattered on the floor.[25]

True, many such stories appeared in the daily and Sunday papers, but there they were at least intermingled with the day's news. The *Gazette* had no redeeming features. Every weekly issue, printed on pale, blush-pink paper, contained only stories of violations of biblical injunctions and was amply illustrated with as many as eight vivid engravings. Seen in nearly every barbershop, saloon, and gambling hall, on news racks, and wherever young men and boys gathered and the mails ran, the *Gazette* was a grievous affront to evangelicals and crusaders for purity who saw it and paperback novels as the personification of evil deliberately corrupting the morals of the young.[26]

To be sure, evangelicals had no behavioral studies to prove the evil effects of impure literature on the young. But their common sense and acknowledgment of their own impure thoughts were enough for them to blame pictures, criminal magazines, and trashy novels for the dissipation and criminal activity of the young people they saw gazing at pictures in cigar-store windows. Certainly they had enough anecdotal evidence of ruined young lives to convince them that vicious publications had led to their downfalls.

Stories of lives destroyed by this literature abounded. Nearly every serious evangelical observer of the problem had an instance or two that demonstrated the connection between trashy literature and the downfall of young people. Joseph Leeds, husband of Deborah Leeds of the WCTU and himself a passionate opponent of impure literature in Philadelphia in the 1880s, had numerous examples. In Philadelphia schools, seven pistols were found on as many young boys who also had in their possessions more than a hundred pernicious publications; in Milwaukee, a "Buffalo Bill organization" of young boys necessitated increasing the police force; and youthful gangs on New York City's East Side constantly menaced property owners. Then there were the young boys who had guns and were headed off to fight Indians. Prisoners in penitentiaries, too, reflected the corrupting influence of insidious publications. Of the 120 prisoners in the Indiana state prison, 76 percent, according to Leeds, blamed their downfall on the vile literature they had read. "There can be no mistaking the direct agency of the cheap and trashy reading matter of the day," he wrote in 1884, "taken in connection with variety theater visitation, in turning out juvenile misdeamants and well developed criminals, and that by wholesale."[27]

It was easier for evangelicals to identify the sources of evil contaminating the young than to find a solution to the problem. Products of the improved communications system and a benign postal policy, neither paperback novels nor, perhaps less understandably, the *National Police Gazette* were considered obscene by the court's definition of obscenity and therefore not removable under the Comstock law. Once Comstock had warned an associate of *National Police Gazette*'s publisher Richard Fox that certain portions of the paper were unsuitable, and those parts were dropped. Later Fox was fined $500 for violations of the postal laws, but to little effect. Sometimes the New York Society for the Suppression of Vice was able to persuade a publisher not to issue a certain work, but the Comstock law was, for the most part, ineffective against these publications.[28]

Forced then to find other ways to halt the dissemination of this pernicious literature, evangelicals, especially the earnest women of the WCTU, undertook to stop what the laws would not. "The land is flooded with evil things," the WCTU purity superintendent said in 1890, "and there is an imperative need that women should lay their hands upon them and destroy them." Actually they were already engaged in this laying on of hands. Throughout the 1880s they could be seen moving about the cities, in and out of shops, in government offices, along streets, and in railroad offices, laboring to persuade newsdealers to remove salacious literature from sales racks, local governments to enact ordinances banning its sale in their cities, and railroad managers to remove it from their cars.[29]

The WCTU's Department to Suppress Impure Literature, although hampered throughout the 1880s and 1890s by changes in leadership and the understandable reluctance of Christian women to unearth "vice and crime," was relentless in its attack upon every kind of impure literature, including reports of the prizefights the *Police Gazette* promoted in the 1880s. From Texas to Maine to Minnesota, the WCTU's attack upon impure literature had become woman's work, as the department's superintendent explained in 1885, and nearly as important as the annihilation of saloons. The survival of pure family life was at stake. "If you would have pure homes in the next generation," the superintendent wrote, "you must care for the moral purity of your children."[30]

That very year, Francis Willard herself took charge of the purity department. Together with the title of her booklet *Social Purity: The Latest and Greatest Crusade* and her leadership of the Purity Conference of 1895, the new responsibility suggested how important the work was to Willard. While she wrote tracts on social purity to be mailed to thousands of mothers, superintendents for the suppression of impure literature in various states continued to urge cohorts to eradicate pernicious literature. When she became superintendent of the Department for the Suppression of Impure Literature in 1888, Deborah Leeds captured the depth of feeling that motivated Christian women to become engaged in such work. In her report of that year, after urging all union members to "be watchful to seize opportunities to discourage or remove trashy and impure reading matter and immoral pictures," Leeds urged young men to protect their "future sons and daughters by the influence of pure and holy lives in your youth. It is possible motherhood," she wrote, "that makes the baby girl sacred in the eyes of the Christian world. It is possible motherhood that hedges the young and innocent maiden about with the watchful care of all lovers of virtue. It is recognition of the fact that motherhood is the greatest source of good or evil to the race, that makes the ethics of marriage a question of such great importance."[31]

Evangelicals did not stop with pleading and education. Fearing contamination of the nation's youths more than abridgement of freedom of speech, they reached beyond their localities to pressure state legislatures to forbid the sale of what they regarded as disgusting, pernicious, and immoral periodicals. Dismayed at the freedom that permitted the press to cast "a moral blight over the youth of the country," the southern *Christian Advocate* struck at the "curse of the printing press," whose "evil was beyond calculation." Supporting the passage of Tennessee's law of 1883 to suppress the sale of such periodicals as the *Police Gazette, Police News,* vicious novels, and repulsive "medical" pamphlets throughout the state, the paper asserted that "such legislation is urgently demanded. . . . For unmitigated devilishment [*sic*] the makers and purveyors of this immoral literature are unsurpassed. In no form does the Satanic element in fallen human nature appear more hideous than in this cold-blooded poisoning of youthful souls for money. On no class of offenders should the strong hand of the law fall more heavily." Urged on by such outrage from the evangelical community and its press, eleven states had enacted laws similar to Tennessee's by 1886.[32]

Still, the presses rolled on, churning out ever more exciting paperbacks, magazines, and health pamphlets and making a farce of state laws forbidding their sales. The WCTU's efforts to purify the environment (and those of others) appeared to Joseph Waddell Cloakey, a Presbyterian minister in New Albany, Indiana, to be all but lost in 1890. Compelled by the widespread but hidden degeneration of the nation's young people to sound a "cry of alarm," he wrote a small but frank book in which he declared, "In our young men, our society is dying at the top."[33]

Cloakey called attention to some seven million of the nation's young men under thirty, only 5 percent of whom belonged to a church and some four million of whom were being degraded by the nation's saloons. Then, citing a mass of statistics gathered from reports of those who counted the young men entering and exiting saloons and brothels, he told of a "multitude of young men . . . going into the hidden chamber of the harlot, and so . . . subjecting themselves to a blight, alongside of which intemperance is mild and gentle." From what he had learned, Cloakey concluded, "the young men of this day, *as a class,* are impure, and licentiousness is rapidly on the increase." Connecting the fall of Greece and Rome to prostitution, he warned that "our modern enterprise and our multitudes of churches will not save us, if this same vice is allowed to capture our youth."[34]

By the time Cloakey's book appeared, evangelists had already perceived that it would take more than local and state laws to eradicate the literature they believed had led so many young people astray. State laws might prevent it from being sold within a state, but they could not prohibit such material from passing through the mail. To prevent that required more congressional control of the nation's principal means of communication than the Comstock law provided. Once again, a move was underway to drive vicious, disgusting literature from the mail.

The Woman's Christian Temperance Union led the way. Fresh from its victory of 1888 in securing a national law for Washington, D.C., and the Territories establishing sixteen as the age at which a girl "might consent to her own ruin" (as the WCTU's petition to Congress read), the organization turned its attention to the problem of eradicating pernicious literature from the mail. At its convention in 1890 the superintendent for the suppression of impure literature announced that the department's first business for the year would be to petition Congress for a law excluding the *Police Gazette* and other stories of crime and criminals from the mail.[35]

At the same meeting, members instructed officers to ask the president, the postmaster general, and the attorney general, "in view of the demoralization of our youth by bad literature disseminated by the United States mails," to construe the Comstock law more strictly in order to drive "obnoxious, obscene, and indecent publications" from the mail. "We beg that this may be done," their memorial continued, "for the sake of the children and youth of whom we, as women, are the natural care-takers, in our glorious country, and who [*sic*] are reached from the cities and towns to the remotest country places by obscene, indecent, lewd, and lascivious books, pamphlets, pictures, newspapers, gambling devices, and many other immoral things disseminated by the United States mails. Everywhere the cry goes up of the debauching of the children and youth of this nation by this means. It has come to be the crying evil of this generation"[36]

Following that plea, the *Union Signal* urged WCTU members to petition the president personally and "when any evil thing came to them through the mail" they were advised to complain about it to postal officials. "Should everyone who feels indignant at the prostitution of the postal service . . . write to the President and the Postmaster General, they would be so effectively snowed under with letters, they would do the thing desired to save themselves from being smothered."[37]

By that time, members of Congress had begun to introduce legislation to squeeze one more amendment into the Comstock law, which only a little more than two years before had been amended for the third time. Thousands of constituents and a variety of organizations demanded purification of the mail, and no less than six bills were submitted between 1890 and 1892 to exclude filthy papers from the mail as well as publications devoted to criminal news, immoral deeds, lust, or crime. Most petitions came from the Midwest, where the mail was the principal disseminator of pernicious literature in small towns and villages and educators were especially disturbed by trashy literature in the mail. One petition was sent by the faculty of Knox College in Galesburg, Illinois, and Newton Bateman, president of the college and a former state superintendent of public instruction in Illinois.[38]

The bill favored by the WCTU was introduced by Iowa's David Henderson, an eight-term veteran of Congress's political wars. A Civil War soldier who had lost a leg in that conflict, Henderson lived in Dubuque and represented a region overflowing with WCTU members. Twice he introduced his measure, which would have made unmailable all kinds of criminal papers and stories. Unfortunately for those who wished to purify the mail, however, both his bill and others like it arrived in the House of Representatives at an unfavorable moment.[39]

Normally, Postmaster General John Wanamaker might have been expected to support Henderson's bill with his customary vigor. In 1891 his assistant attorney general for the post office, James N. Tyner, unable to bar unsavory matter from the mail under the existing law, renewed a recommendation he had made to Wanamaker the year before. "I can not too urgently renew my former recommendation," he wrote, "for more stringent legislation to protect the mails against obscene and indecent matter, much of it in the form of so-called medical pamphlets or 'treatises' describing loathsome diseases and advertising remedies; encouraging evil and immoral practices under the pretense of offering cures." This matter, he wrote, was being sent not to physicians but to the "youth of both sexes, evidently for the purpose of corrupting their thoughts and morals." That was not all, however. "There is also a kind of literature and a class of pictures prevalent," he continued, "intended to demoralize the young and to pander to the gross instincts of older persons, which may be found in almost every mail pouch and post-office."[40]

Wanamaker, a devout Presbyterian, loathed immoral literature, especially that of the French school, which he said depicted "in the most seductive, sometimes in the most repulsive [way], aspects of the decline and fall of women."[41] Indeed, in 1890 he was already involved in ridding the mail of a book thought to be indecent. Early that year, an assistant postmaster in Chicago was apparently skimming through a small red and yellow paperback being submitted for the second-class privilege when he noticed that it concerned adultery. Thinking it might be unmailable, he sent it to the assistant attorney general, who denied it admission to the second-class mail. The book was Leo Tolstoi's *Kreutzer Sonata,* the story of a violist who, after meeting his friend's wife, plays Beethoven's Kreutzer Sonata for her, seduces her, and is killed by her jealous husband. It is a grim tale but scarcely obscene. According to the New York *Times* review, Tolstoi seemed to be attacking a "world that condones impurity in unmarried men and will even shut its eyes to marital infidelity," which was much the same evil the WCTU and others were trying to rectify.[42]

The press blasted Wanamaker for removing Tolstoi's book, which he had not read, and for his presumption in determining, in effect, what people might read. The New York *Times* called him a "jack-in-office"; even Benjamin Flower, editor of *The Arena,* who was kindly disposed toward purity and moral reform, called Wanamaker's action the "most significant step in the despotic censorship of the press." He also professed to see alarming dangers ahead for the freedom of the press and religion if this power were not curbed.[43]

Admitting, in effect, that a mistake had been made, postal officials later permitted *The Kreutzer Sonata* to be mailed. Nevertheless, Wanamaker stood his ground. Pointing out that the law forbade mailing indecent literature and left it, in lieu of action by the courts, to the postmaster general to determine what was or was not indecent, he vowed to enforce the spirit as well as the letter of the law.[44] But the damage had been done. All but one of the several bills like Henderson's were sent to post office committees for quiet burial. The exception was Sen. George Dolph's bill, which the Senate Post Office Committee felt the need to consider because of the many petitions that supported ridding the mail of pernicious literature.

Although he was originally from New England and appeared to have an interest in evangelical matters, Oregon's George Dolph was no surrogate for Sen. Henry Blair, that champion of educational, feminine, and religious causes who had been defeated for reelection in 1890. It was Dolph who had moved, in effect, to kill the day-of-rest bill in 1888. His motivation in introducing a bill in 1892 to make unmailable any publication "devoted to the publication or principally made up of criminal news, police reports, or accounts of criminal deeds, or pictures and stories of immoral deeds, lust, or crime" was obscure.[45]

Whatever his purpose, following the ruckus over *The Kreutzer Sonata* it was virtually inevitable that the committee would reject the bill. And so it did. Congress had the right, the committee said, to determine what could and could not go through the mail, but, in the committee's opinion, Congress had already gone to the very edge of its constitutional authority when it approved existing legislation. In any case, that legislation was sufficient to counteract whatever evils existed. To go further would lead to censorship of the press. Not to be thought insensitive to Christian morality, however, the committee noted that "the most eminent religious bodies" as well as by distinguished moralists shared its view of the matter. Proof was in the Methodist Church's opposition to the Comstock law in 1873.[46]

That virtually ended Congress's effort to purify the mail by amending the Comstock law in the nineteenth century. The conclusion was foreshadowed a year later when the WCTU superintendent for the promotion of purity in Washington, D.C., reported that the Henderson bill, favored by the WCTU, rested in the House Post Office Committee and would "continue to do so unless some persistent effort is made to persuade the Committee to take it up for further consideration."[47]

No such effort was forthcoming, but that did not stop the purity crusade. The movement to cleanse the nation's literature continued, gathering strength as it went. In 1896 it was joined by the National Congress of Mothers, which met in Washington to protest against "all pictures and displays which tend to degrade men and women" and resolved to "exclude from our homes those papers which do not educate or inspire to noble thought and deed."[48]

That same year, Anthony Comstock made an impassioned appeal to the women gathered at the WCTU convention. Their help was needed in the effort to enact postal legislation that would secure pure literature. Comstock pleaded, "Oh, mothers, you who are sitting here secure, how little do you know what secret influences come into your homes and in the school, seminary, and college, through the great avenue of communication, the United States mails. . . . The flood gates are open into our homes through the United States mails, and what we want is that you Christian women, with your thought and with your prayers, may stand by us, so that through the efforts of these societies we may secure legislation, both national and state, that we may have the weapons of defense for our children in our homes and colleges and in all our institutions of learning."[49]

Nothing came of Comstock's pleas, but that same year, as it happened, Congress gave evangelicals one more opportunity to support legislation that would, if adopted, go far toward driving obnoxious paperbacks from the mail.

Notes

1. Gary Hoppenstand, ed., *The Dime Novel Detective* (Bowling Green, 1982), 138–60.
2. Hoppenstand, ed., *The Dime Novel Detective,* 138.
3. *Report of the Postmaster General, 1877,* xxvi–vii, 242–44 (this and subsequent citations to postmasters general reports can be found in the *Congressional Information Service Serial Set Index* [Washington, 1997]).

4. For different views on the background to the report, see "The Loud Bill, Notes on the Hearings before the Committee on Post Offices and Post Roads of the Senate of the United States. . . ," S. Rept. no. 1517, 54th Cong., 2d sess., 95 (Jan. 16, 1897) (hereafter "Loud Bill"); "Second Class Matter," H. Rept. no. 260, 54th Cong., 1st sess., 24–25 (Feb. 5, 1896) (hereafter "Second Class Matter"). On Devens, see *Dictionary of American Biography* (New York, 1936), 3:260–61 (hereafter *DAB*), and Ari Hoogenboom, *Rutherford B. Hayes: Warrior and President* (Lawrence, 1995), 297. Devens's opinion was based on the fact that story papers like the *Ledger,* from which paperback novels derived, had long had the second-class mailing privilege. On story papers, see W. H. Bishop, "Story-Paper Literature," *Atlantic Monthly* 44 (Sept. 1879): 383–93.

5. *United States Statutes at Large* (Washington, 1879), 20:359; for the background to this law see chapter 4 of this volume.

6. *Congressional Record,* 50th Cong., 1st sess., 911–12 (Feb. 2, 1888).

7. The figures are drawn from *Report of the Postmaster General, 1879,* 250, *Report of the Postmaster General, 1880,* 306, *Report of the Postmaster General, 1886,* 672, and *Report of the Postmaster General, 1896,* 40, 563. The weights of second-class mail do not include second-class mail delivered free throughout counties of publication. For the number of publications in second-class mail, see *Report of the Postmaster General, 1894,* 480.

8. "Loud Bill," 49 (quotation), 55. Pre–Civil War publishers published story papers, but their format was not the same as those published in the post–Civil War period although stories ran serially in hundreds of newspapers throughout the era.

9. *Report of the Postmaster General, 1891,* 106; "Loud Bill," 49. These figures were denied by the publishers, and the postmaster general's statement was somewhat ambiguous. On paperbacks, see Raymond H. Shove, *Cheap Book Production in the United States, 1876–1891* (Urbana, 1937), and Frank L. Schick, *The Paperback Book in America* (New York, 1958).

10. "Return of Second-Class Mail Matter," H. Rept. no. 3307, 51st Cong., 2d sess., 2 (Dec. 16, 1890). For an explanation of this practice, see *Congressional Record,* 56th Cong., 1st sess., 3130 (Mar. 21, 1900).

11. Small-town and country editors worked out various ways to use the paperback books. See, for example, the *Lincoln County* (New Mexico) *Leader,* Mar. 22, 1890. A brief account of the paperback business is related in the *Congressional Record,* 54th Cong., 2d sess., 462 (Jan. 5, 1897), and *Congressional Record,* 54th Cong., 2d sess., 504 (Jan. 6, 1897); see also "Loud Bill," 64–65, which contains an excellent description of how the Chicago *Tribune* processed the paperbacks.

12. *Congressional Record,* 54th Cong., 2d sess., 474–75 (Jan. 5, 1897). For the number of issues, see *The Dime Novel Detective,* ed. Hoppenstand, 35, 99; for Robert Bonner's Sons publication, see "Second Class Matter," 27.

13. "Loud Bill," 3–5, 120.

14. "Obscene Mail Matter through the Mails," H. Rept. no. 2676, 49th Cong., 1st sess., 1–2 (May 29, 1886); *Report of the Postmaster General, 1889,* 110–11.

15. *Report of the Postmaster General, 1894,* 33; see *Report of the Postmaster General, 1896,* 7.

16. *Union Signal,* Aug. 5, 1886, 5, May 10, 1888, 5, July 25, 1889, 7; see also Joseph Leeds, *Concerning Printed Poison* (Philadelphia, 1885), 10–15. Beecher's observations are quoted in Ronald G. Walters, *Primers for Prudery: Sexual Advice to Victorian America* (Englewood Cliffs, 1974), 54.

17. Aaron M. Powell, ed., *The National Purity Conference, Its Papers, Addresses Portraits. . . .* (New York, 1896), 113; see also Arthur Schlesinger, *The Rise of the City* (New York, 1933), 157–58n3. Differences between vice in rural America and in the cities were pointed out by a writer for the YMCA in 1863. John Paul Harper, "'Be Fruitful and Multiply': The Reaction to Family Limitation in Nineteenth Century America," Ph.D. diss., Columbia University, 1975, 114–15. In the early 1880s a close connection existed between the WCTU and the Crittendon House for "fallen women." Regina A. Kunzel, *Fallen Women: Unmarried Mothers and the Professionalization of Social Work, 1890–1945* (New Haven, 1993), 14.

18. *Christian Union,* Jan. 1, 1870, 4. On social purity alliances, see David J. Pivar, *Purity Crusade: Social Morality and Social Control, 1868–1900* (Westport, 1973), ch. 3 and 186–90. *Union Signal,* June 3, 1886, 13 (first quotation), Nov. 27, 1890, 7; Nov. 19, 1885, 5 (second quotation). The speaker did not blame the men altogether for moral lapses. She recognized "two thoughtless creatures of strong animal instincts" tempted each other. Some sought to regulate rather than abolish prostitution, but evangelicals would not have that. Members of the White Cross pledged themselves to "maintain the law of purity as equally binding upon man and woman . . ; to spread these principles among my companions and try to help younger brothers, and will use every means to fulfill the sacred pledge: 'Keep thyself pure.'"

19. Pivar, *Purity Crusade,* 116, 120, 136–38. For purity work, see Morton Mezvinsky, "The White Ribbon Crusade, 1784–1920," Ph.D. diss., University of Wisconsin, 1959, 250; for a report of the work of the Department for the Suppression of Impure Literature to 1885 and the instruction of children, see *Union Signal,* Nov. 26, 1885, 2, and Nov. 27, 1890, 7. See also Allison M. Parker, *Purifying America: Women, Cultural Reform, and Pro-Censorship Activism, 1873–1933* (Urbana, 1997), 50–65, for the best work on the WCTU's pro-censorship work in the nineteenth century. Parker dates the creation of this department at 1883.

20. *Christian Advocate,* Oct. 30, 1882, 8 (first quotation); Leeds, *Concerning Printed Poison,* 5–6, 12. *Peck's Bad Boy and His Pa* by George W. Peck was published in book form in 1883; for criticism of the book, see *Union Signal,* Apr. 15, 1886, 5 (second quotation). For a list of the evil contents of paperback and storybooks, see Anthony Comstock, *Traps for the Young* (repr. Cambridge, 1967), 22–27. On the contents of paperback novels see Bishop, "Story-Paper Literature," 411–15.

21. *Union Signal,* April 22, 1886, 5.

22. *National Police Gazette,* Oct. 16, 1845, 57, Nov. 8, 1845, 89, July 11, 1846, 373. The 1846 edition of the newspaper claimed that year as its establishment, but editions had been published the previous year. For the WCTU's fight with the *Gazette* see Parker, *Purifying America,* 55–56.

23. *National Police Gazette,* May 25, 1878, 2.

24. Ibid.

25. *National Police Gazette,* Apr. 27, 1878, 1, 5; Parker, *Purifying America,* 57.

26. For a brief account of the *National Police Gazette,* see Frank Luther Mott, *A History of American Magazines* (Cambridge, 1938), 2:325–37; see also Parker, *Purifying America,* 56–60.

27. Leeds, *Concerning Printed Poison,* 6 (quotation), 24, 30; see also Anthony Comstock, *Frauds Exposed; or, How the People Are Deceived and Youth Corrupted* (New York, 1880), 437–39.

28. Mott, *A History of American Magazines,* 335; see also Records of the New York Society for the Suppression of Vice, 1873–1953, Manuscript Division, Library of Congress, 83–84. State laws banning the *Police Gazette* from sales racks were upheld by state courts. James Jackson Kilptarick, *The Smut Peddlers* (London, 1960), 44.

29. *Union Signal,* Mar. 6, 1890, 7. For an excellent account of the WCTU's activities, see Parker, *Purifying America,* 60–65.

30. *Union Signal,* Nov. 26, 1885, 2. The kinds of activities in which WCTU members engaged to suppress impure literature may be gleaned from directions that the superintendent of the Department for the Suppression of Impure Literature sent to the membership (*Union Signal,* Mar. 29, 1888, 12; Mezvinsky, "The White Ribbon Crusade," 250–55). For the WCTU's views of and attack upon prizefighting, see *Union Signal,* Feb. 2, 1889, 8.

31. *Union Signal,* Nov. 8, 1888, 5.

32. (Southern) *Christian Advocate,* Feb. 24, 1883, 1 (quotation); *Union Signal,* April 15, 1886, 14. *Union Signal* reported that eleven states had passed laws suppressing impure literature by 1886 (Apr. 15, 1886, 14); see also Pivar, *Purity Crusade,* 184.

33. Joseph Waddell Cloakey, *Dying at the Top* (Chicago, 1890), viii, 20. Saying that in her department "there is an immensity of evil whose height, depth, length, and breadth none but God can measure," Deborah Leeds, the superintendent of the WCTU's Department for the Suppression of Impure Literature, urged organization members to know state laws and see that they were enforced (*Union Signal,* May 1981, 12).

34. Cloakey, *Dying at the Top,* 80, 81, 84–85.

35. On the WCTU's huge petition to Congress, see *Union Signal,* Mar. 8, 1888, 5. The age-of-consent bill was introduced by the evangelicals' friend Sen. Henry Blair and enacted by Congress after the age was reduced from eighteen to sixteen (*United States Statutes at Large* [Washington, 1889], 25:658). See also *Union Signal,* Mar. 6, 1890, 12, and Pivar, *Purity Crusade,* 140–41.

36. *Union Signal,* Nov. 26, 1891, 8. Parker (*Purifying America,* 22–23) lists the adjectives used by WCTU members to describe objectionable material.

37. Parker, *Purifying America,* 22–23.

38. *Congressional Record,* 51st Cong., 1st sess., 2871 (Mar. 31, 1890) contains the Bateman petition; for other petitions and for antiobscenity bills introduced, see the indexes of the *Congressional Record* (51st Cong. 1st sess., and 52d Cong., 1st sess.).

39. *Congressional Record,* 51st Cong., 1st sess., 4210 (May 3, 1890); *Congressional Record,* 52d Cong., 1st sess. 128 (Jan. 5, 1892.) On Henderson, see *DAB* (Washington, 1932), 4:233. See also *Union Signal,* Mar. 17, 1892, 12, Mar. 31, 1892, 1.

40. *Report of the Postmaster General, 1891,* 187–88; "Second Class Matter," 25. The courts had forbidden postal officials from banning such material from the mail.

41. "Second Class Matter," 22.

42. *The Independent,* July 7, 1892, 929; Chicago *Tribune,* Aug. 2, 1890, 1; New York *Times,* May 25, 1890, 19; see also Felice Flanery Lewis, *Literature Obscenity and Law* (Carbondale, 1976), 47–48.

43. Benjamin Flower, "The Postmaster General and the Censorship of Morals," *Arena* 2 (Oct. 1890): 540–51; New York *Times,* Aug. 1, 1890.

44. *Report of the Postmaster General, 1890,* 16.

45. "Report to Accompany, S. 2834," S. Rept. no. 747, 52d Cong., 1st sess., 3 (May 25, 1892); on Dolph, see *DAB* (New York, 1930), 3:361.

46. "Report to Accompany S. 2834," 1–3.

47. *Union Signal,* Oct. 27, 1893, 11.

48. The National Congress of Mothers grew out of the mothers' clubs. See Pivar, *The Purity Crusade,* 228–30, for the resolution see Helen A. Richardson, "The National Congress of Mothers," *Arena* 17 (May 1897): 860.

49. *Union Signal,* Dec. 3, 1896, 9.

7 The Post Office, Postage, and the Paperback Controversy

The paperback books do not possess a single one of the attributes which Congress meant to require in publications that shall be entitled to the second-class rate Their "stated intervals" are a parody; their "subscription lists" a fiction; their claim of being published "for the dissemination of information" of a public character, a burlesque.

—Report of the Postmaster General, 1899

Postmaster General William L. Wilson was clearly exasperated when he wrote his last report to President Grover Cleveland in 1896. The postal deficit had risen from just over $6 million in 1890 to more than $8 million in 1896, and his patience with the status quo was exhausted. "THERE IS NO NECESSITY FOR THIS ANNUAL DEFICIT," he wrote. "It has its chief source in the transmission of second-class rates of a large and rapidly increasing volume of matter never in the contemplation of the law."[1]

Postmaster General Wilson was a small, frail man whose appearance scarcely reflected his distinguished career. A person of towering honesty and character, he had a full life as a scholar, Confederate soldier, lawyer, president of the University of West Virginia, and member of Congress from West Virginia. A proponent of low tariffs, he had written a lower-leaning tariff bill while in Congress in 1894 but lost his bid for reelection in that coal mining state where protection was much desired. President Cleveland rescued Wilson from political oblivion by appointing him postmaster general in 1894 to replace Wilson S. Bissell, who resigned in the midst of a controversy over rural free delivery.[2]

Brilliant, amiable, and not easily provoked, Wilson angrily attacked publishers of paperback books and advertising papers, who, he believed, were running up the postal deficit by abusing the second-class mailing privilege. Like his predecessors, he was incensed by their violation of the rules that governed the second-class mailing privilege, something he believed their publications were not entitled to in the first place. Indeed, by the time Wilson became postmaster general the case against the publishers' misuses of the second-class privilege had been so often discussed in the Post Office Department and in and out of Congress that there was little left for him to say.

The unfairness of a postal system that charged some publishers 8 cents a pound to mail their books and other publishers 1 cent seemed too obvious to question. In Congress the prime example of this unfairness was the Holy Bible, which in that age rested in a favored place in many American homes. "You may take this paper-covered book," said Mississippi's Cong. John C. Kyle, an ardent champion of postal reform and member of the Post Office Committee in 1897, "and send it to any part of this country at the pound rate; but if you take the Holy Scriptures or some religious tract and attempt to send it through the mails, you must pay the rate of eight cents a pound."[3]

True, publishers could have put the Bible in paper covers and mailed it for a penny a pound—and some did. But apparently it did not sell well. Perhaps Americans thought that paper covers degraded the Holy Writ; in any case they were accustomed to a Bible that had substantial, preferably leather, binding as befitted the Word of God.

Injustice, however, was one thing, duplicity another. And there was much duplicity to trouble postal officials and members of Congress as they considered the way paperback books and other publications were mailed. To secure the second-class privilege, publishers signed affidavits at post offices of mailing, swearing that their publications had subscription lists and would be issued at least quarterly. Only rarely, however, did the publications fully comply with these requirements. Seldom did they have bona fide subscription lists, nor were they published periodically. Frequently, paperback books were dumped en masse in the mail at various times of the year; certainly they were not mailed periodically, as were authentic periodicals.[4]

How little they cared for the law's provision that they must publish four times a year was disclosed by the fact they mailed dictionaries and almanacs under the second-class privilege. To obtain the cheap postage rate, for example, the first page of the *Arkansas Gazette Almanac* read, "Issued quarterly by the Gazette Publishing Company, at Little Rock, Ark., volume 1, No. 1, January 1896. Subscription price 35 cents a year." Like others of its kind, this was an obvious fraud, for it was unlikely that anyone would subscribe for four almanacs in a year or that almanacs would be published quarterly.[5]

It also sometimes happened that authors who intended to write only one book entered them in second-class mail under the name of a fictitious library and distributed them through the mail for a penny a pound. Fearful of questioning the publisher's integrity, postal authorities admitted the books to the second-class mail without looking behind the affidavit to see if more books would be forthcoming.[6]

Year after year the publishers of such paperback books and other so-called periodicals winked at the letter of the law and sought the second-class privilege for their publications. It was indicative of the massive deception involved in this business that between 1888 and 1894 the Post Office Department accepted into the second-class mail more than twenty-four thousand publications that passed as periodicals. In that same period a standard newspaper directory showed a net increase of only 3,747 newspapers and periodicals, which, presumably, had a legitimate right to use second-class mail.[7]

Of all the publishers' abuses of the second-class privilege, however, the most frustrating to postal authorities was the sample-copy provision, which had been intended to help build circulations. Once awarded the right to mail their publications at the second-class postage rate, publishers were allowed to mail as many sample copies of them as they wished—as long as they did so in good faith. But relying on good faith was like relying on rain in the desert. The fundamental fact was that most papers, large and small, became dependent on the sample-copy privilege. In the end, that dependency caused even the religious press to forsake a bill to ban the paperbacks that evangelicals so detested from the mail.

The most egregious exploiters of the sample-copy privilege were the great mail-order papers of the 1880s and 1890s, particularly those located in Augusta, Maine. Postal laws stipulated that advertising matter should be mailed third class and pay 8 cents a pound. After the definition of second-class matter was broadened in 1879, however, advertising newspapers were—like Cinderella's coach made of a pumpkin—turned into second-class publications almost overnight by scattering a story or two and more general information through some pages and filling the rest with advertising. The February 1898 issue of *Golden Memories, an Illustrated Magazine for All Classes* furnished a good example. A mail-order periodical published in Augusta, Maine, it promised "Instruction, Amusement, and Entertainment" to adhere to the definition of second-class matter and contained sixteen pages composed of six stories for entertainment and amusement; columns on farm, garden, and fashion for instruction; and nearly three hundred advertisements for an undisclosed purpose.[8]

The subscription price for *Golden Memories* was $1 a year—payable in advance. As its masthead explained, however, paying in advance was "not pressed with our preferred list of true and honorable subscribers. We like to and do regard such as our friends." In fact, payment was scarcely required at all. It was much more important to have names on a list that could pass as a subscriber list than bother to collect payment for subscriptions. In fact, only a modest list of actual subscribers gave publishers all they needed to mail thousands of sample copies to would-be subscribers and claim a guaranteed circulation of millions, which made the advertising space in their publications more attractive to businesses and more profitable to the publishers.[9] *Comfort* magazine, one of the best of the Maine mail-order papers, had a dubious subscription list of 750,000 but claimed a circulation of 1,250,000 copies. George Munro's *Fireside Companion* boasted a circulation of twenty-five million with only a fraction of that number being authentic subscribers.[10]

Far from being abashed at skirting the intent of the law by violating the sample-copy privilege, publishers of mail-order papers boasted of their great contributions to the nation's farm families. "In fact," said one, "the whole method of business has been revolutionized in twenty years, and what is called 'mail order trade'—a trade built up by the advertising in papers of general circulation—has put the dweller on the farm where he or she can obtain the same prices and the same goods as at the city store."[11]

That was true, but publishers of advertising papers so abused the sample-copy privilege that postal regulations in 1893 limited the number of sample copies publishers might mail at the low postage rate to half the number of their subscription lists. The limitation, however, was virtually impossible to enforce given the Post Office Department's limited personnel. Publishers ignored the restriction and continued to choke the mail from Maine to California with millions of sample copies.[12]

Like other postal authorities before him, the third assistant postmaster general, H. R. Harris, watching these abuses and the enormous increase of paperback books and advertising papers swelling the mail, warned Congress in 1887 that "unless a check is put to this abuse there is no telling the extent to which it will go." From that time to the end of the century every postmaster general recommended passage of a law to reduce the deficit by depriving paperback books and advertising papers of the second-class mailing privilege.[13]

So powerful were the publishers of these publications, however, that no such law had been able to negotiate the rough passage between both houses of Congress. Between 1888 and 1895 two bills passed the House, one to be defeated in the Senate and the other to be withdrawn by the House itself because of the commotion it had caused. In 1894 the Post Office Department even lost ground in its bid to slow the growth of second-class mail when Congress conferred the penny a pound postage rate on college and university publications as well as on fraternal journals that substituted organizations' membership lists for bona fide subscription lists. The result was more abuse. Quick to see the possibilities of the law, the John Deere Company of Moline, Illinois, financed *The Furrow* as a publication of Augustana College and Seminary. *The Furrow,* much of which was given over to commending John Deere products, had a guaranteed circulation of 250,000, an exceedingly large number for a college publication.[14]

Because of Congress's refusal to restrict the use of the second-class privilege, the loss on the transportation of second-class mail had risen to an estimated $25 million in 1896. That spring Postmaster General Wilson, desperate to reduce the deficit, acted on his own authority to deny the second-class privilege to back issues of paperback reprints on the grounds they were not regularly published as required and had therefore lost their periodicity. Frightened by his ruling, which would prevent the mailing of thousands of paperback books, New York publishers rushed their spokesperson to Washington to convince Wilson of the harm his ruling would do.

The man they chose for this delicate business was John Elderkin, who was to become the publishers' principal spokesperson in the looming fight with the post office. Elderkin had been in the publishing business for a long time. In 1896 he was employed by the New York *Ledger* published by Robert Bonner's Sons, an old firm dating back to pre–Civil War days. Before that he had been with George Munro publications and had edited every copy of the "Seaside Library" until it passed into other hands. Apparently he was persuasive, for Wilson promised to withhold his ruling for sixty days with the expectation that Congress would solve the problem by passing a bill pending before it in late 1896.[15]

The bill he had in mind was the Loud bill, recommended by the House Post Office Committee but named after Eugene F. Loud, a Republican from California and chair of that committee. Designed to undo much of the old law of 1879, it was breathtakingly bold. In less than one page Loud's proposed bill ripped the second-class privilege from publishers of paperback books and advertising papers, removed newsdealers' right to return unsold publications at the pound postage rate, and abolished the sample-copy privilege, the most valued of all privileges by thousands of publishers. It was a bill seemingly made to order for evangelicals. If enacted, it would drive immoral paperback books and detested health pamphlets from the mail and save the government an expected $20 million. Unfortunately, it would also deprive evangelical weeklies of the sample-copy privilege, a fact that weakened their opposition to the bill and gave politicians, advertising papers, and the wily paperback book industry free rein to contest it.[16]

A one-time sailor and Civil War veteran, Eugene Loud had worked his way from menial positions in the California Republican political system to enter Congress in 1891 and remained through five consecutive terms. Conservative enough to believe that people would be better served if the post office were privately operated, testy in debate, often apparently contemptuous of colleagues, Loud seemed an unpromising leader to manage the fight against eastern publishers. And yet no other member of Congress or the post office committee had dared to include a provision eliminating the sample-copy privilege in any bill to restrict the second-class privilege.[17]

It was a provision riddled with hazards. Loud knew how much publishers of the metropolitan newspapers valued the sample-copy privilege, how fearful legislators were of the "great press of the country," and how little chance his bill had of passage without the approval of publishers of major urban newspapers. Determined to be forearmed, in the winter of 1895 he met with the executive committee of the American Newspaper Association for dinner at the Waldorf Hotel, where he explained the immense problem the sample-copy privilege was causing the post office. Appealing to their patriotism, Loud urged the publishers to support his bill, and most did in February 1896 when their association adopted a resolution to that effect.[18]

It was a major victory for Loud, and most unusual. Perhaps publishers acted out of extraordinary patriotism, as Loud maintained, but it could hardly have escaped their notice that eliminating the sample-copy privilege would destroy mail-order papers and others that competed with them for advertising. Furthermore, unlike small rural weekly newspapers in the 1890s, they already had large circulations and no longer particularly needed sample copies.[19]

Whatever the reasons for their capitulation, Loud happily announced their support for his bill at the same time he presented it to a somewhat surprised House of Representatives just before Congress adjourned for the Christmas holidays in 1896. When Congress reassembled on January 5, 1897, the first item of business before the House was the Loud bill.[20]

The wrangle over the Loud bill lasted for three years and exposed the tangled web of interests that swirled around the nation's postal service in the late nineteenth century as publishers, politicians, paper manufacturers, newsdealers, educators, and evangelicals sought to use the mail for their own advantages. At the outset of the debate, the bill's proponents—estimated at ten million—appeared to have the upper hand. In addition to most of the metropolitan press and religious organizations, people with diverse business interests, including educators, ministers, and "every class of good citizens," as a member of the Post Office Committee put it, endorsed the bill.[21]

Moreover, proponents had the better arguments. They were duty bound, they said, to wipe out the abuses of the second-class mailing privilege and reduce the postal deficit. Beyond that, according to Cong. Jacob Bromwell, Congress had an even higher duty. Bromwell, outspoken member of the House Post Office Committee from Cincinnati, believed, as did many evangelicals, that Congress was obligated to protect young people from degenerate paperback books, which the Loud bill promised to do.[22]

Bromwell's question was not whether they should merely remove the second-class privilege but whether they should bar such novels from the mails altogether. According to Loud, it was a "great moral question" that in the beginning of the debate assumed a major role in arguments over the bill. A great stack of paperback books had been piled up in the Post Office Committee room. Lumped together as they were into one great offensive mass, they seemed so indecent to one committee member that he "did not see how there could be any opposition on the floor to this bill." Other committee members agreed. Seemingly appalled that so much trash was being mailed second class to the youth of the nation at government expense, they built their argument for the bill as much upon moral grounds as upon the need to control the mounting postal deficit.[23]

Shortly after noon on an early January day in 1897, Congressman Kyle, standing before colleagues in the House and holding in his hand a paperback, asked if they "would like the Government to put its machinery into operation to convey to your boy a book bearing the title of this book which I show you." The book, *If the Devil Came to Chicago,* had been entered at the Chicago post office as second-class matter.[24] It and one other entitled *If the Devil Came to Congress* had been published by H. M. Howard and were modeled, no doubt, on William Stead's *If Christ Came to Chicago* (1894), a serious study of prostitution. A knowing laugh greeted the mention of Howard's books, but no one—not even opponents of the Loud bill—defended them. Indeed, the most vigorous champion of paperback books in Congress admitted that *If the Devil Came to Congress* should be condemned. Another called it "that miserable Howard book," which he denied having read but which he understood was not much more than a "directory of the houses of prostitution in this city."[25]

For purposes of their argument, it was enough for members of Congress who, like evangelicals, believed paperback books demoralized the young to list representative titles, among them *The Seventh Commandment, Innocent Evils, Diamond Dick's Ride for Life, The Black Mogul,* and *The James Boys.* All were "circulated as a part of the great educational system of this country," according to Ohio's Theodore Burton, son of a Presbyterian minister. It was not the kind of educational literature that the government should be subsidizing.[26]

For these legislators, it was imperative that the second-class privilege be denied to publishers whose inevitable tendency was, as one member of Congress suggested, to issue paperback books of a lower and lower grade. Driven by the competition to satisfy less-refined tastes, publishers would be forced to create racier and racier titles. One list, including *One Night's Mystery, A Wronged*

Wife, The Woman Who Didn't, Bridal Eve, and *Why Men Like Married Women,* seemed to prove the point.[27]

Some emphasized the degradation of paperback books by protesting that such titles were too shameful to read on the floor of the House. One member of the Post Office Committee declared that he "would not insult the ears" of colleagues by reading the titles he held because they were so indecent. Jacob Bromwell averred that he would "not defile the pages of the *Congressional Record* by even naming or giving them [the titles] publicity."[28]

Bromwell was a knowledgeable combatant. More than twenty years' experience as an educator in Cincinnati had convinced him that serial novels tended to demoralize and debase young people rather than educate them. It was an opinion shared by many educators, who in the end were the ones who had to contend with the problems of young people led astray by stories of crime and violence. The Post Office Committee received numerous letters from college presidents, state superintendents of education, and professors, one of them Yale's William G. Sumner, all urging an end to the mailing of the serial novels.[29]

One indictment of serial novels came from the superintendent of schools of Indianapolis, who surmised that "every schoolteacher in the land will rejoice if Congress passes what is called the Loud bill." In his opinion, these and other questionable publications were "an evil of monstrous proportions," and like the evangelicals he longed to see the "Government dissolve partnership with the publishers of this class of publication that depends almost entirely upon the young purchasers." In his view, "there was no more dangerous element in society to-day than the bad influence of bad books of the class referred to, for they give the young incorrect and perverted ideas of life and its duties, and have turned many an honest boy into a criminal career who would otherwise have been a useful and respected citizen."[30]

Educators in the Midwest were especially disturbed by the connection between paperback publishers and the government. It was to their farms and small towns, so far from where the books were published, that the mail brought serial novels. "Tons upon tons of it," the president of Purdue University wrote to the committee, "are sent out from the larger cities all over the country, and our children read it and are demoralized by it." But the East was not immune. The circulation of bad literature in New England was extensive enough to inspire three college presidents and the governor of Massachusetts to urge editors to warn "readers against the peril that besets our youth" from reading the cheap, trashy literature.[31]

But what of the good books that were mailed? Would not the value of one good book passing through the mail outweigh the harm that all the bad ones could do? It was a question posed by California's Hiram Johnson, who was to become a prominent Progressive in the years ahead. He had read both good and bad books and brought a laugh from colleagues when he sarcastically noted that the mail actually carried bad books. For those fighting for purity in the mail the answer was no. Jacob Bromwell spoke for thousands of evangelicals who railed against paperback novels when he said that saving one human soul was "worth all of the intellectual development of the human mind that can be gathered by the use of Dickens' novels or the reading of Thackeray's novels or any other of the standard authors of the world. I say," he continued, "that the evil of such transmission through the mails is so widespread in regard to the serial novels, that the good done, as compared to the evil, is as a grain of wheat to a barrel of chaff."[32]

As presented by members of the House Post Office Committee and postmasters general, the case against abusing the second-class privilege and government subsidization of serial novels seemed irrefutable, and in the debate's first round it was. The Loud bill passed the House that winter of 1897 and moved on to the Senate, where gathering opposition stalled its passage.[33]

Enactment of the Loud bill in the House terrified New York publishers, who envisioned the loss of their second-class mailing privilege and the inevitable crumbling of their multi-million-dollar empires. Rich, influential, and not a little arrogant, the moguls of an industry that entertained so many of the nation's youths gathered in Washington early in 1897 to explain to members of the Senate Post Office Committee why the Loud bill should not pass. Canadian-born George Munro, who died at his summer home in the Catskills on the eve of the hearing, was an instigator of detective novels, and his great fortune had been made on the back of the liberality of postal laws. Virtually all other great publishing houses were represented in Washington, however, as well as the American News Company's ubiquitous Patrick Farewell and spokespersons for the mail-order papers from Augusta, Maine.[34]

In short order they denounced the committee's arguments against their business and countered with their own. Maintaining that the American people would not buy bad books and that they published none, they argued that they had operated within the postal laws and painted a grim picture of the economic chaos that would result from enactment of the Loud bill. It would, if passed, "injure and curtail the periodical literature of the country, limit the field and volume of advertising, and reduce the whole business of the country, and bring bankruptcy and ruin to printers, paper makers, publishers, merchants, and manufacturers."[35]

The Senate hearing was enough to stall the Loud bill but only a prelude to an aggressive lobbying campaign from the publishers. No sooner, in fact, had Loud announced his bill than a committee of New York publishers began to foment opposition to it. Because so many interests depended on the post office, urban eastern publishers, ironically, found support for their position in the heart of Protestant rural America.

The debate over the Loud bill occurred while the acrid smoke of battle created by the presidential campaign of 1896 still lingered in the air. This important turning point in American politics had arrayed the East against the West and South, Populism against conservatism, gold against silver, city against country, old values against new, and industrial enterprise against agriculture. Rural America, therefore, appeared to be an unlikely place for New York publishers to find friends. Yet such were the diverse ways Americans used their postal service that they found common ground with legislators from rural America.[36]

Throughout the presidential campaign of 1896 and in the years preceding it the postal service had been of immense importance to rural politicians. Not only had it served as a model for the public ownership of railroads, something rural politicians espoused, but also, and most important, it was virtually the only means of disseminating politicians' more radical economic views. In a world in which, according to Marion Butler, the Populist senator from North Carolina, "the gold rings, the monopolies, and trusts, already control the avenues and agencies of rapid communication and intelligence," only the postal service had remained open to present another point of view.[37]

In 1894 William H. Harvey, lawyer, rancher, impecunious silver miner, editor of a failed newspaper, and finally spokesperson for the silver interests, obtained the second-class privilege for the mailing of his paperback book *Coin's Financial School* under the library title of the same name. He claimed to have issued one title quarterly under this name as required, but whether that was so made little difference. At least three hundred thousand paper copies of his third book went through the mail at the cheap rate.[38] The book was the *Uncle Tom's Cabin* of the free-silver movement. Because of its wide mail distribution it educated thousands on the virtues of free silver. The prospect of the Loud bill alarmed Harvey. "It strikes," he said, "at censorship, it is a strike at the educational literature of the country."[39]

Still, a paperback book was not the principal means of spreading Populist and Democratic doctrine in the 1890s. That was left to country weeklies that depended on the free exchange of newspapers through the mail, free mailing throughout counties of publication, and, above all, the sample-copy privilege.

The sample-copy privilege Congress had given publishers in 1879 was the beating heart of country weeklies that brought "doings" of farm and fireside to farms and small-town homes across the land. To found such papers publishers had little more than faith, hope, old printing presses, and much charity in the form of the sample-copy privilege. Beginning with only a subscriber or two to secure the second-class privilege, or often with none at all, aspiring publishers mailed sample copies to prospective readers to lure subscriptions that would increase circulation. Every sample copy was mailed for a cent a pound, of course, or even for free in counties of publication. "The ordinary practice is for those who are starting a paper," Cong. Jerry Simpson, the "sockless" Populist from Kansas, explained to colleagues in 1898, "to print a very large number of extra copies and send them out as a prospectus before they have any list of subscribers. That is the method of starting a country newspaper out where I come from."[40]

The sample-copy privilege, however, was scarcely more valuable to the publishers of country papers than it was to politicians running for office. Without wealthy campaign contributors and with few funds of their own, they sought the help of friendly editors, who for a modest price wrote editorials of praise, printed thousands of extra copies of those editorials, and mailed them as sample copies for a penny a pound throughout the congressional district—often for nothing in counties of publication. In this way did the government subsidize both publishers and politicians in rural America.[41]

Aspiring politicians frequently used the sample-copy privilege to establish their own papers and advance their candidacies. "About a certain time of year there is a want felt all over the country," explained one legislator in describing the origin of country newspapers. "It is a long felt want. . . . The ordinary newspapers do not feel the want and proceed in the usual way; but some aspiring man that wants to go to Congress thinks he sees the want, and, perhaps finds some aspiring man who wants to start a newspaper in his interest."[42] After the Civil War, many small rural weeklies began in just that way. Many legislators who helped shape the nation's laws in the late nineteenth century first supped from the government's overflowing sample-copy cup to edit or own a country weekly.

True, postal regulations forbade editors to mail sample copies for someone else at the cheap postage rate and also prohibited free mailing of sample copies throughout the county of publication. Nor was it legal for publishers to mail sample copies without having a subscription list. But no more attention was paid to these postal regulations in the country than paperback publishers paid to them in cities. At election time the mail was filled with sample copies of papers championing the campaign of this or that candidate at government expense.[43]

Thoroughly informed on the uses of the postal system, the Committee of New York Publishers was quick to see the immense benefit of the sample-copy privilege to publishers of country weekly papers and rural politicians. The committee was just as quick to perceive that rustics in the countryside and their representatives in Congress might save their industry from ruin if they could be made to see how dangerous the Loud bill was to their interests. Consequently, early in the debate they sent a frantic circular to publishers of weekly papers to present arguments against the bill, warn of the disaster that awaited them if it passed, and plead for help to defeat the bill. "If you will sign the three protests inclosed," ran the circular letter, "and send one to the Member of Congress of your district, and one to each of the two Senators of your state . . . great good will undoubtedly result." Better still, editors were urged to editorialize against the bill and mail marked copies of those editorials to their legislators.[44]

For those who would enlist in their campaign, the publishers promised rewards. Street and Smith, publishers of the "Sea and Shore Series," mailed hundreds of editorials to publishers of weeklies, offering fifty-two books and a subscription to the New York *Weekly* for a year if they would publish parts of the editorials and send marked copies to members of Congress and to Street and Smith. Some time later, another publisher offered to give four of his company's best books to anyone who would collect ten signatures to a prepared petition opposing the Loud bill, mail the petition to their member of Congress, and send the publisher a notice—printed at the bottom of the page—to indicate they had done so.[45]

Publishers also influenced the efforts of others to stir up trouble for the Loud bill. One editor of a paper that had three hundred subscribers in Tottenville, New York, for example, spent more than he "would make in thirty years," according to Loud, to send editorials against the bill to papers throughout the country. Plainly, he had been paid for his efforts, presumably by New York publishers.[46]

The campaign was incredibly successful. Petitions signed by hundreds of proprietors of weekly newspapers and others who opposed the bill filled the congressional mail and changed debate in Congress from arguments for banning immoral paperback books from the mail to emphasizing the fear of losing the sample-copy privilege. Members of Congress, on the receiving end of torrents of anxious and angry petitions, discovered ample reasons to oppose the bill. The conspiratorially minded among them attacked the hidden motives that they surmised lay behind the proposal. Some charged that it was deliberately designed to stifle Populist-Democratic opposition to the Republican point of view. Others, recalling Loud's statement that the post office would be better managed under private enterprise, claimed that the bill was meant to destroy the post office. Still others said the bill was drawn to favor express companies, which presumably would profit if paperback books had to be mailed at 8 cents a pound instead of 1 cent.[47]

Most of those opposed to the bill, however, from urban and rural districts alike and under pressure from publishers as remote from each another as New York City and Medicine Lodge, Kansas, discovered more than enough arguments to dispel accusations that the second-class privilege had been abused or had caused the postal deficit. Disputing the postmaster general's statistics, they contended that the cost of transporting second-class mail was unknown. In any case, it was paid by revenue (generated by the publications) from first-class business letters and fourth-class packages. The cost of handling second-class matter was largely borne by the Post Office Department's fixed costs, employees and post offices, which had to be paid no matter the size of the second-class mail.[48]

What, then, had caused the postal deficit if not loss of the revenue on second-class mail? Opponents of the Loud bill maintained that no one really knew, but they suggested sources other than second-class mail. Overpayment to railroads for transporting the mail was one, and Congress's franking privilege and the free circulation of papers through counties of publication were others.

But neither the postal deficit nor the abuse of the second-class privilege mattered much to opponents of the Loud bill. Dredging up an argument as old as the 1840s, they contended that the postal service did not need to pay its way. The education of poor children on farms, young people "educating themselves in the best literature of the language, for ten or fifteen cents a volume," was worth the expense.[49]

The rhetoric in the House in favor of preserving a mail system that was bringing the best literature to country boys and girls starved for such reading matter rang with bucolic sentimentality. It also made a wonderfully emotional argument against a bill that would rob the poor of their reading matter. In the course of the debate Houghton Mifflin had thoughtfully provided most members of Congress with a paperback copy of *Evangeline,* which opponents used along with the titles of numerous other well-known reprints to show the kind of literature that mail brought to children in isolated areas. One enthusiastic legislator argued that even advertising sheets, with their little squibs of poetry and philosophy smuggled among hundreds of advertisements in order to obtain the second-class privilege, were helping educate rural children.[50]

Yet in the end, the assault on the Loud bill turned on the provision eliminating the sample-copy privilege. Cunningly, New York publishers had alerted publishers of country papers, and hence their representatives in Congress, to just how much the loss of the sample-copy privilege would affect them. The

Loud bill, they pointed out, required a publisher to have "a legitimate list of subscribers who voluntarily order and pay for" the paper in order to obtain the second-class privilege. On this point hung the fate of the Loud bill. It was futile for its supporters to point out that this had always been the law. For those in the Heartland it was a change that would deprive them of their most valuable resource. There the law had always been "so construed," as Simpson tactfully put it, to give publishers "the privilege of sending out sample copies without a subscription list." The supposed change in the law, which really was no change at all, stood in the way of enacting the Loud bill, and Congress argued over it for hours.[51]

Because it threatened to destroy their principal means of campaigning for public office, eliminate the opportunity for aspiring young publishers to begin their own papers, and reduce the number of country weeklies, the loss of the sample-copy privilege made the Loud bill unacceptable to members of Congress from rural areas. Moreover, the bill would ruin the small-town editor, for whom the House chamber rang with encomiums. "The rural editor—God bless him!—is the most persistent of teachers," extolled Missouri's Champ Clark in a great burst of oratory. In a eulogy that evoked the portrayal of love in St. Paul's thirteenth chapter of First Corinthians, Clark went on to describe the country editor's contributions. "He is the pack horse of every community, the promoter of every laudable enterprise, the worst underpaid laborer in the vineyard. Counting his space as his capital, he gives more to charity, his means considered, than any member of society. He is a power in politics, a pillar of the church, a leader in the crusade for better morals. He is preeminently the friend of humanity."[52]

Clark's eulogy was long remembered by his colleagues, many of whom had been publishers of rural weeklies themselves. Although the remarks played well back home, they were not needed to galvanize country editors' opposition to the bill. They as well as editors of weekly papers everywhere, including editors of religious weeklies, rallied to the destruction of the bill. Hundreds of editorials reflected what editors believed (and had been told): The loss of their sample-copy privilege would mean the loss of their papers. Wilbur Crafts had told senators that most of the religious press would support the bill for moral reasons. If some did, many did not, and more than a few publishers signed petitions opposing the bill. Not even the WCTU's *Union Signal,* which had so vigorously attacked paperback books, supported the Loud bill, which would have destroyed the industry surrounding those books. Religious publishers, like all those of weekly papers, had become dependent upon the sample-copy privilege. Most apparently lost interest in banning immoral paperbacks and criminal papers when doing so meant losing the sample-copy privilege as well. The Protestant *Independent,* which had ventured the opinion that the Loud bill had some excellent features, editorialized that it was "unreasonably illiberal as to sample copies by which publishers advertise their newspapers."[53]

Indeed, talk of purifying the mails, which had been one purpose of the Loud bill and much discussed in the earliest debate, faded during the ruckus over the sample-copy privilege. True, Congressman Bromwell was still there in 1900 to condemn a list "of the vilest publications that were ever permitted to be published in this country," which he found advertised on the back of a paperback book, and even opponents of the bill occasionally regretted the mailing of such books as *Sapho,* a paperback by a French author whose principal character was a harlot. Allegedly, it was being mailed by the tons at the second-class rate. No doubt most publishers of religious papers lamented the mailing of such a book, but if so they still felt compelled to oppose the Loud bill or remain silent. In any case it seemed strange that at the end of the century the managers of a play based on *Sapho* were arrested along with actress Olga Nethersole in New York for "violating public decency" yet the book was allowed in the mail at the pound postage rate.[54]

By 1900 the Loud bill had been presented to the House of Representatives three times and debated at length as often. Several times efforts had been made to amend the bill and make it acceptable to rural publishers. At one point the Post Office Committee offered to permit them to mail as many sample copies as 10 percent of their subscription lists, not to exceed one thousand copies. Mailing a thousand sample copies with each issue of a paper was also proposed, provided they were mailed at the same time as the regular issue. Finally, in desperation, the Post Office Committee agreed to accept amendments that would permit publishers to mail as many sample copies outside their counties as the number of their regular subscription list, up to two thousand copies. No restriction at all would apply to the number of sample copies they might mail inside the county of publication. Champ Clark, once a vigorous foe of the Loud bill, proposed these last amendments, which he believed vastly improved the original bill and "were as good as we are likely to get, if we are ever to pass a law excluding from the 1-cent-pound-rate privilege the fake periodicals which have produced a huge deficit in the postal revenues and which have brought the whole business into disrepute."[55]

Clark's amendments appeared to give publishers of country papers all they needed to advertise their publications, and the support Clark gave the bill after so long opposing it seemed to assure its passage. As it turned out, the chief obstacle to the Loud bill was not rural publishers but politicians, New York publishers, and newsdealers. As finally amended, the bill would not have provided for the thousands of sample copies that rural politicians might need for a successful campaign. Nor did it give New York publishers of paperback books or mail-order papers the right to mail their publications for a penny a pound. Moreover, it did not give newsdealers the right to return unsold papers at the second-class postage rate. Failure to overcome these issues doomed the Loud bill.

In the three years of debate on the bill, only once—in 1897 when the focus of the debate had been on the viciousness of paperback books that the law of 1879 had brought into the mail—did the Loud bill even so much as pass the House. The next year, following the Committee of New York Publishers' campaign against it, and again in 1900, legislators who had once voted for the bill changed sides. The bill failed, leaving the post office to mail paperback books for 1 cent a pound. As one disgusted postmaster general said, "[Paperbacks] do not possess a single one of the attributes which Congress meant to require in publications that should be entitled to the second-class rate. Their 'stated intervals' are a parody; their 'subscription lists' a fiction; their claim of being published 'for the dissemination of information of a public character' a burlesque." In the end, Congress left postmasters general of the next century to do what it would not.[56]

Following the last vote on the bill in 1900, both *The Independent* and *The Outlook,* those standard Protestant religious weeklies of the late nineteenth century, commented, apparently without regret, that the Loud bill had lost by a larger majority than before. Although *The Outlook* remarked that the "general aim of the bill was good," neither it nor *The Independent* seemed troubled by the failure to drive paperback books and criminal papers from the mail. Nor did they seem disposed, as so many evangelicals did, to ban periodicals scattering advertisements of "immoral things" throughout the country for 1 cent a pound.[57]

Notes

1. *Report of the Postmaster General, 1891,* 8; *Report of the Postmaster General, 1896,* 5 (these and subsequent citations to postmasters general reports can be found in the *Congressional Information Service Serial Set Index* [Washington, 1997]).

2. *Dictionary of American Biography* (Washington, 1936), 10:351–52 (hereafter *DAB*); see also Allan Nevins, *Grover Cleveland:; A Study in Courage* (New York, 1941), 566–67.

3. *Congressional Record,* 54th Cong., 2d sess., 468 (Jan. 5, 1897). Years before the WCTU superintendent for the suppression of impure literature had protested this injustice to the postmaster general (*Union Signal,* May 9, 1889, 5).

4. *Congressional Record,* 54th Cong., 2d sess, 469, 474 (Jan. 5, 1897); see also *Congressional Record,* 54th Cong., 2d sess., 515–16 (Jan. 6, 1897) for a specific case of fraud.

5. *Congressional Record,* 55th Cong., 2d sess., 2383 (Mar. 2, 1898).

6. Ibid.

7. *Report of the Postmaster General, 1894,* 35–36; see also *Congressional Record,* 55th Cong., 2d sess., 2430 (Mar. 3, 1898).

8. *Golden Memories: An Illustrated Magazine for All Classes* 19 (Feb. 1898): passim.

9. *Golden Memories,* 1.

10. *Congressional Record,* 54th Cong., 2d sess., 188 (Dec. 15, 1888); *Congressional Record,* 55th Cong., 2d sess., 2334 (Mar. 1898).

11. "The Loud Bill, Notes on the Hearings before the Committee on Post Offices and Post Roads of the Senate of the United States . . . ," S. Rept. no 1517, 54th Cong., 2d sess., 130 (Jan. 16, 1897) (hereafter "Loud Bill").

12. "Loud Bill," 132.

13. *Report of the Postmaster General, 1887,* 902, *Report of the Postmaster General, 1888,* 679–80; *Report of the Postmaster General, 1892,* 69; *Report of the Postmaster General, 1894,* 31; *Report of the Postmaster General, 1896,* 9; *Report of the Postmaster General, 1897,* 7.

14. "Rate of Postage on Certain Periodicals." H. Rept. no. 513, 53d Cong., 2d sess., 1–2 (Mar. 1, 1894). This report accompanied H.R. 5188, which was a bill to restrict the second-class privilege; it was attached to the post office appropriation bill for 1895 and passed. *Congressional Record,* 53d Cong., 2d sess., 3642 (Apr. 10, 1894); *Congressional Record,* 54th Cong., 2d sess., 464 (Jan. 5, 1897). For the law on fraternal journals and educational institutions, see *United States Statutes at Large* (Washington, 1896), 28:105, and "Loud Bill," 26–27; on the 1890 proposal to restrict, see *Congressional Record,* 54th Cong., 2d sess., 474 (Jan. 5, 1897).

15. *Report of the Postmaster General, 1896,* 3, 7; New York *Times,* Mar. 28, 1896, 9; "Certain Rulings of the Post Office Department," S. Doc. no. 22, 54th Cong., 2d sess., 2 (Dec. 15, 1896). On Elderkin, see "Loud Bill," 47–48.

16. *Congressional Record,* 54 Cong., 2 Sess., 184 (Dec. 15, 1896).

17. On Loud, see *Biographical Dictionary of the United States Congress, 1774–1989* (Washington, 1989), 1392 (hereafter *BDAC*); see also Eugene F. Loud, "The Need for Postal Reform," *North American Review* 166 (Mar. 1898): 342ff.

18. *Congressional Record,* 54th Cong., 2d sess., 186–87 (Dec. 15, 1896); *Congressional Record,* 54th Cong., 2d sess., 476 (Jan 5, 1897).

19. For the suggestion that publishers could eliminate some of their competition if the no sample copies section were allowed in the mails, see *Congressional Record,* 54th Cong., 2d sess., 475 (Jan. 5, 1897).

20. Ibid., 187. Loud was charged with hiding the bill until the moment he presented it to Congress. He did not deny that charge.

21. *Congressional Record,* 54th Cong., 2d sess., 468 (Jan. 5, 1897). For the Christian organizations in support of the bill, see "Loud Bill," 165–66; see also *Congressional Record,* 56th Cong., 1st sess., 3090 (Mar 20, 1900) for Loud's estimation of the number of supporters.

22. *Congressional Record,* 54th Cong., 2d sess., 474 (Jan. 5, 1897).

23. *Congressional Record,* 54th Cong., 2d sess., 509, 516 (Jan. 6, 1897). Loud's position on the "great moral question" was uncertain. He never went beyond noting that it was a moral question, but left others to argue the point.

24. *Congressional Record,* 54th Cong., 2d sess., 467 (Jan. 5, 1897).

25. Ibid., 473, 511.

26. Ibid., 467–69; on Burton, see *DAB* (New York, 1944), supp. 1, 141.

27. Ibid., 469; "Loud Bill," 38.

28. *Congressional Record,* 55th Cong., 2d sess., 2383 (Mar. 2, 1898).

29. *Congressional Record,* 54th Cong., 2d sess. 474 (Jan. 5, 1897). On Jacob Bromwell as an educator, see *Congressional Record,* 55th Cong., 2d sess., 2884 (Mar. 2, 1898), and *BDAC,* 679.

30. *Congressional Record,* 54th Cong., 2d sess., 468 (Jan. 5, 1897).

31. *Congressional Record,* 55th Cong., 2d sess., 2384 (Mar. 2, 1898).

32. *Congressional Record,* 54th Cong., 2d sess., 471, 474 (Jan. 5, 1897). For a grudging review of the value of reading paperback novels, see W. H. Bishop, "Story-Paper Literature," *Atlantic Monthly* 14 (Sept. 1879): 419–21.

33. *Congressional Record,* 54th Cong., 2d sess., 519 (Jan. 6, 1897).

34. "Loud Bill," 3. On Mucro as instigator of "trash novels," see *Publishers' Weekly,* June 16, 1900, 1188. On Mucro's death, see New York *Times,* Apr. 25, 1896, 1. The *Times* reported that Mucro was an ardent, liberal-minded Presbyterian who contributed generously to his church.

35. "Loud Bill," 54.

36. John D. Hicks, *The Populist Revolt: A History of the Farmers' Revolt* (Lincoln, 1962), 340–41; Lawrence Goodwyn, *The Populist Movement: A Short History of the Agrarian Revolt in America* (New York, 1978), 245–46; Stanley L. Jones, *The Presidential Election of 1896* (Madison, 1964), 23–24.

37. "Loud Bill" (minority report), 3.

38. On Harvey, see Hicks, *Populist Revolt,* 240–41; see also Hicks, *Populist Revolt,* 24.

39. "Loud Bill," 24.

40. *Congressional Record,* 55th Cong., 2d sess., 2375–76 (Mar. 2, 1898).

41. Ibid., 2375.

42. Ibid., 2394. It was no coincidence that a significant number of Populist members of Congress were, or had been, editors of country papers.

43. "Postal Regulations," H. Mis. Doc. no. 90, 52d Cong., 2d sess., 120–21 (Washington, 1893).

44. "Loud Bill," 64–65.

45. *Congressional Record,* 55th Cong., 2d sess., 2329, 2332 (Mar. 1, 1898); *Congressional Record,* 56th Cong., 1st sess., 3088 (Mar. 20, 1900). Much fraud was involved in the collection of the ten names. Some were allegedly signed by family members, and in some cases one person signed all names.

46. *Congressional Record,* 55th Cong., 2d sess., 2332 (Mar. 1, 1898).

47. *Congressional Record,* 55th Cong., 2d sess., 471–72, 505 (Jan. 6, 1897); "Loud Bill," (minority report).

48. *Congressional Record,* 54th Cong., 2d sess., 462–66 (Jan. 5, 1897); see also *Congressional Record,* 56th Cong., 1st sess., 3095–96 (Mar. 20, 1900).

49. "Loud Bill," 43–44.

50. *Congressional Record,* 55th Cong., 2d sess., 2390 (Mar. 2, 1898).

51. Ibid., 2336; "Loud Bill," 65.

52. *Congressional Record,* 55th Cong., 2d sess., 2379 (Mar. 2, 1898).

53. On the fame of Clark's speech, see *Congressional Record,* 56th Cong., 1st sess., 319 (Mar. 27, 1900); "Loud Bill," 13. For a sampling of the opposition of religious papers to the bill, see petitions in the *Congressional Record,* 54th Cong., 2d sess., 484 (Jan. 5, 1897); *Congressional Record,* 54th Cong., 2d sess., 523 (Jan. 7, 1897); and *Congressional Record,*

54th Cong., 2d sess., 705 (Jan. 12, 1897). For one religious paper, the *Michigan Christian Advocate,* for the bill, see *Congressional Record,* 54th Cong., 2d sess., 448 (Jan. 5, 1897), and *The Independent,* Mar. 10, 1898, 311. For the *Union Signal*'s use of the sample-copy privilege, see *Union Signal,* Nov. 15, 1888, 13.

54. *Congressional Record,* 56th Cong., 1st sess., 3185 (Mar. 22, 1900). The New York *Evening Post,* blasted the book, which was permitted in the mail. "It is not necessary to soil the columns of this paper," the *Post* reported, "with a particular account of the sickly sentimentality of Mr. Dadoed's book or the reeking compost of filth and folly that the crude and frivolous Mr. Clyde Fetch had dug out of it, with which to mire the stage." As quoted in Mark Sullivan, *Our Times: The Turn of the Century* (New York, 1926), 518.

55. *Congressional Record,* 55th Cong., 2d sess., 2327 (Mar. 1, 1898); *Congressional Record,* 55th Cong., 2d sess., 2435 (Mar. 3, 1898; *Congressional Record,* 55th Cong., 2d sess., 3193 (Mar. 22, 1898).

56. *Congressional Record,* 54th Cong., 2d sess., 519 (Jan. 6, 1897); *Congressional Record,* 55th Cong., 2d sess., 2447 (Mar. 3. 1898); *Congressional Record,* 56th Cong., 1st sess., 3199 (Mar. 22, 1900). See also Chicago *Tribune,* Jan. 7, 1897, 8, Mar. 4, 1898, 7; *The Outlook,* Mar. 31, 1900, 699. In 1898 forty-seven Republicans, many of whom had previously voted for the bill, joined Democrats and Populists to defeat the measure (Chicago *Tribune,* Mar. 4, 1898, 7). For the rulings of the postmaster general, see *Report of the Postmaster General, 1902,* 28–29, 567–76. The bill of 1900 was further complicated by college presidents who feared that their college publications that had sneaked into the second-class mails under the law of 1894 would be deprived of that privilege if the law passed. *Congressional Record,* 56th Cong., 1st sess., 3089, 3101–2. For the postmaster general's quote, see, *Report of the Postmaster General, 1899,* 8.

57. *The Independent,* Mar. 29, 1900; *The Outlook,* Mar. 31, 1900, 699–700.

8 For the Preservation of the American Family

For this is the will *of God, even your sanctification: that ye should abstain from fornication: That every one of you should know how to possess his vessel in sanctification and honor; not in the lust of concupiscence, even as the Gentiles which know not God. . . . For God hath not called us unto uncleanness, but unto holiness.*

—First Thessalonians 4:3–7

When the women of the WCTU asked the president, the attorney general, and the postmaster general in 1891 to interpret the Comstock law more narrowly in order to increase the list of unmailable matter, they specifically requested that "immoral things" be banned from the mails. Too repulsive for the women to call by name in the nineteenth century, the "immoral things" they had in mind were devices to prevent conception and induce abortion, which, in fact, were already banned but circulated through the mails in spite of the ban.

Of all the moral problems the evangelical moral majority confronted in their efforts to purify the mail and preserve the nation's Christian character, none was more troublesome or more difficult for them to grapple with than that relating to birth control. It was an issue they rarely addressed directly, and in the 1890s, after a half century of struggle, it was no easier for Christian women—or men for that matter—to speak of contraceptives or abortifacients than it had been in 1850.

Until midcentury not many of the "immoral things" or even publications relating to reproductive control had passed through the mail. To be sure, methods of family limitation had been publicized in England in the 1820s, and two books on the subject were published in the United States in the 1830s. One, by Robert Dale Owen, was entitled *Moral Physiology; or, A Brief and Plain Treatise on the Population Questions;* the other, *Fruits of Philosophy; or, The Private Companion of Young Married People,* was written by Dr. Charles Knowlton. These were followed by other pamphlets, papers, and lectures relating to reproductive control, and by midcentury all methods of birth control had been written about in one place or another. That included the condom, which after the vulcanization of rubber in 1839 and subsequent improvements became the most widely used artificial birth control device of the nineteenth century.[1]

Nearly all this information had been made public by freethinkers, those perennial foes with whom evangelicals so often broke lances in the nineteenth century. Freethinking in everything except Christianity, upon which their minds were closed and which they saw as the source of humanity's troubles, only they were bold enough, and perhaps knowledgeable enough, to broach the subject of birth control in the 1830s. Both Knowlton and Owen were typical of the freethinkers. Knowlton, a fervent agnostic, was a physician in Ashfield, Massachusetts, and had been educated at what was to become Dartmouth College. Robert Dale Owen, son of Robert Owen, founder of the anti-Christian community at New Harmony, Indiana, was the publisher of the *Free Enquirer,* a freethinking paper he coedited with the iconoclast Frances Wright until she became pregnant out of wedlock and returned home to Scotland.[2]

Many if not most of the freethinkers' publications were probably originally purchased by other freethinkers scattered in small groups around the country and were sold by agents, in bookstores, or directly by their authors. Some publications no doubt went through the mail, but in the 1830s and 1840s the post office was of limited use to them. True, the postal system had expanded wonderfully during those years, but until the 1850s publications such as the *Free Inquirer* required an additional half-cent postage if mailed across state lines, books had not yet been admitted to the mail, and there was no parcel service. Pamphlets and periodicals could be mailed, but at 2.5 cents for each one-ounce copy and 1 cent more for every additional ounce it was not cheap to do so.[3]

From the 1850s until the 1870s, however, birth control information flowed unrelentingly and unimpeded through the mail, along with an enormous tide of publications of all kinds. In 1850 the 2,526 newspapers in the nation had a circulation of no more than five million. Ten years later, there were 4,051 newspapers, and circulation had reached 13,663,409, with a print run of nearly 927,000,000 copies. At the beginning of the next decade, 5,871 American newspapers had a circulation of more than twenty million and a print run of a billion and a half copies.[4]

This extraordinary escalation of newspapers, to say nothing of the proliferation of new magazines such as *Harper's New Monthly Magazine* and transient pamphlets and circulars of all kinds, has been attributed to Richard Hoe's steam cylinder rotary press and to the telegraph, the Associated Press, and the growth of towns and cities as well as Americans' craving for news. Indispensable to this growth were the expanding arms of the post office, as well as changes in the postage laws of 1851 and 1852 that permitted weekly newspapers to be mailed free throughout the county of publication, opened the mail to books, and reduced postage on both newspapers and periodicals to a flat rate of 1 cent per three-ounce copy mailed to any part of the nation. Even that cheap postage rate was reduced by half if prepaid. And there was more. Small papers could be mailed to one address in one eight-ounce package for a half-cent an ounce if prepaid, even if the papers in the package would cost more if mailed singly.[5]

The post office had kindled the growth of this astonishing array of publications in the 1850s, but paid advertisements sustained the newspapers and magazines themselves. Advertising was at least as old as writing, but no society had used it as widely as did Americans after the massing of publications in the 1850s. From simple advertisements placed by businesspeople in local papers, to paid agents whose business it was to sell space in newspapers and other publications, to agencies that made an art of advertising, the trade flourished during the 1850s. Hand in hand with the bustling business activity of the decade and the broad dissemination of new publications, advertisements for the products that were bursting from teeming American businesses appeared in thousands of newspapers, circulars, and advertising publications.[6]

Among those most prominently advertised were patent medicines that promised cures for all the ills of humanity. Finding a vast market among a trusting people who had so few remedies for their physical frailties, producers of patent medicine filled the mail with transient matter—pamphlets, books, and circulars—as well as newspapers, all brazenly advertising miraculous cures. Because the law's definition of a newspaper was vague, all were mailed at the newspaper-periodical postage rate, which, cheap as it was, often went unpaid. "On much of this kind of matter sent in the mails," the postmaster general complained in 1855, "no postage at all is collected. The greatest abuse in this respect pertains to lottery and patent medicine circulars and pamphlets with which the mails in every part of the country are burdened. In some instances from thirty to forty bags of this matter have been received in one day for distribution at a single office."[7]

Included among the many patent medicine advertisements were those for products to prevent conception or induce abortions. Until these advertisements began to find space in many newspapers, little attention had been paid to abortion (or feticide as it was sometimes called) in America. As in England, abortion in the United States was governed by the common law, which made its practice legal before the quickening of the fetus. Exercised without penalty in the century's early years, and generally—it was believed—by unmarried women and prostitutes as a last desperate solution to their plight, abortion was not widely regarded as a means of family limitation.[8]

Near midcentury, however, more suddenly than gradually, the silence that had enveloped abortion like a dark cloud lifted to expose a lucrative and burgeoning business. The growth of the new enterprise was partly the result of aggressive competition among abortionists. But it was no coincidence that it occurred simultaneously with the cheapening of the postage rate and expansion of the postal service, which allowed abortionists to advertise over ever-lengthening mail routes. It was, in fact, the rapid expansion of this business over the extended lines of communication that spawned in just five years an anti-abortion crusade led by physicians, many of whom were enraged by the lack of a Christian conscience that ignored the destruction of babies in the womb.[9]

The crusade was led by Horatio Robinson Storer, a one-time Harvard Medical School professor and gynecologist and son of David Humphrey Storer, professor of obstetrics at the Harvard Medical School. In 1855 the elder Storer had written a paper citing abortion as a cause of uterine disorders and criticizing women of fashion for selfishly destroying their babies. The paper was suppressed, but two years later, Horatio Storer, whose ancestors were Puritans, began where his father had left off.[10]

Already known in the early 1850s for his interest in abortion and abortion laws, Storer was appointed in 1857 by the American Medical Association to chair a committee to investigate abortion in the United States. Two years later, the association adopted the committee's report, which Storer had written, and passed resolutions encouraging state medical associations to press their legislatures to enact or revise anti-abortion laws. The phenomenal effect of this report, and physicians' subsequent powerful agitation to outlaw abortion, was reflected in some forty anti-abortion laws enacted in twenty-seven states over the ensuing years.[11]

The roots of the crusade have been traced to Storer's ambition to be recognized in his profession, the physicians' efforts to eliminate the competition of untrained abortionists with the help of state laws, the elevation of the status of the medical profession, the prevention of injury or worse to women at the hands of the untrained, the attempt to confine women to traditional roles, the desire for fewer children among women of old Puritan stock, and even to "psychodynamic factors" among the reformers. Capitalism, too, has been urged as a source of the increased use of contraception and abortion.[12]

Missing from that list is the fact that Christian impulse drove so many crusades of the time. It may have been that ambition lay behind Storer's campaign against abortion. But the moral outrage of that son of Puritanism at the prevalence of a practice he considered anti-Christian and sinful permeates his writing on the subject, as does his unrestrained anger at the press that carried the advertisements of quack practitioners of abortion and their products over mail routes. "Hardly a newspaper throughout the land," he wrote, "that does not contain their [abortionists'] open and pointed advertisements." Knowledge of abortionists' activities was "brought home to all our women, no matter how purely minded, and despite every care to the contrary, through the medium of the daily press; few papers, however professedly respectable or religious, proving able to refuse the bribe." Storer also cited druggists as accomplices in the crime of abortion, although newspapers bore the primary responsibility for the scourge. "The press," he believed, "if it choose, may almost annihilate the crime; it now openly encourages it."[13]

Of course, women themselves, particularly Protestant women, were not blameless. It was not, Storer discovered, only young, unmarried women who resorted to abortion and read the advertisements to take advantage of the increasing exposure of the trade. Very often it was married women, frequently women of fashion and privilege, who aborted their young for matters of convenience or image. Sometimes they even boasted of having an abortion and recommended doing so to friends, and thus "the wretch whose account with the Almighty is heaviest with guilt" became heroines. "If these wretched women," Storer wrote in 1868, "these married, lawful mothers, ay! and these Christian husbands—are thus murdering their children by the thousand, through ignorance, they must be taught the truth; but if—as there is reason to believe is too often the case—they have been influenced to do so by fashion, extravagance of living, or lust, no language of condemnation can be too strong."[14]

Storer's list of reasons for the spread of abortion included the failure of the Protestant clergy and their congregations to take a stand against it. To Storer, the protection of infants in the womb was a clear Christian duty and their destruction a sin. It grieved him that he was compelled to admit that "Christianity itself, or at least Protestantism, has failed to check the increase in criminal abortion."[15]

The charge was more true than untrue. Perhaps the first prominent member of the clergy to speak against contraception and abortion was Horace Bushnell, the controversial Congregational minister and theologian who condemned both in a speech in 1837. John Todd, another Congregational minister, went further and bitterly attacked abortion in his book *Serpents in the Dove's Nest* (1867). Moreover, the Congregational churches in Connecticut and Maine openly opposed the practice in the 1860s, as did the Old School Branch of the Presbyterian Church in 1869. Yet for the most part both the Protestant clergy and the religious press remained silent on the subject in spite of vigorous efforts on the part of physicians to enlist them in what they believed was a Christian cause.[16]

Just as abolitionists had to teach Americans the evils of slavery, so physicians found it necessary to sensitize them to the evils of abortion. Yet it did seem odd that it was physicians, wrapping their arguments against contraception and abortion in Christian rhetoric, who did so rather than Protestant ministers. It was odder still that evangelicals, many of whom had been Sabbatarians and among the leaders against slavery, were not at the forefront of the battle against abortion. Perhaps their reluctance to believe that Christian women in their congregations were engaging in such a practice was partly responsible for the ministers' silence.[17]

Most likely, however, ministers feared to address such delicate sexual matters from the pulpit. Their aversion was suggested by John Todd, who began his book by saying that "nothing less but an imperative duty could induce me to pen what I am about to write." Indirectly apologizing for writing about abortion, which he called "fashionable murder," he asked women who might complain about his book's indelicacy to consider that the practice of abortion was "fearfully common."[18]

That hesitancy was observed and criticized by Henry Ward Beecher, the most prominent Protestant minister of the day, whose own alleged affair with his friend's wife had perhaps made him more aware of his colleagues' neglect of a serious problem. "'So inveterate is the prejudice against introducing the subject of licentiousness,'" he wrote in *Twelve Lectures to Young Men,* "'that ministers of the gospel, knowing vice to be singularly dangerous and frequent, have yet by silence almost complete, or broken only by circuitous allusions, manifested their submission to the popular taste.'"[19]

Silence, however, in no way meant that evangelicals approved of either contraception or abortion. Not much is known about the pressures or motivations that led state legislators to enact anti-abortion laws during the declining years of the nineteenth century, possibly because they, like their constituents, hesitated to speak out on the subject. The rapidity with which they passed those laws once the fire was lit, however, suggests that they shared a belief that abortion was an unchristian evil of immense proportions. Many considered it to be lashed to the sins of fornication, adultery, lust, and greed.[20]

Perhaps Alexander Andrus Alcott bespoke the attitude of most evangelicals toward sex, contraception, and abortion in the nineteenth century in *The Physiology of Marriage* (1855). Alcott, cousin of Bronson Alcott, the novelist's father, was born in the little village of Wolcott, Connecticut. Imbued with that Puritan urge to help humanity, he hoped to improve society through education and began his career as a teacher. Ill-health encouraged him to study medicine, and that led him, in turn, into counteracting "Satan's plans" by educating young people on sex and marriage. His book on the subject, however, unlike those by Owen and Knowlton, was written in a Christian context and instructed readers on what might be called a Christian view of sexual matters and the marriage relationship.[21]

Contrary to what has sometimes been said, Christians did not hate sex. Nor did Alcott. But like most Christians of the time, he did fear its unbridled power. Like the Puritans, Alcott taught that a sovereign God had given men and women a powerful appetite to enjoy and use to replenish the earth. But it was not to be appeased either by fornication, which would lead to the downfall of pure women, or by destructive self-abuse. Sex was to be reserved for that divinely inspired institution of marriage, and men and women, Alcott believed, had a duty, even a religious duty, to marry. "Bad as the world now is," he wrote, "how much worse would it be but for matrimony? It is, so to speak of it, the golden chain that binds society together. Remove it and you set the world ajar."[22]

To be successful, marriage required perseverance and self-denial. Alcott understood that the arrival of children and the occasional physical incapacities of women burdened marriage, and he raised the question of whether, under certain circumstances, means might not be taken to prevent conception. Some rare conditions, Alcott grudgingly granted, might make coitus interruptus, the cyclical method, or even total abstinence necessary. But he was clearly uncomfortable with that advice and would not go farther. He would have nothing to do with the artificial means of contraception, which might be used by the unmarried as well as the married. Dismissing Knowlton's book, which taught "people, both in married life and elsewhere, the art of gratifying the sexual appetite without the necessity of progeny," Alcott proclaimed it the work of a physician "of much greater practical skill than strict integrity, especially towards God."[23]

As for abortion, Alcott, like Storer, abhorred the practice. He called the various means of abortion "Crimes without Name" and suggested that the public was unaware of how prevalent they were "against Nature and Nature's God." He was especially incensed by the most common. "Of all the measures for accomplishing these results which I have called *crimes without name,"* he wrote, "none are more common, I think, than the use of poison of one kind or another, and that of instruments; and certainly none of these are more reprehensible."[24]

For Alcott, the proper approach toward sex was celibacy until marriage and restraint or self-denial thereafter for the well-being of both partners. "God did not intend marriage to be unlicensed indulgence," he wrote. Its purpose was, in part, to teach "self restraint and self-denial." Although he was hesitant about prescribing a rigid rule regarding the frequency of intercourse between married couples, it was clear that he believed once a month was sufficient. Real gratification, he observed, came less from frequency than from infrequency.[25]

That Alcott's views regarding sex, contraception, and abortion were not far from those of most evangelical Protestants in the nineteenth century was reflected in the nation's postal laws, which, in effect, pronounced contraception and abortion immoral and obscene in 1873, a stigma that long persisted in the evangelical mind.

Among the 182,000 obscene photographs and five tons of obscene books and pamphlets that Anthony Comstock had seized in his raids on bookstores in 1872 were more than thirty thousand "immoral rubber articles" and seven hundred pounds of lead molds for their manufacture. Discovered in pornographic shops, where they were sold along with a vast array of obscene literature and catalogs advertising obscene materials (much of which was mailed to young students in academies, colleges, and seminaries), they were clearly intended for the use of the unmarried. "For be it known," Comstock wrote in 1873, "that wherever these books go, or catalogues of these books, there you will ever find, as almost indispensable, a complete list of rubber articles for masturbation or for the professed prevention of conception."[26]

In reproductive control other than self-restraint Comstock saw, as did many other evangelicals, a threat to the purity of the young, the destruction of the family, and an affront to Christian morality and the Christian nation. No doubt he worried, like Alcott, that sexual gratification without fear of pregnancy would destroy the institution of marriage and bring about the unraveling of society. In any event, frustrated by previous legislation that gave him no authority to remove contraceptive devices from the mail or destroy abortionists' trade, he had written into his proposed law comprehensive provisions that would deny abortionists and peddlers of contraceptive devices the use of the mail. "In no case," wrote his biographers, "did he show a more passionate zeal than in the fight against purveyors of contraceptive remedies or devices."[27]

When Comstock brought it to their attention in 1873, some members of Congress professed to be appalled at this sweeping use of the mails to advertise and sell "immoral appliances," which, together with other obscene materials, one legislator described as "of so low and debasing a nature that it would seem that the brute creation itself would turn from in disgust." Although most legislators were presumably unaware of how widespread the use of the mail to spread contraceptive information was, they could hardly have been ignorant of the traffic in this invitation to promiscuity or of the ravages of abortion. Even as they met in early 1873, a story appeared in the news about an abortionist who, in a flawed attempt to abort her fetus, had killed his client and shipped her body off in a trunk.[28]

The abortionist, Jacob Rosenzweig, was only one of a number of practitioners who had recently killed their patients, and the role of newspapers in fostering the practice of abortion was condemned in the New York *Times.* In January 1873, when Comstock was exhibiting his collection of "immoral things" and presenting his bill to members of Congress, the *Times* attacked the New York *Herald* for its "medical" advertisements, through which abortionists had "been enabled to reach their victims, and make profits large enough to warrant the purchase of luxuriously furnished houses at the seaside, and in the fashionable thoroughfares of New York." The *Times* went on to note that three abortionists had recently been sent to prison, and in every case "the evidence of the principal witnesses went to show that the 'medical' columns of the daily and weekly journals had brought together the murdered women and their slayers."[29]

It was against that background of the killing of mother and child and the profusion of advertisements of a booming business, as well as the anti-abortion crusade proclaiming the immorality of the trade that Congress, not blindly but deliberately, included contraceptives and abortafacients among the obscene material to be banned from the mail in 1873. What they agreed to in enacting the Comstock law of that year was not just the removal from the mails of obscene, lewd, and lascivious publications but of "any article or thing designed or intended for the prevention of conception or procuring of abortion" and "any article or thing intended or adapted for any indecent or immoral use or nature."[30]

Nor was that all. Such was their aversion to these twin means of reproductive control that legislators proscribed from the mail "any written or printed card, circular, book, pamphlet, advertisement or notice of any kind giving information directly or indirectly, where or how, or of whom, or by what means either of the things before mentioned may be obtained or made." Moreover, "any person who shall knowingly deposit, or cause to be deposited, for mailing or delivery, any of the hereinbefore-mentioned articles or things, or any notice, or paper containing any advertisement relating to the aforesaid articles or things, and any person who, in pursuance of any plan or scheme for disposing of any of the hereinbefore-mentioned articles or things, shall take, or cause to be taken, from the mail any such letter or package, shall be deemed guilty of a misdemeanor."[31]

Following passage of the bill, Comstock at first seemed pleased with the new law. In its wake he was able to cause the arrest under federal law of numerous abortionists by securing from them either information of their business or an actual abortifacient through the mail. One of these was Ann Lohman, the infamous "Madame Restell," whose fabulous home at the corner of Fifty-second Street and Fifth Avenue in New York City attested to the wealth she had amassed. Arriving there to arrest her, Comstock encountered the distraught wife of a prominent man. The mother of four was seeking an abortion and asked Comstock to protect her privacy. Comstock agreed to say nothing, but he was less agreeable to Madame Restell, who offered him $40,000 not to arrest her. Comstock was not for sale, and when Restell was confronted with the possibility of a term in jail, which she had already once endured, she committed suicide.[32]

The new law also diminished the number of abortionists' advertisements appearing in the nation's newspapers. A New York *Times* editorial observed that the law had forced the *Herald* to weed out "advertisements which have brought ruin to the souls and bodies of countless human beings."[33] Meanwhile, Comstock was encouraged by the prospect of other papers following the *Herald*'s example. The truth was, however, that abortionists were still at work long after passage of the Comstock law, and quack advertisements still appeared in the *Herald.*

In March of 1875, almost exactly two years after the law banning contraceptive and abortionist advertisements from the mail had been enacted, the sad story appeared in the *Times* of a married woman whose illicit affair had resulted in her pregnancy and a botched abortion. Seduced by a married man who had heard her sing in the choir of an uptown church, she revealed as she lay dying that she had "searched the columns of a morning journal for relief" and was attracted by the advertisement of Mme. Annie J. Ihl, a long-time practitioner who performed the abortion. The woman's subsequent death led the *Times* to again attack the New York *Herald* for its role in the event. "It is to be hoped," ran the editorial, "that the proprietor of the *Herald* will one day be brought to see the necessity of refusing to publish advertisements of a certain horrible class of male and female 'doctors.' . . . One case should have been enough," the editorial continued, but "still the traffic goes on."[34]

Such incidents were still occurring in the centennial year when Congress considered an amendment to the Comstock law that would correct an omission in the law of 1873. By that time, however, Comstock's vigorous attacks on abortionists and editors of newspapers that carried advertising for abortions had disturbed the nests of so many special interests that some members of Congress were more concerned about clauses outlawing such advertising than correcting omissions in the original bill.[35]

No changes in those clauses were proposed in the amendment, but the outraged complaints of Comstock's victims, whom he had dragged into court or otherwise forced to give up lucrative advertising, made legislators acutely aware that the original law not only banned contraceptive and abortion advertisements from the mail but also prevented publications from mentioning where (or how, or of whom, or by what means) such contraceptives or abortions might be obtained. Reacting to that seemingly belated discovery, some legislators protested that the law was too vague, that the wording "of things adapted for any indecent or immoral purpose" was too broad, that it exposed the press to danger, and that the penalty for violating the law was too severe. Others complained that merely publishing a paper that advertised the place where proscribed articles or abortions were to be found subjected both editor and reader to unwarranted punishment.[36]

Still, those who objected to the amendment, fearful of being thought supportive of contraception and abortion, quickly denied that they opposed the purpose of the law. No one, indeed, opposed the amendment outright in spite of irate complaints against Comstock's heavy-handed enforcement of it. Instead, they urged that the law be recommitted to the Post Office Committee and amended to protect the innocent, which it was. When it reappeared, however, it was but little changed. A few phrases of the original were missing, but the penalty for knowingly mailing or receiving matter relating to contraception and abortion was still a fine of not less than $100 nor more than $5,000, or imprisonment for not less than a year or more than ten, or both fine and imprisonment. Passed with virtually no debate, the legislation laid to rest any ambiguity about Congress's desire to control the mailing of contraceptive information or concern that the Comstock law had gone beyond what Congress essentially intended. The view that these were unmitigated evils in the American society had gained general acceptance among a moral majority that did not include freethinkers.[37]

Few issues divided freethinkers and evangelicals in the late nineteenth century more sharply than the question of reproductive control. It was an issue made to order for unbelievers. It gave them an opening to pummel the hated Christian morals and obscenity laws with reasonable and appealing arguments on the virtues of contraception. Ignoring abortion, of which they generally disapproved, and unbound by Christian apprehensions of uncontrolled sex, the freethinkers, almost alone of all Americans, promoted reproductive control.

Whether from Valley Falls, Kansas, where Moses Harmon published *Lucifer, the Lightbearer,* Princeton, Massachusetts, where Ezra Heywood issued *The Word* and *Cupid's Yokes,* or New York City, where DeRobigne Mortimer Bennett put out *The Truth Seeker,* freethinkers' publications preached the blessings of contraception. Scorning Christian marriage as prostitution in the pages of *The Word* and again in *Cupid's Yokes,* Heywood enlightened readers on the means of contraception. Less radical than Heywood, Bennett made the case for contraception in *The Truth Seeker* and in his book *Champions of the Church: Their Crimes and Persecutions.*[38]

Comstock's arrest of both men, and their subsequent imprisonment for their allegedly obscene publications, had understandably left both Bennett and Heywood with a boundless hatred of Comstock, and they heaped coals of fire upon him in their publications. In *Champions of the Church,* after summarizing the misery Comstock had inflicted upon undeserving victims who had written about or advertised contraceptive devices or related matters, Bennett wrote a reasoned defense of contraception and prophesied its future acceptance. "The question of preventing conception is one which is bound to be discussed and passed upon by the American public as it has been by the people of Great Britain," he wrote. "It will be canvassed in all its aspects, and it will be examined into with a view to decide whether it is criminal or not." Predicting that Comstock's law would not "stand through all coming time," Bennett went on to describe the many instances in which contraception could be used to prevent suffering, including limiting population growth, which seemed especially desirable in view of the fear in some circles that the world's population would soon outstrip its food supply. Moreover, he struck a blow for women's rights. "Is it not right," he asked, "for any wife or mother to decide for herself whether she wishes to bear more children or not?"[39]

Because evangelicals had been brought up to believe that sex outside marriage was sinful and that fornication as well as adultery were violations of God's law and threats to the American family and a Christian nation, the question of contraception was of immense importance to serious Christians who studied the Bible and believed its every word. But unlike freethinkers, who actively promoted contraception, they waged no campaign from pulpit or Christian press against it as they had against Sunday newspapers and the violation of the Sabbath. Nor did they refer directly to contraceptive devices except to call them "articles of indecent and immoral use."[40]

That did not mean that evangelicals shunned sexual subjects altogether. Sex—unbridled, illicit sex—loomed large among the evils they saw about them. "'The use of the reproduction function,'" J. H. Kellogg, a leader of the purity crusade, wrote in 1877, "'is perhaps the highest physical act of which man is capable; its *abuse* is certainly one of the most grievous attacks against nature which it is possible for him to perpetrate.'" Their answer to the problem was not condoms or syringes but sexual self-restraint, a theme that runs like a charted path through their writings. Indeed, the sex manuals of the late nineteenth century, written in a religious context, brim with instructions to young men on how to restrain the sexual impulse—including everything from diet to exercise to temperance and employment—with no mention of contraception.[41]

Such manuals contain frank discussions of sexual matters, as did WCTU publications with respect to errant sex and prostitution and the costly consequences of ruined lives and venereal disease. Members of the WCTU were proud of the boldness of their attack on these problems. "Not more than two score years ago," one member wrote in 1898, "not one of the literary or religious publications of that day dared speak openly of the great truths based upon natural law, an ignorance of which dooms the youthful victims to disease, mental degradation and moral death, the result of solitary and social sins, which then as now exist everywhere." Even the Reverend Todd's *Student Manual,* according to her account, "yielded to the false shame of his day," hiding behind the Latin tongue the "wise counsel which every boy should be given." Rather than fearing a discussion of prostitution and venereal disease, as so many did, the WCTU had ushered in the "dawn of a new day" and unfolded the "truths" to boys and girls, "purely and delicately."[42]

Even so, evangelicals remained reticent about speaking of contraception and abortion or naming the devices by which these might be accomplished. It was as if they feared that the mere mention of contraception or to the devices used for that purpose would give those things a legitimacy that would lead to the impurity of individuals they would make pure. Left, then, to attack indirectly what they could not strike directly, they taught young people to be pure and abstinent, showed them how to restrain sexual impulses, and struggled to create a pure environment throughout the 1880s and 1890s. Everywhere they worked together—in reform associations, White Shield and White Cross organizations, and church groups such as the Epworth League and the WCTU—to enforce the Comstock law and strengthen it in order to prevent the postal service from spreading "immoral things" throughout the country.

The post office was a major obstacle to containing this perceived threat to marriage, a stable family life, and a Christian nation. Not only did it circulate newspapers and periodicals that carried advertising for contraceptives and abortifacients through every urban and country post office and then on to nearly every home, but it also conveyed contraceptive devices as well.

In 1872 Congress created the post office's parcel service more by accident than design, and the story of its development is replete with the usual conflict of interests that spun around so many postal innovations. Beginning with the mailing of seeds to constituents in the late 1850s, by 1872 Congress had added ores, metals, and general merchandise to the list of matter that might be mailed. That was followed by a prolonged contest among urban merchants, seedsmen, express companies, and small-town shopkeepers who feared the competition of mail-order stores to determine the weight and postage rate of a parcel that could be mailed. To appease all interests, especially express companies, in 1876 the weight of a mailable parcel was set at four pounds and the postage rate at 1 cent an ounce.[43]

Restricted as it was, the parcel post system did wonders for the mercantile trade of large urban department stores and mail-order stores like Montgomery Ward. It was hardly less of a boon to dealers in contraceptives and abortafacients and publishers of those advertising magazines whose pages informed the public that they could order and receive by mail the devices so detested by evangelicals. Not only did the package service provide them with a way to reach the nation's heartland where such unwelcome urban products were not otherwise usually available, but it also permitted anxious customers to receive goods clandestinely. Secrecy was important in making such purchases. One manufacturer, for example, assured customers that their correspondence was "treated with the utmost confidence, and no names of our patrons are divulged under any circumstances." [44]

To mail such goods was illegal, of course, and involved some risk. Postal regulations required that mailed packages must "admit of easy examination," and even registered packages were to be examined before registration. In the busy post offices where most of the packages were mailed, however, a careful examination of every parcel thrown into the mail was impossible. Postal clerks were no more able to prevent all contraceptives and abortifacients from being mailed than postal inspectors were to screen all advertising for them.[45]

The most common device to be mailed was rubber condoms, which virtually all manufacturers of contraceptives offered. For women, cleansing by means of a syringe appeared to be the favorite method of contraception. "'They [women] seem to have the information,'" the Kansas City *Medical Record* reported in 1884, "'that in this way fecundation may generally be prevented. How this knowledge had become so widespread we are unable to say.'"[46]

Greater familiarity with the advertising and devices that passed through the mail would have explained to the *Record* how it was that women had such knowledge. In the mail were thousands of notices advertising a remarkable number of syringes designed for contraceptive purposes. Among them was one that, according to the company's blurb, could be used in bed. Composed of the "best material" and "constructed upon the most scientific principles," it had two tubes, one that brought fluid in and the other that took it out. The device came either "with a bulb syringe attachment" or "with a Fountain Spring Attachment." Used with a weak alkali solution or water and alcohol, the Universal Safety Syringe would "eventually cure" congestion and inflammation. Should women wish to "bring about a cure in a short time," the company recommended a preparation called "Nonmoral," also to be used with the syringe, which would "cure the ills in from 5 to 20 days." The price was "$1.50 a bottle (mailed.)" The Woman's Medical Company of Chicago, which sold the device, also boasted that its institute made a "specialty of 'Diseases' of Women'" and even treated patients "by mail." "Write us your troubles," urged the advertisement. "Thousands cured at home by correspondence. All cases treated confidentially."[47]

If two or three syringes were not enough, some manufacturers offered a more extensive variety. At a cost of $2, the "Lady's Friend," for example, was advertised by E. Edwards and Company of New York as "the only perfect vaginal syringe in the world." That same company also offered the "Emerald Fountain Syringe," the "Niagara Water Bottle Fountain Syringe," the "Diamond Syringe No. 10," and the "Family Fountain Syringe." All of these, the company pledged, were packed for mailing in boxes "with plain sealed wrapper," and postage was paid on all orders. An address form at the bottom of the advertisement requested that patrons list only name, town, county, and state, which revealed that the company's appeal was to rural Americans and suggested how much it depended upon the mail for business.[48]

Besides syringes, E. Edwards and Company also sold rubber pessaries that were "an absolute preventative and safeguard against a certain unpleasant feature relating to women only." But in the event this was not used, the company had the "Celebrated French Apple Pills," which were "the most successful emmenagogue ever put on the market." They were "the only absolutely reliable female pills," capable of "restoring the menstrual period or monthly sickness." Moreover, they were said to *"never disappoint."* The cost was $2, prepaid, and the box came by mail in a plain wrapper.[49] It was these "immoral things"—the numberless advertisements for them in the newspapers and advertising periodicals that continued to pass through the mail in spite of the Comstock law—that evangelicals hoped to drive from the mail with additional restrictive legislation.

The distress such advertisements caused among Christian families in the late nineteenth century was no better illustrated than in the anger of an anguished mother, the wife of an Illinois state senator, whose daughter had received a letter containing an advertisement for an "Antiseptic Vaginal Suppository." "Our SUPPOSITORIES" ran the notice, "contains the most reliable and harmless antiseptics. By introducing one of them into the Vagina pushing it well up against the cervex about five minutes before intercourse the Coco butter will melt, setting the drug free, which acts as an effective germicide."[50]

Outraged by this insult to her daughter, the woman asked the postmaster general to suppress such advertising. "I think it a duty as a mother," she observed, "to enclose this letter which came sealed with 2c stamp to my daughter a young girl." She was writing, she said, not only for her two daughters, who were "pure & lovely in character," but also "for the sake of young innocent girls, who no doubt have had the same letters," which were written for money by "unprincipled men who would mark their ruin." Worried lest many girls be led astray by such "dangerous advice," she asked, "Am I asking too much of you who stands at the helm, and who has so many weighty matters pressing upon him, to give this a serious thought & use means to suppress such vileness to our young children being sent broadcast through the land[?]" Requesting the postmaster general not to mention her name, she concluded by noting that the advertisements "were not sent to a married woman . . . but to a maid. They [the perpetrators] hunt up the catalogues for names and scatter them all over the land."[51]

Advertising for abortion-related items and services was particularly pernicious. Few women reading the *Family Ledger* in the 1890s, for example, would have had trouble deciphering an advertisement "for all ladies, safe, quick cure, confinement at home." Nor could they possibly have misunderstood Dr. H. M. Rogers's advertisement of his "monthly regulator" that "brought happiness to hundreds of anxious women." "Have never had a single failure," ran the notice. "Longest cases relieved in 2 to 5 days without fail; positively safe; by mail or at the office, $2."[52]

Nor did they misunderstand, although some may have been skeptical. Believing that because Rogers had post office box 36 the postmaster must know him, one woman wrote to ask for more information. "I should like to be informed by you," she said, "if he is a reliable doctor. I wrote to him to say, that I am three months pregnant, that my husband had left me, and that I was a poor woman working out. Dr. Rogers writes in answer that he wants $2 for certain relief. I have no $2 to throw away, as I have to work a long week for it. But if you can honestly recommend him I shall certainly send him the $2."[53]

Other advertising for contraceptives was more circumspect. Apparently hoping to circumvent the law, manufacturers of contraceptives often advertised their products as remedies for ills common to women, suggesting only incidentally their real purpose. "Femica's Celebrated Tampons," for example, was cleverly designed for "Diseases Peculiar to Women" but carried the warning that they were not to be used "just before or immediately after sexual congress, as they will invariably prevent conception."[54]

Accompanying that advertisement was an article, distributed but not mailed, throughout Lexington, Kentucky, in 1897. It was made to resemble a newspaper clipping and allegedly quoted physicians on the means of preventing conception without resorting to the dangers of abortion. "All physicians know something of the prevalence of criminal abortion in any community," read the article, "but particularly in large cities. Every practitioner is aware of ruined physical health of many women because of their practicing criminal feticide, and gynecologists reap their greatest harvest from the uterine maladies engendered by instrumental abortion as the results of frequently repeated confinements at close intervals, with the inevitable accidents and concomitant injuries to the uterus under such conditions." To avoid that unwelcome result, the alleged physicians recommended, *"the prevention of conception,"* even in the face of the "anathemas of the church in its every faction." The best prevention was, of course, "Dr. Femica's celebrated Tampon, sold by the Femica Supply Co. of Indianapolis, Ind."[55]

Many notices that publicized contraceptives and abortifacients appeared in advertising papers that Congress subsidized with cheap postage and refused to remove from the second-class mail, even though their subscription lists were suspect and their abuse of the sample-copy privilege was notorious. The papers were virtually mail-order catalogs, and the center of their publication in the nineteenth century was Augusta, Maine, probably because of its easy access to paper mills. There, one publisher alone had five such papers and another four, all flourishing because of the sample-copy privilege that swelled their numbers and enabled the publishers to guarantee huge circulations to businesses that advertised with them.[56]

Provided with such down-home titles as *Golden Memories, Sunshine, Happy Hours,* and *Hearth and Home* and directed at farm families, the periodicals seemed the very essence of wholesomeness. Four of the two publishers' nine publications, however, were banned from the Canadian mail in 1891 because they carried, according to a Canadian official, advertisements "of an immoral or indecent tendency."[57]

One of those banned was *Vickery's Fireside Visitor,* a paper of twenty-four pages in 1897. It was one of John H. Hill's four publications and had been living off the sample-copy privilege, 1 cent a pound postage, and unsavory advertising for twenty years. To the anguish of evangelicals, neither it nor the others were barred from the U.S. mail. Protesting against these advertisements, the superintendent of the WCTU's impure literature department in 1892 remarked that the *Kreutzer Sonata,* which Postmaster General John Wanamaker had banned, did not compare in filthiness to the "ads" in some newspapers; nor was it so corrupting in its intention. "The *intention* of the 'ads,'" she wrote, "is bad and is *meant* to be bad and bad alone."[58]

It might have been supposed that the Comstock law forbidding mailing advertising for products that promised to prevent conception or produce abortion was detailed enough to bar them from the mail. But that was not always so. When postal inspectors brought offenders to court for such violations, they often pleaded innocent on the grounds that the products they had advertised would neither prevent conception nor produce abortions. Some judges, but not all, ruled that the government must prove the products actually did what they were supposed to do.[59]

Had evangelical America been less concerned about the threat contraception and abortion seemed to pose to families and morals, a busy Congress might have overlooked that evasion of the law. As it was, the Senate passed another amendment to the Comstock law in 1886, declaring unmailable "every article or thing designed or intended, or adapted, or *purporting to be for any indecent or immoral use, and every article or thing so advertised or offered for sale as to suggest or lead to the use of the same for the purpose of preventing conception, or the procuring of abortion.*" For good measure the words *filthy and disgusting* were added to the adjectives describing unmailable matter in order to remove the various disgusting magazines that a House committee claimed advertised "alleged specific diseases" but that, in keeping with evangelical reservations about such matters, the committee said "would be nameless."[60]

The amendment was introduced by James Wilson, senator from Iowa. Wilson's political career had been a distinguished one. As chair of the Judiciary Committee in the House of Representatives during the Civil War and Reconstruction he had played an influential role in much of the Reconstruction legislation. The New York *Times* called Wilson the "Slave's Friend" for his bill to enfranchise slaves in Washington, D.C., and for his resolution to forbid the return to slavery of those who had attached themselves to the Union Army. A one-time harnessmaker, lawyer, and prohibitionist, Wilson was typical example of the moral majority that sought to maintain a Christian nation.[61]

Wilson's bill passed the Republican Senate without debate and moved on to the Democratic House, where its counterpart was being fashioned in the Post Office Committee by Truman Merriman, an independent Democrat from New York City. Explaining how "dealers in obscene and filthy matter" had evaded the law against mailing contraceptive and abortive information, Merriman proposed a bill similar to the Senate measure that would make the law against contraceptive and abortifacient advertisements so definite it could not be evaded. But perhaps because freethinkers were in Washington that year demanding abolition of all Comstock laws, or possibly because the Democrats had opposed sumptuary laws in their platform of 1884, the House ignored the bill.[62]

Two years later, however, when Congress did amend the Comstock law for the third and last time, it no longer needed to include the words *purporting to be* because the courts had finally concluded that it was no defense to argue that the products being advertised to prevent conception or procure abortion did not work. The amendment did include, however, an unprecedented provision stipulating that anything—article, pamphlet, advertisement, or whatever—intended to prevent conception or procure abortion, *"whether sealed as first class matter or not,"* was unmailable.[63]

Helpful as it was, this law, like the others, failed to prevent purveyors of birth control devices from advertising through the mail or even mailing their goods. The words *filthy and disgusting* describing unmailable matter, which had been in Wilson's Senate bill two years before and would have broadened the postmaster general's power to drive some contraceptive matter from the mail, were stripped from the amendment. Aside from that, the market for the goods was too widespread, contraceptive advertisements were too lucrative for publishers to reject, profits were too inviting, and publications were too numerous for postal inspectors to eradicate all advertising that evangelicals found obnoxious.

Failure of the law, however, brought only renewed evangelical efforts during the early 1890s to rid the mail of contraceptive information and devices. In the spring of 1892, several bills before Congress were designed to drive what the WCTU superintendent of purity called "cancer planters" from the mail. One proposed that "upon the continued mailing of newspapers or periodicals containing advertisements, or other articles or items forbidden by this bill to be transmitted in the mails, the Postmaster General is authorized to declare such publication including future issues thereof unmailable."[64]

Claiming she had letters from throughout the United States and Canada imploring her to "do something to stem the flood of vile and corrupting matter" passing through the mail, WCTU superintendent Emilie D. Martin rallied members to support such legislation, noting that those who had proprietary interest in "advertising and selling abominations" would oppose it. But the bills to strike at those who dealt in contraceptives also struck at publishers of paperback books, and all failed of passage that spring.[65]

The tangled interests of postal service users—publishers of paperback books and advertising papers, merchants, abortionists, and manufacturers of contraceptives—made purification of the mail in the late nineteenth century virtually impossible. A law regulating a single interest such as contraception and abortion could seemingly not be written without touching another interest. Moreover, the demand for contraceptive material, the help given to the trade through cheap advertising, and the convenience of the parcel system was so great that it was easier to stop the flow of obscene literature than that of contraceptive devices and information. Yet continued public pressure of a moral evangelical majority forced Congress to take one more step to suppress the spread of contraception and abortion.

In 1894 Wisconsin's Sen. William F. Vilas introduced a measure to prevent express companies from "the carrying of obscene literature and articles designed for indecent and immoral use from one State or Territory to another State or Territory." Without debate the Senate passed the measure and sent it to the House, where it languished until 1897 when it was brought forward and passed with no debate. When Vilas again brought it before the Senate, however, it was temporarily held up by Edward Wolcott of Colorado, who had not read the bill. But like every member of Congress who had ever had reservations about such bills, he assured the Senate that he did not "wish even to appear to object to the passage of a bill of this sort." After the bill was retained for a day it was passed—again without debate.[66]

Senator Vilas's law confirmed the national consensus at the end of the nineteenth century: Material related to contraception and abortion would not be tolerated in the mail if law could prevent it. Because this was not a regulation of the government's mail service but the first control of a private carrier's right to carry obscene matter, it affirmed that Congress, responding to its sense of evangelical Christian morality, would go far to destroy the nation's trade in contraception, which it linked with pornography and obscenity. Only a firm belief that obscene publications and contraceptive materials could harm young people and the family structure could have induced Congress to undertake such a step.[67] Yet neither this law nor the Comstock law could stop the mailing of abortifacients and contraceptive devices that people desired. In an urban world in which the Sabbath was rapidly becoming a day of pleasure instead of worship and rapid communication was obliterating the divisions between urban and rural America, the evangelical effort to purify an increasingly secular American society was a hopeless dream.

That is not to say the laws forbidding the transmission of birth control information had no effect, for they did slow its flow. But as the century ended more and more physicians were moving away from the American Medical Association's rigid standard on contraception. Some were explaining that contraception was not harmful, that abortions could be performed without injury, and that physicians who opposed vaginal douches for contraception but not for other purposes were merely making statements for "the religious public." Although the upending of the anticontraceptive and anti-abortion laws was years away, a trend toward that goal was already apparent. In the end, perhaps the most important effect of evangelicals' long campaign to close the mail to abortionists and those who dealt in contraceptives was to stigmatize their practice and convince many Christians of its sinfulness. In much the same way their campaign to prevent the mail from being used to promote lotteries was to stigmatize gambling in the nineteenth century.[68]

Notes

1. James Reed, *From Private Vice to Pubic Virtue: The Birth Control Movement and American Society since 1830* (New York, 1978), 6–17; Janet Farrell Brodie, *Contraception and Abortion in Nineteenth-Century America* (Ithaca, 1994), 59–86; on the condom, see Nor-

man E. Himes, *Medical History of Contraception* (New York, 1963), 191–202, 224–30. See also John Paul Harper, "'Be Fruitful and Multiply': The Reaction to Family Limitation in Nineteenth Century America," Ph.D. diss., Columbia University, 1975, 5–23. The WCTU's use of the term *immoral things* for abortifacients may have given the impression that the organization "rarely alluded to this type of advertisement." Alison M. Parker, *Purifying American: Women, Cultural Reform, and Pro-Censorship Activism, 1873–1933* (Urbana, 1997), 41.

2. Sidney Ditzion, *Marriage, Morals, and Sex in America: A History of Ideas* (New York, 1953), 318–22; Brodie, *Contraception and Abortion,* 89–90, 119–25, 137–43. In his youth, Knowlton was sickly and weak, and he suffered, mentally at least, from self-abuse. Robert Riegel, "The American Father of Birth Control," *New England Quarterly* 6 (Sept. 1933): 470–92. Although prosecuted for the publication of his book and scorned, Riegel notes that in time his practice grew along with his respectability and rapid sale of his book. On Knowlton, see also Harper, "'Be Fruitful and Multiply,'" 17–23.

3. "Compilation of Laws of the United States, Showing Changes in Domestic Rates of Postage, etc.," S. Misc. Doc. no. 88, 44th Cong., 1st sess., 11 (Apr. 3, 1876). Because of the limitations, the use of mail by freethinkers was probably not as widespread in the early period as Brodie indicated (*Contraception and Abortion,* 162–63, 166–67, 231–33). It is unclear exactly how the Shakers carried on a mail-order business, as Brodie suggests, or how contraceptive "devices and medical products could be ordered and received by mid century through the post." Postal laws made no provision for transporting merchandise until 1872, although seeds, bulbs, and cuttings had been made mailable in 1861. Books, however, by Knowlton and Owen could have been mailed in pamphlet form if mailed at all before 1852.

4. *Compendium of the Ninth Census* (Washington, 1872), 510.

5. *United States Statutes at Large* (Boston, 1851), 9:588–89; *United States Statutes at Large* (Boston, 1855), 10:38–40. The eight-ounce packet provision was designed to accommodate religious tracts. For the passage of these postage laws, see chapter 4 of this volume; on the beginning of "junk mail," see Richard R. John, *Spreading the News: The American Postal System from Franklin to Morse* (New York, 1995), 161.

6. On the rise of the advertising agent and agencies, see Ralph M. Hower, *The History of An Advertising Agency: N. W. Ayer & Son at Work, 1869–1939* (Cambridge, 1939), 7–24. See also Daniel J. Boorstin, *The American: The Democratic Experience* (New York, 1973), 137–150, and Alan Trachtenberg, *The Incorporation of America: Culture and Society in the Gilded Age* (New York, 1982), 135–39.

7. *Report of the Postmaster General, 1855,* 29 (this and subsequent citations to postmasters general reports can be found in the *Congressional Information Service Serial Set Index* [Washington, 1997]); see also James D. Norris, *Advertising and the Transformation of American Society, 1865–1920* (Westport, 1990), 14. On the vague definition of the newspaper, see *Report of the Postmaster General, 1861,* 10.

8. James C. Mohr, *Abortion in America: The Origins and Evolution of National Policy, 1800–1900* (New York, 1978), 17. Mohr (46–50) places the increase in newspaper advertisements for abortion and the consequent public information about abortion in the 1840s, but the nationwide circulation of this information followed the changes in the postage laws.

9. Mohr, *Abortion in America,* 46–50. Mohr, whose book is the best account of abortion in America to date, makes no mention of changes in the postal system and sets the

date for the beginning of the increase in abortions in the 1840s rather than the 1850s when the business was given greater publicity. See also Brodie, *Contraception and Abortion,* 224–31.

10. Other physicians in New York had opposed abortion in the 1840s as well. Harper, "'Be Fruitful and Multiply,'" 60–61.

11. Mohr, *Abortion in America,* 200. Storer's ancestor on his mother's side was Thomas Dudley, governor of Massachusetts Bay colony. *Dictionary of American Biography* (New York, 1936), 9:95–96 (hereafter *DAB*). For state laws, see also C. Thomas Dienes, *Laws, Politics, and Birth Control* (Urbana, 1972), 42–47, appendix B. For details of some of state laws and for Storer's work, see Harper, "'Be Fruitful and Multiply,'" 26–30, 59–60, 66–67, 83–84, 119–21, and ch. 5.

12. Mohr, *Abortion in America,* 160–70; Brodie, *Contraception and Abortion,* 268–74. On birth control and capitalism, see the feminist-Marxian interpretation of Linda Gordon, *Woman's Body, Woman's Right: A Social History of Birth Control in America* (New York, 1976), 14–17, and Carroll Smith-Rosenberg, *Disorderly Conduct: Visions of Gender in Victorian America* (New York, 1985), 217–44. Most historians have apparently been reluctant to believe that leaders of the anti-abortion crusade were motivated by Christian principles in their fight, as their rhetoric suggests, and so have attributed the sources of the campaign to a wide variety of other causes. Mohr, *Abortion in America,* 164–67.

13. Horatio Storer, *Criminal Abortion: Its Nature, Its Evidence, and Its Law* (Boston, 1868), 55, 101–2.

14. Storer, *Criminal Abortion,* 65–68, 98, 134. It was true that middle- and upper-class women were adjusting to a changing world. Their routines were different, and so were their husbands' expectations of them. Moreover, new opportunities opened before them. Although it may have been that husbands in some instances forced them to have an abortion, the choice was, at last, theirs for whatever reason. For a woman's point of view, see Smith-Rosenberg, *Disorderly Conduct,* 242–44.

15. Storer, *Criminal Abortion,* 69. Others also noted the Protestant clergy's reluctance to engage in the crusade. Harper, "'Be Fruitful and Multiply,'" 139. Storer remarked upon the Catholic Church's stand against abortion and noted that immigrant women, most of whom were Catholic, had large families. The Catholic Church was noticeable, however, for its opposition to the mailing of contraceptives and abortifacients.

16. Mohr, *Abortion in America,* 182–96. Mohr's account of the failure of the Protestant clergy and churches to take a stand against abortion is a thorough one. He does not, however, deal with Christian organizations such as the YMCA and Woman's Christian Temperance Union, which protested the mailing of contraceptives and abortifacients. On Bushnell's statement, see Harper, "'Be Fruitful and Multiply,'" 24, and John Todd, *Serpents in the Wilderness* (Boston, 1867).

17. See Harper, "'Be Fruitful and Multiply,'" 146, on the Christian rhetoric of physicians' arguments against abortion.

18. Todd, *Serpents in the Wilderness,* 3–4.

19. As quoted in Ronald G. Walters, ed., *Primers for Prudery: Sexual Advice to Victorian America* (Englewood Cliffs, 1974), 25.

20. On the state laws, see Mohr, *Abortion in America,* ch. 8; Brodie, *Contraception and Abortion,* 253–58; and Dienes, *Laws, Politics, and Birth Control,* 42–47. That Dwight Moody, the great evangelist of the period, was accused of "lowering the pulpit" when he spoke out on the violations of the Seventh Commandment may suggest why Prot-

estant ministers were fearful of preaching on sexual matters. *The Independent,* Jan. 21, 1897, 82.

21. On Alcott, see *DAB* (New York, 1936), 1:142–43; for his purpose in writing, see William Alcott, *The Physiology of Marriage* (Boston, 1855), v–vi. Alcott was one of those Christians who, like Sylvester Graham in the antibellum period, was interested in reforming the body to maintain a Christian nation and save the nation from moral decline. On body reforms, see the excellent chapter of that name in Robert H. Abzug, *Cosmos Crumbling: American Reform and the Religious Imagination* (New York, 1994), 163–82.

22. Gordon, *Woman's Body, Woman's Right,* 9–10; Alcott, *Physiology of Marriage,* 14 (quotation), 50–54, 64, 66–74, 98–99. See also Edmund S. Morgan, "The Puritan and Sex," in *Pivotal Interpretations in American History,* ed. Carl Degler (New York, 1966), 1:1–16.Morgan wrote his article to show that a considerable amount of illicit sex existed in Puritan America, but the larger point was that sex should be reserved for marriage and even then should not be indulged in to the exclusion of God, who must be accorded the higher place in one's thoughts.

23. Alcott, *Physiology of Marriage,* 15–17, 180, 189–91.

24. Ibid., 184, emphasis in the original.

25. Ibid., 118–26, quotation on 120.

26. *Congressional Record,* 42d Cong., 3d sess., 168 (Mar. 1, 1873), appendix. Comstock, of course, did not discover contraception and abortion. New York city authorities had convicted a substantial number of abortionists before Comstock became involved. Harper, "'Be Fruitful and Multiply,'" 154–73.

27. Heywood Broun and Margaret Leech, *Anthony Comstock: Roundsman of the Lord* (New York, 1927), 133, 148. By citing Comstock's wealthy supporters, an effort has been made to tie his motivations in ridding the mail of contraceptives to the preservation of privileged and middle-class families. Nicola Beisel, *Imperiled Innocents: Anthony Comstock and Family Reproduction in Victorian America* (Princeton, 1997), ch. 5.

28. *Congressional Record,* 42d Cong., 3d sess., 169 (Mar. 1, 1873), appendix; New York *Times,* Feb. 11, 1873, 2, Feb. 14, 1873, 6.

29. New York *Times,* Jan. 30, 1873, 4.

30. *United States Statutes at Large* (Boston, 1873), 17:599. Brodie (*Contraception and Abortion,* 263–66) offers a detailed account of the Comstock law and suggests that Congress was ambiguous about criminalizing abortion. See Dienes, *Law, Politics, and Birth Control,* 31–42, for another analysis of the abortion portion of the Comstock law.

31. *United States Statutes at Large* (Boston 1873), 17:599.

32. The story of Comstock and Madame Restell is well known. See Broun and Leech, *Anthony Comstock,* ch. 11, and Beisel, *Imperiled Innocents,* 35–36, 46–48; see also Harper, "'Be Fruitful and Multiply,'" 35–38, 57–65, and manuscript pages for Feb. 11, 1875 (11–12), in Records of the New York Society for the Suppression of Vice, 1873–1953, Manuscript Division, Library of Congress.

33. New York *Times,* Mar. 12, 1873, 4.

34. New York *Times,* Mar. 17, 1875, 7, Mar. 18, 1875, 6, Mar. 20, 1875, 12 (quotation).

35. For the background to this law, see chapter 5 of this volume. A number of Comstock's "persecutions" appear in Harper, "'Be Fruitful and Multiply,'" 187–91, 194–204, and in DeRobigne Mortimer Bennett, *Champions of the Church: Their Crimes and Persecutions* (New York, 1878), 1025–76.

36. *Congressional Record,* 44th Cong., 1st sess., 695–96 (Jan. 27, 1876).

37. Cf. *Congressional Record,* 44th Cong., 1st sess., 695 (Jan. 25, 1876), and *United States Statutes at Large* (Washington, 1877), 19:90. Because of some peculiarities surrounding passage of the Comstock law, one historian has suggested that the law reflected ambiguity about the desire to control contraception and "went far beyond what most legislators, presumably, wanted." Brodie, *Contraception and Abortion,* 263, 65

38. Hal M. Sears, *The Sex Radicals: Free Love in High Victorian America* (Lawrence, 1977), 28, 53–64, 164.

39. Bennett, *Champions of the Church,* 1076–77. In his widely known book *Population* (1798), Thomas Malthus had suggested that population growth would outstrip the world's food supply.

40. Referring to certain forms of evil that curse the young, Samuel Colgate, president of the New York Society for the Suppression of Vice, cited obscene literature and "articles of indecent and immoral use" (*The Independent,* Mar. 3, 1892, 298). St. Paul's instructions to the church at Corinth on sexual matters (I Corinthians 7:1–40) were obviously persuasive in Protestant thought on the subject.

41. John Harvey Kellogg, *Plain Facts about Sexual Life* (Battle Creek, 1877), as quoted in *Primers for Prudery,* ed. Walters, 44 (quotation, 114–16; John Cowan, *The Science of New Life* (New York, 1880).

42. *Union Signal,* Aug. 4, 1898, 4.

43. *United States Statutes at Large* (Washington, 1877), 19:82; *United States Statutes at Large* (Washington, 1879), 20:360. For the efforts of members of Congress from rural areas to mail packages to constituents at the rate of 1 cent an ounce, see *Congressional Record,* 44th Cong., 1st sess., 655 ff. (Jan. 28, 1876). The four-pound package service lasted until 1913, when the present parcel post system permitting mailing of larger parcels was established.

44. Box 142, no file number, Correspondence and Reports Relating to Criminal Investigations, Nov. 1877–Dec. 1903, Records of the Post Office Department, Bureau of the Chief Inspector, National Archives (hereafter Case Files). For an excellent account of the contraceptive business, see Brodie, *Contraception and Abortion,* ch. 7.

45. "Postal Regulations," H. Misc. Doc. no. 63, 50th Cong., 1st sess., 155–60, 378 (Oct. 20, 1888).

46. As quoted in Brodie, *Contraception and Abortion in America,* 68.

47. Box 104, file no. 150, Case Files.

48. Box 142, no file number, Case Files. Towns with population of fewer than ten thousand had no free delivery addresses; the mail for inhabitants in smaller places went only to their post offices. For them, as for the farm population, the county was needed in the address.

49. Ibid.

50. Ibid.

51. Ibid.

52. Box 107, file no. 198, and box 149, no file number, both in Case Files.

53. Box 149, no file number, Case Files.

54. Box 147, no file number, Case Files.

55. Ibid.

56. "Loud Bill, Notes on Hearings before the Committee of the Post Office of the United States Senate . . . ," S. Rept. no. 1517, 54th Cong., 2d sess., 131–32, 140 (Jan. 16,

1897). Publishers of advertising catalogs, or sheets, thought of their publications as newspapers and were disturbed when they were referred to as "sheets."

57. *Union Signal,* Nov. 26, 1891, 8, Feb. 4, 1892, 4.

58. *Union Signal,* Feb. 4, 1892, 4.

59. On the problems involved in enforcing the law, see Dienes, *Law, Politics, and Birth Control,* 55–59.

60. *Congressional Record,* 49th Cong., 1st sess., 5448 (June 9, 1886). Additions to the old law are in italics. "Obscene Matter through the Mails," H. Rept. no. 2676, 49th Cong., 1st sess., 1 (May 29, 1886).

61. New York *Times,* Apr. 24, 1895, 12; *DAB* (New York, 1936), 20:332–33.

62. "Obscene Matter through the Mails," 1–2

63. *United States Statutes at Large* (Washington, 1889), 496–97, emphasis added. The decision involved was *Bates v. United States,* cited in postal regulations.

64. *Union Signal,* Mar. 17, 1892, 12 (first quotation); S. Rept. no. 747, 52d Cong., 1st sess., 1–4 (May 25, 1892) (second quotation).

65. *Union Signal,* Mar. 17, 1892, 12.

66. S. Rept. no. 476, 53d Cong., 2d sess., 1 (May 25, 1894); "Carrying of Obscene Literature, etc., from One State to Another," H. Rept. no. 1363, 54th Cong., 1st sess. 1 (Apr. 18, 1896); *Congressional Record,* 54th Cong., 1st sess., 1680–81 (Feb. 13, 1897); *Congressional Record,* 54th Cong., 1st sess., 1395 (Feb. 1, 1897); see also *United States Statutes at Large* (Washington, 1889), 25:496.

67. On the constitutionality of this law, see Dienes, *Law, Politics, and Birth Control,* 63.

68. For this trend, see Harper, "'Be Fruitful and Multiply,'" 213–28. On the crisis of the family at the turn of the century, see Christopher Lasch, *Haven in a Heartless World: The Family Besieged* (New York, 1977), 8–12.

9 The Postal Power, Protestants, and the Lottery

If it can be demonstrated that to prey upon one's fellow-men by means of a lottery is a fundamental right, the Decalogue, and the Sermon on the Mount, not to mention the Declaration of Independence ought to be re-written at once.

—Argument before the Supreme Court, 1892

The horrors of the awesome battle of Gettysburg were still as fresh in American minds as the day's news when, in 1867, a New York merchant and his associates secured a license from the Pennsylvania legislature to conduct a lottery. Their purpose was to raise money to build an asylum at Gettysburg for the brave men whose bodies had been mangled in that great battle. Ostensibly it was a noble cause that most Americans in the North could support. Gen. George Meade, commander of the Union Army at the battle, had lent his name to the project, and President Andrew Johnson's postmaster general Alexander Randall urged postmasters throughout the nation to support what he called this "truly patriotic and beneficent enterprise."[1]

Designed to be a great national lottery, it was intended to raise $1,200,000. Prizes worth $100,000 were being offered to fortunate ticket holders, and managers of the lottery promised several grand concerts to enhance ticket sales. The last of these was to be held April 23, 1868, when the drawing would take place.

The wartime tax on lotteries was suspended for this great national undertaking, and citizens across the country were given the opportunity to help in a laudable enterprise by purchasing chances for the rich prizes. In New York City, where a ticket office had been established at 546 Broadway, a huge sign advertising the lottery had been strung across the street, and placard-bearers, enticing passersby to purchase a chance for the grand prize, paraded outside the office.[2]

The first concert was held in New York City's Irving Hall in early February 1868 and drew an overflow crowd. A celebrated orchestra and a distinguished female vocalist performed magnificently, and the manager of the lottery and an army officer gave stirring speeches urging the crowd's participation in this philanthropic endeavor.[3] Alas, however, a congressional investigation earlier that year had found that the noble effort was primarily arranged to recover the wealth of a New York merchant who had lost a fortune investing in fraudulent diamonds and to enrich his associates. According to the congressional committee, "Experts of large experience . . . who were valuable by reason of their knowledge of the devices whereby the laws against gambling could be evaded, the credulous entrapped, the moralist and Christian assured that vice was only exterior under cover of which piety and charity might be fully developed" had been chosen to manage the affair. The grand prize was to be a farm, valued by the managers at $60,000 but scarcely worth $6,000. Other prizes were to be diamonds of little value. The lottery, said Charles Van Wyck of New York, who had uncovered the scandal, was "one of the most infamous frauds and swindles that has ever been . . . perpetrated under the guise and mantle and pretense of charity for our disabled soldiers and for the children of deceased soldiers."[4] The scandal ripped through the country and left the hopeful hopeless. Scarcely a year after it had granted it, Pennsylvania revoked the lottery's license. General Meade and the postmaster general withdrew support, and the busy lottery office at 546 Broadway closed.[5]

Once, in the 1820s and 1830s, such lotteries had been commonplace as the nation endured a lottery frenzy in the age of the common man. Spurred on by the poorest of Americans, who sought to be uncommon by winning a fortune in one turn of the wheel, and by an expanding post office that advertised lotteries in a growing number of newspapers and conveyed letters and money for tickets through the mail, lotteries had left a trail of lost fortunes, broken homes, despair, drunkenness, stolen money, and suicide by the 1830s.

In that age of the Second Great Awakening when so many reforms were abroad it was but a matter of time before evangelical Christians, witnessing the lottery's ill-effects upon people, would declare lotteries to be immoral. In 1827 Lyman Beecher, ever the reformer and then minister of the Hanover Street Church in Boston, condemned lotteries in a fiery speech to the Hanover Association of Young Men. Three years later, a resolution of the General Assembly of the Presbyterian Church proclaimed lotteries to be "immoral in their nature, and ruinous in their effects upon individual character and public welfare."[6]

But it was Job Robert Tyson, a Philadelphia Quaker, who stirred the American conscience with his small book *A Brief Survey of the Great Extent and Evil Tendencies of the Lottery System as Existing in the United States* (1833). Replete with statistics of lottery debts and pitiful stories of ruined lives, Tyson's book, condemning states that condoned lotteries, was mailed by the thousands throughout the nation. It stigmatized gambling and lotteries as sins and inspired a national evangelical campaign from New England to California to abolish lotteries by law. The constitutionality of such laws was affirmed by the Supreme Court in 1850. The fact that Justice Robert Cooper Grier ruled in favor of Virginia's anti-lottery law that year indicates the moral majority's abhorrence of lotteries, which the mail had nurtured. "Experience has shown," he wrote, "that the common forms of gambling are comparatively innocuous when placed in contrast to lotteries. The former are confined to a few places, but the latter infests the whole country; it enters every dwelling; it reaches every class; it prays upon the hard earnings of the poor; and it plunders the ignorant and single."[7]

Aside from its law of 1842, which banned them in Washington, D.C., Congress had been little concerned with the crusade to abolish lotteries. Until the Civil War the anti-lottery fight had been waged by states that either banned them constitutionally or by law. Some of the states that had done so, however, did not enforce those laws. Consequently, lottery dealers, taking advantage of the expanding postal service, stuffed the mail from coast to coast in the 1860s with lottery material. A resurgence of the gambling spirit could only be quelled by excluding such items from the mail, evangelicals thought. For more than thirty years they drove Congress to stretch the postal power until it had banished from the mail every lottery ticket, every lottery circular, every newspaper carrying a lottery advertisement, every letter, registered or ordinary, addressed to a lottery, and every money order drawn to the favor of a lottery.[8]

That was no easy task, and Congress got off to a shaky start. At first, it attempted to take advantage of existing lotteries in 1864 by imposing a war revenue tax on them, exempting from the tax those lotteries whose proceeds were to be used for the "relief of sick and wounded soldiers, or to some other charitable use." True, it did give lip service to the anti-lottery sentiment by amending the law to say that nothing in it was to be "construed to legalize any lottery." Inescapably, however, the law gave an aura of respectability to lotteries and an invitation to create them for "charitable use."[9] Almost assuredly it was this exemption that inspired the New York merchant to launch his ill-fated Gettysburg lottery.

By coincidence that same year Congress inadvertently gave more assistance to the lottery business when it provided for a postal money order system. The successful operation of the money order system in England and European countries during the 1840s had led the nation's postmasters general in the 1850s to recommend establishing such a service to protect money in the U.S. mail. Wary of such experiments, however, the best Congress would do was provide for the registration of letters in 1855. That did little more than point thieves to the letters most likely to contain money, as one legislator remarked, and money lost in the mail was a never-ending problem for postal officials.[10]

During the Civil War, however, when southern legislators were unable to object, the money order system's time had come, as it had for so many other postal innovations. What had once seemed impractical in so large a country suddenly appeared possible and even necessary. Now, it was said, the money order system would protect not only businesses' money in the mail but also the funds that patriotic soldiers in the field mailed to their families. Not to be overlooked was the fact that the money order system was likely to produce revenue "now so much needed," as one legislator suggested, "to put down this gigantic rebellion, to sustain the Constitution, and preserve the Union," which in the dark days of early 1862 may have seemed uncertain to some members of Congress.[11]

After the money order bill was introduced, it took Congress two years to pass it. When it did, it limited the amount of a money order that could be purchased to $30, too low, some thought, to be useful to business. But if that was a handicap to businesspeople, it was not to the lottery enterprise into whose coffers money orders much smaller than $30 tumbled en masse after 1864, sometimes in registered letters but often enclosed in ordinary letters. Most were sent in response to lottery circulars or newspaper advertisements that people found in their mail; many, perhaps most, were the products of fraudulent enterprises. The National Protective Union, for example, was a gift concert that promised monthly drawings for prizes for lucky ticket holders and a distribution at the Eagle Hotel in Vernon, New Hampshire, on December 30, 1865. There was no Vernon, New Hampshire, however, and consequently no Eagle Hotel, and hence no distribution.[12]

Other swindling enterprises in addition to fraudulent lotteries also advertised by means of circulars and newspapers. Unscrupulous firms in New York City and elsewhere received money orders totaling large amounts every day for cheap imitations of the goods they advertised. Often they sent no merchandise at all, in which case they blamed the post office for losing goods they had "mailed." Local officials were powerless to prevent fraud in the mail, of course, and in 1866 the mayor of New York City, overwhelmed by what he called "outrageous swindles" and the complaints of constituents, asked the postmaster general to withhold letters and money orders going to fraudulent concerns.[13] That had already been tried, however. Letters thought to be intended to dishonest businesses were withheld under the authority of postal regulations. Postmasters were hesitant to enforce the regulation, however because it was not firmly based on a law. To solve the problem the assistant attorney general for the post office drafted a law that would give the postmaster general the actual authority to remove such spurious matter from the mail.[14]

The bill was immediately introduced in Congress, but two years went by before it acted on the matter. When it did act in 1868 it passed a timid law that made it unlawful "to deposit in any post-office, to be sent by mail, any letters or circulars concerning lotteries, so-called gift concerts, or other similar enterprises offering prizes of any kind on any pretext whatever." No penalties were given for violating the law, and the Senate's effort to strengthen it by allowing postmasters to withdraw suspicious packages and letters was throttled in the House, where legislators feared giving them so dangerous a power.[15]

In that same year and less than a month after the law was signed, the Louisiana legislature, as if in deliberate defiance of the law, chartered the Louisiana State Lottery to run until 1894 and gave it a monopoly of the lottery business in the state. To be sure, conditions in Louisiana contributed to this affront to the nationwide anti-lottery sentiment. Its government, then being reconstructed by northerners and former slaves, was impoverished by the war, torn by violence, honeycombed with corruption, and scarcely concerned about the immorality of lotteries. The state's legislators created the Louisiana State Lottery to prevent, they said, the drainage of money from their state by other lotteries and to establish "a solvent, reliable home institution . . . to insure perfect fairness and justice in the distribution of prizes."[16]

Actually, motives for the establishment were less exalted. The moving force behind the lottery was Charles T. Howard, a lottery agent for some twenty years who was employed by C. H. Murray and Company, an old Kentucky lottery. Surmising that business might be better in Louisiana, he and Murray moved there in 1866 and began immediately to work on the legislature to secure a charter for a lottery company. It took two years, but eventually the votes of the members of the lower house of the legislature were apparently purchased for $100 a head and those of the senate for stock in the new company. The charter was granted in 1868. With it in hand, Howard and his associates, C. H. Murray, John Morris, and Z. E. Simmons, took control of the company. Howard became president and the others directors, but in time the largest stockholder and most important figure was Morris, a quiet, behind-the-scenes operator and race-horse devotee who lived lavishly in New York, New Orleans, Maryland, and Texas during the 1880s. Contracting among themselves to run the business for 50 percent of its profits, they issued $100 million worth of stock, one-half to be divided among themselves and the rest reserved for stockholders. On January 1, 1869, they began their lucrative business.[17]

Here matters stood when Congress began to codify the postal laws in 1872. Forced to strengthen the impotent anti-lottery law of 1868, Congress paused. One legislator from California, a state built on a gamble, saw no harm in organizing gift concerts, and he wanted to permit circulars and letters for them in the mail. A legislator from New York who defended the idea of preventing lotteries from using the mail opposed giving postmasters the power to seize lottery letters and money orders as a measure of prevention. "It is, sir," he said, "a power which ought never to be granted by the Congress . . . to the Postmaster General." He believed it would "expose the correspondence of the people to a scrutiny and espionage of a most dangerous character."[18]

Nevertheless, in 1872 Congress rewrote the law of 1868 that closed the mail to material relating to gift concerts, lotteries, and other such enterprises and strengthened it by adding a fine of not more than $500 and not less than $100 for violations. Moreover, the bill gave the postmaster general power to stop registered letters and money orders addressed to a lottery.

But the law was not a complete victory for lottery abolitionists. Some way had to be found to preserve the right of states to establish a lottery if they wished to do so. The hoary doctrine of states' rights was not yet as irrelevant as it was to become, and Congress had to accord it some attention. It did so by banning every *illegal* lottery from the mail and permitting the postmaster general, upon "evidence satisfactory to him," to deny registered letters and the payment of money orders to *fraudulent* lotteries only.[19]

This bow to states' rights obviously removed the postmaster general's power to stop the mail of those lotteries that could claim legal establishment, and circulars and letters promoting them were being mailed from one end of the country to the other. Lotteries appeared to be everywhere in the early 1870s, in Texas, Wyoming, Kentucky, Mississippi, and Missouri. Some had only shadowy claims to legality and others had none, but there were so many that postmasters could not tell the legal from the illegal. Two Kentucky lotteries, for example—the Commonwealth Distribution Company of Louisville and the Kentucky State Lottery—claimed legality under charters granted by the state in 1839 although they had long since raised the money for which they had been chartered.[20]

Clearly, the interest in gambling that had been subdued before the war had returned with a vigor that disturbed evangelicals. "Even the church (unwitting, no doubt)," the *Christian Statesman* editorialized in 1873, "is sometimes found doing the work of the devil. Gift concerts, gift enterprises and raffles, sometimes in aid of religion or charitable objects, but often for less worthy purposes, lotteries, prizes, packages, etc. are all devised to obtain money without value received. Nothing is so demoralizing or intoxicating, particularly to the young, as the acquisition of money or property without labor."[21]

Congress was not insensitive to such complaints or to fraudulent businesses' use of the mail, and in 1876 many members were disposed to wipe the word *fraudulent* from the law. It was necessary, said Maine's Senator Hannibal Hamlin, in support of the proposal, "to treat all lotteries, whether legal or illegal, alike, as precisely the same, or as a system of gambling which a wise course in legislation will not only justify but demand at our hands shall be stopped."[22]

Coming as it did in that centennial presidential election year when the "bloody shirt" was again being waved and partisan feelings ran high, this proposal touched off angry debate in the Senate. Not that anyone actually defended lotteries. Nearly all agreed that they were demoralizing. But the doctrine of states' rights still cast a shadow over the debate. Louisiana's Senator J. Rodman West, a Republican who had returned to the South from California after the war, claimed to be opposed to the lottery in his own state. He was even more opposed to the government's attempt to control morality by restricting the use of the mail to patronize a lottery a state had established. "If we once adopt that policy," he said, "and embark upon it, there is no end whatever to the jurisdiction of the Congress . . . over the morals of the people in their State enactments."[23]

West's was a troubling argument. Constitutionally, of course, the people of Louisiana had a right to say what was moral and what was immoral and to establish a legal lottery if they wished. Confined to Louisiana, doing so would have created no problem. But the mail, like tendrils of a poisonous vine, spread the temptations of a lottery throughout America, and evangelical morality had long since condemned lotteries as immoral in virtually every state except Louisiana. Could Congress's power to regulate the post office be stretched to prevent the lottery from circulating throughout the country? Could Congress, in effect, use the postal power to regulate morals?

That had already occurred, West admitted, when Congress banned obscene literature from the mail. He contended, however, that there was a difference between withdrawing obscene material from the mail and seizing letters to stop lotteries. No state, he said, approved of mailing obscene literature. That difference was lost on other senators, who responded with a spate of rebuttals. Samuel Bell Maxwell from Texas, who regarded lotteries "as one of greatest curses that ever was inflicted upon the American people," asserted that "if the Congress . . . has the power to prevent the passage of obscene books, pamphlets, and pictures through the mails . . . it has the power to prevent any other thing which is immoral in its tendencies."[24]

John Logan from Illinois went beyond that. He believed it was not only "the right and province but the duty of Congress" to ban lottery matter from the mail. Standing before his colleagues, an impressive figure with coal-black hair and a black beard, Logan warmed to his subject as he denounced what he called the nation's greatest swindling business. "Lotteries," he said, "call them by what name you please, when legalized are legalized gambling, and they can only be legalized in States that are in favor of gambling; and wherever a community is so demoralized that they are in favor of gambling they will then legalize lotteries, and not till they are so."[25]

A Civil War veteran who had risen in the ranks from private to general, had twice been wounded, and was a founder and three times president of the Grand Army of the Republic, Logan came from a Methodist background and was no doubt sincere in his hatred of lotteries. Whether he was or not, he was on the side of the angels in this fight. Congress swept aside the doctrine of states' rights as if it did not exist and passed the law of 1876, which prevented all lotteries, legal or illegal, from using the mail. Unfortunately, it neglected, either carelessly or willfully, to erase the word *fraudulent* from those sections that permitted the postmaster general to seize registered letters and money orders pertaining to lotteries.[26]

This seemingly straightforward effort to ban lottery material from the mail had been in effect for only a short time when Orlando Jackson, a petty gambler in New York, violated it by mailing a lottery circular. He was arrested, quickly convicted, fined, and jailed until he paid the fine. From jail, however, he appealed his conviction on the grounds that the law was unconstitutional. Among other things, it deprived him of his right to post what had been mailable at the time the Constitution was adopted. The Supreme Court thought otherwise. In *Ex Parte Jackson* (1878) it reasoned that "the power possessed by Congress embraces the regulation of the entire postal system. The right to designate what shall be carried necessarily involves the right to determine what shall be excluded."[27]

Because it gave Congress the constitutional right to determine what could or could not be mailed, *Ex Parte Jackson* was perhaps the Supreme Court's most important decision regarding the mail in the nineteenth century. It did not, however, make it easy for the postmaster general to enforce the anti-lottery law. Indeed, the Court warned that enforcement would be difficult because Congress's right to censor the mail did not extend to the postmaster general's right to open letters.[28]

The postmaster general had already found the anti-lottery law to be filled with loopholes and all but impossible to enforce. David Key, President Rutherford B. Hayes's postmaster general from Tennessee who had been appointed as part of a compromise to make Hayes president, had hardly begun to issue fraud orders against various and sundry concerns than Attorney General Charles Devens warned him against seizing letters without a warrant and without knowing their contents. That ruling almost negated the law, for opening letters to examine their contents exacted a harsh penalty that made their seizure on the suspicion that they contained lottery material risky for postmasters.[29]

Devens's ruling was confirmed in 1878 by the assistant attorney general to the post office, and although Postmaster General Key continued to issue fraud orders he was wary of his power to do so. Then a new assistant attorney general, A. A. Freeman, ruled in October 1879 that the mere mailing of letters to lottery companies or their agents constituted evidence enough to withhold them. Emboldened by that ruling, Key ordered postmasters to refuse to mail or register letters or circulars addressed to lottery companies or their agents. It was an order "so sweeping," warned the New York *Times,* that it might "lead to serious trouble and possible litigation." And it did.[30]

Key's order brought a swift and angry reaction from lottery directors. In October and into November they gathered in Washington with their lawyers and lobbyists, some of whom were former members of Congress, to plead with Congress and the postmaster general for a suspension of the order. Failing that, Kentucky lotteries joined to support the Commonwealth Distribution Company in its suit to force the postmaster at Louisville to deliver its letters.[31]

The lottery managers' arguments were based on a maze of legal opinions that went as far back as 1819 and were as recent as 1877. Their lotteries, they said, were legal and therefore not fraudulent and hence not subject to the law. Some, like the Kentucky lotteries, argued that they had been chartered by the state and that their charters were contracts that could not be broken. Consequently, their companies were legal. They also found refuge in the jumble of the Fourteenth Amendment, which gave freedmen their citizenship, guaranteed their privileges and immunities and equal protection under state law, and protected their property against seizure without due process. As it turned out, it was this last, akin to Devens's ruling and guaranteed by both the Fifth and Fourteenth amendments, that was the arrow for the lottery managers' bow.[32]

Postmaster General Key made his way through this tangle of arguments as best he could. He steadfastly refused to rescind his order and in 1879 asked Congress to erase the word *fraudulent* from those sections of the revised statutes, 3929 and 4041, in order that he might have the authority to seize registered letters and refuse payment of money orders directed to all lotteries. He also ordered his assistant attorney general to defend the Louisville postmaster in the suit brought against him by the Commonwealth Distribution Company.[33]

While that suit was still pending, however, the Supreme Court was hearing a case in which the state of Mississippi was attempting to remove the charter of a lottery company chartered years before. In its defense, the lottery company asserted that it had been chartered by the state and that its charter was a contract that could not be broken. But the Supreme Court held that the right of the state to preserve morality through its police power could not be bargained away and was sufficient to authorize revocation of the charter. Admittedly, those police powers were vague, the Court said, but they applied to all matters affecting public morals and lotteries. "They [lotteries] are a species of gambling and wrong in their influences," noted the Court. "They disturb the checks and balances of a well ordered community. Society built on such a foundation would almost of necessity bring forth a population of gamblers, living on the expectation of what 'by the casting of lots, or by lot, chance or otherwise,' might be 'awarded' to them from the accumulation of others."[34]

Following that decision, the Kentucky Commonwealth Company's suit against the Louisville postmaster withered. Fraud orders were issued against the company, it was denied use of the mail, and eventually it disappeared, as did others to whom fraud orders were issued. Matters were different, however, with regard to the Louisiana Lottery, which that state's legislature had chartered and rechartered.

By 1879 the Louisiana Lottery had been in operation for eleven years, and it had grown enormously rich and powerful. Each week its office in New Orleans at the corner of Charles and Union streets received some two thousand ordinary letters, 630 registered letters, and—in the quarter ending September 30, 1879—6,966 money orders worth $23,542. Scattered throughout the city were between two and three hundred ticket agents, some of them local politicians who could be relied upon for help against the lottery's foes. The city's postmaster estimated in 1879 that as many as three thousand people in New Orleans were dependent upon the sale of tickets for their livelihoods.[35]

Masters of publicity and keenly aware of the need to ameliorate the stigma attached to their enterprise, the lottery's directors had employed Generals Jubal Early and P. G. T. Beauregard, Confederate heroes, to preside over its monthly drawings and spread an aura of patriotism and respectability over the tainted business. At drawing time and in a room filled with anxious spectators, the two old men would stand, their bearing dramatic, beside a rotating drum and at a precise moment pick a ticket from it and read the numbers located thereon. After each monthly drawing the company would mail about five thousand letters, presumably containing prizes and announcements of the results of the drawing.[36]

The activity at New Orleans, however, was only a fraction of the company's business. Much of its operation was carried on at the office of its president, Maximilian A. Dauphin, at 319 Broadway, an ordinary second-floor office. No sign indicated the kind of trade carried on there, and only newspaper advertising gave any indication of its business. Every week, however, between a thousand and 1,500 registered letters were addressed to M. A. Dauphin at that location. Although addressed to Dauphin, who, as people in New Orleans knew, was only an employed company lackey, they were picked up at the New

York post office's delivery desk by B. Frank Moore, whom Anthony Comstock had arrested several times for his participation in the gambling enterprise. An estimated $150,000 a month was being drained from the credulous of New York City through the mail and through the sale of tickets by company agents scattered throughout the city.[37]

The power of the lottery in Louisiana was made obvious in 1879 when delegates to a constitutional convention gathered to write a new constitution to replace the old carpetbag government's document. Earlier that year the state legislature, incensed by the ignominy the lottery had brought upon Louisiana, abolished it. A judge's ruling quickly thwarted the law, but many convention delegates wished to abolish lotteries via the new constitution. Alarmed by that possibility, lottery directors, who had money to pass around, were able to buy enough delegates to secure a charter in the new constitution until 1895. But the constitution, bowing to evangelical morality, did declare lotteries to be a vice and provided for their destruction in 1896. Moreover, lottery directors had to agree to give up their monopoly and pay to support the charity hospital of New Orleans.[38]

The confirmation of its charter left no doubt about the lottery's legality in Louisiana and placed it in a strong position to meet the blanket fraud order issued by the postmaster general in October 1879, an order that some one hundred or so fraudulent concerns had failed to obey by the beginning of 1880. Nevertheless, Postmaster General Key had gathered evidence "satisfactory to him," as the law demanded, that the Louisiana State Lottery Company was engaged in fraudulent activities. On November 13, 1879, he issued a fraud order against Maximilian A. Dauphin, ordering the postmaster at New Orleans to deliver no registered letters to Dauphin and redeem no money orders sent to him.[39]

It was the opening blow in a struggle that was to last for more than a decade. The southern *Christian Advocate* assured Postmaster General Key that in his "war against the lotteries" he had "the sympathies of all Christian men and women." The *Christian Union,* too, was encouraged by this turn of events and by the prospect that the postmaster general would ask Congress for a law prohibiting the mailing of publications that advertised lotteries and seduced the unwary to gamble. Noting that Louisiana and Kentucky were the only states to license lotteries, it remarked that "the rest of us cannot save these States from self-inflicted disgrace, but we can at least refuse to participate in a business which invites us to a share of the dishonor . . . by asking us to carry advertisements of the business."[40]

The federal government, the Mobile *Register* snapped, was "'not endowed with the power of determining what is moral and what is immoral,'" which was the view of southern members of Congress and, of course, that of the lottery's managers. In December 1879 Dauphin brought suit in the federal court of the District of Columbia against Postmaster General Key, pleading for an injunction to forbid the execution of Key's order. He averred that he was not engaged in a fraudulent business and that the act of Congress and its enforcement by the postmaster general were abuses of the postal power that deprived him of his rights, privileges, and property without due process. The court ruled, however, that there were no constitutional limits on Congress's use of postal power and declared that "it cannot be said that the citizen of the United States has an absolute constitutional right, or, in other words, that it is one of the privileges of his citizenship that his letters should be carried by the United States mail at all."[41]

Dauphin appealed that decision to the Supreme Court, but before it could be heard Key resigned to become a federal judge in Tennessee. He also withdrew, or revoked, the order against Dauphin, apparently because he was uncertain that the company was engaged in fraudulent activity. After that, further court action on Dauphin's appeal was postponed or dropped, and an unusual chain of circumstances followed.[42]

It all began with the presidency of James Garfield in 1881 and his appointment of Thomas James to be postmaster general. James, the former postmaster of the New York City post office, had always been wary of being able to prove fraud against the lottery. Consequently, he ignored the matter and busied himself with rooting out the culprits who had defrauded the government in the 1870s by manipulating their bids for star routes. When Garfield was assassinated James resigned and was followed by Timothy Howe, former senator from Wisconsin. Like James, Howe, before he suddenly died in 1883, found no evidence that the Louisiana State Lottery was guilty of fraud. He was succeeded by William Gresham, a resolute former soldier who had found favor with Ulysses S. Grant at the battle of Shiloh and upon whose recommendation he had been appointed brigadier general.[43]

By the time Gresham, a former judge, took office, three years had elapsed since Key had issued the fraud order against Dauphin. The Louisiana Lottery, unmolested by the post office, had grown so rich and powerful by use of registered letters and money orders that it had, for all practical purposes, ignored the state's constitution and regained its monopoly of the lottery business in Louisiana. To be sure there was opposition, The New Orleans *Morning Star* called the lottery "a grievous curse" and commented that "every vice, encouraged and legalized, is a rallying point for every other vice." The *Southwestern*

Presbyterian lamented the "Lottery of infamy, which now holds such a leading if not controlling place in our State politics." Still, "Mr. Howard's Lottery," as it was called in Louisiana, continued to dominate the legislature.[44]

Postmaster General Gresham, however, was unafraid of its power. Discovering how Key's fraud order and the subsequent case against Dauphin had been left hanging, he renewed the fraud order against Dauphin on September 13, 1883, "in pursuance of the finding of Postmaster General Key, which finding remains in full force."[45]

Just then, however, the wily lottery managers advertised in the papers that all correspondence previously addressed to Dauphin should be mailed instead to the National Bank of New Orleans. It was a clever scheme that would mix bank and lottery letters together, making it impossible to tell one from the other without opening them, which postmasters, of course, could not do. Gresham was outraged that a national bank would lend itself to this perfidy and declared that it could not be made to stand in for the lottery. "This is a defiant scheme on the part of M. A. Dauphin and the New Orleans National Bank," he wrote the postmaster at New Orleans, "to evade the orders which have been addressed to you . . . to protect the mails and the public against a business which is vicious and immoral, and in the main preys upon the ignorant and credulous." "You will," he continued, "deliver to the New Orleans bank no registered letter and redeem no money order payable to it."[46]

Again there was defiance. The lottery secured an injunction from a district court staying the postmaster general's order. The post office was forced to appeal on behalf of the New Orleans postmaster to the U.S. Circuit Court in New Orleans. The appeal was to be heard after Christmas. In the meantime, tension mounted in New Orleans as people awaited the judge's decision and papers speculated about the outcome. The *Daily Picayune* called the postmaster general's order against the New Orleans National Bank an abuse of power and accused him of leaving Washington to avoid meeting with directors of the Louisiana State Lottery and its lawyers. And the New York *Herald* questioned the postmaster general's authority to issue orders against the lottery for fraud. "'But a lottery,'" it said, "'however objectionable or demoralizing it may be, is not necessarily fraudulent.'"[47]

That, in essence, was the opinion of the judge of the federal circuit court, who upheld the district court's decision to stop Postmaster General Gresham's order against the bank. The judge ruled that Gresham could not use Key's findings against Dauphin but must investigate the bank's relationship to the lottery on his own, which he had not done. He had no evidence of fraud, nor had he charged the company with fraud. Therefore, the company was free to pursue its business, and the lottery law was virtually dead.[48]

Disappointed in the ruling, the New York *Times* claimed the case had been decided upon a technicality and not its merits. But because of the ambiguity of the law, Judge Don Albert Pardee's decision was warranted. To make the law effective, Congress needed to erase the word *fraudulent* from sections 3929 and 4041 of the revised statutes so that those sections would be congruent with the rest of the law, which forbade mailing letters from all lotteries, legal or illegal. Only then could the postmaster general stop all registered letters and money orders directed to lotteries without having to find them fraudulent. Three postmasters general had asked for such legislation. Newspapers were still mulling over the judge's decision when in the spring of 1884 a bill was proposed in the House to erase the word *fraudulent* from sections 3929 and 4041 and a Senate bill would have banned newspapers and other publications carrying lottery advertising from the mail.[49]

Both bills ran headlong into the time-worn doctrine of states' rights. In 1876 Congress had easily overcome the states' rights arguments of weak representatives from carpetbag governments to declare all lotteries illegal. By 1884, however, Democrats controlled the House of Representatives, and southerners of Confederate heritage had redeemed their governments and sent to Congress unreconstructed legislators who breathed fire and trumpeted states' rights, for which they claimed to have fought. It was as if the South, not the North, had won the war. Almost to a man, the new legislators had served in the Confederate Army or in the Confederate government, were among the last to be pardoned by the amnesty act of 1876, and were serving only their first or second terms in Congress.

They were often in the minority in their own postal committees, but such was the vehemence of their rhetoric against the abuse of the postal power that they were able to beat back the passage of the bills by using arguments reminiscent of John C. Calhoun's. Using that power to "protect the morality of the people against the pernicious effect of lotteries" would, they asserted, lead to paternalism. Moreover, it would cause centralization of power, usurpation of the rights of the states, and subversion of "the whole theory and character of our national system as originally formed."[50]

They did concur with the majority, of course, that lotteries were "a pernicious species of gambling, exerting an evil and demoralizing influence upon the people," but they held that the general government had no authority to suppress gambling or prevent legalization of a lottery. That power belonged to the states, which had ample authority to deal with it. For proof they pointed to the majority's own argument that thirty-five states already had statutes or constitutional provisions outlawing lotteries. As for the bill to prohibit mailing publications that advertised lotteries, it would violate the First

Amendment guaranteeing freedom of speech. The bill to erase the word *fraudulent* from sections 3929 and 4041 would give the postmaster general the right to seize a company's mail on "evidence satisfactory to himself" without bringing charges, without a trial, and without the right to appeal. It was an effort to coerce states into adopting "standards of Congressional morality."[51]

The arguments urged in these congressional reports scuttled the bills, possibly because of the influence of the lottery in Congress but more likely because Congress was not altogether confident of the reach of postal power. In the House, the bill to amend sections 3929 and 4041 was left in committee, but a roll-call vote on the Senate bill to ban publications bearing lottery advertising from the mail suggested the political source of moral reform in the nineteenth century. It was of more than passing significance that all of those who voted for the bill were Republicans from northern states; of those opposed, all but one was a Democrat and all but five were from southern states. Seemingly, the willingness to use the power of the national government to achieve moral reforms, which had characterized the Republican Party at its birth, still lingered, whereas the Democratic Party clung to the past and abjured sumptuary laws.[52]

Despite their defeat in 1884, anti-lottery members of Congress and senators from the Midwest kept the two bills before every Congress for six years. In each, Sen. James Wilson, that champion of moral causes from Fairfield, Iowa, introduced his bill to forbid the mailing of publications advertising lotteries, and just as often bills were offered to amend sections 3329 and 4041 of the *Revised Statutes*. Once the Republican Senate passed a bill to amend the two sections of the anti-lottery law with little debate, and once it also passed a bill to forbid the mailing of newspapers or other publications that advertised lotteries. Both failed in the Democratic House of Representatives, however.[53]

One reason for their failure in those years was the return of the Democrats to the White House in 1885. Grover Cleveland's postmaster general William Freeman Vilas, an avid and wealthy supporter of the president, recommended in 1885 that Congress deny the second-class mailing privilege to publications that carried lottery advertising. He never mentioned the lottery again in any of his reports, however, nor did President Cleveland refer to it in his messages to Congress. Vilas, a lawyer and prominent Democrat from Wisconsin, had a New England background and was not averse to using the postal power for moral purposes. Presumably, however, he realized the futility of attempting to use it to demolish the Louisiana Lottery during a Democratic administration.[54]

Whatever the reason, the administration remained silent on the subject in spite of the petitions against the lotteries that were reaching Congress in increasing numbers and in the face of attacks of the religious press against gambling of all kinds and lotteries in particular. Striking out at the "lottery nuisance" in 1890, the *Christian Union* called gambling one of "the most formidable, subtle, and ruinous sins of the American people. It creeps into the home, the church, the college, the workshop, the store, the bank, the farmhouse, and even into the backwoods hamlet, leaving behind a train of evils which are often drowned in the wine-cup or by suicide." Of all forms of gambling, the lottery was the worst. "The whole effect of this species of gambling is demoralizing to the community and disastrous to the individual. . . . Young man," the editor warned, "let this thing alone. Be satisfied with the slow and moderate improvement of your finances."[55]

In the meantime, the power and wealth of the Louisiana State Lottery had reached immense proportions. With a virtual national monopoly of the lottery business, it was raking in an estimated $30 million a year, 93 percent of which came from out of the state. In Washington, D.C., where bills to prevent the sale of lottery tickets and the advertising of lotteries had failed in Congress, the company's sales multiplied like the locusts of ancient Egypt. The lottery mailed approximately fifty thousand letters each month and received about as many at the post office. Its clerks worked night and day, hauling outgoing mail in express wagons and furniture carts, often at night to conceal the identifications of those who bet. According to the postmaster general, the amount of mail the lottery generated "had no parallel in the history of the Post Office Department."[56]

The Louisiana Lottery's malevolent presence was everywhere, corrupting the state's legislature and financial institutions and even demoralizing and tainting trusted postmasters, mail carriers, and postal clerks. Railway mail clerks were particularly susceptible to the seductive opportunities the lottery afforded them and often succumbed to the temptation to open letters addressed to the Louisiana Lottery and take whatever was of value from them. That postal inspectors were kept busy tracing lost money and money orders to the most skilled of all postal employees was a confirmation, certainly, of the lottery's baneful influence.[57]

Regardless of its demoralizing influence, the lottery seemed untouchable in 1890, and only the realization that its charter would run out in 1893 gave hope to evangelicals and others. The expectation that the infamous business would soon end, however, vanished in the spring of 1890 when John Morris, by this time a multimillionaire, asked the Louisiana legislature to enact a measure that would permit people to vote on amending the state constitution to extend the lottery's charter for twenty-five years. In return, the lottery would make a payment of $1,250,000 annually. Consternation at this request spread swiftly among those in Louisiana who had looked forward to the lottery's end. Whatever chance opponents of the measure had to defeat it was lost, however, when a flood destroyed levees at New Orleans, and the company, with a great show of generosity, donated money to alleviate the suffering that ensued. Thus helped by the elements and its usual bribery of legislators, the company pushed its bill through the legislature in 1890. The date for the referendum was set for the next year.[58]

John Morris, perhaps misled by the hordes of Americans who spent money on his lottery, had misjudged the depth of the moral outrage that evangelicals had generated at the continuance of the lottery and at gambling in general. The immense importance they accorded the referendum's outcome was articulated by their most important journals. The editor of the *Christian Union* prophesied darkly that a win for the lottery would "continue to be . . . as it has been in the past, the blackest blot upon the fair name of the United States." That Louisiana would do this seemed almost incomprehensible. "Will she alone," he asked unbelievingly, "encourage and legalize one of the most ruinous and debasing species of vice which the ingenuity of humanity has ever produced? Will she ensnare, impoverish and degrade, not only her own citizens, but those of her sister States?" It was time to end a great fraud. "The American people want this gigantic evil abolished. It is sapping the prosperity of the working masses of the country over. Its agents are to be found in all the great cities and large towns. Month after month and year after year those who can least afford to do so give up a considerable portion of their hard-earned wages for worthless scraps of paper which they surely hope will bring them fortune."[59]

The Independent was equally concerned. The lottery's managers, it explained, were fearful that voters would end their lottery in Louisiana and had tried but failed to bribe legislators in the newly organized state of North Dakota into licensing a lottery. Now, the editor feared, they might try to persuade the new states of Montana and Idaho to permit establishment of a lottery and so "renew the lease of evil and sin which Louisiana might not be willing to allow." To this there was only one remedy, and evangelicals had turned to it time and again. "So we revert," the editor wrote, "to the only power that can rise above and control States rights on which the lottery depends, and that is the power of Congress over the mails."[60]

When *The Independent* spoke out, the election of 1888 had returned Republicans to power in Washington. In the White House sat Benjamin Harrison, a Presbyterian elder and grandson of a former president. At the Post Office Department was Postmaster General John Wanamaker, an advocate of moral reform and a devout Presbyterian. Both houses of Congress, too, belonged to the Republicans. The time had come to ignore the states' rights argument and drive a stake into the heart of the Louisiana State Lottery.

Postmaster General Wanamaker led the way. In his first report to the president in 1889 and again in a long letter to him the next summer, he reviewed the history of the post office's inability to control the lottery. Affirming that the postal power gave Congress the right to say what could or could not be carried in the mail and that whatever it ruled in this regard was "final and conclusive," he asked for the passage of the stalemated laws to eliminate the word *fraudulent* from sections 3929 and 4041 and to exclude from the mail publications displaying lottery advertising. More than that, he wanted a law that would apply to lottery agents as well as managers and permit him to stop lottery letters, whether at points of origin or along routes and at places of delivery, and to try offenders in districts in which offenses occurred.[61]

The president, too, urged Congress to enact the bills. Informing Congress that North Dakota's recent effort to authorize a lottery, the Louisiana State Lottery's drive to extend its life, and the Mexican lottery on the nation's border had called attention to "an evil of vast proportion" in which the mail system was "made the effective and profitable, medium of intercourse between the lottery company and its victims," Harrison asked for severe and prompt legislation to put an end to it.[62]

Having tried for so long to enact such bills without success, Congress needed no more to stir it into action. In the summer of 1890 no less than eleven bills to bar publications carrying lottery advertising from the mail and erase the word *fraudulent* from sections 3929 and 4041 spilled into congressional hoppers. Nor was that all. New Hampshire's Senator Henry Blair, who bore the brunt—and ridicule—of moral reform in those years, introduced a constitutional amendment making lotteries unconstitutional. Finally, numerous petitions from constituents against the lottery convinced reluctant legislators that the time for action had come.[63]

Even so, in the House, where the proposed measures were rolled into one, a fading states' rights sentiment lingered to stymie the quick passage of the bill—and not without reason. The new bill did test the limits of postal power. It narrowed freedom of the press; closed the mail to all lotteries, games of chance, and fraudulent schemes; enlarged the powers of the postmaster general; stipulated punishments for offenders; and, to prevent violators from being tried before juries sympathetic to lotteries, provided for such trials in either the district where the offending material had been mailed or where it was finally delivered.[64]

The bill was a reflection of how far Congress, spurred by evangelical fervor, was willing to expand the postal power to crush the Louisiana State Lottery. Support for the legislation was overwhelming, although states' right southern Democrats, denying they opposed it, sought to weaken the bill. The path they chose was to remove that section of the bill that permitted postmasters to remove from the mail registered letters and money orders directed to an agent of a lottery or fraudulent company, "whether such agent or representative" was "acting as an individual or as a firm, bank, corporation, or association of any kind."[65]

The stipulation that an individual could be considered an agent if a lottery merely announced that remittances might be made to him gave opponents of the bill an opportunity. William Henry Crain of Cuero, Texas, labored earnestly to find that clause dangerous and unconstitutional by raising the unlikely possibility that a lottery might designate him an agent without his permission."What authority has any man or any corporation," Crain argued in support of his amendment to eliminate this section, "to constitute me his agent unless I acquiesce in that agency?" Such a prospect fed his apprehensions. "It deprives me of the right to receive my money-orders through the post-office," he said. "It deprives me of the right to receive my registered packages."[66]

Crain, a lifelong and devout Catholic, had been educated in Catholic schools and supported Catholic causes. Unlike the majority of his colleagues, he was uncertain that lotteries were immoral. If they were, he urged that they be suppressed in a "legal and constitutional manner." He did not explain how that might be done, but he was not alone in fearing that he (or someone else) might be named an agent and have no recourse to clear his name. Even the New York *Times,* no friend of lotteries, questioned whether the national government, without police power to govern morals, could provide one citizen with mail service and not another. More support for Crain's position came from other southerners, one of whom, James Henderson Blount from Georgia, had been an enemy of the lottery for years. In this case, however, he argued that the section Crain wanted to eliminate was not needed because the postmaster general already had the power, on "evidence satisfactory to him," to single out a lottery agent. This section as it stood, he thought, might even limit the postmaster general's determination of an agent to someone publicly advertised as such when there might also be other agents who were not advertised. For that reason, Blount thought, Crain's amendment should be adopted.[67]

But Republicans, bent on destroying the lottery, were in no mood to temporize. "Mr. Speaker," exclaimed one member of Congress, "the mail service of our country should not be used as the agent of vice and criminality." Remembering how the Louisiana Lottery had made the New Orleans National Bank its agent, he and others harshly attacked Crain's amendment. Some thought it would remove the most essential part of the bill, and others insinuated it was an attempt to destroy the bill. A legislator from New Hampshire, explaining how lotteries in the early years were products of the French code of morals "based on the toleration of vice rather than its suppression," warned the "gentlemen on the floor, if they mean to crush this hydra-headed monster, which is demoralizing the young, the poor, and the needy throughout the country, as no other institution in America had ever done, to beware of the insidious suggestion involved in the amendment of the gentleman from Texas."[68]

Discerning certain defeat but assured by a proviso that a lottery's public announcement naming an agent constituted no acknowledgment of that person actually being an agent but only prima facie evidence, Crain withdrew his amendment. Following that, the House hastily sidestepped the sticky constitutional question of whether it had authority to bar newspapers carrying lottery advertising from the mail and passed the bill in a spirit of self-congratulation that the doctrine of states' rights had been overcome. "We have reached, sir," exclaimed Blount, once chair and a long-time member of the House Post Office Committee, "a point where the [postal] power is clear, and, the power being clear to exclude the instrumentalities of this corporation to continue its crimes, the moral sentiment of the country is about to be responded to by legislation in pursuance of it. . . . Mr. Speaker," he continued to the applause of members, "I think we can congratulate ourselves and the country upon the fact that we are about to consummate a great moral act in the interests of the best people and the best sentiments of the country."[69]

The bill moved on to the Senate, where it was passed without debate in September 1890. Postmaster General Wanamaker immediately issued directives to some sixty thousand postmasters, explaining the bill and issuing instructions on how to enforce it. Care was to be taken not to make the bill obnoxious by immediately prosecuting newspapers and charitable organizations that promoted guessing games and gave prizes, although such activities were now illegal. The full power of the law, however, was to be used to crush the Louisiana State Lottery. In just two months, registered letters to the lottery company and money orders drawn to its order had virtually ceased, and business at the New Orleans post office had fallen by one-third.[70]

Meanwhile, a titanic struggle was taking place in Louisiana as foes and friends of the lottery fought over whether it should be extended for twenty-five years. As in all struggles over moral issues, emotions ran high. Although the lottery continued to operate on a limited scale in 1891 and drew the usual paid supporters to its cause, opponents banded together to form an anti-lottery league, publish a newspaper, and persuade the people of Louisiana of the disgrace the lottery had brought upon the state. Such was the intensity of the issue that the parties split over it. Louisiana's Presbyterian ministers rallied to demand of Congress a constitutional amendment that would end all lotteries, which, they said, had "blunted the moral sense of the community." They were joined in their fight by the WCTU, which at its 1891 convention adopted a resolution "that we unite with all good people in protesting against the legalizing of the Louisiana lottery."[71]

As it turned out, however, it was a Supreme Court decision and not a vote of the people that brought the lottery to its knees. As was bound to happen, the constitutionality of the anti-lottery law of 1890 was tested in 1892 when the editors of two newspapers were arrested for mailing lottery advertising. Ignoring the question of the lottery's immorality, their lawyers resorted to the old contention that Congress had no more power to suppress lotteries than it had to suppress other businesses. The law, they said, reached beyond a legitimate end, violated the Tenth Amendment, abridged freedom of the press, and deprived their clients of a fundamental right.[72]

Chief Justice Melville Fuller accepted none of these arguments in his decision *Ex Parte Rapier*. Congress, said he, repeating an old ruling, has the right to say what shall and shall not be carried in the mail and may refuse its facilities for the distribution of material harmful to the people. The refusal to transport publications advertising lotteries did not abridge the freedom of the press. "The circulation of newspapers is not forbidden," he wrote, "but the government declines to become itself an agent in the circulation of printed material which it regards as injurious to the people." Nor did the chief justice regard the right to operate a lottery as a fundamental right. In this he seemed to agree with the Post Office Department's attorney that "if it can be demonstrated that to prey upon one's fellow-men by means of a lottery is a fundamental human right the Decalogue, and the Sermon on the Mount, to say nothing of the Declaration of Independence, ought to be re-written at once."[73]

John L. Rapier was president of the Register Company, which owned the Mobile, Alabama, *Daily Weekly Register*. His lawyer, Hannis Taylor, one of the nation's preeminent constitutional authorities and author of a prestigious book on the English constitution, was so outraged at this decision that he wrote a scathing article in the *North American Review*. In it he denounced the Court for depriving a citizen, "without a legal trial, of the right to send his communications *through the mail,"* thereby taking away "the only substantial right the First Amendment was ever intended to guarantee him." Taylor had no doubt that "neither the Congress nor the Supreme Court could have permitted themselves to be dragged into this grotesque position, so dangerous to the future liberty of the country, had not both bodies been seduced by the fatal argument that the vastness of a temporary evil which they were called upon to suppress, and which they alone could suppress, justified the sacrifice."[74]

Taylor was right. Only what was perceived to be a vastness of evil could have forced Congress to enact such a law, but he was wrong about it being only temporary. When Congress passed the law with near-unanimity in 1890, the possibility existed that the evil might continue for at least twenty-five more years and that the immorality might spread to other states—something neither evangelicals nor Congress could abide. It was a measure of the widespread belief in the lotteries' immorality that even the nation's press, which lost considerable advertising revenue by the law's enactment, had acquiesced to it.[75]

However the constitutionality of the law might be regarded, the Supreme Court's decision ended the lottery in Louisiana. When the law was announced in 1892, John Morris declared that it would be obeyed. He withdrew the proposed referendum to extend the lottery for another twenty-five years and noted that the lottery would expire on December 31, 1893.[76]

But the end of the Louisiana Lottery was still to come. In reptilian fashion it had shed its name but not its business. In 1893 Morris was on his ranch in Texas, preparing to move some seventy-five of his ninety Thoroughbred mares to his training stables in Maryland. Questioned there about the future of the lottery, he replied that it would not go out of business—and indeed it did not. By 1894 the lottery, now known as the Honduras Lottery, had moved to that country, where allegedly it was given a charter for fifty years, an island on which to operate, the right to lay a cable to the United States, concession for a steamship line from Honduras to any part of the world, exemption from taxes, and exemptions from military service for its employees.[77]

To survive, however, the Honduras Lottery needed the patronage of gullible players in the United States. Taking advantage of a Florida law that banned state lotteries but not foreign ones, its managers established a headquarters at Tampa in 1893. There they formed the Graham Printing Company to print the lottery's advertising and other publications, including lists of prizes drawn in Honduras and brought to Tampa by steamship. From there, their own Central American Express Company and other express companies scattered the material to agents throughout the country, who in many instances accepted express money orders for payments and used the express companies' offices to sell lottery tickets and award prizes. "The carrying business of the lottery companies done by express companies," wrote the post office's assistant attorney general in 1894, "has increased in the direct ratio of the decrease of that business through the mails."[78]

Lottery managers denied using the mail for business, of course, but in fact they were. Many of the ordinary letters that passed through the mail in 1894 addressed to the Central American Express Company contained orders for lottery tickets and the money to pay for them. These the postmasters were powerless to open or stop, because the anti-lottery law of 1890 applied only to registered letters.[79]

Unimpeded, then, by either postal authorities or laws controlling interstate traffic, the Honduras Lottery flourished. So did "bond investment companies," lotteries of a different name that sprang up all over the country in the wake of the disappearance of the Louisiana Lottery that had gobbled the available lottery money. It was, however, the Honduras Lottery that remained the focus of evangelicals' indignation, and their press swarmed to attack it. Even before the lottery began its operation, *The Outlook,* one of the most outspoken Christian foes of the lotteries and gambling, demanded that Congress pass a law "prohibiting under the heaviest penalties, the bringing of lottery matter within our territory." "Christian manhood and womanhood" should petition Congress to extinguish this "international crime," and the paper promised to use its offices to forward such petitions to the president and secretary of state.[80]

After the election of 1892, however, moral reformers faced a Democratic Congress for the first time since the Civil War, a situation that put in doubt the enactment of a new anti-lottery bill. Consequently, it was not a Democrat who introduced the new restrictive bill in the Senate. Nor was it an evangelical senator. It was left to a Republican member of the Senate Judiciary Committee, Massachusetts Senator George Hoar, a Unitarian, to bring before the Democratic Senate a bill that was to doom the Honduras Lottery. Introduced in February of 1894, the proposed legislation had a broad sweep. It used Congress's power to control interstate commerce to shut down express companies' traffic in interstate and foreign traffic commerce and once again broadened the postal power to permit the postmaster general to stop the use of ordinary as well as registered letters in conducting the lottery trade.[81]

There were now no long arguments about infringing states' rights and abusing the postal power, for it was clear they would be of no avail against the insistent demand of the "best people" to stop the Honduras Lottery. "There are few Congressmen," *The Outlook* prophesied, "who dare vote against it, if brought to a vote." Knowing that to be true, Democrats who opposed the bill, which was not on the regular order, adopted a strategy to prevent it from coming to a vote. Sen. Arthur Gorman, a powerful voice in the Democratic Senate from Maryland, led the way. Arguing that the bill would end church raffles and charitable festivals, the senator, who, as one man remembered, "spun webs of exceeding finess," objected to a vote on the bill.[82]

But evangelicals were building a fire under the bill's opponents. Urging that "the efforts of moral citizens . . . for the passage of Hoar's bill, be intensified," *The Outlook* printed two petitions, one to the Senate and one to the House, and asked subscribers to send one of each to Congress. "Do not hesitate to forward your petitions," it advised, "because you do not believe your representative is not in sympathy with moral measures." He would be, the paper suggested, if he heard from constituents. The result of this effort was a massive outpouring of evangelical petitions from congregations large and small, seminaries, ministers, and educators; their communications were scattered across more than 150 pages of the *Congressional Record.*[83]

That was enough to secure passage of the bill in the Senate but not in the Democratic House. Four times in 1894 Case Broderick of Kansas offered the bill for passage, and four times objections were made against it. Once Congressman Hayes of Iowa, whom *The Outlook* singled out as the lottery's man and who, for whatever reason, had vigorously opposed the anti-lottery law of 1890, objected. Three times Robert Charles Davey of Louisiana, "indifferent to the impression his objection made," objected. "It suited him to uphold the interests of the lottery people," the New York *Times* reported, "and at that stage of the proceedings the easiest way in which he could do this was to object." The tactic was successful. Before the bill could be presented again, time had run out on the second session of the Fifty-second Congress.[84]

Time was also running out on the Democratic control of Congress, for that party had been badly defeated in the midterm election of 1894. Still, it controlled the third session of the old Congress, and gloom over the prospect of passing the anti-lottery bill settled over the editorial pages of *The Outlook* as Congress met for the short session in January 1895. The lottery was promising money to the political campaigns of those who would oppose the bill, and fears arose that the Congress would end before it had time to pass the anti-lottery law. "Not a dozen men in the House," fumed the weekly's editorial, "would vote against it in the open, but its enemies seem to have power to prevent a vote." The paper chided churches for their inactivity, noting "the moral forces of the country have not shown themselves strong enough to secure consideration for the only distinctively moral measure presented to the present Congress."[85]

Nevertheless, the foes of the lottery refused to give in, and a Boston Institute of Technology professor named Woodbridge who had assumed control of a national drive to secure memorials and petitions for the anti-lottery bill focused on the districts of legislators who had the most influence over the proposed bill. That proved decisive. Speaker Charles Crisp, a southern Democrat in favor of the bill, recognized Broderick, who presented his bill, and it was swiftly passed. But it was not a total victory. The bill was returned to the Senate for its approval, where once again it was introduced by Senator Hoar and objected to by Senator Gorman.[86]

And now a great test of wills took place between Senator Hoar—a Republican of Puritan ancestry and the Harvard-educated, grandson of Roger Sherman of Connecticut—and Senator Gorman, a Democrat and grandson of an Irish immigrant, "without claim to a great ancestral line" or college education. Busily completing appropriation bills, Gorman objected to Hoar's bill, claiming there was no time to present it, and from two in the afternoon until two the next morning Hoar waited. When the last appropriation bill had been passed and before Gorman could prevent it, Hoar was recognized and presented his bill, which was immediately passed by a voice vote.[87]

It was a dramatic finish to a long battle that had vastly extended Congress's postal power to prevent use of the nation's communications system for disseminating material the evangelical moral majority considered immoral. "The long fight for anti-lottery legislation," *The Outlook* exulted, "which began in several states sixty years ago, has now triumphed in every State in the Union and in the national government." Explaining that the law forbade forwarding any mail whatsoever to any person engaged in the lottery business, the paper declared, "The lottery is now an outlaw, from one end of the country to the other end of our country." Lottery letters, advertising, and publications of all kinds had joined the long list of immoral mail that evangelical Christians were also responsible for banishing.[88]

Notes

1. *Congressional Record,* 40th Cong., 2d sess., 162 (Dec. 12, 1867) (quotation); New York *Times,* Dec. 13, 1867, 1.

2. New York *Times,* Apr. 11. 1868, 2; "Gettysburg Lottery," H. Rept. no. 12, 40th Cong., 2d sess., 1–5 (Jan. 22, 1868). On the wartime tax, see "Gettysburg Asylum Lottery," H. Exec. Doc. no. 61, 40th Cong., 2d sess., 1 (Dec. 17, 1867).

3. New York *Times,* Feb. 9, 1869, 5.

4. "Gettysburg Lottery," 2 (first quotation); *Congressional Record,* 40th Cong., 2d sess., 162 (Dec. 12, 1867) (second quotation).

5. New York *Times,* Feb. 12, 1868, 8, Apr. 11, 1868, 2.

6. For notice of Beecher's speech, see John Samuel Ezell, *Fortune's Merry Wheel: The Lottery in America* (Cambridge, 1960), 180–82. The General Assembly's resolution is in Jane Garrett, "The Delaware College Lotteries, 1818–1845," *Delaware History* 7 (Sept. 1975): 303. For the immorality of lotteries and an account of an evangelical reformer and former gambler, see Ann Fabian, *Card Sharps, Dream Books, and Bucket Shops: Gambling in Nineteenth-Century America* (Ithaca, 1990), 70–107, 113–28. Thomas Jefferson reasoned against the the immorality of lotteries in the last year of his life when he proposed one to relieve him and his family of his enormous debt. If lotteries were immoral, he argued, so were most enterprises—for almost all were gambles. *The Writings of Thomas Jefferson,* ed. Paul Leicester Ford (New York, 1899), 10:362–73.

7. Job Roberts Tyson, *A Brief Survey of the Great Extent and Evil Tendencies of the Lottery System as Existing in the United States.* (Philadelphia, 1833), 23–27. Justice Grier's opin-

ion is found in *Cases Argued and Decided in the Supreme Court of the United States,* ed. Stephen K. Williams (Rochester, 1901), 5:262–444 (quotation on 279). For a list of states that had banned lotteries in the constitutions see A. R. Spoffard, "Lotteries in American History," *Annual Report of the American Historical Association for the Year 1892* (Washington, 1893), 193.

8. Even in the 1850s the postmaster general had complained about mailbags filled with lottery advertisements. *Report of the Postmaster General, 1855,* (this and subsequent citations to postmasters general reports can be found in the *Congressional Information Service Serial Set Index* [Washington, 1997]), 29.

9. *United States Statutes at Large* (Boston, 1865), 13:279.

10. For accounts of money being lost in the mail, see *Report of the Postmaster General, 1854,* 625–26; see also *Congressional Globe,* 37th Cong., 2d sess., 951 (Feb. 26, 1862). For the registration of letters, see *United States Statutes at Large* (Boston, 1855), 10:642.

11. *Congressional Globe,* 37th Cong., 2d sess., 951 (Feb. 25, 1862).

12. *Congressional Globe,* 38th Cong., 1st sess., 1659 (Apr. 26, 1864); *United States Statutes at Large* (Boston, 1866), 13:76–79; New York *Times,* Mar. 1, 1866, 8. Gift concerts were lotteries of a different name. Many lotteries featured concerts that took place at the time of a drawing. After raising a certain amount of money by selling tickets for listed "prizes" or "gifts," managers of gift concerts promised to have a concert at the time of the drawing when the "gifts" would be distributed. *Frank Leslie's Illustrated Newspaper,* Jan. 5, 1867, 255.

13. "Letter of the Solicitor of the Post Office Department to the Postmaster General in Regard to Fraudulent Lottery Enterprises . . . by Using the Mails of the United States," S. Misc. Doc. no. 57, 39th Cong., 1st sess., 1–4 (Feb. 14, 1866) (hereafter "Letter of the Solicitor"); New York *Times,* Mar. 1, 1866, 8.

14. "Letter of the Solicitor," 4.

15. *Congressional Globe,* 40th Cong., 2d sess., 4412 (July 24, 1868).

16. "The Use of the Mails for Lottery Purposes," H. Exec. Doc. no. 22, 46th Cong., 2d sess., 16 (Jan. 13, 1880) (hereafter "Use of the Mails"). Louisiana's governor, Henry Clay Warmouth, whose salary was $8,000 a year but was believed to have made $100,000 in one year, let the bill become law without his signature. Kenneth Stampp, *The Era of Reconstruction, 1865–1877* (New York, 1965), 174. On violence in Louisiana, see Allen W. Trelease, *White Terror: The Ku Klux Klan Conspiracy and Southern Reconstruction* (New York, 1971), 127–36.

17. New York *Times,* Jan. 7, 1884, 1.

18. *Congressional Record,* 41st Cong., 3d sess., 35 (Dec. 7, 1870).

19. *United States Statutes at Large* (Boston, 1872), 17:302. See sections 3929 and 4041 for the postmaster general's power to seize fraudulent lottery letters and money orders.

20. *Congressional Record,* 44th Cong., 1st sess., 4662 (June 30, 1876); "Uses of the Mail," 13–16. Nearly thirty fraud orders were issued under the law of 1873.

21. *Christian Statesman,* Jan. 16, 1873, 2.

22. *Congressional Record,* 44th Cong., 1st sess., 4262 (June 30, 1876).

23. Ibid. In January of 1876 Congress was preparing to grant amnesty to all Confederates who did not have it when the speaker of the House, James G. Blaine, reawakened sectional animosities when he proposed to amend the bill to prevent amnesty for Jefferson Davis, whom he accused of being the author of the "great crime of Andersonville." H. Wayne Morgan, *From Hayes to McKinley: National Party Politics, 1877–1896* (Syracuse, 1969), 65–66.

24. *Congressional Record,* 44th Cong., 1st sess., 4262–63 (June 39, 1876).

25. Ibid., 4262.

26. *United States Statutes at Large* (Washington, 1876), 18:758; but see sections 3929 and 4041. On Logan, see *Dictionary of American Biography* (New York, 1933), 6:363–65 (hereafter *DAB*).

27. Williams, ed., *Cases Argued and Decided,* 9:878–79.

28. Ibid.

29. *Report of the Postmaster General, 1879,* 35, 334–37; New York *Times,* Oct. 5, 1879, 5. See the New York *Times,* Oct. 8, 1879, 1, for the uneasiness of the Philadelphia postmaster regarding withholding the letter. On Deven's ruling, see "Letter of the Postmaster General in Regard to the Use of the Mails by the Louisiana Lottery Company," S. Exec. Doc. no. 196, 51st Cong., 1st sess., 1 (July 29, 1890) (hereafter "Letter of the Postmaster General").

30. *Report of the Postmaster General, 1879,* 35; Comstock made good use of the law in New York with a number of arrests. New York *Times,* Oct. 11, 1879, 8 (quotation), Oct. 15, 1879, 3, Nov. 12, 1879, 8; see also Records of the New York Society for the Suppression of Vice, 1873–1953, Manuscript Division, Library of Congress (hereafter RNYSSV).

31. New York *Times,* Oct. 23, 1879, 1, Nov., 27, 1879, 1; *Report of the Postmaster General, 1879,* 35–36.

32. See A. A. Freeman's argument against the Commonwealth Distribution Company in *Report of the Postmaster General, 1879,* 339–40, and *Dauphin v. Key* in *Report of the Postmaster General, 1880,* 529–42. The idea that a charter was a contract had been established in *Dartmouth v. Woodward* (1819).

33. *Report of the Postmaster General, 1879,* 35–36.

34. Williams, ed., *Cases Argued and Decided,* 25:1080–81; *Report of the Postmaster General, 1880,* 37–39.

35. "Use of the Mails," 17–18.

36. Ibid.; see also Marshall Cushing, *The Story of Our Post Office: The Greatest Government Department in All Its Phases* (Boston, 1893), 512–15.

37. "Use of the Mails"; New York *Times,* Nov. 12, 1879, 8; RNYSSV, Nov. 11, 1877, 141–22; Anthony Comstock. *Traps for the Young* (repr. Cambridge, 1967), 68–69.

38. Jonathan Wycliffe, "The Louisiana Lottery: A History of the Company," *The Forum* 12 (Jan. 1892): 569–76; Frank McGloin, "Shall the Lottery's Charter Be Renewed?" *The Forum* 12 (Jan. 1892): 555–68. Lottery managers worked hand in hand with those who were "redeeming" the government from carpetbaggers. C. Vann Woodward, *Origins of the New South,* vol. 9 in *A History of the South,* ed. Wendell Homes Stephenson and E. Merton Coulter (Baton Rouge, 1951), 11–14.

39. *Report of the Postmaster General, 1880,* 39; "Use of the Mails," 3.

40. (southern) *Christian Advocate,* Feb. 7, 1880, 8 (quotation), 19, 1880; *Christian Union,* Nov. 19, 1879, 410.

41. Mobile *Register* as quoted in the *Daily Picayune,* Nov. 19, 1879, 4; *Dauphin v. Key,* in *Report of the Postmaster General, 1880,* 529–46 (quotation on 532–33).

42. *Daily Picayune,* Feb. 27, 1884. There was much confusion over whether Key had suspended or revoked the order against Dauphin, but his apparent uncertainty over the order seemed to indicate that he had revoked it

43. On James and Howe, see *DAB* (New York, 1932), 5:245–46, 297–98; on Gresham, see *DAB* (New York, 1932), 4:607–8.

44. *Daily Picayune,* Nov. 13, 1883, 2.

45. *Report of the Postmaster General, 1883,* 30–31.

46. Ibid., 56.

47. *Daily Picayune,* Sept. 21, 1883, 1, Sept. 22, 1883, 1; New York *Herald,* as quoted in the *Daily Picayune,* Sept. 29, 1883, 2.

48. The full decision appears in the *Daily Picayune,* Jan. 6, 1883, 10.

49. New York *Times,* Jan. 7, 1884, 1; "Delivery of Registered Letter and Payment of Money-Orders," H. Rept. no. 472, 48th Cong., 1st sess., 1 (Feb. 23, 1884) (hereafter "Delivery of Registered Letter"); *Congressional Record,* 48th Cong., 1st sess., 4380 (May 22, 1884).

50. *Congressional Record,* 48th Cong., 1st sess., 4382–83 (May 22, 1884).

51. Ibid.; "Delivery of Registered Letter," 3.

52. *Congressional Record,* 48th Cong., 1st sess., 4384 (May 22, 1884). Twenty-five senators did not vote.

53. *Congressional Record,* 48th Cong., 2d sess., 105 (Dec. 9, 1884); *Congressional Record,* 49th Cong., 2d sess., 2390 (Feb. 28, 1887).

54. On Vilas, see *DAB* (New York, 1936), 10:270–71.

55. *Christian Union,* Apr. 4, 1890, 419.

56. *Congressional Record,* 51st Cong., 1st sess., 8706 (Aug. 13, 1890); "Letter of the Postmaster General," 2.

57. "Letter of the Postmaster General," 2; *Congressional Record,* 51st Cong., 1st sess., 8717 (Aug. 16, 1890).

58. McGloin, "Shall the Lottery's Charter Be Renewed?" 576; *Congressional Record,* 51st Cong., 1st sess., 8715 (Aug. 16, 1890).

59. *Christian Union,* July 3, 1890, 5.

60. *The Independent,* Mar. 13, 1890, 347.

61. *Report of the Postmaster General, 1889,* 39–41; "Letter of the Postmaster General," 4.

62. "Letter of the Postmaster General," 1–2. The president also urged the passage of laws in his State of the Union address in December 1889. James R. Richardson, comp., *A Compilation of the Presidents, 1789–1897* (Washington, D.C., 1899), 9:80.

63. *Congressional Record,* 51st Cong., 2d sess., index.

64. *United States Statutes at Large* (Washington, 1891), 26:465–66. For the original bill, see *Congressional Record,* 51st Cong., 1st sess., 4698 (Aug. 16, 1890).

65. Strangely, only Walter M. Hays, a member of Congress from Iowa and normally the source of moral crusades, opposed the bill with the old states' rights doctrine intact. *Congressional Record,* 51st Cong., 1st sess., 8703 (Aug. 16, 1890).

66. Ibid., 8699.

67. Ibid., 8700–702; New York *Times,* Aug. 18, 1896, 4. On Crain's life, see memorial speeches, *Congressional Record,* 54st Cong., 1st sess., 4437–45 (Apr. 25, 1896).

68. *Congressional Record,* 51st Cong., 1st sess., 8710 (first quotation), 1805 (second quotation) (Aug. 16, 1890).

69. Ibid., 8720. Blount, once a Confederate soldier, was best known as Cleveland's commissioner to Hawaii in 1893 for a report criticizing the American role there. *DAB* (New York, 1931), 1:388–89. The bill also provided that the postmaster general might determine a lottery agent in other ways than by a public announcement.

70. *Report of the Postmaster General, 1890,* 14–15, 96–100.

71. Wycliffe, "The Louisiana Lottery," 571–74: McGloin, "Shall the Lottery's Charter Be Renewed?" 558–68; "Memorial of Members of the Presbyterian Clergy of New Orleans Praying an Amendment to the Constitution to Prohibit Lotteries," S. Misc. Doc. no 57, 51st Cong., 2d sess., 1–2 (Feb. 3, 1891) (first quotation); *Union Signal,* Dec. 10, 1891, 16 (second quotation).

72. Williams, ed., *Cases Argued and Decided,* 36:93–102.

73. Ibid., 36:99.

74. Hannis Taylor, "A Blow at the Freedom of the Press," *North American Review* 155 (Dec. 1892): 700, emphasis in the original; New York *Times,* Feb. 5, 1892, 4.

75. *Congressional Record,* 51st Cong., 1st sess., 8721 (Aug. 16, 1890) gives the vote on the bill. The ayes and nays were not taken, although a friend of the bill wanted a vote to show the unanimity with which the measure passed. For one newspaper's approval see Chicago *Tribune,* Aug. 19, 1890, 4.

76. New York *Times,* Feb. 5, 1892, 4.

77. New York *Times,* Jan. 18, 1893, 1. The grant was for twenty-five years

78. New York *Times,* Feb. 21, 1894, 4, Mar. 6, 1895, 4; see also *Congressional Record,* 53d Cong., 3d sess., 2356 (Feb. 22, 1894). To secure agents, lottery managers sent lottery material and tickets to influential men and asked them to be agents. Some packets wound up in the hands of the editor of *The Outlook* (formerly the *Christian Union*). See, for example, the issue of Apr. 7, 1894, 614–15; and *Report of the Postmaster General, 1894,* 63.

79. New York *Times,* Mar. 6, 1895, 4.

80. *Report of the Postmaster General, 1894,* 17–18. One journalist commented on the great increase of various kinds of gambling in 1894. *The Outlook,* Nov. 18, 1893, 883.

81. *Congressional Record,* 53 Cong., 2 Sess., 2211 (Feb. 15, 1894); *Congressional Record,* 53d Cong., 2d sess., 4313 (May 2, 1894); *Congressional Record,* 53d Cong., 2d sess., 4986 (May 19, 1894); On Senator Hoar's religion, see George F. Hoar, *Autobiography of Seventy Years* (New York, 1903), 2:437–40. In the long fight to reform the postal system, Senator Hoar is the first Unitarian to emerge as a leader of a postal reform effort. In general, Unitarians were not conspicuous in the movement to reform the postal system.

82. *The Outlook,* Mar. 10, 1894, 438; *Congressional Record,* 53d Cong, 2d sess., 3883 (Apr. 20, 1894); on Gorman, see Thurston Peck, *Twenty Years of the Republic, 1885–1905* (New York, 1913), 278–79.

83. *The Outlook,* Feb. 24, 1894, 383 (quotation), Mar. 10, 1894, 438. A sample of petitions appers in *Congressional Record,* 53d Cong., 2d sess., 2408 (Feb. 26, 1894); see also the index to *Congressional Record,* 53d Cong., 2d sess., 11–257 passim.

84. *Congressional Record,* 52d Cong., 2d sess., 3631 (Aug. 26, 1894); *Congressional Record,* 52d Cong., 2d sess., 8667 (Aug. 28, 1894); *The Outlook,* Feb. 9, 1895, 218; New York *Times,* Oct. 1, 1894, 6.

85. *The Outlook,* Feb. 16, 1895, 258 (first quotation), Feb. 23, 1895, 297–98 (second quotation). On the election of 1894 and its ramifications, see Morgan, *From Hayes to McKinley,* 476–78

86. *The Outlook,* Mar. 9, 1895, 382; *Congressional Record,* 52 Cong. 3 Sess., 3100–101 (Mar. 2, 1895).

87. Peck, *Twenty Years,* 279 (quotation). For Hoar's ancestry, see Hoar, *Autobiography of Seventy Years,* 7–37; for Gorman's, see *Congressional Record,* 59th Cong. 2d sess., 2081ff. (Feb 1, 1907); see also *The Outlook,* Mar. 9, 1895, 382, for the New York *Post*'s description

of the passage of the law, and *Congressional Record,* 53d Cong., 3d sess., 3130 (Mar. 2, 1895).

88. *The Outlook,* Mar. 9, 1895, 382. In 1897, at the culmination of the evangelicals' efforts to reform the post office, Charles Sheldon, a Congregational minister in Topeka, Kansas, wrote a book entitled *In His Steps* (repr. Tulsa, 1998). In it, characters confront all the social problems against which the evangelicals had campaigned—everything from Sunday newspapers, to advertising harmful products, to gambling and pornography—by asking, "What would Jesus do?" It is estimated that the book has sold more than fifteen million copies over the years. It is still being reprinted and stands as a reflection of evangelical efforts to maintain a Christian nation.

10 Immoral Mail and the Enforcement of Evangelical Morality

If the facts of the business of obscene publications and indecent articles could be published here, a shock would be given to the sensitive and decent in the community that would make their blood run cold, while a wave of indignation would roll over the country that would sweep away any person found engaging in the business.

—*Anthony Comstock,* Traps for the Young *(1882)*

On March 1, 1897, Postal Inspector F. M. Betz was in the little town of Eaton, Ohio, investigating the mailing of obscene letters. For two years, "vile anonymous letters" had been mailed to three of the town's young women and to the son of the superintendent of public schools, who, the letters accused, was having illicit relations with one of the three women. Besides the letters, obscene notes had been left during the night on the veranda of one of the women's home, a high school senior whose father was a member of the school board. Suspecting that the letters had been written by a student, the inspector asked the superintendent to determine if by chance their handwriting matched that of someone in high school. Subsequently, and at his request, the young woman at whose home the notes had been left kept watch on her front yard for the possible return of the writer. She had not long to wait. Shortly after her vigil began, she saw the superintendent's son cautiously approach the front gate of her home and loft another note into the yard.

When the note was retrieved it was clear that its handwriting was identical to that of the other obscene notes and letters. The author of all was none other than the superintendent's son, who had tried to avoid being a suspect by mailing letters to himself. Confronted by the inspector, he sobbingly confessed and asked to speak to the young woman, with whom, the letters alleged, he had illicit relations and who, it was understood, had been his sweetheart. In a tearful meeting he admitted his guilt to her and begged her forgiveness, upon which, after weeping copiously, she forgave him with "her whole heart."

The inspector was less forgiving. Suspecting that the young man's purpose was "to pollute the minds of these young women in the hope that he might subsequently be able to induce them to have carnal relations with him," he had him arrested for the federal offense of mailing obscene letters. Brought before the U.S. commissioner, he was bound over to the grand jury and freed on a $500 bond. The school board member whose daughter had received both the letters and the notes demanded that the superintendent expel his son from school.[1]

Following postal inspection procedures, Betz wrote a report of the affair to the inspector-in-charge of his division, and that report subsequently came to rest in the National Archives, where boxes repose that are filled with similar reports detailing the underside of American life in that Victorian age of civility and polite speech. There—in formal reports secured with rubber bands that crumble to the touch, newspaper clippings yellowed with age, salacious books, advertisements, and photographs, and in letters that disclose people's most private thoughts—are the remnants of that odious mail against which the evangelical moral majority struggled for more than a quarter of a century.

From the 1870s to 1890, evangelical agitation to purify the American mail drove Congress to ban the mailing of all "lewd, licentious, and obscene" writing and pictures, all advertisements regarding abortion and contraception, all abortifacients and contraceptives, all advertisements of lotteries and games of chance, all letters aimed at purchasing lottery tickets, and all money orders directed to lotteries. For good measure, all obscene sealed letters and sealed obscene stylograph material were also excluded, although, of course, such letters could be opened only by the addressee.

To investigate and bring to justice all those who mailed such matter was an enormous task for which the Post Office Department had developed an elite force of efficient postal inspectors like F. M. Betz. That corps had been years in the making. In the beginning, inspectors were known as "special agents." Their duties included the hands-on work of the department: establishing post offices, instructing postmasters, investigating their characters and accounts, exploring the reasons for delays in the mail, reporting the failure of mail contractors to keep their schedules, tracing lost mail, and the much publicized task of finding and arresting mail depredators. In short, they were to do all the fieldwork necessary to keep the mail flowing.[2]

Special agents were the eyes and ears of the department as they traveled the post roads. Invaluable as they were, however, they were for years only temporary employees, kept so by a Congress that feared they might be used for political purposes if given permanent status. That apprehension became justified as year after year they performed political chores, along with their regular duties, for whatever president and political party were in power.[3]

Given the nature of the American post office in the nineteenth century, that was inevitable. For those who belonged to the president's party, the post office was a virtual cornucopia for political exploitation. It had advertising to give to loyal newspaper publishers, mail contracts to favored stagecoach owners, contracts for postal supplies to friendly businesses, and thousands of postmasterships, to say nothing of postal clerk positions, for faithful legislators eager to build political machines in their districts. As it turned out, the responsibility for delivering many of these political favors fell to the special agents who traveled the countryside selecting post office sites, removing postmasters and recommending their successors, overseeing the work of mail contractors, and sniffing the political winds for the incumbent administration.

That was especially true after the Jacksonian era. Upon entering the presidency in 1829, Andrew Jackson found many of his political adversaries entrenched in postmasterships throughout the nation. Intending to remove them, Jackson appointed as his postmaster general the pliant William T. Barry of Kentucky, who established the Office of Instruction and Inspection, seeded it with temporary special agents, and sent them out to remove politically obnoxious postmasters. After some thought, this policy was called "rotation in office," designed, supposedly, to give all good Americans an opportunity to serve their government.[4]

However democratic it might have been to give every citizen an opportunity to serve the government, the rotation in office policy did not proceed without complaint. The temporary agents Barry had employed were paid from contingency funds, which was especially objectionable to Sen. John Clayton of Delaware, whose state had sacrificed sixteen postmasters on the altar of rotation in office. "Sir," he asked in 1831, "is it possible that it can escape a thinking intellect, how easy a part of these immense sums might be paid away to a hireling agent for an electioneering tour, under pretense of public duty? Is it, dare it, be denied that there are secret agents in the employment of this chief [Barry] whose compensation defrayed out of the public purse, is regulated by his sole control, and whose services are never made known to the public, or their representatives here?"[5]

It could not be denied, of course, and out of the turmoil over special agents, postmaster removals, and the scandals in the Post Office Department that occurred in the Jacksonian administration came an act in 1836 that reformed the post office. By its provisions, special agents were given permanent positions and presumably no longer paid from contingency funds.[6]

Rotation in office, more commonly called the "spoils system," has been interpreted as a gesture toward democracy in the age of the common man, and there was merit to the argument. Whether for good or ill, however, it established a precedent that would be followed through the rest of the century and beyond. After each change of administration special agents would help rebuild the post office in the image of the political party in power by replacing political enemies with friends in the nation's postmasterships.[7]

Nor did special agents become less political after the Civil War. Because of their long tenure in office during and after the war, Republicans controlled the post office and normally favored special agents, more than once coming to their rescue when their status was endangered. Democrats, however, were less enamored. Long out of command of the central government during the years of the Civil War and Reconstruction, they had seen special agents come and go in their districts, reestablishing vanished post offices here and there and making recommendations with which they did not agree. It was no surprise, then, that when Democrats again controlled the House of Representatives they reduced appropriations for special agents and may even have intended to destroy their bureau.[8]

Yet in 1885, when Democrats at last ruled over the post office during President Grover Cleveland's administration, they dismissed Republican special agents (called "inspectors" after 1881) and appointed in their place Democratic inspectors, who gave the post office a partisan cast. Democratic postal officials were loud in their praise of the new inspectors as they went about removing Republican postmasters and recommending good Democrats to replace them. Their investigations and removal of Republican postmasters, however, were still underway when Republicans returned in 1888 to put a Republican stamp on the postal system once more.[9]

These rapid transformations occurred again in 1893 and 1897, when the administrations once more changed hands. By 1897 the postal inspection corps, which had always been instrumental in changing the cast of characters involved in this political drama, had itself undergone major alterations. In 1888 President Cleveland classified the postal inspectors, forcing them to pass a civil service examination before they received an appointment. Consequently, the inspection corps was much less political than it once had been, as was evident from its composition in 1896. That year 105 inspectors, fifty-eight Republicans and forty-seven Democrats, composed the corps. They had been drawn largely from the ranks of the very best postal employees, railroad mail clerks and postal clerks of long experience in the great city post offices, and were, as one member of Congress boasted, a class of men "who had the confidence of the country." The employment of a Republican chief postal inspector in a Democratic administration gave emphasis to the nonpolitical character of the corps.[10]

Other changes made through the years had brought the Division of Mail Inspection, as it was called in the 1890s, to a degree of efficiency rare among government bureaus. Placed under the fourth assistant postmaster general for administrative purposes, it was headed by a chief postal inspector who had overall charge of postal inspectors scattered in twelve divisions throughout the nation. Each division had an inspector-in-charge and its own contingent of inspectors, who were required to live in the division to which they had been assigned. Each year they were responsible for the investigation of thousands and thousands of cases, which were systematically divided into the categories *A, B, C,* and *F.* In the A category were complaints involving registered letters; in B, those involving ordinary letters; C concerned miscellaneous violations of the postal laws; and F dealt with foreign charges against the postal service.[11]

As grievances over lost letters and reports of such outrages as post office burnings and burglaries and robberies of mail stages and trains—in addition to rumors of countless violations of postal laws and regulations—poured into the Office of the Chief Clerk of the Post Office Department, they were forwarded to the applicable A, B, C, or F clerk. That person then jacketed them with the name and location of the violation and sent them on to the division where the offense had occurred. There they were assigned to an inspector. It was this system that enabled postal inspectors to complete investigations of 100,205 cases out of the 108,037 received in 1896. Of these, well over 1,500 involved breaches of the nation's antiobscenity laws.[12]

In 1881 the third assistant postmaster general in charge of the dead-letter office was gratified to find upon opening unmailable letters and packages that the U.S. mail was being used less and less for the mailing of obscene material. "No obscene book has been received during the year," he wrote, "and to find an indecent photograph is a rare occurrence." The next year even Comstock noted that "the danger is not as great as it was ten years ago." Sixteen years later, however, in addition to the 1,500 cases of obscene matter given to postal inspectors for investigation, officials in the dead-letter office destroyed more than five million letters and packages containing unmailable enclosures, many of them of an obscene nature. Cheap postage, postal innovations, the expansion of the mail service, and the American appetite for the obscene—all fed by the avarice of those outside the evangelical moral structure who were willing to risk prison for profit—combined to produce a furtive but pervasive national and international trade in pornography. Not for nothing had Anthony Comstock warned women attending the American Purity Alliance conference in 1896 of the dreaded material flowing through the mail when he urged their help in strengthening postal laws against unseemly material.[13]

The postal innovations that sped newspapers, periodicals, and books through the mail in the name of educating the American people were, of course, as useful to those trading in pornography during the nineteenth century as to the public, and they made the most of them. They used money orders, the registry system, and the package service and profited immensely from safeguards that protected the privacy of the mail.

In 1885 Congress had raised the weight limit on first-class letters from one-half to a full ounce, and thousands of businesspeople began mailing advertising circulars in first-class mail. The change was made to order for purveyors of pornography, who sent thousands of obscene circulars in sealed envelopes to dealers in pornography, to those on one of the mailing lists they had obtained, and to young people whose addresses were gleaned from catalogs of boarding schools and academies. The flyers contained titles of all the works familiar to those who consumed pornography. "I hand you herewith," ran one of many such circulars in 1897, *"specimen pages,* printed from the plates of some of my high-class *original obscene books.* . . . Each book contains a large assortment of steel cuts of *Male and Females,* many colored to correspond to the stories."[14]

This collection of lewd books—one entitled *Rose d'amour* and listed as "very vile"—was large and included three booklets, *Only a Girl, Love a Passion,* and *Only a Boy,* which Comstock called "as filthy as filth can be." They were possessed by nearly every large and small dealer in obscene publications in the nation and proved, if proof were needed, the existence of a national network of the pornography trade that the postal system had made possible by the 1890s. No place in the nation was too small to have a place where these and other similar works might be found—not LaHarpe, Illinois, where two dealers advertised obscene songs and music for sale, or Murdoch, Ohio, where a woman shopkeeper's small store featured *Love a Passion* and *Only a Boy* as well as a nationally distributed illustrated booklet entitled *The Bride's Confession.*[15]

A large portion of the obscene material advertised in the trade consisted not only of explicit sexual stories, songs, and poetry but also playing cards, plain cards, watch charms, men's pocket cases containing pictures, and photographs of women in all stages of dress and undress. Only their bodies were described, and in much the same way as female slaves on the auction block had once been advertised. One typical broadside read, "CABINET PHOTOS—Of Lovely Women taken from Nature in careless and bewitching attitudes. There are short Women, tall Women, fleshy Women and graceful Women, they were taken in a warm room and are dandies, Fresh, Rosy, Plump, and Pretty."[16]

Many of the obscene photographs of female torsos originally came from the Netherlands, Amsterdam in particular, and France as part of an international trade that had been illegal since 1842. Once smuggled into the United States, they were reproduced again and again in small photography shops around the country, such as the Photo Publishing Company of North Dunbarton, New Hampshire. There photographs were "manufactured" in a room located above the North Dunbarton post office, as one postal inspector ironically explained. From his bustling business the photographer mailed between three and five hundred letters and packages every day.[17]

The reproduction of obscene publications and photographs was the very life of the trade. Improvements in cameras and photographic equipment by the 1890s made possible the success of numerous studios like the Photo Publishing Company, just as printshops with small handpresses flourished and were able to reprint thousands of the trade's publications. Comstock had written in 1882 that printing plates of 163 of the 165 pornographic books manufactured in New York City and Brooklyn in 1872 and mailed to some four thousand dealers across the country had been destroyed, but there was never an end to the reproduction of such material. Printers across the country, who often did legitimate printing for local businesses in their modest shops, also secretly reproduced pornographic material from the nation's store of obscenity. Even a small publishing business could reprint as many as five hundred obscene books a day on a small handpress. From the early 1880s into the 1890s, the same poems, such as "On the Delaware," and booklets like *Only a Boy* were kept alive by such businesses. Occasionally a new title did appear. One shop, for example, offered wholesale customers a book said to be new and promised to illustrate it with half-tone photographs similar to those in *Love a Passion.* But that was unusual. Judging strictly by the pornographers' circulars, original obscene books and pamphlets were as rare as clothes in the photographs they distributed of women. It was as if pornography did not lend itself to the creative imagination beyond the obscene plots and situations already in print.[18]

The names of the authors of the vulgar books and pamphlets that sold in the trade do not usually appear on their work, and little is known about them. One mercenary merchant of lascivious "literature" announced that the author of *A Night in a Turkish Harem* was also the author of *Love a Passion* and that *The Romance of a French Bedstead* was written by the author of *May Howard* and *Old Tricks.* Who the authors were, however, was unknown, except, no doubt, to those in the trade who knew enough about *Love a Passion* or *Old Tricks* to be intrigued by books by the same authors. In any case, authors did not matter much, and language and plots were monotonously repetitive. Written at an adolescent level, the stories and poems were largely aimed at the nation's youth, who, as Comstock and the evangelicals had contended, constituted pornographers' great market. Still, the material was purchased in large quantities and served as "adult literature," either for "adult" purchasers or among the young, who in their innocence found it palpitatingly exciting.[19]

Typical of the genre was *Only a Boy,* perhaps the most popular obscene book of the period. A paperback with drawings on its blue cover, it was the simple story of a middle-class married couple vacationing for the summer in a rented cottage by the sea. They permit a mature female guest to share their twelve-year-old son's bedroom. Sexually aggressive, she spends her nights and most of her days teaching her young and susceptible roommate the delights of lust and the secrets of womanhood. Through some thirty or forty pages the lessons continue until the author, his imagination apparently exhausted, ends the vacation.[20]

Profits from the sale of pornography were immense, as much as 100 percent according to one observer. List prices on brochures and circulars varied, of course, but usually ran from 50 cents to $1 and more. There was always room for bargaining, however, and prices varied with the size of the order. *A Night in a Turkish Harem* sold for $1 on one list, but $5 would buy ten copies if all were purchased at the same time. Large orders of books and photographs were sold at a fraction of the retail price. Books that cost $1 in a bookstore could be sold by the printers who reproduced them for 10 cents a copy or less if a customer purchased five hundred copies or more.[21]

Profits were great, but so were the risks pornographers took in conducting business through the post office. Their greatest hazard was in revealing their return addresses, which, of course, was necessary if they were to transact business. Because a return address was as visible to postal inspectors as to patrons, pornographers devised various schemes of concealment. Typically, they used fictitious names and box numbers at post offices within reach with the expectation that by doing so they could remain anonymous and take mail from the box unobserved. In 1893 two dealers in LaHarpe used the name "George Simpson" of box 307 at the local post office to receive orders for the words and music to twenty-five obscene titles listed in their circular. The songs cost 5 cents each, or 75 cents for the twenty-five. A note at the bottom of the circular advised, "Any of these goods will be POST PAID upon receipt of the price named."[22]

In large cities, private letter boxes installed in places of business for the benefit of those who wanted, for whatever reason, to correspond secretly were as useful to pornographers as they were troubling to postal officials. To secure a private letter box it was necessary only that a place have a street address. Mail carriers were required to deliver to that address, but once there mail was placed in private letter boxes rented by people unknown to the post office. At this point the post office lost control of the mail, to the discomfort of postal officials. Post office regulations gave control of the delivery of mail to minors to their parents or guardians in order to prevent them from receiving salacious mail, but the department could not enforce that regulation when mail went to private letter boxes.[23]

For years postal authorities pleaded with Congress to abolish private letter boxes, and throughout the 1890s Pennsylvania's Henry Bingham, a longtime member of the House Post Office Committee, introduced legislation that would have done so. But the bills reached no farther than the Post Office Committee, thereby—unintentionally no doubt—supporting the pornography trade. During the 1890s, one pornographer conducted a thriving New York City business of "CHOICE BOOKS, FANCY PHOTOS, ETC., FOR MEN ONLY" through five letter boxes at addresses such as the "Bowery Book Co., #57 Bowery" and the "Holland Publishing Co., #256 West 14th St."[24] Usually that kind of address was not given on the envelopes in which the circulars were mailed. Nor was it listed on the circulars themselves. Wary dealers would enclose self-addressed envelopes along with flyers describing their offerings and provide instructions to "remit in the enclosed envelope." If a business were fraudulent and the dealer had no intention of delivering the advertised material, he might add, "No personal checks or Registered Letters accepted."[25]

It was all but impossible, however, for owners of large, and presumably respectable, bookstores secretly engaged in the obscenity trade not to advertise their holdings and give their business addresses. The usual method was to risk giving addresses and openly advertise "racy material" for sale, mentioning only one or two popular obscene books. To prospective customers they promised to send, by express, a catalog of their grossest holdings, thereby hoping to avoid the laws against mailing obscene material.

Until the passage of the Vilas Act in 1897, which forbade express companies from transporting obscene material across state lines, those companies had always been useful to pornographers. One circular mailed from Chicago to "GENTS AND SPORTS" advertised "a set of twelve, full-length Cabinet Photogaphs of *nude females . . . everything revealed, nature as plain as day"* and illustrated how pornographers used the express and were wary of mail. The photographs were to be sent "BY EXPRESS ONLY." "Remember," the circular cautioned, "we positively cannot send these photos by mail, we send *only by express. You Pay Express,* which will amount to about 25c." Expecting a national market, the huckster suggested that the express cost "to the far Western States will not exceed 40c." The rest of the business, however, was to be done through the mail. Further instructions advised "HOW TO SEND MONEY—Get a $1.00 bill, a postal note, or stamps, as is most convenient to you, inclose it with this circular in a SEALED ENVELOPE, containing your name and address and we will know what you want."[26]

Such efforts to evade antiobscenity laws, however, were met step by step by the Post Office Department's inspectors. The ways they had developed over the years of trapping lawbreakers and enforcing the purity laws aroused angry protests against "entrapment" by those found to be corrupting the mail. Wise as serpents, they scanned the papers, particularly advertising papers in cheap, second-class mail, for pornographers' blurbs, wrote decoy letters to them from distant places, ordered what they had to sell, and paid for it with marked money. When the merchandise would arrive via mail, inspectors could have the offenders arrested. Often they would wait long hours at post offices for the malefactors of the mail to retrieve letters and packages from post office boxes. Proficient at comparing handwriting, inspectors frequently used that skill to identify violators of antiobscenity laws by the way they formed loops in the letters of the alphabet. They would also spend days, weeks, months, and even years on a single case, traveling night and day on trains and stagecoaches to collect evidence and bring about arrests. They were handicapped, however, by being unable to make the arrests themselves after tracking quarries to post offices. Efforts to give them the power to do so in 1897 failed in a Congress still wary of postal inspectors. Awkward as it sometimes was, however, they were usually able to "cause the arrest" of a violator, as their reports said, and they gave the evidence they collected against that person to a U.S. attorney. Upon his decision to try the offenders for violations of the postal laws, the inspectors would testify against them in court.

The Post Office Department depended heavily on two postal inspectors—Anthony Comstock and R. W. McAffee—for enforcement of antiobscenity laws. "In closing this report," the chief postal inspector wrote to the president in 1886, "it affords me pleasure to commend to your favorable consideration the valuable aid rendered this Department in suppressing the publications of obscene literature and suppression of numerous frauds . . . by Messrs Anthony Comstock of N.Y. N.Y and R. W. McAfee of St. Louis, Mo." Both men were associated with societies for the suppression of vice and both were postal agents. But they had a singular status within the department. They were not removed for political purposes as were the regular inspectors, nor were they usually involved in the mundane investigations of post offices and postmasters.[27]

It is a mistake, however, to suppose that they did this work alone. Comstock and McAfee had the help of an elite corps of postal inspectors as well as thousands of evangelical citizens for whom obscenity in all forms was repugnant beyond measure and freedom of expression only a distant right in comparison. Many of these people were members of societies for the suppression of vice scattered throughout the nation, organizations whose burden it was to stamp out pornography before it reached the nation's youth. But there were also many thousands of private citizens who, upon receiving a circular advertising obscene material, informed their postmasters, who then relayed the information to postal inspectors.

The first information that pornographers were operating out of LaHarpe, Illinois, for example, had come from a "well-intentioned" person in Michigan who sent the pornographers' flyer to the postmistress at LaHarpe, not knowing that a woman would read it. From there the complaint reached the inspector-in-charge of the Chicago division, and then it went on to the postal inspector, who spent two years finding that "George Simpson" was really Frank and John Campbell. "I have expended a great deal of time and labor in it [the case]," the inspector wrote. After all that, he was able only to secure fines of $110 for each man because he could not recover the actual poems and because the U.S. attorney did not want to proceed further.[28]

It was also a citizen of Murdoch, Ohio, who informed inspectors that he had received a notice, concealed in second-class mail, of obscene material for sale from a Bertha Wyman of that town. Encouraged by inspectors to make further inquiries, he soon had provided enough information to make their case to a U.S. attorney, who issued a warrant for her arrest. An investigation of her store proved unnerving. "Her place," the inspectors wrote, "is but a few doors from the Public Library and is visited by hundreds of children and youth every day, and is a most vile and demoralizing place."[29]

Nothing so disturbed postal inspectors in that age when the protection of youth was paramount as finding that pornography was accessible to young people, as was the case in Murdoch. In February 1894 obscene material appeared at the Swett Grammar School in San Francisco, distributed, apparently, by a young male student to whom it had been sent. Its source was unknown for a time, even though the secretary of the San Francisco Society for the Suppression of Vice made repeated efforts to find it. Then, on April 14, 1894, an advertisement appeared in *California World* announcing that the Metropolitan Book Company and Purchasing Agency at 26 Stockton Street in San Francisco was the "Headquarters for Sensational Books." Among its holdings were *Only a Boy, Bride's Confession,* and *Love a Passion.* The Division of Mail Inspection quickly ordered an investigation, labeling the case "No. 179.718 C." By April 30, the matter had reached San Francisco and Postal Inspector James W. Erwin, whose subsequent investigation of the Metropolitan Book Company was a model of the methods inspectors used to snare pornographers.[30]

Erwin first sent a decoy letter to the company, postmarked from Arcata, California, expressing interest in the books advertised in *California World.* When he received a price list of the company's obscene holdings, he returned a registered letter containing a marked $1 bill and a half dollar to pay for one book and a photograph. Erwin gave the letter to a mail carrier and instructed him to deliver it to 26 Stockton Street. When the carrier arrived, Inspector Erwin was there, examining books. He saw the letter delivered to Solomon

Levin, the owner of the store; moreover, he saw Levin read it and deposit the marked money in the cash drawer. Erwin then went outside and met an Inspector Gordon, to whom he gave a $5 gold piece. Gordon was asked to make a small purchase and request paper dollars in change. Acting on those instructions, Gordon retrieved the marked $1 bill that Erwin had mailed in the registered letter. The next day, Erwin went to the express company office where he had been informed that his order had been sent. There he received a package, which he opened in the presence of the clerk who initialed the envelope. In it he found the obscene book and photograph he had ordered.

Ordinarily, that would have been enough evidence to bring Levin to trial. Erwin, however, was anxious to convict Abraham Levin, who was Solomon Levin's brother, and Isadore C. Wood, a younger man deeply involved in the company's business. For this purpose he recruited Charles A. Lee, a reporter for the San Francisco *Daily Report.* Lee was to spend several days in the bookstore, buying books and winning the confidence of the Levin brothers and Wood. After several days, Lee expressed interest in a large purchase of books and photographs and made an appointment with Wood to examine the company's stock, which was kept in another building at 25½ Stockton Street and never for more than two days in the same room. On the day of the appointment, Wood and Lee, distantly followed by Inspector Erwin and a deputy U.S. marshal, entered a room filled with obscene books and photographs spread out across a bed. There Wood was arrested, and the entire stock of some four hundred photographs and many boxes of books and pamphlets were seized. A short time later, the Levin brothers were arrested. All three were freed on a $3,000 bond and subsequently bought to trial.

At the trial, it became obvious that the sordid material circulating at John Swett Grammar School had come from the Metropolitan Book Company and Purchasing Agency. "Levin and Wood were shown to have been in the business of distributing the most filthy and vile books and pictures, for gain," the *Daily Report* exclaimed, "and in the sphere of their operations they included even the public schools of this city. . . . As compared with fellows who would deliberately and sordidly carry on dissemination of indecent literature—among school children at that—the burglar, footpad, counterfeiter, or smuggler is a gentleman."[31]

After a trial of four days, Solomon Levin and Isadore Wood were convicted of violating federal antiobscenity laws. In order to secure the vote of one juror for conviction, however, the jury was forced to recommend a punishment of extreme mercy. The judge, steeped in nineteenth-century evangelical morality, was uncertain. As he told the weeping Levin, "The character of the offense is not one that appeals to the mercy of the court. It is an offense which is far-reaching in its consequences on the youth and public morals. No words of mine can add to the condemnation of all right-minded men for it. . . . I have some doubt about what should be done as to sentence. You have an aged mother and brothers in business here. You have not only disgraced yourself but have brought disgrace upon your family. . . . The sentence should be such as to deter others from committing a like offense. The public must be protected. You will, therefore, be confined to the County Jail of Alameda county for a term of one year and pay a fine of $500."[32]

Charges were dropped against Abraham Levin, but Wood received the same sentence Solomon Levin had been given. According to the *Daily Report,* Wood remained unmoved at the sentence, but "Levin sat down and wept, and his wife laid her hand on his shoulder and joined him in shedding tears, until both were removed to the Marshal's office."[33]

At first it was thought that the obscene material in the company's possession had come from Chicago, but an investigation of the company's records pointed to a small printshop in Ukiah, California, as its source. Another investigation and more decoy letters led to Fernando Broback, a crippled printer in that town, whose public printing business was conducted from a shop in his wealthy father's home to disguise the covert reproduction of thousands of obscene publications, many of which he sold to Solomon Levin, who had encouraged him in the business. When arrested, he had some 1,500 books ready for delivery and another eight hundred in preparation. Broback pleaded guilty to violating the antiobscenity laws and was sentenced to a six-month term in the county jail at Ukiah and a fine of $500.[34]

The light sentence suggested that courts and juries did not regard such offenses seriously. In this instance, however, as in the Levin-Wood case, there were mitigating circumstances. "Broback is a cripple," Postal Inspector Erwin wrote, "unable to walk, and but for his physical condition he would undoubtedly have received a more severe sentence." Likely that was true, for judges and juries could exact harsh penalties for such deliberate violations of antiobscenity laws. Jacob Riblett's was a case in point. The proprietor of the Hub, a book and stamp exchange at 602 South Adams Street in Peoria, Illinois, was one of those crafty salesmen of salacious goods who sought to circumvent the law by using the mail to advertise and an express company for deliveries. In 1894 he advertised in Lum Smith's *Public Herald,* an advertising paper, that his store had "racy books" for sale, among them the usual *Only a Boy, Only a Girl,* and *Bride's Confession.* For 50 cents he promised to send, by express, his catalog of obscene holdings, which contained graphic scenes of the female anatomy and copulation. For this he was arrested, held in jail in default of a $3,000 bond, and in time tried, convicted, and sentenced to four years in the penitentiary in Joliet, Illinois.[35]

An even more severe punishment was given to William P. Hanke, owner of the Hanke Book and News Company in St. Louis, who had the misfortune in 1897 to have violated the laws against mailing obscene material in addition to the new Vilas Act of that year banning express companies from transporting such material across state lines. Hanke's newsstand was located near Number 2 North Eighteenth Street in St. Louis, close to the city's Union Station, but his business went beyond his stand. His agents sold his obscene books on the Burlington Railroad, and it was their indiscretion that led Postal Inspectors McAffee and George A. Dice to discover Hanke's business, which led to his arrest.

Hanke at first refused to admit his guilt, saying that the obscene books, more than a hundred different publications, had been left at his store by someone else. When evidence mounted against him, however, he tried to change his plea to guilty. The judge in the case denied that request, and Hanke was tried and found guilty. Because his wife was ill and their children depended on him, a plea for mercy was made. The judge was unmoved. He delivered a scathing lecture to the accused, sentenced him to five years at hard labor at the penitentiary at Jefferson City, and fined him $1. This, wrote the exultant Inspector McAfee, was the first conviction in the West for a violation of the Vilas Act. The result could not "fail to have a salutary effect and will doubtless cause dealers in this class of articles to either cease using the forbidden means of distribution or pursue their unholy business with great secrecy and care."[36]

Throughout the 1880s the center of the pornography trade, like the lottery business, had been driven from the East, where it began, to the Midwest and beyond, largely through the efforts of the redoubtable Comstock. "Mr. Comstock proved energetic and tireless," the Chicago *Telegram* reported in 1883, "in hunting up criminals and bringing them before the 'bar of justice.' Today Anthony Comstock's name is known throughout the breadth of the land, as a savior to public morals, and a fearless officer of justice." The paper bemoaned the fact that Chicago had no Comstock to drive out the "thieves, blacklegs, and gamblers" who had recently arrived there after "their Imprisonment in New York Prisons." But Comstock still had work to do. Like a man on a mission, which, of course, he was, he tenaciously pursued violators of the contraception laws. Using both state and federal laws against gambling, he closed policy shops, arrested lottery dealers, and made New York City inhospitable to the gaming industry.[37]

If upon occasion in the 1890s pornographers did use the mail in Comstock's division for their business, they quickly drew his attention. In February of 1895, after an unsuccessful five-week effort of another postal inspector to find the "W. C. Walker Photo Co.—the Photo Pub. Co. of North Dunbarton, New Hampshire," a manufacturer of obscene photographs, the case was turned over to Comstock. He arrived in Concord within days and in the company of a U.S. marshal took a sleigh from that city to North Dunbarton, found Walter C. Walker, the postmaster's son, and had him arrested. Moreover, at the end of that year he successfully tracked down and arrested Charles Hall, an especially clever New York City pornographer who, Comstock admitted, conducted his business in a "shrewd manner."[38]

Because of his use of five private letter boxes, Hall was able to evade Comstock's pursuit for more than six months, but in the end he fell victim to one of Comstock's famous—infamous in the view of many—decoy letters. Wily as ever, Comstock had written to offer to buy some of the obscene publications Hall had advertised. Baiting the trap, Comstock did not at first reply to Hall's return letter, which revealed his eagerness to sell the goods. As Comstock expected, Hall wrote again, this time mailing a circular advertising his obscene publications and offering to sell Comstock choice works worth $3 at a bargain. "For $1.00," he wrote, "I will send you either Book No. 1 or 2 on the enclosed circular, any two of the pamphlets, one Sample Cabinet Photo, One sample card Photo, and Five samples of the transparent cards." He explained that he would be willing to send samples free of charge but for the fact that everyone would want them "just to have some fun with and carelessly expose them to the Public." Wary of postal officials, Hall noted that he "did not care to receive any orders for less than $1.00, there is just as much risk and not profit enough to pay for wrapping papers."[39]

Hall's address, which he gave to Comstock in his letter, was "E. Hall, 4040 40 6th Ave., NYC," one of his private letter boxes. Knowing that Hall also received registered mail at the New York City post office, however, Comstock found him there and had him arrested. Hall pleaded guilty and was sentenced to the Ludlow Street jail for only three months and a fine of $1. Comstock, uncharacteristically, accepted the light decision calmly, believing that the business had been stopped.[40]

By 1897 Anthony Comstock was rounding out twenty-five years of "standing at the mouth of a sewer," as he said. Fervent in his evangelical faith and zealous in the pursuit of corrupters of youth, he had been threatened by enemies, beaten, scarred, pilloried in the press, scorned, and ridiculed—often for his views on art. Through it all he had won a host of friends who loved him for the enemies he made. To them he was a "moral hero" who fought the good fight against immorality for the sake of the youth of America, and they gathered that year at Carnegie Hall to pay tribute to his twenty-five years of service against the forces of evil. Praises were heaped upon him, and he spoke of his quarter-century of work on behalf of young people. In the end, his good friend Morris Jesup was there to praise him and present him with a check for $5,000, given on behalf of a number of friends for his long service.[41]

In all those years, Comstock left behind him a trail of suicides and broken lives as well as a long string of convicted transgressors of the postal laws and a throng of bitter enemies. He was, wrote his biographers, "hated as few men have been hated." His bitterest enemies, however, were generally anarchistic, freethinking, and anti-Christian. Frequently, they were the National Liberal League members he had arrested at one time or another for violating antiobscenity laws and whose enmity he could discount. They were not pornographers outright but reformers of sexual practices, and their publications were forthright in violations of antiobscenity laws. Animated by a hatred of Christianity, they had written what Comstock had regarded as blasphemous articles as well as produced publications that advocated anarchism, free love, and contraception and attacked marriage. Ignoring their cries of freedom of the press, which meant to them the right to use the mail to distribute their publications, he had long before arrested Ezra Heywood and D. M. Bennett, two champions of these views.[42]

It was not Comstock, however, who arrested other freethinking publicists for violating antiobscenity postal laws. Like pornographers and lottery dealers, publishers of the anarchistic, free-love, and anti-marriage papers advocating contraception moved west, and the postal laws followed them. In the 1880s Moses Harman, an advocate of free love in Valley Falls, Kansas, was publishing *Lucifer, the Lightbearer,* "one of the most filthy publications that ever came to the Department," according to the contemporary historian of the post office. Taking advantage of generous postal laws to undercut the prevailing moral standard with his message, he entered the paper into cheap, second-class mail and sent it postage-free through the county of publication. By 1887, and with a subscription list of scarcely seven hundred, Harman distributed some two thousand papers free of charge through the sample-copy privilege. When the Post Office Department received numerous complaints against Harman's message, and because he was in the St. Louis postal division, he was apprehended by Postal Inspector McAfee and eventually imprisoned for violating the nation's antiobscenity laws.[43]

The West, indeed, had inherited the free-love publications of the East. In 1896 J. F. Jones was arrested, indicted, found guilty, and fined $100 for mailing a "lewd and obscene" publication, *The Non Partisan,* from Los Angeles. The next year, three anarchists were arrested in Portland, Oregon, for mailing from there *the firebrand for the Burning Away of Cobwebs of Ignorance and Superstition,* a "dangerous publication," according to Postal Inspector W. P. Robinson, "that openly and freely advocated Anarchy, Communism, Social Reform, and Free love." To be sure, subscribers were few and revulsion against such papers' message was widespread. The anger of those who did support them, however, was intense. The arrest of the three *Firebrand* publishers precipitated threatening letters, and publications from across the country warned the U.S. attorney in the case and the judge who had incarcerated the men about "their interference in the freedom of the 'Press' and for the illegal arrest of those anarchists."[44]

Then there was the case of Lois Waisbrooker, a one-time editor of *Lucifer* and notorious for the "horse penis affair." In *Lucifer,* Waisbrooker had compared a Department of Agriculture article on that part of a horse's anatomy to a letter in the paper that had been declared obscene because it made reference to a similar anatomical appendage. She was also the publisher of a free-love paper, *Foundation Principles,* which she was mailing from Topeka, Kansas, in 1896. Arrested there that year, she was indicted for mailing an obscene paper. A motion to quash the indictment against her on the ground that her paper was not obscene failed, and she pleaded guilty. Because of Waisbrooker's age and infirmity, however, and because she had ceased to publish the paper, a motion to suspend judgment was granted. She was not appeased. "She was very bitter in her denunciation of the government and all its officers," Postal Inspector McAfee wrote, "for interfering with her claimed right to publish filth and distribute same thorough the mails of the United States. She is, I think, over seventy years of age and is quite feeble physically. She has been a standing candidate for martyrdom and I am of the opinion that the suspended sentence during good behavior is a wise move."[45]

Unfortunately for the publishers of publications such as *Foundation Principles,* it was easier for postal inspectors to enforce obscenity laws against them for mailing their views on marriage, free love, and contraception than it was to find, arrest, and convict the hundreds who advertised contraceptives and abortifacients in the nation's newspapers during the 1890s and sold their "immoral things" through the mail. After all, publishers like Harman were forthright reformers, martyrs to the principle of free speech, and their publications were easy to target. They were advocates of ideas rather than manufacturers of quack medicines whose sly advertisements promised to prevent conception or, failing that, produce abortion. Demand for these instruments was unceasing, and advertisements to supply that demand appeared in so many small papers and weekly advertising publications throughout the United States that it was impossible for postal inspectors to find them all or convict the perpetrators when they did.

Most of those in the business of contraception sold condoms, of course, or "rubber goods," as they were called, but insofar as advertising revealed the market for contraceptives the burden of preventing childbirth fell heaviest upon women. For them, pseudophysicians and manufacturers had pills, tampons, syringes of all kinds, emmenagogues, pessaries, suppositories, and reams of information on marriage. The booklet *Maternal Secrets,* for example, included "Worry and Doubt," a section on maternity that explained "how and when to avoid it" and the "limitation of Off-spring."[46]

Most who advertised such products were frauds who preyed upon the desperate and gullible. Those who spent $2 for Dr. J. H. Leroy's "GREAT SECRET" of how to prevent conception ("HERETOFORE KNOWN ONLY TO THE ELITE OF FRANCE") were surely disappointed when they received in return a small card picturing a couple sleeping apart. Disillusionment, too, must have been the lot of those despairing and dejected women who bought "French Apple Pills" (an emmenagogue discovered by a "French physician and chemist") in the hope that they would "bring about the menstrual secretions or monthly sickness." The advertisement may have been particularly seductive because it was apparently common belief that the apple root, from which French Apple Pills were presumably made, was an abortifacient.[47]

Postal inspectors encountered evidence of a considerable amount of sexual dysfunction among American males in the 1890s, measured at least by those arrested for supplying supposed cures for that condition. The bogus scientists were particularly adept at advertising preparations purported to enlarge penis size, and they played upon the fears of those who believed they required such help. "Many men from infantile diseases, bad habits in youth or sexual excesses," ran the circular of Boston's Santa Rita Medical Company in 1894, "are affected with Atrophy or a shrunken undeveloped state of the sexual organs." Happily, to correct this problem the company had "Dr. Chalco's Magnetic Developer," which would be mailed to the buyer "in plain, sealed packages on receipt of price, $5.00 a package." Dr. Chalco's brilliant discovery of a cure had only come after "many trials and costly experiments" and was "the only natural means whereby the sexual organs of man can be developed and enlarged. . . . It is put up in the form of a lotion to be applied externally, only directly to the parts, being rubbed in every night, a few drops at a time being sufficient. . . . Failures are impossible when directions are strictly followed. It is a veritable boon to mankind."[48]

Penis size, of course, was said to be related the problem of impotence, which Dr. Chalco's product and similar preparations were designed to cure. To merely enhance the sexual experience, the Much Joy Company of New York City offered twenty applications of "Pleasure Powder" for $1. "LAST AND

GREATEST DISCOVERY, Great Excitement Prevails Over the Effect," the company's circular trumpeted in 1895. The reason for such exhilaration was clear: "Not one in ten enjoy the bliss of married life," but Pleasure Powder, applied to "head and neck . . . an hour or so before you are ready to enjoy life . . . prevents a premature emission." The result, of course, is married bliss.[49]

More evidence of male sexual problems in the late nineteenth century was apparent in magazines and books filled with advertising for pseudoremedies for sexual diseases, loss of sexual drive, night emissions, and problems resulting from masturbation. These were the publications that evangelicals and congressional bills termed "filthy and disgusting." Because they were not regarded as obscene, however, postal inspectors were unable to stop their circulation. The WCTU's Department for the Suppression of Obscenity had protested vigorously in the early 1890s against mailing this material, which, it was believed, the nation's youths read only to satisfy prurient interest. Throughout the 1890s the Post Office Department continually asked for a law that made it unmailable, but the law never came.[50]

The failure of Congress to enact such legislation was indicative of the changing attitude toward birth control and the consequent faltering enforcement of that part of the Comstock antiobscenity law relating to contraceptive information in the mail. Again and again during the 1890s cases developed by postal inspectors against offenders of these laws were dismissed with an admonishment not to offend again or with a fine and payment of legal costs. Unlike traffickers in pornography, they rarely went to jail for their offense, although the penalty was the same for both. Publishers of small weeklies and advertising papers were treated especially lightly. They often pleaded that they did not know the contents of the advertising their papers carried, an argument that was acceptable to some judges and exonerated the publishers.

The trial of the publisher of the *Manistee Advocate* in Manistee, Michigan, was typical. The papers had advertised "Dr. Lane's Female Pastiles, warranted to cure all female diseases" in 1896. In court, in spite of the postal inspector's testimony to the contrary, the publisher denied that he knew the contents of the advertisement. Upon his word and the judge's charge to the jury emphasizing that they must be convinced beyond a reasonable doubt before finding the defendant guilty, the publisher was found not guilty. "I trust," wrote the disappointed postal inspector, "it will not be necessary to try any more such cases in that district during the reign of the present Judge."[51]

Even when found guilty, the most obviously fraudulent promoters of abortifacients or contraceptives scarcely felt the effects of their punishment. The owner of the Santa Rita Medical Company, after pleading guilty to the obscenity charge in 1894, paid only the legal costs for his trial. He was freed with the understanding that his case was to be kept on file and he would forgo use of the postal service when mailing advertising for his product. Similarly, when Franklin Crouse, owner of the Much Joy Company, pleaded guilty to advertising Pleasant Powder he was fined only $100.[52]

Punishment for more serious venders of contraceptive devices was little different. In 1897 the owners of the North Dakota Chemical Company, which had mailed a circular describing its "ANTISEPTIC VAGINAL SUPPOSITORIES" to a young woman whose outraged mother had written a letter of protest to the postmaster general, pleaded guilty and were each fined but $25. More illustrative of the court's reluctance to punish those who offended the laws against mailing advertising for contraceptives as the century drew to a close was the postal inspector's case against the Woman's Medical Company of Chicago in 1894.[53]

The company apparently did a very large business in "Instruments and Appliances for the medical and surgical treatment of all Uterine Diseases, Displacements, Tumor, Cancers, Sterilitis, and Irregularities, All Acute, Nervous, Chronic and Skin Diseases." Many of its advertisements for "appliances" preventing contraception, however, violated the antiobscenity laws. The company's owner, a man named Hanselmair, was arrested, indicted, and convicted. The verdict, however, was set aside by legal maneuvers, and Hanselmair was fined $100 and costs. The postal inspector, R. W. McAfee, who had seen punishments in a number of such cases evaporate, was outraged. "The evidence showed conclusively on its face," he wrote, "that Hanselmair knew he was violating the law as he warned his correspondents to keep the communications secret as they were sent in violation of the Postal Laws and they were jointly liable to prosecution for receiving same." Observing what had become obvious nearly everywhere, he noted, "This class of offenses is of very small importance in the estimation of the present U.S. Attorney in this district. It is discouraging," McAfee concluded dispiritedly, "to try to enforce the law under such circumstances."[54]

By 1888 postal inspectors had been waging war against publishers of obscene literature and the contraceptive trade for fifteen years. They were overwhelmed, however, when they tried to enforce the law of that year forbidding mailing obscene letters. The huge mass of these letters soon dwarfed the number of all other obscene matter in the mail during the 1890s. Although it is little-noted by the press or historians of censorship, the fact is that a vast majority of obscene letters were not investigated by Anthony Comstock and R. W. McFee but by other postal inspectors to whom the letters were referred.

The purpose of the law had been to prevent first-class mail from being used for blackmail and scurrilous attacks on debtors and by pornographers who stylographed instead of printed their publications. When Congress passed the law, however, it is doubtful that any of its members suspected the magnitude of obscene letters that poured through the mail. Nor did they have any idea of the purposes of such letters until enforcement of the new law disclosed them. Letters, it was discovered, were often intended to arrange assignations, promote blackmail, aggravate bitter relationships, secure vengeance, intimidate enemies, and give voice to youthful sexual fantasies, all wrapped in obscenities and profanity.

The preponderance of obscene letters involved sexual harassment in one way or another. "The loafers around village stores," an inspector wrote in the file of two different Iowa men who had written an obscene proposal to a woman they believed might be an easy prey, "in some places have nothing to do but to discuss the character of the ladies they may know." Often letters were forthright propositions for a sexual encounter. Others were more subtle, "well designed . . . to seduce," as an inspector explained of one such letter, and "couched in lewd and lascivious phrase." They were frequently written over a number of weeks and so cleverly that several were needed to decipher the writer's true intentions. Sometimes the letters were addressed to a number of women or girls in the hope, apparently, that one or two of them would accept an indecent proposal. The most graphically obscene of all such letters of harassment were those from young men. Such letters reflected mounting sexual fantasies and grew more graphic, sprinkled with four-letter words and even obscene drawings on occasion, as their authors pictured the girl or woman to whom they wrote and perhaps recalled a meeting in which they had played "museums" or some other erotic game. It was as if using U.S. mail to send their inmost thoughts to the objects of their passion gave them some kind of sexual release.[55]

Occasionally, letters were angry and threatening as well as obscene. After being rejected for making indecent proposals, one man wrote a violent letter threatening to shoot his intended lover "on sight" and to seize her, "forcing her into a closed carriage, chloroforming her,—carrying her to a Chinese Opium Den and there while in this unconscious condition he would 'violate her person and have the Chinaman to repeat the process.'" An eighteen-year-old, apparently disturbed by some action of the principal of his school, wrote a torrid letter replete with obscene drawings to indicate what he would do to the principal's wife.[56]

Unfortunately, the law, intended to purify the mail, had unintended consequences. Learning, as they gradually did, that mailing an obscene letter was punishable by the government, those who wished to inflict pain on another, for whatever reason, used the obscene letter they had received from the offender for that purpose. Estranged married men or women often wrote bitter, obscene letters to their spouses, which were quickly presented to postal officials in the hope of inflicting a prison sentence or fine upon the writers. Parents, too, more than once used obscene letters written to a susceptible daughter to destroy a relationship between the daughter and her prospective lover. Jilted lovers, too, sought redress by signing the names of those who had wronged them to obscene letters certain to find their way to the postal inspectors. A young woman, for example, wrote a number of obscene letters to various people in Gettysburg, Pennsylvania, in 1897 and signed them with the name of her former suitor or the name of the woman with whom he was then involved. No doubt the inspector had seen it all before. In any case, it did not take him long to discern that she had written the letters "with a view to getting them into trouble."[57]

Letters could be used not only to exact revenge for some slight but also for extortion, as the scheme of a young Ohio woman and her cousin illustrates. Seeking to retaliate for the wrong done her, the disappointed lover, whose admirer, Thomas Jefferson Smith, had ceased to write to her, permitted her cousin to insert obscenities between the lines of a sentimental letter Smith had written to her when love bloomed. Then, threatening to expose the obscene letter, the cousin extorted $25 for it from the "'soft' and 'verdant'" former lover and $15 for her "quitclaim deed to his affections" (as the postal inspector wryly put it).[58]

One of the purposes of the law of 1888 had been to prevent the mail from being used for blackmail of this kind. No doubt it did give extortionists pause, although, of course, it could not stop them all. In Chicago in December 1894, a physician appeared in the office of Post Office Inspector James Stuart to complain that a former business associate, a lawyer, was blackmailing him. The lawyer had addressed an obscene six-page letter to the physician's wife concerning her husband's infidelities. The lawyer had not signed the letter with his own name, nor had he mailed it to the woman. Instead he had mailed it to the doctor's clerk, where it hung over the physician's head. The lawyer, knowing he could not be prosecuted without another witness to their conversations, took "fiendish delight" in admitting that he had written the letter and asking the physician, "Well, what are you going to do about it?'"[59]

In desperation, the physician had at last appealed to Inspector Stuart for help in the hope that the obscene-letter law could somehow be used against his tormentor. Because there was no evidence, the case at first seemed hopeless until the postal inspector and his helpers devised an ingenious strategy to secure the needed evidence to arrest the conspirator. Stuart knew that the only way to obtain evidence would be to have a witness other than the physician hear the lawyer admit he had written the letter. With the help of an electrician, he arranged to equip the physician with a telephone that would be concealed inside the man's tall hat when he met the lawyer at a secluded and guarded room. A nearly invisible wire stretched from the physician's telephone and battery to that of the inspector, who waited outside the room to overhear the conversation between the lawyer and the man he was blackmailing. The strange mechanism worked perfectly. The inspector heard the lawyer's confession, wrote it down, and had the lawyer arrested.

The Chicago *Evening Post* headlined the story "Trap in a Silk Hat" and gave an account of the sensational use of a tool invented only a few years before. In addition to illustrating the possibilities of eavesdropping in a new age, the story also indicated the extraordinary lengths to which postal inspectors would go in enforcing the law against mailing obscene letters, legislation that Congress, pressed by evangelical voices from the Heartland, had passed. They would work for days and expend every effort to find the authors of anonymously written obscene letters or to locate and cause the arrest of writers who signed someone else's name. It took Inspector Guy T. Gould, for example, from July of 1893 to February of the next year to trace an obscene anonymous letter from the dead-letter office to a post office in Willmar, Minnesota, first to a family that did not send it and, finally, to the guilty son of the owner of the town's lumberyard by a clever comparison of the handwriting in the lumberyard's ledgerbooks and the obscene letter.[60]

Many time-consuming, expensive investigations were aimed at clearing the mail of obscene letters. In December of 1894, George F. Bundy was tried in Helena, Montana, for writing an obscene letter. It had been a costly experience that Postal Inspector C. L. Wayland had taken the trouble to itemize. Bundy had been arrested in June 1894, and the U.S. marshal had traveled 746 miles at 20 cents a mile to detain him; two witnesses had traveled 270 miles to Billings and returned at 15 cents a mile; and the U.S. attorney had gone 476 miles to Billings and returned, also at 20 cents a mile. Bundy had been held in jail for six months, and the U.S. marshal had traveled 476 miles to transfer him from Billings to Helena. "It took three days of my time," the inspector wrote, "to attend the hearing at Billings, and a visit to Helena to procure the indictment and another . . . two days time at the trial. It took one day's time of the U.S. Court, with all its clerks, officers, and bailiffs." All of this was to acquit a man who, in the opinion of the inspector, was guilty.[61]

The inspector made a plea for a bill then being considered in Congress to empower the U.S. commissioner to try police court cases such as this in the belief the commissioner would not ignore the evidence and would be more likely to convict the guilty. But that was doubtful. In most cases judges imposed either no punishment on those found guilty of mailing an obscene letter or a small fine of $10 and costs and possibly sixty days in jail. Women who wrote obscene letters were often considered "mentally unsound," rarely punished, and almost never jailed. Lenient punishment in obscene-letters cases, indeed, was a hallmark of Judge Peter S. Grosscup's decisions. This judge, so ready to issue an injunction to stop the strike against the Pullman Company in 1894 and keep mail flowing, regarded violations of the obscene-letter law no more seriously than he did violations of anti-contraceptive laws. He fined a young man who had written an obscene letter to the principal of his school only $10 and the cost of the prosecution. In one case Grosscup did assess a fine of $50, but the fine for obscene letters written by a married man trying to seduce a young girl was so inconsequential in comparison to the immensity of the crime (in the view of the postal inspector) that he noted in his report, "How discouraging it is to spend time in trying to suppress this class of violations."[62]

Yet even Judge Grosscup could come down hard on those he regarded as serious offenders of antiobscenity laws. When Joseph R. Dunlop, editor of the Chicago *Dispatch,* was brought before him in early 1896 for filling that paper with advertisements such as "THREE YOUNG LADIES—Two blondes and [a] brunette with nice forms, wish to meet their friends at 2012 State Street, first flat, right," it was too much for the judge. He overruled every legal maneuver that Dunlop's lawyer made and would listen to no plea of mercy for the defendant, who had suffered a stroke. Nor did the press sympathize with Dunlop. In the end, according to the *Sunday Times Herald,* when asked if he had anything to say, Dunlop "stood up before the court a trembling wretch, leaning on a table for support. He mumbled a few words in a frightened voice. . . . With the sinking of his heart his tones faded away until they choked him, and left a sentence half finished, and he sat down with a quivering frame and lips moving in pitiful impotence." In the end, Judge Grosscup sentenced Dunlop to two years in prison and told him that although every family could shut its door to servants and visitors offensive to family moral standards, "the United States mail service penetrates to every chamber of the house, and it is no light obligation to see that it is kept clean."[63]

If Judge Grosscup's rulings were less severe in cases involving obscene letters than they were in the case involving Dunlop, the same could not be said for other judges, some of whom did assess harsh penalties against those who wrote obscene letters. A young woman and her cousin who blackmailed a man in Ohio by inserting obscenities into his letters were given prison sentences—she for one and a half years and he for four years at hard labor in the penitentiary at Columbus. Although perjury and blackmail as well as an obscene letter were involved in this case, a sentence of six months in the county jail or even a year for writing an obscene letter was not uncommon. In a sensational case in the little town of Mt. Pleasant, Iowa, in 1893, in which the lawyers for the defendant tampered with the evidence, Theodore Michaels was sentenced to spend twelve months in the Lee County jail and made to pay a $300 fine for writing a number of obscene letters to May Harding, whom the inspector called "a highly respectable young lady." Like most who wrote obscene letters, Michaels received little sympathy from public opinion or the press. "She [May Harding] had no father to protect her," the *Daily Gate City* reported, "from his [Michael's] repeated insults and the government must protect her in her rights. . . . When a man attacks the virtue and chastity of home," the paper continued with an almost universal evangelical opinion of the age, "he strikes the deadliest blow at our national life and institutions. . . . Mr. Palmer [the defense attorney] says it was but a lover's quarrel and indulges in unjust insinuations against her character. . . . He says the prosecuting witness brought the trouble upon herself and let her abide the consequences. All this is manifestly unjust. There is but one issue for the jury to consider and that is, 'Is it [the letter] obscene?'"[64]

But the issue in determining the punishment for those who wrote obscene letters was often more complicated than whether the letter was obscene. What, for example, should be the punishment given young men who were prompted to write obscene letters because of their habit of masturbation? Were they to blame when this "secret vice"—rarely called by its real name in that era—had driven them to lose their minds as was believed to be the case?

Masturbation, or "self-abuse" as it was called, was a youthful habit that weighed heavily upon the evangelical mind in the nineteenth century, not only because it was considered impure but also because they believed it was so widely practiced. "Lust begins its degrading work in the libidinous desires and vision of the heart, and in the practice of self-abuse," the Rev. Waddell Cloakey wrote in 1890. "This unclean devil possesses far more than any one has dreamed of." Few things, indeed, seemed more certain to Anthony Comstock, an expert on the subject, than the fact that the circulars advertising obscene literature that were invading Christian homes led young people to the "habit of secret vices" and inspired them to write obscene letters.[65]

Comstock and Cloakey were by no means alone in their denunciation of "self-abuse" and its tragic results. Medical opinion generally agreed that continued masturbation led to insanity. So commonly accepted was this opinion that it affected the punishment of those whom the postal inspectors had arrested for writing obscene letters. In 1893 an Atlanta man was arrested on that charge and pleaded guilty. He was sentenced to twelve months in the penitentiary, but when it was claimed that he "was of unsound mind, that he was a sexual pervert and a victim of masturbation or self-abuse," the judge took his bond for $500 and suspended the sentence. Postal Inspector William C. Baird, who had investigated the matter, looked askance at the judge's decision, but it was a judgment compatible with the conventional wisdom of the time.[66]

For six months that same year, the young women of Argentine, Kansas, had been receiving obscene letters when the postal inspector caused the arrest of William O'Connor. O'Connor confessed to writing the letters and had in his pockets at the time of his arrest "a large amount of obscene writings and memoranda showing that his mind was much occupied with licentious thoughts." His attorney entered a plea of insanity for him, and the family physician testified that he had examined the young man. "I found the young man has been for nearly four years practicing masturbation," he reported. "Part of his time he has used mechanical means to effect emission. This has produced such inroads upon his nervous system that the young man now dreams of copulation, thus effecting emissions. The long continued abuse indulged in by this young man, together with his having read the spurious literature on this subject so often thrown broadcast upon the public for the purpose of captivating the weak, afflicted, and unfortunate, rob them of their money and fill our asylums with inmates has not missed this unfortunate boy's hands. I have found in my practice young men afflicted with the same trouble that would sacrifice their entire fortune and almost at the verge of committing suicide from the effect this literature produced upon their minds, together with this trouble. In my judgement Mr. William O'Connor has been subject of both of these vices, and their effect upon his mind has unbalanced him."[67]

To such an end, it was commonly believed, had the pornography pouring through the mail driven many a young man in the nineteenth century. It was to prevent such wasted lives, protect the structure of the American family life, and preserve a Christian country, that the evangelicals had urged the passage of and supported the antiobscenity and lottery laws throughout the era.

Notes

1. Box 140, file 317, Correspondence and Reports Relating to Criminal Investigations, Nov. 1877–Dec. 1903, Records of the Post Office Department, Bureau of Chief Inspector, National Archives (hereafter Case Files). These files usually contain the postal inspector's report of his investigation and material relating to the case: circulars, photographs, and newspapers clippings. Hence they offer a complete story in themselves. The citations in the notes that follow refer to all the material in the numbered file and box number from Record Group no. 28 in the National Archives. Occasionally the file number is missing, but the box number is always cited.

2. *American State Papers, Post Office Department, 1789–1833* (Washington, D.C., 1834), no. 8, 18 (Jan 8, 1799) (hereafter *ASP: P.O.D.*). For the general nature of their work see

"Post Office Department—Permanent Employees," H. Doc. no. 170, 27th Cong., 2d sess., 1 (Mar. 31, 1842). It is possible to trace the origin of the inspection corps to colonial times and to Benjamin Franklin's postmaster generalship. E. J. Kahn, Jr., *Fraud: The United States Postal Inspection Service and Some of the Fools and Knaves It Has Known* (New York, 1954), 5–6; James Jackson Kilpatrick, *The Smut Peddlers* (London, 1961), 37–38. Richard R. John, *Spreading the News: The American Postal System from Franklin to Morse* (Cambridge, 1995), 77, includes a brief survey of their work.

3. *The Debates and Proceedings in the United States; with an Appendix etc. . . ,* 11th Cong., 2d sess., 1723 (Apr. 12, 1813); see also *ASP: P.O.D.,* no. 22, 41–42.

4. Jackson elevated Postmaster General McLean to the Supreme Court when McLean refused to remove postmasters without cause. Dorothy Ganfield Fowler, *Cabinet Politician: The Postmasters General, 1829–1909* (New York, 1943), 190–99. For the policy of "rotation in office," see "Letters of William T. Barry, 1806–1810, 1829–1831," *American Historical Review* 16 (Jan. 1911): 333; for Barry's establishment of the Office of Instruction and Inspection, see *ASP: P.O.D.,* no. 91, 242, no. 95, 256, no. 100, 304. Jackson's "rotation in office" policy is well told in John, *Spreading the News,* 214–42.

5. *Register of Debates in Congress,* 21st Cong., 2d sess., 156 (Feb. 9, 1831).

6. *United States Statutes at Large* (Boston, 1856), 5:81. Under this authority Postmaster General Kendall placed special agents in the Office of Instruction and Mail Depredations as Barry had done, put Daniel Coleman in charge, and summarized their many duties. *Report of the Postmaster General, 1836,* 520 (this and subsequent citations for postmasters general reports can be found in the *Congressional Information Service Serial Set Index* [Washington, D.C., 1997]). For the post office scandal in the Jackson administration, see chapter 2 of this volume.

7. Following the Jacksonian policy in 1841, Whigs summarily dismissed "unfit" Democratic postmasters, shocking Democrats who had begun the process. *Report of the Postmaster General, 1841,* 445; "Post Office Department—Persons Employed," H. Doc. no. 170, 27th Cong., 2d sess., 2 (Mar. 31, 1842); *Congressional Globe,* 23d Cong., 1st sess., 609–10 (May 25, 1844). For a favorable view of "rotation in office," see Robert Remini, *Andew Jackson and the Course of American Freedom* (New York, 1981), 190–92.

8. Between 1876 and 1880 Democrats reduced appropriations for the Office of Inspection and Mail Depredations from $160,000 to as low as $135,000 in 1876 and would have decreased it much more had not the Republican Senate intervened. *Congressional* Record, 44th Cong., 2d sess., 2992 (May 4, 1876); *United States Statutes at Large* (Washington, 1875), 18:314, 19:78; see also David B. Parker, *A Chautauqua Boy* (Boston, 1912), 235. Parker, who had served President Abraham Lincoln, was appointed chief of the Office of Special Agents and Mail Depredation. It was he who accused James Blount of Georgia of attempting to abolish the Postal Inspector Corps.

9. *Report of the Postmaster General, 1886,* 45–48; see also Fowler, *Cabinet Politician,* 228–30, 252, and Carl Russell Fish, *The Civil Service and the Patronage* (Cambridge, 1920), 222–23.

10. *Report of the Postmaster General, 1889,* 17–18; *Congressional Record,* 54th Cong., 1st sess., 2533 (Mar. 6, 1896). A nonscholarly overview of the Postal Inspection Corps is given in E. J. Kahn, *Fraud: The United States Postal Inspection Service and Some of the Fools and Knaves It Has Known* (New York, 1954), ch. 1.

11. "Report of the Select Committee," S. Doc. no. 507, 50th Cong., 1st sess., 34–35,

46 (Mar. 8, 1889). The Office of Fourth Assistant Postmaster General was established in 1891, and it took charge of the Inspection Corps in 1892. *Report of the Postmaster General, 1892,* 6.

12. *Report of the Postmaster General, 1896,* 565.

13. *Report of the Postmaster General, 1881,* 356. The word *pornography* was not commonly used in late-nineteenth-century reports and is used here only for convenience. A detailed derivation of the word appears in Joan Hoff, "Why There Has Been No History of Pornography," in *For Adult Users Only: The Dilemma of Violent Pornography,* ed. Susan Gubar and Joan Hoff (Bloomington, 1989), 18–23. Of the many books on pornography in America, none deal at length with pornography in the Gilded Age. Felice Flannery Lewis, *Literature, Obscenity and Law* (Carbondale, 1976), 20, notes that until the twentieth century little obscene fiction by American authors was published. Presumably, she was thinking only of what might be considered literature, because the mail was filled with pornographic fiction and poetry.

14. On the increased use of first-class mail for mailing circulars, see *Report of the Postmaster General, 1886,* 642. Mail-order pornography had not changed much to 1960 and could still invoke outrage (Kilpatrick, *Smut Peddlers,* 3–6, 49). The circular cited is found in box 142, no file number, Case Files.

15. Box 92, file no. 12, and box 127, file no. 137, both in Case Files. A list of the titles of obscene books Comstock had earlier seized appears in Heywood Broun and Margaret Leech, *Anthony Comstock: Roundsman of the Lord* (New York, 1927), 16, only a few of which turn up in postal inspectors' later reports. For Comstock's description, see box 186, file no. 196, Case Files. In the 1900s two apparently harmless pamphlets intended to give "wholesome" advice to the young were given "catchy titles" to promote sales: *Only a Boy* and *Only a Girl.* No doubt the publisher hoped buyers would believe these to be the old (and obscene) books. In any case, the Post Office Department banned them, giving Theodore Schroeder, champion of the free press, an argument against censorship. Theodore Schroeder, *"Obscene" Literature and Constitutional Law: A Forensic Defense of Freedom of the Press* (New York, 1972), 67.

16. Box 127, file no. 122, Case Files. The superintendent of the WCTU's Department for Social Purity expressed outrage at such pictures in 1888, declaring that "the picture of the nude or partially nude form of woman . . has been so degraded by men who seem to forget that the creature to whom they owe their existence was a woman, and that they are degrading her by the base use of the form of one of her sex" (*Union Signal,* Nov. 8, 1888, 6). It took feminists nearly one hundred years longer to discover that pornography made women "invisible as human beings, visible only as things or objects." Susan G. Cole, *Pornography and the Sex Crisis* (Toronto, 1989), 21. In modern secular society, feminists' discovery of pornography's degradation of women is not founded on Christian beliefs, as was the WCTU's viewpoint.

17. Box 129, file no. 148, Case Files. That so many obscene photographs of women came from Europe suggests the reluctance of American women to pose for such pictures.

18. Box 127, file no. 124, Case Files; Anthony Comstock, *Traps for the Young* (repr. Cambridge, 1967), 141–42. Comstock was aware that much of what he had destroyed was being reprinted. See also Broun and Leech, *Anthony Comstock,* 268–69, on the monotony of pornographic literature.

19. Box 127, file no. 122, Case Files. See Broun and Leech, *Anthony Comstock,* 268–69,

on the difficulty in finding originality in pornography; see also Steven Marcus, *The Other Victorians: A Study of Sexuality and Pornography in Mid-Nineteenth-Century England* (New York, 1966), 279.

20. Box 142, no file number, Case Files. Such paperback books did not, of course, have the second-class mailing privilege but were mailed first class in sealed envelopes.

21. Box 127, file no. 124, Case Files.

22. Box 92, file no. 12, Case Files.

23. *Report of the Postmaster General, 1896,* 160–61.

24. *Congressional Record,* 52d Cong., 1st sess., 197 (Jan. 1892); Box 127, file no. 122, Case Files.

25. Box 142, no file number, Case Files.

26. Box 147, no file number, Case Files.

27. *Report of the Postmaster General, 1886,* 48. On postal inspectors' methods, see Anthony Comstock, J. M. Buckley, and O. B. Frothingham, "Suppression of Vice," *North American Review* 135 (Nov. 1882): 485, and Kilpatrick, *Smut Peddlers,* 47–8.

28. Box 92, file no. 12, Case Files. Because he sponsored the antiobscenity law and was especially visible in its enforcement, Comstock became the whipping boy for the National Liberal League and for historians of censorship who have not examined the postal records. He was only one of a number of postal inspectors who enforced the law, however, and, in spite of the attacks upon him, he was generally supported by Congress and the American people. For a commonly misleading view of Comstock and his work, see Walter Kendrick, *The Secret Museum: Pornography in Modern Culture* (New York, 1987), 131–45.

29. Box 127, file no. 137, Case Files. The Murdoch, Ohio, post office was perhaps the victim of consolidations that took place after the advent of rural free delivery. In any case, it was no longer in existence in 1903.

30. Box 106, file no. 186, Case Files.

31. Ibid.

32. Ibid.

33. Ibid.

34. Box 127, file no. 124, Case Files.

35. Box 114, file no. 277, Case Files.

36. Box 144, no file number, Case Files.

37. Box 3, file no. 154, Case Files. For Comstock's attack upon the gaming industry, see Records of the New York Society for the Suppression of Vice, 1873–1953, Manuscript Division of the Library of Congress, passim.

38. Box 129, file no. 148, Case Files.

39. Box 127, file no. 122, Case Files.

40. Ibid. Comstock's reports often give the impression that he personally made arrests, although postal inspectors were not permitted to do that. In enforcing the federal law, at least, arrests were made by federal marshals or some other authority.

41. Broun and Leech, *Anthony Comstock,* 187.

42. Ibid., 213–14.

43. Hal D. Sears, *The Sex Radicals: Free Love in High Victorian America* (Lawrence, 1977), 29, 57, 99, 112. Not without some reason, Sears blames Comstock for the attack on the "sex radicals," but the Post Office Department, in view of the many complaints it received from orthodox Americans against their publications, was as anxious as Comstock

to ban such papers from the mail. Sears insists (116) that McAfee was Comstock's agent, whereas he was a postal inspector in his own right. For the prevalent nineteenth-century view of Harman's work, see Marshall Cushing, *The Story of Our Post Office: The Greatest Government Department in All Its Phases* (Boston, 1893), 612. That Harman's paper could obtain a second-class mailing privilege indicates postmasters' reluctance to reject publishers' applications for this service.

44. Box 127, file no. 134, and box 146, no file number, both in Case Files. Two of the anarchists pleaded not guilty to the charge of violating postal laws, but the third refused to plead, saying "he recognized 'no law' nor any 'power on earth' but his own will." The charge against one of the men was dismissed, and the other two were found guilty.

45. Box 108, file no. 226, Case Files. On Waisbrooker's background and the horse penis affair, see Sears, *Sex Radicals,* 229–33.

46. Box 142, file no. 10, Case Files. See, for example, the several circulars included in the postal inspectors' reports (Box 147, no file number, Case Files).

47. Box 5, file no. 191, and box 142, no file number, both in Case Files. A letter to a pregnant woman from her lover advising her to drink a tea made from apple root and other ingredients to relieve her condition suggests a belief in the curative powers of apple root. Box 113, file no. 262, Case Files.

48. Box 104, file no. 155, Case Files.

49. Box 127, file no. 124, Case Files.

50. *Union Signal,* Oct. 27, 1893, 11; *Report of the Postmaster General, 1896,* 61, 102, 489; see also chapter 6 of this volume.

51. Box 127, file no. 121, Case Files. A similar case in Los Angeles resulted in the publisher of the *Family Ledger* receiving only a day in prison and $1 in fines after the jury found him guilty. Box 107, file no. 198, Case Files.

52. Box 104, file no. 155, and box 127, file no. 124, both in Case Files.

53. Box 142, no file number, Case Files; see chapter 8 of this volume for the mother's letter.

54. Box 103, file no. 140, Case Files.

55. For examples, see box 141, file no. 335, box 139, files no. 142 and 287, box 129, file no. 151, box 103, file no. 139, and box 128, file no. 151 (all in Case Files). The 1888 law banning obscene letters from the mail was, of course, tested in the courts and found constitutional. Kilpatrick, *Smut Peddlers,* 40–41.

56. Box 92, file no. 6, and box 107, file no. 202, both in Case Files.

57. Box 145, no file number, Case Files.

58. Box 142, no file number, Case Files.

59. Box 113, file no. 267, Case Files.

60. Box 103, file no. 146, Case Files.

61. Box 107, file no. 203, Case Files.

62. Box 139, file no. 287, Case Files. In 1894 a woman in Savannah, Georgia, wrote a string of obscene letters to various people in that city, which greatly upset the community. She was not only poor but also believed to be "a little unsound mentally," apparently considering herself "a 'regulator' for a large section of the city." No one, however, wanted to testify against her in a trial that would expose all the obscene letters. Box 107, file no. 188, Case Files. On Judge Grosscup, see Samuel Yellin, *American Labor Struggles* (New York, 1936), 125–27, and *Dictionary of American Biography* (New York, 1932), 4:21–22.

63. Box 185, file no. 97, Case Files. For the judge's admonishment, see also Chicago *Tribune,* Feb. 9, 1896, 13.

64. Box 93, file no. 26, Case Files.

65. Waddell Cloakey, *Dying at the Top* (Chicago, 1890), 82; Comstock, *Traps for the Young,* 136.

66. Box 92, file no. 6, Case Files. For the nineteenth-century medical opinion on masturbation, see John S. Haller, Jr., and Robin M. Haller, *The Physician and Sexuality in Victorian America* (New York, 1974), 195–211.

67. Box 103, file no. 139, Case Files.

EPILOGUE

At the end of the nineteenth century, the moral majority of evangelical Protestants could look back with some satisfaction on the laws they had supported to govern unmailable matter. Setting out at the beginning of the century to preserve what they believed to be a Christian nation and maintain an evangelical moral order, they had met headlong the postal innovations and expansion that brought unsavory mail into American homes. They had also been able, by law at least, to cleanse the mail of much that offended Christian morality. In doing so they had sensitized the American people to the evils of obscenity and cast an aura of sinfulness over gambling, masturbation, contraception, and birth control that would last to the middle of the next century.

Such laws were indeed a reflection of nineteenth-century Christian morality and perhaps helped give evangelicals confidence that the United States was "still a Christian country." Even the Supreme Court seemed to agree that was so. Ruling on a law forbidding the importation of contract labor in 1892, the Court, citing the manifestations of Christianity in the nation's history, contended that "these and many other matters, which might be noticed, add a volume of unofficial declarations to the mass of organic utterance that this is a Christian nation." Therefore, the law was not applicable to the church's importation of a Christian minister.[1]

Still, evangelical reform of the post office was incomplete. American post offices remained open on the Sabbath as they had since 1810, and the Sabbath was increasingly desecrated by Sunday travel and pleasurable excursions, Sunday newspapers, baseball games, and empty pews. Many times judges did not seriously enforce laws against mailing contraceptives, abortifacients, and advertising for them. Moreover, the *Police Gazette,* loathsome health magazines, and dime novels still circulated through the mail to sear the hearts of evangelicals. So, too, did sensational Sunday newspapers, and the detailed stories of infidelity they carried were believed to have caused the divorce rate to soar and endanger family life in the Republic. Nor did there seem to be a way to stop the erosion of family life. Renewed evangelical efforts toward the century's end to secure a national divorce law had failed, as had a constitutional amendment to place the name of God in the Constitution's preamble.[2]

But if evangelicals had less to show for their long struggle to preserve a Christian nation than they wished, their crusade to purify the mail had revealed much about the nation's people of faith, its fundamental law, and its culture in nineteenth-century America. Their engagement with Congress over the operation of the mail on the Sabbath was the first in the nation's history to test the breadth of the Constitution's freedom of religion clause. Tested, too, in the struggle were its Tenth Amendment; the lengths and limits of its freedom of speech clause; and the boundaries involved in using postal power to ban lottery and contraceptive matter, Sunday newspapers, paperback books, salacious magazines, and material that was deliberately obscene.

Inevitably, the evangelical challenges to what went through the mail disclosed the changing culture of the nation as it moved from farm to city. It was the culture of the city in the late nineteenth century—illuminated in dime novels, advertising magazines, and especially Sunday newspapers that had coverage of sports, the theater, and society and stories of divorce and seduction—which was purveyed through the mail and which raised evangelical protests and revealed how far the nation had drifted from its rural past. Actually, the postal innovations themselves—city free delivery, special delivery, fast trains, money orders, and railway post offices that produced the communications revolution—testified to the rise of a commerical, urban-oriented society inimical to old evangelical values.

It said much about the remaining strength of evangelical religion in American life in nineteenth-century America that Congress was willing to stretch the postal power as far as it did to exclude from the mail much that a putative evangelical moral majority considered immoral. But it said even more about the waning of Puritanism and the fading dominance of Protestantism at the turn of the century that Congress could not be persuaded to stop the mail on Sundays or exclude Sunday newspapers, salacious periodicals, and dime novels from the mail even though the cost of mailing the latter was huge and its second-class privilege, at least for dime novels, questionable. Rooted in the old biblical morality of a rural society, the evangelical moral majority was no match for the power of the publishers of Sunday newspapers, dime novels, and salacious magazines brought into being by the nation's post office. For good or ill, the post office promoted a new national culture, and in it evangelical

Christian verities would lose their power to steer the nation's bark away from a looming paganism.

Notes

1. See Anson Phelps Stokes, *The Church and State in the United States* (New York, 1950), 2:572, for the quotation and decision; see also Robert T. Handy, *Christian America: Protestant Hopes and Historical Realities* (New York, 1977), 8–12.

2. An organization to protect children had been established in 1890, and it tried, without success, to secure a constitutional amendment that would permit Congress to pass a national divorce law. *The Outlook*, Apr. 22, 1900, 902–3. On family crises in 1900, see Christopher Lasch, *Haven in a Heartless World: The Family Besieged* (New York, 1977), 8–12.

INDEX

WAYNE E. FULLER was educated in a country school and at the University of Colorado, Denver University, and the University of California, Berkeley. During World War II he served as an Infantry officer in Normandy, was wounded, and spent four years in army hospitals. From 1955 to 1988 he taught American history at the University of Texas at El Paso. He is the author of *R.F.D.: The Changing Face of Rural America, The American Mail: Enlarger of the Common Life, The Old Country School: The Story of Rural Education in the Midwest,* and *One-Room Schools of the Middle West: An Illustrated History.*

The University of Illinois Press
is a founding member of the
Association of American University Presses.

Composed in 9/13 Stone Serif
with Stone Sans display
by Jim Proefrock
at the University of Illinois Press
Manufactured by Thomson-Shore, Inc.

University of Illinois Press
1325 South Oak Street
Champaign, IL 61820-6903
www.press.uillinois.edu